Federico Fellini

Federico
FELLINI

a guide to
references and resources

A
Reference
Publication
in
Film

Ronald Gottesman
Editor

Federico

FELLINI

a guide to
references and resources

JOHN C. STUBBS

with
Constance D. Markey
and
Marc Lenzini

G.K. HALL & CO.

70 LINCOLN STREET, BOSTON, MASS.

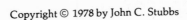

Library of Congress Cataloging in Publication Data
Stubbs, John Caldwell.
    Federico Fellini: a guide to references and resources.

    (A Reference publication in film)
    Bibliography: p.
    Includes indexes.
    1. Fellini, Federico.   I. Series.
PN1998.A3F3644   791.43'0233'0924   78-1638
ISBN 0-8161-7885-2

This publication is printed on permanent/durable acid-free paper
MANUFACTURED IN THE UNITED STATES OF AMERICA

To
June and Leda

Contents

PREFACE   xi

BIOGRAPHICAL BACKGROUND   1

CRITICAL SURVEY OF OEUVRE   17

THE FILMS: SYNOPSIS, CREDITS AND NOTES   45

WRITINGS ABOUT FEDERICO FELLINI 141

WRITINGS, PERFORMANCES AND OTHER FILM RELATED ACTIVITY 313

ARCHIVAL SOURCES 329

FILM DISTRIBUTORS 333

FILM TITLE INDEX 335

AUTHOR INDEX 341

Preface

This book is a reference guide to the works of Federico Fellini. It seeks to provide information about Fellini that will be useful and interesting to both the film scholar and the general viewer. The first two chapters are background essays. Chapter One gives biographical information about Fellini with particular emphasis on those elements that have played a part in his filmmaking, and Chapter Two is a critical overview of the eighteen movies written and directed by Fellini. Chapter Three offers synopses, credits, and notes on the eighteen films. The fourth chapter is the heart of the book, an annotated bibliography of criticism about Fellini in English, French, and Italian. The fifth chapter contains an annotated list of published screenplays of the eighteen movies written and directed by Fellini, a list of Fellini's various jobs as script writer, assistant director, and actor, and a list of materials of interest related to his filmmaking. Chapter Six gives information on study centers, and Chapter Seven, information on distributors of 16mm. prints of Fellini's films.

Every bibliographer would like his bibliography to be exhaustive for the years covered. In Fellini's case, that is impossible. Virtually each newspaper in each city has offered a review of each Fellini film since the mid-1950's. What I have tried to do is give extensive coverage to English language criticism and broadly representational coverage to the criticism in French and Italian. (Some important works in German from the Diogenes Press of Zurich are also included.) My method was as follows. I gathered references from these standard bibliographical sources: Vincent J. Aceto, Jane Graves, and Fred Silva, Film Literature Index, 1973, 1974, 1975. Albany: Filmdex, Inc., 1975, 1976, 1977; Stephen E. Bowles, Index to Critical Film Reviews. New York: Burt Franklin, 1974; John C. and Lana Gerlach, The Critical Index: A Bibliography of Articles on Film in English, 1946-1973. New York and London: Teachers College Press, 1974. Richard Dyer MacCann and Edward S. Perry, The New Film Index, 1930-1970. New York: E. P. Dutton, 1974; Michael Moulds, International Index to Film Periodicals, 1972, 1973. New York and London: R. R. Bowker, 1973, 1974; James M. Salem, A Guide to Critical Reviews. Part IV: The Screenplay from "The Jazz Singer" to "Dr. Strangelove." 2. Metuchen, N.J.: Scarecrow Press, 1971;

Preface

Mel Shuster, Motion Picture Directors: A Bibliography of Magazine
and Periodical Articles, 1900-1972. Metuchen, N.J.: Scarecrow Press,
1973. These works gave good coverage of criticism in English and
some coverage of international criticism through 1973. The journals
treated in the above bibliographies were, then, searched by means of
The Reader's Guide to Periodical Literature, indexes in the journals
themselves, and tables of contents for the years 1974 to 1976. The
sixteen items published in 1977 included here are items that came
readily to hand to the bibliographer interested in Fellini. The
latest ones are the two articles from Film Quarterly of the summer of
1977. However, neither 1976 nor 1977 should be considered thoroughly
researched because indexes for the journals were unavailable for
those years. To expand the coverage of criticism in French and
Italian, the following journals were searched from 1950 to 1976:

French	Italian
Avant-Scène	Bianco e nero
Cahiers du Cinéma	Cineforum
Cinéma (Paris)	Cinema nuovo
Écran	L'espresso
Études Cinématatographiques	Filmcritica
Image et Son	Ikon
Positif	Oggi
Télé-ciné	

To expand further the references, the card catalogues or director
files of the following archives and libraries were consulted: Amer-
ican Film Institute, Beverly Hills, California; British Film Institute,
London, England; Centro sperimentale di cinematografia, Rome, Italy;
Film Study Center, Museum of Modern Art, New York, New York; Margaret
Herrick Library, Academy of Motion Picture Arts and Sciences, Beverly
Hills, California; Special Collections Library, Doheny Library,
University of Southern California, Los Angeles, California; Theater
Arts Library of UCLA, Los Angeles, California; University of Illinois
Library, Urbana, Illinois. Still further expansion came from bibli-
ographies, footnotes, and references found in the books and articles
obtained through the above methods. A few articles and reviews were
excluded from this bibliography when I found them too slight to be
useful.

Some articles, reviews, and interviews have been published in
different journals, at different times, and sometimes in different
languages. This is especially true of interviews with Fellini and
the reviews of popular reviewers. I have tried to trace these items
back to their earliest publication. The annotation of the item is
given with the earliest publication entry. Later publication entries
are given, and the reader is referred back to the earliest date for
the annotation. Also, at the earliest entry date, the reader is
referred to later versions of the article which may be more conven-
ient for him to obtain or in a language he prefers.

A small number of entries could not be located in the United States, but were found in other countries. (Alberto Moravia's early reviews in L'espresso are examples.) Wherever this was the case, I have indicated it in parenthesis and have given a location to which the reader might write.

In the titles of bibliographical entries I have followed the capitalization practices of the country in which an item was published. In the texts of the annotations, however, I have anglicized the titles of Fellini's movies. Anything else seemed to me pretentious. So Fellini's 1959 movie may appear as La dolce vita in the title of an Italian article and as La Dolce Vita in the annotation, and his 1965 movie as Giulietta degli spiriti in the one and as Juliet of the Spirits in the other.

Some material in Chapter Two, "Federico Fellini: A Critical Survey of Oeuvre," I published earlier as part of an article entitled "8½: A Guide to Study," which appeared in the Journal of Aesthetic Education, 9, No. 2 (April 1975), 96-108, c 1975 by the Board of Trustees of the University of Illinois. The material is revised, and it appears as a part of a much longer essay. I wish to thank the Board of Trustees for permission to use the material in this manner.

Two doctoral candidates at the University of Illinois worked with me on this project, Constance D. Markey of the Department of Spanish, Italian, and Portuguese and Marc Lenzini of the English Department. Constance D. Markey read and annotated most of the items in Italian and worked on the synopses of Toby Dammit and Fellini: A Director's Notebook. Marc Lenzini searched through the standard film bibliographies mentioned above, tracked down library locations of material, gathered factual data on film credits and film distributors, and worked on synopses for A Matrimonial Agency, La Strada and Casanova. He helped with the indexing and proofreading of the book and with other tasks. Their assistance was invaluable. All their work was subject to my editorial supervision. Responsibility for errors, therefore, must necessarily fall on me, while credit for successes must be shared. My thanks to the Graduate College of the University of Illinois for grants which made possible the assistance of these two doctoral candidates.

I was also helped enormously by directors, librarians, and staff members at several research centers. I would like to thank especially the following people for their helpfulness and patience with me: at the American Film Institute, Anne G. Schlosser; at the British Film Institute, Gillian Hartnoll; at the Centro sperimentale di cinematografia in Rome, Lodoletta Lupo, M. Luisa Pintauro, Franca Riccomagno, and Angelo Urban; at the Film Studies Center of the Museum of Modern Art, Charles Silver; at the Margaret Herrick Library, Bonnie Rothbart; at the Special Collections Library at USC, Robert Knutson, Sandra Bailey, and Edward Comstock; at the Theater Arts Library of UCLA, Audree Malkin; and at the University of

Preface

Illinois Library, Nancy Allen, Constance Fairchild, Susan Bekiares, Emma Davis, Martha Landis, Carol Penka, Richard Smith, Paula Watson, and Amy Wilson.

The screenwriters Tullio Pinelli and Bernardino Zapponi, the critic and editor Renzo Renzi, and the assistant director Liliana Betti offered me advice on items to include in this book. Professor Ronald Gottesman of USC read my manuscript and offered suggestions for its improvement. Irene Wahlfeldt typed the manuscript with accuracy and cheerfulness. My wife June accompanied me to libraries in exotic lands in search of the rare bibliographical item and urged on the hunt with her interest. I extend my thanks to these people.

JCS

Biographical Background

There is a strong autobiographical strain in the movies of
Federico Fellini. We see his persona as a child at the circus in
The Clowns. He is frightened and stimulated by the cruelty of the
clown acts, and we are witness to early stirrings of imagination. In
Amarcord, the persona is an adolescent in a small resort town in Italy
in the thirties. His fantasies, affections, sexual longings, and
growing consciousness of the distinctive qualities of other individ-
uals are presented to us. I Vitelloni treats the group closeness and
high spirits of young men in the provinces. The persona, however,
grows aware of the irresponsibility and the limitations of the group.
Roma treats the amazement and excitement of the provincial newly
arrived in Rome. In La Dolce Vita, the persona is older, in his
thirties. He knows Rome. He prowls it in his job as reporter. But
he retains, as various critics have pointed out, a provincial's sense
of estrangement from the decadence and the vitality of the city. In
this work, the reporter is an artist-manqué. In 8½, the persona is a
director of some stature who wishes to make a movie that will be an
honest representation of his life. His mind goes back to the secure
love, the introduction of sexuality, and the severe religion of his
childhood. He must deal, in the present time, with the attractions
various kinds of women have for him, his longing for an ideal, the
question of middle age, the role of the artist, and the function of
his imagination. These protagonists form a continuous line of self-
portraits of Fellini, some, of course, based more closely on biographical facts than others. Fellini is a man absorbed with telling
and retelling his life, analyzing and reshaping his experiences.
This being the case, consideration of the materials of his life is
especially important. Yet because Fellini uses his life so often as
a fictional base and is constantly reshaping factual events, it is
often difficult to distinguish between a myth of his life created by
him and his life as he actually lived it.

* * *

Fellini's childhood and adolescence were spent in Rimini on the
Adriatic Sea. He was born there on January 20, 1920. Rimini was and
is a town with two distinct seasons. In the summer, tourists come to
visit the beaches, the Roman ruins, and the medieval churches. The

1

summer has the atmosphere of a festival. In the winter, with tourists gone and with cold drizzles and fogs in from the sea, Rimini becomes more simply a commercial city, and, in Fellini's youth, it became a quiet provincial town. The family, the church, and, during the 1930's, the Fascist party were important societal structures. For Fellini, Rimini seems to have supplied an almost inexhaustible amount of happenings and people that stimulated his imagination. He has said: "Rimini: what is it? It is a dimension of my memory (among other things an invented, adulterated, second-hand sort of memory) on which I have speculated so much that it has produced a kind of embarrassment in me. And yet I must go on talking about it.... Rimini: a word made up of sticks, of soldiers in a row. I cannot make it objective. Rimini, a nonsense story, confused, frightening, tender, with that great breath of its own and its empty sea."

Fellini's family was solidly in the middle class. His father, Urbano Fellini, was a salesman in groceries, preserves, confectionery, and coffee. He travelled in his job, and Fellini has commented, "My father had an eye for women, and this led to many bitter quarrels between him and my mother." Fellini suspects that his father was beaten by black shirts during the Fascist era, but chose not to speak of the event in front of his son. The father died of a heart attack in 1956. The lack of closeness between father and son seems to have bothered Fellini. In La Dolce Vita, at the end of the father's visit to Rome, Marcello, the son, urges him to stay on: "We can be together all day and talk. We never see one another." This lack of closeness seems to have existed also between Fellini and his mother, Ida. He has described her as "a good housewife who has had too much cause to worry over me." And she has commented to interviewer Eugene Walter: "Federico and I have never had a talk. Oh, he's played tricks on me, and he's always made me laugh--we're good friends!--but I don't feel as I really know him." Fellini has a brother Riccardo, a year younger, who played a role as one of the boys in I Vitelloni, and a sister Maddalena, seven years younger. Fellini was thin and shy as a boy. His friends called him "Gandhi," and his mother referred to Riccardo and him as "big heads." Although he participated in a number of escapades as a boy and had many friends his own age, he describes himself as one who lived "a life apart." In his reminiscences, there is often the sense of Fellini as an onlooker to his own life. Not an onlooker detached to the extent he cannot respond to what he sees, but rather the opposite. Fellini seems to have been someone with the capacity to step back from the events and people around him, to separate out the interesting, the startling, or the important from all the rest, and to respond strongly to what he focused on.

Certainly during his youth, Fellini was drawn to those things which stimulated his imagination and his capacity to fantasize. In his essay, "Rimini, My Home Town," he describes his discovery of an acting troupe at rehearsal of a Grand Guignol production in a theater next to a house where Fellini lived as a boy. One of the actors brought Fellini onto the stage. He comments: "I saw the gilded boxes, and, right over me, the belly of a railway engine hanging from the flies, among red, white and yellow gels." The boy was entranced. Two evenings later, his parents took him to see the play, and Fellini recounts the event: "My mother says I never moved throughout the performance. The train came forward from the darkness, about to run over a woman tied to the tracks, until she was saved, and an enormous, soft, heavy red curtain fell on her. My excitement lasted all night. During the intervals I had seen the wings, the stalls, the velvet and brass, the passages, mysterious warrens I dashed along like a mouse." His first view of the circus struck him with as much or even more force. The circus was a travelling one directed by the clown Pierino. Its acts, especially the clown acts, terrified as well as fascinated Fellini. He has commented on Pierino: "From that first moment, I was totally fascinated by the clown. For he embodies, in a fantastic character, all the irrational aspects of man, the instinctive part of him, the touch of rebellion against the established order which is in each one of us. He is a caricature of the most animal, most childish aspects of man, the victim of jokes and the joker. From that first meeting I wanted to be like him." Fellini has given to various of his early interviewers accounts that he ran away to the circus when he was approximately ten years old. In most accounts, the boy sees a woman performer with large, beautiful legs sewing her costume; he is asked to carry water to help nurse back to health a sick zebra; he is befriended by Pierino and made to feel a part of the circus group. The story has been called into question by biographer Angelo Solmi. (Fellini's mother denies the event took place at all.) Whatever the truth, the story testifies, at the very least, to the strong wish on the young Fellini's part to become a part of the world of the circus spectacle.

In his childhood, Fellini enjoyed putting on puppet shows. As a boy, he was attracted by the fantasy world of the comic strips, at first the humorous ones like Happy Hooligan and Bringing Up Father, then later the adventure strips like Flash Gordon. He went occasionally to movies at the town's Fulgor theater. With his school friends, he acted out endlessly stories of the Trojan War from the Iliad and stories of intrigue from the works of Edgar Wallace. And as an adolescent, his imagination was fired by the spectacle of summer dances at the town's resort hotel, the Grand: "On its terraces, curtained by thick rows of plants, the Ziegfield Follies might have been taking place. We caught glimpses of barebacked women who looked marvellous to us, clasped in the arms of men in white dinner-jackets, a scented breeze brought us snatches of syncopated music, languid enough to make us feel faint." All these things bear witness to Fellini's extraordinary interest in fantasy.

Numerous people from Rimini have stamped themselves in Fellini's memory. He has used some of these people as characters in his films. His essay "Rimini, My Home Town" is a virtual gallery of Rimini townspeople. Giudizio, the town idiot, Fellini relates, functioned as a self-appointed, "second" nightwatchman who would follow the regular nightwatchman on his rounds. Where the nightwatchman would hang a sign "Visited," Giudizio would add his own sign "Me too." "E guàt" was a man who reenacted battle scenes in the streets after seeing World War I films. Gigino was the town bully who wàs finally beaten badly by the town barber after Gigino had interfered in a romantic liason between the barber and a girl. "Ronald Colman" wàs the owner of the movie theater who wore a raincoat even in the heat of the summer and kept his moustache groomed to emphasize his resemblance to the movie star. Fafinon was an old man who would sit naked in the water of the drainage ditch whistling to the birds. "Gradisca" was the town vamp. She was the first to wear false eyelashes and the first to have a permanent wave in her hair. Her walk past the Cafe Commercio, in her black skirt, was an event eagerly awaited each day by the male customers of the cafe. These inhabitants of Rimini peopled Fellini's imagination.

Fellini has described himself as a child who liked to draw attention to himself by means of staged "scenes." On a radio interview, he recounted that he used to crouch immobile for long periods of time on a high window sill in the house in order to puzzle the adults who came into the room. His behavior would prompt them to wonder what was going on in his mind. One of his uncles, however, could always see through his "scenes." Fellini says that once he stained his forehead with red ink and arranged himself at the foot of the stairs in a position designed to arouse alarm in any one who would come upon him. The young Fellini remained in position three-quarters of an hour only to be discovered by the uncle who merely glanced at him, nudged him with his cane, and told him to go wash his face.

Fellini obtained his education at the primary level from a school run by the nuns of San Vincenzo. For the next level he was sent to a small boarding school run by the Carissimi Fathers at the nearby town of Fano. As Edward Murray has suggested in his biographical essay, these schools did much to shape Fellini's anti-clerical attitudes. Fellini remembers the school at Fano as an enormous building with long, dimly-lit corridors. Discipline was severe. Students were rapped on the hands. They were made to kneel on kernels of corn. When Fellini scored zero on pieces of work, he was made to wear a placard of the zero. Fellini has said that the strong sense of guilt that he carries with him has come from his education at Fano. He returned to school in Rimini in Via al Tempio Malatestiano for his education at the more advanced level. Fellini speaks of this experience with good-natured affection. He describes a headmaster nicknamed Zeus as a man with "a foot as big as a Fiat 600, which he aimed at us children, giving kicks that could break your back," and he recalls, "We were the despair of the teachers, especially of poor Don Bastianelli, the scripture teacher, whose life we certainly shortened." He did well in Italian, poorly in mathematics, and he states that the only subject which he enjoyed was the history of art. At this stage, Fellini participated in the public activities of the Fascist youth groups--parades and ceremonies--as did the others of his age group.

He insists, however, that he held himself back from commitment: "At
Fascist meetings, I never had a complete uniform: I always lacked
something--black shoes, grey-green shorts, the fez. This was a sort
of lukewarm sabotage, to stop me looking wholly Fascist: the protest
of an off-beat temperament, instinctively averse to that militaristic,
foreboding atmosphere and all those processions."

   Some of his time in the summer was spent at his grandmother's
house in the small country town of Gambettola in the Romagna area.
Fellini admired his grandmother. He says of her: "My grandmother
always carried a cane and made the men jump with it; it was just like
a cartoon film. The men were day labourers she employed to work the
land, and she certainly kept them at it. In the morning we would hear
loud laughter and noise. Then, when she appeared, those violent men
suddenly looked respectful, as if they were in church. My grandmother handed out coffee-and-milk and asked about everything." The
grandmother's house is recreated in 8½ as a place of nourishing
maternal love and as a place of beguiling magic. But Gambettola was
also a place where gypsies and strange itinerant workers passed
through, and these figures also made an impact on Fellini. He remembers in particular the gelder of pigs who would appear suddenly in
the town each year wearing a black coat and an old-fashioned hat.
The man bedded several of the unmarried girls, and once left pregnant
a poor idiot girl. It was said by the people of the town that the
baby was the devil's child. Fellini used this man as the model for
the seducer in his episode The Miracle, and he thinks the man may
have served also as a model for the brutish Zampano in La Strada.

   Fellini claims that he made the discovery of sex in his eighth
year when he and a group of friends paid a prostitute to reveal herself to them on the beach. She was a prostitute who offered her
services to fishermen, and she was known as "la Saraghina." Fellini
has described her as "an unbelievable mountain of white--a kind of
Moby-Dick that didn't scare me at all, even though I couldn't talk
for at least fifteen minutes afterward." Fellini also saw the bi-
weekly parade of carriages of new prostitutes for the "closed house"
on Via Clodia near the river in Rimini. The drive in the carriages
was designed to show off the new prostitutes. Fellini remembers them
as "painted women wearing strange, mysterious veils, smoking gold-
tipped cigarettes." The episode with Saraghina, Fellini has treated
in 8½, and the carriage ride of the prostitutes, in Amarcord. Both
events presented sex to the young Fellini as exciting, mysterious,
and, above all, illicit. His first love affair, however, seems to
have been polite and almost courtly. He fell in love with Bianchina
Sorianis, a girl two years younger who lived in the house across the
street. "Bianchina was a dark little girl," Fellini has said. "I
could see her from my bedroom. The first time I saw her she appeared
at the window, or else--I can't remember--she was wearing her Fascist
youth movement uniform, with fine heavy, already motherly, breasts."
Many years later, Bianchina told biographer Angelo Solmi about the
relationship: "Our greatest escapades consisted of a few romantic

5

walks outside the Porta d'Augusto, a few bicycle rides--with myself
on the crossbar whilst Federico pedalled--around the outskirts of
town.... He loved to be elegant, in summer he always dressed in
white or wore a close-fitting jacket over white trousers as was then
the fashion." The love affair ended when Bianchina moved to Milan.

Fellini had a talent for sketching. When he was a boy, he made
caricatures of movie stars and exhibited them in various store windows. As payment, he received passes to the movie theater. Later
with a friend, Demos Bonini, he began a business of sketching ladies
in their homes or, during the summer, on the beach. He drew cartoons
also and submitted them to the humor magazine 420 published in
Florence by the editor Nerbini.

* * *

In the fall of 1938, after graduating from high school, Fellini
left Rimini and went to Florence for a period of six months. His
father wanted him to become a lawyer, and Fellini seems to have made
vague promises that he would enroll in a university. (He did enroll
later in the Law Faculty in Rome, but he never attended classes.)
Fellini went instead to Nerbini and took a job with 420. There he
ran errands, corrected proofs, and drew cartoons. Then he got a job
with the comic strip magazine Avventuroso, also issued by Nerbini.
The magazine printed American, science fiction strips, including
Flash Gordon and Mandrake. During this period, however, publication
of materials from the U.S.A. was banned by Mussolini. Nerbini,
therefore, gave Fellini and artist Giove Toppi the job of inventing
an Italian version of the adventures of Flash Gordon. Fellini rel-
ished the assignment.

Fellini, however, moved from Florence to Rome in the spring of
1939. If Rimini, the provincial town, has been the most important
source of material for his imagination, Rome, the eternal city, has
been certainly the next most important. As Fellini made clear in
the film Roma, he was raised on classroom accounts of the glories of
the Roman empire. He saw mythical-historical versions of Rome in the
movies. Furthermore Rome was the city of his mother. He thought of
it as an archetype of mother and home. But perhaps more than any of
these things, it was to him at that time a complement to provincial
experience, a testing ground where he could try himself against new,
more risky possibilities. Sketches Fellini has made in his dream
notebook show him in this period as a stick figure threatened by
large, overpoweringly sexual women or, in one instance, a sinister
male offering Fellini his "wives." "Rome as I knew it then," he has
written, "was a tiny casbah of furnished rooms around the main station, with a jumbled population of frightened immigrants, prostitutes,
confidence tricksters, and Chinamen selling ties. The fact that it
was close to the station gave me a feeling of home, made me feel less
far from Rimini. If things go wrong, a voice inside me kept saying,
the train's there."

Fellini wanted to become a journalist. He told an interviewer, "I had seen so many American films in which newspapermen were glamorous figures.... I liked the coats they wore and the way they wore their hats on the back of their heads." He located a job in Rome on the newspaper Il popolo. His task was to collect news items from the local courts and from the police blotters. He found the work routine and uninteresting and gave it up after three weeks.

To support himself he formed a partnership with a friend, Rinaldo Geleng, who is now a successful illustrator, to draw caricatures of customers in cafes. Fellini would draw the outline, and Geleng would color it in. Once when business was poor, as Fellini tells the story in "Via Veneto: dolce vita," they made an attempt to put advertisements on shop windows with oil paint. Fellini found a store owner on the prestigious Via Veneto who was willing to hire him. Geleng had gone off to paint another shop window, but he had left Fellini a sketch of a curvaceous girl to copy onto the window. A crowd gathered to watch Fellini work. He had trouble, however, transferring the sketch to a larger scale and made the top of the girl too large and the bottom disproportionately small. Trying to correct his error, Fellini asked the shopgirl for a wet rag and began rubbing out the painting. Rather than taking off the paint, he spread it in smears over the whole of the window. A small boy advised him that he would have to use turpentine. At that point, the owner came to inspect the work, and Fellini in a panic gathered up his paints and brushes and ran off. The owner chased him down, and then took pity on him and paid him for his time.

While working with Geleng on the caricatures, Fellini also submitted cartoons and stories to the weekly satirical magazine Marc' Aurelio. His efforts here were more successful. He got a position on the magazine's editorial staff. He wrote a number of columns including "Third Year in High School" (based on his own school experiences) and a series about the comic situations of a young married couple "Cico' and Pallina." Due to his sucess with the magazine, he was invited to write sketches for the radio and to work as a gag writer on movies. In 1939 and 1940, he wrote jokes for the comedian Macario in the movies Lo vedi come sei? [Do You Know What You Look Like?], Non me lo dire [Don't Tell Me], and Il pirato sono io [I Am the Pirate], all directed by Mario Mattoli.

In 1939, Fellini met the comedian and actor Aldo Fabrizi and formed a friendship that proved very important. Fellini was taking surveys for the fan magazine Cinemagazzino, as assignment which lasted a few months, and he arranged an interview with Fabrizi backstage in the theater where he was performing. According to Fellini's account, the two men went to the restaurants of Rome together; Fellini told Fabrizi some ideas for comic routines; and Fabrizi invited Fellini to tour the provinces with his troupe for six months as writer and general factotum. Fellini claims that the troupe put on a tacky, second-rate revue called Sparks of Love, that they travelled

the length of Italy, and that six of the eight female dancers fell in
love with him. Fabrizi's account differs. He denies that Fellini
accompanied him on any tour of the provinces. He states more simply
that a friendship sprung up between them and that they spent many
nights together at the Bar Castellino in the Piazza Venezia. Fabrizi
told Fellini in innumerable conversations about his life in the variety halls and on the stage. Whichever story is true, and Fabrizi's
is certainly the more believeable, it is clear that Fellini gained
access to a backstage view of the entertainer's world, a subject he
treats in different ways in Variety Lights, 8½, and The Clowns.

Fabrizi helped Fellini gain access also to screenwriting jobs between 1941 and 1943. Specifically, Fabrizi had Fellini collaborate
with him on the writing of Avanti, c'è posto [Come On, There's Room],
Campo dei fiori [Field of Flowers], and L'ultima carrozzella [The Last
Merry-Go-Round]. Other screenwriting jobs done by Fellini during
this period, without collaboration with Fabrizi, include Documento Z3,
Quarta pagina [The Fourth Page], Chi l'ha visto? [Who Has Seen Him?],
Apparizione, and Tutta la città canta [The Whole City Sings]. Of
these films, Fellini said to Angelo Solmi: "They weren't much, but
they foreshadowed neorealism with small scenes and social sketches
depicted in a good-humored fashion. In short, I think I had gone
beyond the paraphernalia of white telephones and the mawkish situations of that era."

Italy entered World War II in 1940. Fellini escaped the draft at
first because of his position on the Marc' Aurelio, which was well
regarded, at least for awhile, by the Fascist party and because of a
disability certificate for a heart murmur which he obtained through
friends or bribery. An ironic letter to a soldier at the front which
he published in Marc' Aurelio jeopardized his situation. In the
beginning of 1943, when Fellini went to a military hospital to renew
his disability certificate, he received a stringent examination with
German soldiers observing the procedures of the doctors, and he was
pronounced fit to serve in the army. Fellini tore up his papers.
Then realizing the danger of being without papers, he went to friends
who made him a new set. Fellini arranged for another examination.
As he explained it to Angelo Solmi, an air-raid began while he was
waiting his turn. A bomb hit the hospital. Fellini slipped away
slightly injured, and the records of the hospital were destroyed. He
was safe at least for awhile.

In June, 1943, Fellini met the actress Giulietta Masina who
became his wife. Giulietta came from a middle class background. She
was born in 1921 in San Giorgio di Piano near Bologna. Her father
was a school teacher. She was an arts graduate of the University of
Bologna, with her fourth-year thesis on archaeology. At the University, she entered into amateur theatrical productions, and, after
graduation, she went to work professionally with the Ateneo Theater
group in Rome. At the time of her meeting with Fellini, she had
taken on the part of Pallina in a radio series written by Fellini

based on his column in <u>Marc' Aurelio</u>. Fellini knew her only by her voice over the radio. One day, however, he saw her picture in a fan magazine, phoned her, and invited her to lunch. Attempting to establish the <u>figura</u> of a suffering artist, he told her that scars on his wrist were marks of a suicide attempt. (The marks were really caused by an accident at a drinking bout.) Giulietta told Angelo Solmi that she pretended to believe Fellini's account of his despair and agreed to meet him again. In approximately one month, they became engaged.

During the time of their engagement in the summer and fall of 1943, the country suffered a complete upheaval. The Allies landed in Sicily and moved into southern Italy. Mussolini's resignation was forced by the Fascist Grand Council. He was arrested, escaped, and attempted to set up his Italian Social Republic at Salò in the North. The King and his new anti-Fascist government fled to the South. The northern and central parts of Italy, including Rome, came to be essentially under German control. The movie studios in Rome were shut down. (Mussolini tried to reorganize the industry in Salò.) Fellini was cut off from his main source of income, and he and Giulietta were living in a city in turmoil. Nevertheless, they decided to marry. The ceremony took place on October 30 in the apartment building where Giulietta lived with her aunt. To save money, the couple stayed on with the aunt in her apartment. Giulietta became pregnant and gave birth in the summer to a son, "Federichino." The son, however, lived only three weeks, and the couple has since remained childless.

Giulietta Masina has appeared in seven films directed by Fellini and in three others on which he served as writer. Fellini has stated: "Giulietta is a special case. She is not just the main actress in a number of my films, but in a very subtle way their inspiration as well." Her greatest gifts as an actress are her abilities at mime, gesture, and facial expression. Her most successful movies, accordingly, are the two which allow her often to use these abilities, <u>La Strada</u> and <u>Nights of Cabiria</u>. Fellini has said: "Giulietta, my wife, has the gift for evoking a kind of waking dream quite spontaneously, as if it were taking place quite outside her own consciousness. With her clown-like gift for mimicry, she embodies in our relationship my nostalgia for innocence." She appears in clown make-up in her act with Zampano in <u>La Strada</u> and wears a clown's painted-on tear in the corner of her eye in a shot near the end of <u>Nights of Cabiria</u>. But even when not made up specifically as a clown, her face usually has something of the clown's mask-like quality. Her face is round ("like an artichoke," says the Fool in <u>La Strada</u>). It is usually whitened with powder, and her expressive features (eyes, eyebrows, and mouth) are emphasized. Giulietta Masina is short. Her size is often played off against taller foils such as Zampano in <u>La Strada</u> and Wanda, Matilda, and the actor in <u>Nights of Cabiria</u>. In her last film with her husband, <u>Juliet of the Spirits</u>, she was required to play a betrayed housewife, a role more realistic or wider in range than her parts in <u>La Strada</u> and <u>Nights of Cabiria</u>, and she was less effective.

9

Shortly after the wedding, as Fellini has recounted to interviewers, he was arrested by Fascists while he was walking in the
Piazza di Spagna. The incident was part of a roundup of young men
not in uniform. He was put in the back of a truck at gunpoint along
with other young men already under the guard of German soldiers.
Fellini caught sight of two German officers talking on a sidewalk.
While the truck was moving slowly, he jumped out and rushed up to the
German officers as if he knew them. No shots were fired at him, and
the truck did not stop. The officers pushed him away in annoyance,
and he escaped. The incident resembles to some extent the scene of
the arrest of the resistance worker in Rome, Open City, a film on
which Fellini was to work as a screenwriter.

Rome was liberated in June, 1944. Fellini along with friends
from the Marc' Aurelio opened a series of "Funny Face Shops." In the
shops beneath the banner (in English), "Look out. The most ferocious
and amusing caricaturists are eyeing you. Sit down and tremble,"
Fellini and his friends would draw caricatures of Allied soldiers.
They also photographed soldiers in cut-outs and recorded their voices
on cheap discs. The items were usually mailed by the soldiers to
their girl friends and parents. Fellini recalls that the records
were of such poor quality that they would wear out after one playback.
When occasionally a soldier would test the record more than once
before mailing it off, he would return to the shop and cause a row
that would have to be broken up by the military police. Fellini
states emphatically that the shops were good money-makers.

In the main shop on Via Nazionale, Fellini met Roberto Rossellini,
and Fellini's involvement with the project for the neorealistic film
Rome, Open City began. Rossellini sought out Fellini as an inter-
mediary to persuade Aldo Fabrizi to act in a short documentary on
Don Morosini, a priest who had worked in the resistance. The film
had been commissioned by a wealthy woman. Rossellini and Alberto
Consiglio had already done a script. Rossellini was to direct it.
Fellini agreed to help. While he was negotiating with Fabrizi,
Rossellini tried to persuade his backer to finance a second short film
on the harassment Roman children had done to the Germans during the
war. Screenwriter Sergio Amidei suggested to Rossellini that the
idea for the second film might be combined with the story of Don
Morosini to make a feature-length film. In a week of furious work in
Fellini's kitchen ("the only warm place in the house," he said),
Rossellini, Amidei, and Fellini wrote a new script. The result, Rome,
Open City, was a landmark in establishing the neorealistic movement
in Italian films. It is celebrated for its use of real locations,
its use of actors with realistic appearances, especially Fabrizi and
Anna Magnani, its grainy film stock, and the overall documentary feel
to it.

Fellini continued to work with Rossellini on his next project,
Paisan (1946), this time as a screenwriter and as an assistant director. The movie consists of six episodes, each set in different parts

of Italy and each dealing with different aspects of war and occupation. Fellini summed up the experience as follows: "With Paisan I
went all over Italy with Rossellini, because...the action stretches
right from Sicily to the Po, and it was a very exciting discovery,
because the war had just ended, and we were surrounded by a whole new
race of people, who seemed to be drawing hope from the very hopeless-
ness of their situation. There were ruins, trees, scenes of disaster
and loss, and everywhere a wild spirit of reconstruction. In the
midst of which we did our tour.... Living in amongst this mass of
new impressions which were so extraordinarily rich in suggestive
power, was like filling my lungs with oxygen." Fellini directed some
of the scenes himself, especially in the Florence sequence on the
battle between the Germans and the partisans, and he contributed most
as a writer to the sequence in a monastery in the Apennines where the
religious outlooks of three army chaplains are compared with the med-
itative faith of the monks. Along with the other collaborators,
Fellini received an Oscar for the screenplay.

Fellini collaborated three more times with Rossellini. In 1948,
he wrote and acted in The Miracle, one of the episodes in Rossellini's
two-part film L'amore. The episode concerns a simple peasant girl
who is made pregnant by a passing stranger. She is certain the
stranger was St. Joseph and that the baby will be the Holy Child.
Anna Magnani played the part of the woman, and Fellini with his hair
dyed blond, the part of the stranger. He does not speak. The story,
as mentioned earlier, was based on the story of the pig gelder which
Fellini had heard in Gambettola. When he first told the idea to
Rossellini, however, he presented it not as original, but as taken
from a Russian story. Perhaps, he did this out of shyness, as he
claims, or perhaps he did it to insure Rossellini would take the idea
seriously. Fellini also worked as screenwriter and assistant director with Rossellini on Francesco, giullare di Dio [Flowers of
St. Francis] (1949) and with him briefly as a collaborator on the
story treatment of Europa '51 (1952) in which Giulietta Masina played
a secondary role. During the years 1946 to 1952, Fellini worked as a
screenwriter and/or assistant director with two other directors
identified with the neorealistic movement, Alberto Lattuada and Pietro
Germi. With the former, he did Il delitto di Giovanni Episcopo [Flesh
Will Surrender] (1947), Senza pietà [Without Pity] (1948) in which
Giulietta Masina made her film debut in a secondary role, and Il
mulino del Po [Mill on the Po] (1948). With the latter, he worked on
In nome della legge [In the Name of the Law] (1948), Il cammino della
speranza [The Path of Hope] (1950), La città si difende [Passport to
Hell] (1951), and Il brigante di Tacca del Lupo [The Brigand of Tacca
del Lupo] (1952). As his "apprenticeship" period drew to a close,
Fellini was best known as a screenwriter, and he was strongly identified as a figure in the neorealistic movement.

Rosselini demonstrated to Fellini the importance of film as a
medium and was a pivotal figure in his life. Fellini has said:

And here is the real lesson I learned from Roberto:
this humility before the camera and in a certain sense
this extraordinary faith in things photographed--in men,
in faces.... Humility in one's attitude toward life,
not presumption, not to say: "I'm telling my fantasies,
my stories." No: "I'm trying to tell what I have seen."
And then immense faith in the human, the plastic material itself. What struck me most and finally made me
understand was that seeing things with this love was
really my profession and my trade, this communion which
is created from time to time between you and a face,
between you and an object.

From the neorealistic movement in general, Fellini took several things.
First, the knowledge that form could be open and episodic. This characteristic began to appear in Fellini's own films with I Vitelloni
and has become increasingly important. Second, a use of desolate or
lonely locale. This characteristic is most important in early films
such as La Strada, Il Bidone, and Nights of Cabiria. Even here,
though, Fellini usually adds or finds a unique element--such as an
isolated tree, a piece of drainage pipe, a swayback horse, a jungle
gym of pipes--to make the landscape more evocative of mystery than is
normally the case in neorealistic films. (In recent films, he has
moved completely away from realistic representation to an insistence
on studio artificiality.) Third, a concern and tenderness for characters at the bottom or on the fringes of society. Again this trait
is most noticeable in his early films. Despite these influences,
Fellini's linkage with neorealism was an encumbrance to him in some
ways. As he deviated from neorealism's program of clear and direct
social relevance to more personalized and even mystical views of the
human condition, critics branded him a traitor to the cause. It is
clear from interviews Fellini gave in the late fifties and early
sixties that he was troubled and hurt by these attacks, but it is
also clear that Fellini was determined to make his movies in his own
manner. (See also the scene of the debate between the activist students and Fellini in Roma.)

* * *

Variety Lights, made in 1950, is generally considered to be
Fellini's first film. He co-directed it with Alberto Lattuada and
collaborated with Lattuada, Tullio Pinelli, and Ennio Flaiano on the
screenplay from the story treatment by Fellini. As far as the directing was concerned, Fellini worked mainly with the actors, and Lattuada
concentrated on the technical aspects of capturing the performance on
film. But because the veteran director Lattuada was always present
to be leaned on for support, Fellini himself has stated over and over
that he did not become a director in the fullest sense of the word
until he began making The White Sheik as sole director in 1952. He
has recounted the following story of the moment when he feels that he
first took command of a film: "One day I noticed that I was a

director.... One morning I found myself on a boat taking me from Fiumicino to a motor-cutter which was out at sea with the cast and crew of The White Sheik on board. At what was still almost crack of dawn I had said good-bye to Giulietta with that same accelerated heart-beat and that same anxiety with which one goes into an exam. I had even gone into church and had tried to pray. I was driving my little Fiat and, on the way to Ostia, one of the tires blew.... I had to shoot a particularly complicated scene between Sordi and Brunella Bovo. As I approached the motor-cutter I could see the faces of the film crew.... I couldn't stop asking myself; What am I going to do? I couldn't remember the film; I couldn't remember anything. I only had a strong desire to run away. But I had hardly set foot on the ship than I was giving instructions, demanding this, that, and the other, looking through the camera.... In the few minutes' voyage from the harbor to the ship, I had become an exacting, pedantic, self-willed director...."

The team of Tullio Pinelli and Ennio Flaiano played an extremely important role in Fellini's career up to 1967. They worked with him on his films from Variety Lights through Juliet of the Spirits. Pinelli came from a noble family in Turin. His first collaboration with Fellini was on Senza pietà. He is described by Angelo Solmi as a man "greatly absorbed by mysticism." He is a playwright, and he is very skilled at writing dialogue. Flaiano was from the Abbruzzi. He was a playwright and prose writer. Fellini has called him "the delicate humorist, the ardent chronicler of Italian life." He was known for his gift for satire. Variety Lights was Flaiano's first film with Fellini. (Flaiano died in 1972.) The two men were, in Fellini's words, "temperamentally quite different, but...basically complementary." Fellini has described his method of working with them this way: "When I start getting an idea for what may be my new film..., I talk about it without dramatizing it at all.... Starting from there, we try to arrange our meetings in the least dramatic way possible. We try to meet as little as possible, and when we do meet, we behave in such a way as to avoid the heavy, formal atmosphere of a working session. We chat...well, we chat around the subject, and develop it.... Then, when the story begins to have a fairly precise thread in it, we often divide up the work. Pinelli takes some scenes, Flaiano others, and I take others myself, but we do all we can to give this creation...the greatest possible freedom." To this team of writers, Fellini added other craftsmen and collaborators with whom he felt comfortable working. Music composer Nino Rota joined him in 1952 on The White Sheik; editor Leo Cattozzo in 1954 on La Strada; and art director Piero Gherardi in 1956 on Nights of Cabiria. Otello Martelli was Fellini's cinematographer on Variety Lights, I Vitelloni, La Strada, Il Bidone, Nights of Cabiria, La Dolce Vita, and The Temptations of Doctor Antonio, and Gianni di Venanzo on A Matrimonial Agency, $8\frac{1}{2}$, and Juliet of the Spirits. These people formed the nucleus of Fellini's team in the first half of his career. Their highest point of success, with di Venanzo as cinematographer, was certainly $8\frac{1}{2}$ in 1963. The film won many international awards,

including seven silver ribbons from the Italian film critics, the
Grand Prize at the Moscow Film Festival, and two American Academy
Awards (one to Fellini for best Foreign Language Film and one to
Gherardi for Best Achievement in Costume Design of a Black and White
Picture).

In 1967, Fellini was taken seriously ill and was hospitalized.
His illness was diagnosed as pleurisy or a rare virus. The experience deeply frightened him. He has described his stay in the hospital
as follows: "At night, the passages are full of flowers: flowers,
flowers, flowers, which they put outside the patients' rooms, as if
it were a cemetery. The low lights: in the darkness, when you open
your eyes, you see a head floating in the air, lit from below. A nun
or a nurse is holding a flashlight to read a thermometer. The floating faces slide silently along the passages. Sometimes the nuns give
you an injection without waking you, like an assassin hired by Cesare
Borgia: then you see them, back view, slipping away into darkness.
Often, weird images loom up at me: sudden visions from heaven knows
where." When the illness ended, however, Fellini felt renewed. He
revamped his team of collaborators and plunged into work with great
energy.

Prior to his illness, he had been working on a projected film
called The Voyage of G. Mastorna, with avant-garde writer Dino
Buzzatti as a co-writer. The movie was to show a sensitive 'cello
player's journey into fantasy. Marcello Mastroianni, the leading
actor in La Dolce Vita and 8½, was cast in the role of the 'cello
player. (An airport set, constructed for use in the film, is shown
at the beginning of Fellini's documentary Fellini: A Director's
Notebook.) After his convalescence, Fellini scrapped The Voyage of
G. Mastorna. Perhaps it was too much like 8½ and Juliet of the
Spirits. Instead, he began work on the Toby Dammit episode of
Spirits of the Dead, based on Edgar Allan Poe's story "Never Bet the
Devil Your Head."

After his illness, Fellini did not again resume working with
Pinelli and Flaiano. The reasons for the break up are not known, but
a desire on Fellini's part for a complete self-renewal seems to have
been a major factor. Fellini took on screenwriter Bernardino Zapponi,
a Roman, as his principal collaborator. His interests lie in the
strange and the unusual. His favorite authors are Edgar Allan Poe
and Franz Kafka. He has worked on all of Fellini's movies since 1967
except Amarcord. (The novelist Tonino Guerra was Fellini's sole collaborator on the story treatment and screenplay of Amarcord.) For
other reasons, Fellini had to replace other members of his group.
Cinematographer Gianni di Venanzo died tragically at the age of forty-
five in 1966. Production designer Piero Gherardi died in 1971. Editor
Leo Cattozzo invented a simplified home editing machine and retired
to live on the proceeds. Fellini built up a new group with Giuseppe
Rotunno as cinematographer, Danilo Donati as production designer, and
Ruggero Mastroianni (Marcello's younger brother) as editor. With

this new group, Fellini has seemed to work more with costume, artificial sets, color, and vast spectacle. All these, however, are elements that were important earlier in Juliet of the Spirits. But with Zapponi and these others, Fellini has made subjective-documentaries and "free" adaptations of literary works, two genres he had not tried previously.

Through all the changes in his group, Fellini has maintained the same manner of bringing a movie into existence. He describes the process as having seven stages. The first stage is when he gets his initial idea: "The first time [a film] appears, it is cloudy, vague and indistinct. Any contact one has with it is in the imagination: it is a nocturnal sort of contact. It may be, indeed it is, a friendly contact. At this point the film seems to have everything, it seems to be entirely itself, whereas in fact it is nothing. It is a vision, a feeling." The second stage is the arranging of finances: "The contract comes into being, involving lawyers and handshakes. Coca-cola is drunk, and toasts in champagne." The third stage is the writing of the screenplay. Working with his collaborator or collaborators, Fellini tries to convert his mental images to what he calls "literary rhythm" and to set down dialogue. "In this third phase," he says, "the film seems to be pulled along by the hair, and puts up some resistance. It has to be persuaded in some way. Sometimes I expand the literary part in full consciousness of my bad faith, at others I leave pages and pages blank." The fourth phase is the casting stage. Fellini enjoys this phase enormously. "At this point I wish I could see all the faces on this planet," he says. He publishes a call for actors and amateurs and sends his own scouts out looking for people to match the characters he has envisioned. It is the physical presence, especially the face, which interests him: "One fascinates me with a facial tic. Another interests me because of his spectacles. Sometimes I add a new character to the screenplay to accommodate the new face I have discovered." The fifth stage is the production work. Here Fellini works with his production designer on costumes, locations, and sets. Often he sketches his ideas and gives the sketches to the designer. The sixth stage is the actual directing of the actors. Fellini tries to tell the actors as little as possible about their roles. He prefers to have actors work scene by scene, with him telling them what emotion, gesture, or facial expression he wants. He will not allow the actor's interpretation of a character to clash with his. Of the actor Marcello Mastroianni, Fellini has remarked, "The way Marcello really helps me is not just by being professionally good, but by abandoning himself confidently to me." The seventh and final stage is the editing. Fellini works closely with his editor in putting the final version of the film together. At this point, he has to compare the realized film with his original mental images. The film usually seems to him diminished, less somehow than he had hoped it would be, and he must force himself to finish the editing.

15

Fellini now lives with his wife Giulietta in a house they have built in Fregene near the Tyrrhenian Sea, twenty miles outside of Rome. He also keeps an apartment in Rome, and when not working, he loves to prowl the streets of the city. More and more, however, Fellini has come to define his life in terms of work on his films. It is while making films that he feels most alive. He has said: "What I know is that I want to tell stories. I am not saying this out of modesty, but simply because telling stories seems to me the only game worth playing. It is a game which makes its own demands on me, on my imagination and my nature. When I am playing it, I feel free, away from all embarrassment. And I am lucky in this, that I can play with that toy, the cinema. The dark set, when all the lights are out, exerts a fascination over me which has some very obscure origin. To put up some of the scenery with my own hands, to make up an actor, to dress him, to urge him to some movement, to some unforeseeable reaction, involves me totally, sucks out all my energies. I know the unreality of it all: its limitations, the feeling of exultation and extravagance which it brings, the dangerous romantic risks, but outside the cinema I know no other way in which I can feel at ease, and in tune with my own self."

Acknowledgment of Major Sources:

Camilla Cederna, "Confesso Fellini," L'espresso-mese, 1, No. 3 (July 1960), 54-63 & 108-109.

Jacques Delcorde, ed., Entretiens avec Federico Fellini (Belgium: Radio-diffusion télévision belge, 1962), 69 pp.

Tullio Kezich, "The Long Interview," in Juliet of the Spirits, translated by Howard Greenfeld (New York: Orion Press, 1965), pp. 11-65.

Edward Murray, Fellini the Artist (New York: Frederick Ungar Publishing, 1976), 256 pp.

Renzo Renzi, Federico Fellini (Guanda: Parma, 1956), 63 pp.

Lillian Ross, "10½: A Movie in Technicolor," New Yorker (30 October 1965), pp. 63-68, 73-90, 95-102 & 105-107.

Angelo Solmi, Fellini, translated by Elizabeth Greenwood (New York: Merlin Press, 1967), 183 pp.

Christian Strich, ed., Fellini on Fellini, translated by Isabel Quigley (New York: Delacorte Press/Seymour Lawrence, 1976), 180 pp.

Eugene Walter, "The Wizardry of Fellini," Films and Filming, 12, No. 9 (June 1966), 18-26.

Critical Survey of Oeuvre

The movies of Federico Fellini are festive and explosive. They seem to overflow their bounds. Fellini has said, "I love hearing about amazing things. My capacity for marvelling is boundless. I am not blasé about anything. On the contrary, I am careful not to confine my imagination." This attitude is reflected in his films. The term most often applied to his style is "baroque," and to his form, "open." His work is "baroque" in the sense that it is intricate, full of details, movements, and changes, yet immediately accessible in its emotional impact on the viewer. It is "open" in two senses. First, his films are episodic. They contain sequences which are virtually stories in themselves and could almost be viewed independently. Arguably, the parts of a Fellini movie could be considered better than the whole. But certainly his films could be expanded or contracted by the addition or subtraction of such episodes. Second, his movies are filled with secondary characters who enter the film, present their piece of the whole, and depart, each one taking with him a story we might well want to follow. Similarly, Fellini takes up in his films a variety of themes and subjects. He treats staged illusions, spectacles, circuses, and religious ceremonies, and he treats quiet moments of loneliness. He is concerned with life in the provincial town and life in the city. There is a Franciscan quality to some of his films and an anti-clerical quality to others. The internal life of the imagination and the memory interests him, and so does the external life of mannerisms, foibles, and forms. Early in his career, he was concerned with the ideas of self-sacrifice and communication with others, and later with those of individual self-definition and liberation. Recently the themes of mutability, age and death have become important to him. He is fascinated with adolescents, social outsiders, grotesques, con men, performers, clowns, and troubled creative artists, but he can treat also, albeit usually satirically, characters who are "norms" in their societies. The movies of Fellini are a rich, important part of modern cinema.

* * *

Fellini's first three movies were comedies. Variety Lights (1950, co-directed with Alberto Lattuada) is a story about a vaudeville comic who tries to take under his wing a young, female singer-dancer on her way up; a fairly typical "show biz" tale. What saves the movie from the banal, though, are scenes, semi-comic and semi-humiliating, where the vaudevillians have to cope with a horse-cart driver who insists on his money before he will transport them, a hostile audience who want the "redhead" from the chorus line and no one else, a theater manager who demands to know why the troupe is so small, and a wealthy lawyer who kicks them out of his house when he finds he can't spend the night with the young singer-dancer. The tacky side of vaudeville has never been better detailed. Here Fellini probably drew on stories told him by his comedian friend Aldo Fabrizi about life on tour. The White Sheik (1952) treats a newlywed couple who come to Rome for their honeymoon. The wife wishes to find her romantic hero of the fumetti. (The fumetti are Italian comic books; their pictures, though, are photographs of actors in staged poses, instead of drawings.) She sneaks off to the location for the photo-graphing of the strip The White Sheik, and again Fellini reveals the behind-the-scenes maneuverings of a staged, entertainment world. The husband looks forward to a papal audience arranged by his well-connected relatives. He must stall off the relatives until he can relocate his wife, or he will lose face. The wife is naively romantic and the husband foolishly proper; they are natural comic adversaries. For this movie, Fellini could draw on his experiences with the humor magazines 420 and Marc' Aurelio. I Vitelloni (1953) is a noticeably more ambitious comedy. It deals with a group of delayed adolescents in a seaside resort like Fellini's Rimini. Despite the fact they are pushing thirty, these males have not taken on the responsibilities associated with adulthood. They live with parents, attempt romantic conquests together, joke together, dream together, and, above all, seek to avoid work together. At least three of the group receive severe jolts. Alberto, the most fanciful, is upset the morning after the Carnival ball when his sister, who had supported Alberto and the mother, leaves home with her lover. Responsibility is thrust at Alberto after his night of play and disguise at the ball, when he least expects responsibility. Leopoldo, the pretentious playwright of the group, presents his manuscript to the traveling actor Sergio Natali, leads his friends backstage after the actor's performance, and discovers to his ecstatic delight the actor's interest in his manuscript and in him. Later that night, by the edge of the sea, from Natali's leer, Leopoldo learns that the actor's interest in him is primarily a homosexual one, and Leopoldo runs off, clutching his manuscript to him. Fausto, the ringleader of the group, is forced into marriage when he makes pregnant the sister of one of his pals. Months later, after Fausto takes to bed a singer from Natali's tour-ing show, Fausto's wife runs away for a day, causing Fausto sharp concern until he finds her safe and earning him a beating from his angry father. I Vitelloni follows a rhythm of emotional ups and downs. It is the most episodic, or "open," of the early comedies.

In the early comedies there are two kinds of sequences which have become set pieces Fellini uses over and over. The first is a party which builds up to a frantic pitch and then winds down to the separateness and loneliness of the participants; the second is a meeting in a deserted town square at night, all the more lonely, as critic Geneviève Agel has noted, because during the day the square is the center of community activity. Parties wind down to abject conclusions in Variety Lights and I Vitelloni, and there are lonely meetings in squares in The White Sheik and I Vitelloni. In the later movie Il Bidone, Augusto's hopes of getting into a night club venture with the successful Rinaldo fade as the New Year's Eve party peaks in excitement and moves to its conclusion in the dispute among Augusto, Roberto, Picasso, and Iris in the street littered with confetti. The famous orgy sequence of La Dolce Vita ends at dawn with the desultory trek to the beach and a look at the bloated jelly fish by members of the smart-set with whom Marcello has cast his lot. And in 8½, the frantic pace of the harem fantasy gives way to Guido and Luisa sitting separately in the audition hall. The moment when Gelsomina is taunted by drunks in a nearly deserted square is an especially strong scene in La Strada. Powerful, too, are the scene in the village square between Guido and Claudia in 8½, when Guido tells her that he has no part for her in his movie and the final sequence in Roma, when the motor-cyclists drive through the otherwise deserted main squares in Rome late at night.

In all of the three early comedies, there is a look at staged illusion and at the reality behind it. Variety Lights begins with the show performed by the vaudeville troupe and then reveals the petty squabbles, betrayals, and difficulties of the troupe off-stage. The wife's first view of the White Sheik shows him at his illusory best and his most romantic. She sees him in costume, swinging lightly on a trapeze high above her. He seems almost to fly to her. Only after he hits ground, shows his fear of the horse he must mount, bungles the sailing of his craft, and climbs tamely on the vespa behind his mountainous wife does the heroine see behind the facade of his role. Similarly, Natali and his troupe perform an energetic, if hammy, pageant and impress Leopoldo in the audience, before Natali reveals his homosexual designs on Leopoldo later that night. In these early comedies, Fellini wishes, of course, to debunk the facade and glamour of staged illusion. But much more interesting than this is the sense of genuine wonder Fellini can create that the staged illusion does, in fact, work, despite its commonplace practitioners and materials. Each of the staged illusions in the early comedies works quite clearly for its audience inside the film and very probably for its audience outside the film. The theme of the staged spectacle is one that has continued to fascinate Fellini. The more vociferous the audience inside the film, the greater the wonder when they are subdued and caught up by illusion. This is the case in Nights of Cabiria, where the audience hoots at Cabiria and then watches her in subdued silence as she acts out her romantic longings under hypnosis. And it is the case in Roma when one of the most critical and maliciously witty audiences ever assembled gets caught up in the patriotic fervor of the master of ceremonies and the energetic dancing of the girls in sailor suits. European critics, in particular, have commented on Fellini's concern with the interrelationship of illusion and reality in 8½. They put him in the tradition of Pirandello. The American critic Stuart Rosenthal has commented that staged spectacle gives Fellini the means to expand the scale of the emotion and signif- icance of a life or an event. Beyond these points is the additional one that group spectacle gives the individual an opportunity to be caught up in a sense of community emotion, to feel more than an indi- vidual alone. This seems an important effect of the various pageants in Amarcord.

The theme of adolescence as presented in I Vitelloni is especially interesting. On the surface, the film is an attack on the young males for delaying too long at the adolescent stage. Moraldo, who like Fellini leaves the provincial town, condemns Fausto openly for his irresponsible behavior toward Moraldo's sister. Fausto must attempt to seduce every attractive woman who crosses his path. He is incapable of considering points of view other than his own for more than a few minutes. He is unwilling to make sacrifices for long- ranged goals. His is a world of instant self-gratification. Leopoldo revels in his deluded dream of becoming a playwright. Alberto un- thinkingly exploits his sister for money, and misses completely her painful moment with the mother, in his rush to find a hat to wear to the ball. As a group, the vitelloni harass a forty-year-old prosti- tute and mock Moraldo's job. That is the surface of the film. But, there is also a "sub-text," and, like so many "sub-texts" in litera- ture, this one runs counter to the surface meaning. When Fausto plays the mambo record he brought from Rome, he and Alberto can dance to it without inhibition in the main street. They respond simply and directly to the music. The moment is one of spontaneous joy. That the vitelloni are capable of such immediate and complete response is their most appealing aspect. Moraldo forgets the "Miss Siren Contest" and enjoys the thunderstorm at the movie's beginning. Riccardo and Alberto forget momentarily the search for Sandra and lose themselves in interest over the call of a bird. When Alberto and the others dress up for the Carnival ball, they are not just escaping reality, they are also exercising their wit and inventiveness through play. The vitelloni can discover a tin can in the street and instantly launch a rousing soccer game. There is an interesting mixture of rapport and competitiveness in the group. They can enjoy each other's successes and mock each other's mistakes, but in either case, they offer each other the comfort of membership in a group. Compared to the joylessness in the work routines and in the codes of duty of the adults, the emotional spontaneity, the playful inventiveness, and the group sense of the vitelloni give their adolescent life-style a certain, real value.

* * *

La Strada (1954), Il Bidone (1955), and Nights of Cabiria (1956) comprise Fellini's trilogy of loneliness. The main characters are social outsiders. The basic themes in each work are the separateness

20

of people and the need for a spirit of self-sacrifice and love which can overcome this separateness. In an open letter on the subject of La Strada, Fellini has said: "Our trouble, as modern men, is loneliness, and this begins in the very depths of our being. No public celebration or political symphony can hope to be rid of it. Only between man and man, I think, can this solitude be broken, only through individual people can a kind of message be passed, making them understand--almost <u>discover</u>--the profound link between one person and the next." Fellini describes himself as a religious, but anticlerical man. Especially in his trilogy of loneliness he exhibits a strong Franciscan belief in the value of self-sacrifice and in the capacity to love.

<u>Nights of Cabiria</u> is the story of a guileless prostitute who goes through a series of episodes in which her expectations of a better, less lonely life are aroused, only to be dashed. For instance, in the last sequences, Cabiria enters a theater where a magician is performing. He hypnotizes her and tells her to carry on a courtship with an imaginary man named Oscar. After the performance, a con man seeks her out, and, telling her his name is Oscar, begins to court her. The courtship ends abruptly after she draws her savings from the bank. Oscar takes her money and deserts her in a forest. The final shots show Cabiria walking back to town. She looks into the camera and begins to smile. It is Cabiria's human resiliency that Fellini celebrates. He has put it: "Cabiria...is fragile, tender and unfortunate; after all that has happened to her, and after the collapse of her naive dream of love, she still believes in love and in life."

Like <u>I Vitelloni</u>, <u>Nights of Cabiria</u> is an episodic movie, and also like the earlier movie, it follows an alternating rhythm of hope and disappointment. <u>Nights of Cabiria</u> is the first film Fellini made with editor Leo Cattozzo, and the film is often praised for its editing. Sequences alternate, with some regularity, between night and day, reinforcing the cyclical rhythm of hope and disappointment. After each disappointment, Cabiria is plunged into a new adventure with an abruptness that helps curtail excessive sentimentality. Fellini and Cattozzo begin new sequences often with "disorientation" shots, that is, close-ups which jar the viewer. For example, a sequence involving prostitutes on the <u>Passeggiata Archeologica</u> starts with a close-up of a woman's pacing legs. The camera, then, pulls back to reveal to us the entire scene in long shot, and we discover the appropriateness of the opening shot. The jarring effect of the close-up which we can't immediately "place" serves to pull us away from considerations of what had happened previously and to make us extremely attentive to what will happen next. Fellini and Cattozzo have used the device quite effectively also in <u>La Dolce Vita</u> and 8½. Consider the close-up of the Siamese mask of the dancer, which introduces us to the sequence in the night club in <u>La Dolce Vita</u>, or the close-up in silhouette of Carla's head, which introduces us to the bedroom sequence in $8\frac{1}{2}$. The jarring effect is similar to the effect gained by the "jump-cutting" in French New Wave films made shortly after Nights of Cabiria.

Il Bidone deals with a small-time swindler. (The title means literally the swindle.) The method of Augusto, this swindler, is to play on the greed of his victims. His favorite swindle is the buried treasure ruse. Augusto disguises himself as a priest and goes to a rural family with the story that a dying criminal has buried his loot on the family's property and confessed the whereabouts to the priest-swindler. If the family will pay for masses to be said over the criminal, the loot will go to the family, according to the criminal's last request. The pickings for the swindler and his henchmen are small because they cheat relatively poor people. Throughout the movie, we become increasingly aware of the precariousness and the loneliness of the swindler's life. Augusto is separated from his wife and daughter. His situation is contrasted to that of Picasso, another con man, who withdraws from swindling in order to keep his marriage intact. At the movie's end, Augusto holds out money from his henchmen—presumably to give it to his daughter, before whom he has been humiliated by an arrest in the recent past. The henchmen beat him and leave him to die. Augusto's failed attempt to do something for his daughter is his one act of kindness—perhaps a redemptive act.

The last shots of Il Bidone are highly symbolic. They clash severely with the tone of the movie which has been realistic or comic until the death scene. The final shots show the swindler crawling up the side of a rocky hill to die. There is agony on his face. A patch of blood on his forehead. His arms are spread. It would be hard to imagine a more Christlike death. Certainly Fellini is enamored of symbolic endings which externalize his hero's final state of mind. When the endings are forced, as in Il Bidone, they are "groaners." But when they successfully mirror the hero's condition and sum up accurately the tone of the work, they can be haunting. Such is the case with Cabiria's smile, or the circus ring ending of $8\frac{1}{2}$, or the waltz on the frozen canal at the conclusion of Casanova.

The best of Fellini's trilogy of loneliness is La Strada. The film won the Grand Prize at the Venice Film Festival and an Academy Award in the United States. It was Fellini's first big financial success. As Fellini tells it, the film began with his idea of portraying the lonely travels of a medieval knight. The idea of the knight, however, gave way to the notion of a gypsy couple when, during the filming of Variety Lights, Fellini saw such a couple camped by the roadside. The woman stirred a pot of soup. The man waited for his dinner, standing apart from her. The couple never spoke. Fellini found the loneliness of two people living together, but not communicating, very starkly presented by the pair. Perhaps such loneliness is finally a deeper one than the loneliness of a single person, because it seems accepted by choice.

As he had done in <u>The White Sheik</u>, Fellini contrasts in <u>La Strada</u> two diametrically opposed types: a brutish strongman, Zampano, who performs the single trick of breaking a chain by inflating his lungs, and a soft, almost simple-minded waif, Gelsomina, who serves as the strongman's assistant. Gelsomina's face is moon-shaped, her eyes enormous, she wears bangs, and she is very short. She is an archetypal underdog. Zampano is tall and massive, with dark, thick eyebrows. He is an archetypal bully. Most of the action is presented from Gelsomina's point-of-view. When Zampano performs an act independently from her, we usually return to Gelsomina for her reaction. At the beginning of the movie, Zampano buys her from her family, takes her to bed with him as his wife, and trains her to act as his assistant in his travelling show. Like many of Fellini's childlike characters, Gelsomina has the capacity for spontaneous joy. She delights in the applause of the crowd. In a field, she throws her arms wide in imitation of a tree. Given a few free moments, she plants tomato seeds, although she knows she can't stay to harvest them. Quickly, intuitively, she learns to play musical instruments with extraordinary skill. But with Zampano, she is lonely. To her questions about his past and about his relations with other women, he gives no answers. And he falls asleep when Gelsomina tries to tell him of her loneliness. Twice Zampano leaves Gelsomina while he goes off with other women he finds more sexually attractive. Gelsomina's loneliness is demonstrated in two, brief, almost silent scenes which are among the best in Fellini's movies. In the first, Gelsomina sits on a curb, deserted by Zampano for a night of love-making. Toward dawn, a horse plods down the middle of the street, passes Gelsomina without noticing her, and disappears. Probably, the horse is returning by rote to its barn after a night at pasture. In the dawn light, however, it seems almost a phantom. As it approaches, it raises expectations that somehow it will be important or comforting to Gelsomina. Such, unfortunately, is not the case, and Gelsomina seems the more alone when these expectations fail. Mainly, though, the solitary horse is a mirrorlike equivalent of Gelsomina's emotional state, her loneliness. The second scene achieves a similar effect. At a marriage feast, some children lead Gelsomina to the room of a retarded child. They ask her to entertain the child, and she tries to do so. But when she can draw no reaction, she goes closer and stares at the white mask of the child's face. Fellini has commented: "The apparition of this creature who is so isolated, and a prey to delirium--and who thus has an extremely mysterious dimension--it seems to me that uniting him in close-up with Gelsomina, who comes right next to him and who looks at him with curiosity, underlines with rather great suggestive power Gelsomina's own solitude."

In the middle section of the film, the character of the tight-rope walker, known as the Fool, appears. He is Fellini's <u>eiron</u>. He intensifies the situation. At every opportunity, the Fool attacks Zampano's self-complacency. More importantly the Fool gives direction and purpose to Gelsomina's attempts to communicate with Zampano and to reach him emotionally. The Fool explains to Gelsomina his theory that everything in the universe, even a pebble, does have a purpose. Maybe Gelsomina's purpose, the Fool suggests, is to bring love to Zampano. The Fool's words cheer Gelsomina, and she redoubles her efforts with Zampano. "I wanted to leave you once," she tells Zampano, "but now you're my home." Unfortunately, Zampano's brutal acts destroy the relationship. He tries to force Gelsomina to help him rob a convent where they have spent the night, and Zampano kills the Fool in a brawl. Shocked beyond recovery, Gelsomina withdraws into herself, and Zampano abandons her.

The ending of the movie is controversial. It has drawn a great deal of attention from critics who attempt to explain and justify it on thematic grounds. To many viewers, however, the emotional "heft" of it seems wrong. The last sequence takes place five years after Zampano's abandonment of Gelsomina. In a provincial town, Zampano hears a song Gelsomina hummed and played. He learns that she died in the town. In a rage, Zampano picks a fight in a cafe and then goes to the beach, falls on his knees, and cries out in agony. Critics have argued that Zampano has been moved at last by Gelsomina and has been humanized by her. Ironically, this humanizing, they argue further, has come through Gelsomina's death, and Zampano is cut off from the kind of sustaining relationship he now realizes he needs. This reading seems valid. But two problems remain. The first is structural. Fellini has changed points-of-view. Whereas we have seen most of the action of the film through Gelsomina's eyes up to the ending, we see the last sequence from Zampano's viewpoint. The switch is a daring one. But we may well feel cheated by it, for we have come to identify closely with Gelsomina as we have looked through her eyes. The second is thematic. The ending asks us to accept as very important the fact that Zampano has been humanized by Gelsomina's sacrifice. But if we weigh the loss of Gelsomina's life and her gift for enjoying life against this consequence, it may be difficult for us to accept such an attitude. To accept it, we must virtually bring to the work a Franciscan belief in the value of sacrificing one's self for another. If we do not bring such a belief to the work, it may seem to us that Fellini has sought to look away at the end from the tragic consequence inherent in the relationship between Gelsomina and Zampano—her destruction at his hands.

La Strada made clear to reviewers and viewers in Italy Fellini's separation from the neorealistic movement where he had served his apprenticeship. The characters are from the sub-proletariat. But the movie does not show their problem as a class problem, nor does it follow a documentary style. The movie depicts Gelsomina and Zampano as symbolic characters in an existential drama of communication. Fellini's vision is a highly personal, almost mystical one. Accordingly, the movie was attacked by Marxist critics. And because of the Franciscan spirit of Gelsomina's sacrifice and the general Christian stance of the film, it was praised by Catholic critics.

Fellini's movement away from the "documentary" or "objective" style could have been observed in the short episode A Matrimonial Agency which Fellini did in 1953 before the shooting of La Strada. The episode was made for the anthology film Love in the City organized by neorealist writer Cesar Zavattini. (Other directors who contributed were Michaelangelo Antonioni, Dino Risi, Francesco Maselli, Alberto Lattuada, and Zavattini. An episode on prostitution by Carlo Lizzani was cut by the censor.) The film was to resemble a journalistic enquiry with each director doing a documentary on different aspects of love in the urban situation. Unlike the other episodes, Fellini's segment is invented. It is about the findings of a reporter who goes to a matrimonial agency and claims to be seeking a wife for a patient who thinks he is a werewolf. To his surprise, he finds a young woman willing to consider marrying this patient. The fantasy involved in Fellini's episode indicates a separation between Fellini and the neorealists. The loneliness of the young woman willing to consider such a strange union, though, links the short episode to the themes of Fellini's trilogy of feature length films on loneliness.

* * *

With La Dolce Vita (1959), Fellini broke away from making movies of social outsiders and turned in the opposite direction to make a satire of modern society itself. The movie was described by Fellini as an attempt to "take the temperature" of society. He asked that the movie be considered more as a "fresco" than as a traditional narrative. Important to Fellini in conceiving the film were conversations he had with reporters and photographers who covered the personal lives of the celebrities frequenting the outdoor cafes of the Via Veneto in Rome. He has written: "I spent many evenings with the photographer-reporters of the Via Veneto, chatting with Tazio Secchiaroli and the others, and getting them to tell me about the tricks of their trade. How they fixed on their victim; how they behaved to make him nervous; how they prepared their pieces, exactly as required, for the various papers." Fellini's protagonist, Marcello, would like to be a serious writer, but he is, in fact, a reporter who covers assignments on celebrities and sensational events for the tabloids. The movie itself has often the visual impact of a tabloid picture-spread. Fellini puts Marcello and the women of the film in inky black clothes, with dark wigs often for the women. Their faces are lit to make them appear often glaringly white. Fellini uses telephoto lenses to make the principle figures stand out against blurred backgrounds. The total effect is that of a series of newspaper feature photographs in strong blacks and whites. In the movie, the photographers, the paparazzi, contrive situations so that they can present them to their readers as real, and they reduce real, human tragedy, on the other hand, to the clichés of sensationalism. The journalists and the photographers are as much a part of Fellini's satire as the people and events they cover.

Fellini treats two different, staged spectacles in the film, the promotion of the movie star Sylvia and the TV filming of the children who claim to have seen the Virgin. Sylvia arrives by airplane in Rome and makes the traditional march down the steps blowing kisses to newspapermen. She is presented with a pizza pie by her producer. At her press conference, prompted by her secretary, she gives the programmed responses of the sex goddess: "I sleep in only two drops of French perfume... I like a lot of things, but there are three things I like most: love, love, love." So far the sequence is amusing. A pleasant collusion between the star, the newspapermen, and the unseen readers who will get a good story. The joke deepens. We learn that Sylvia does have, in fact, an enormous physical vitality when she races to the top of St. Peter's, dances with Frankie Stout at the Baths of Caracalla, and splashes in the Fountain of Trevi. Marcello responds to her as if she were a deity. "You are the first woman on the first day of creation," he tells her. But the sequence ends sadly with Sylvia's troubled relationship with her fiancé Robert. He slaps her. She cries and tells him, "You shouldn't do things like that, especially in front of people." The facade is gone. We see a hurt woman, worried about her image. The TV filming sequence follows a similar pattern, but does so on a level of more intensity. Two children claim to have seen the Virgin by a tree in a field and have predicted her return. A crowd gathers for the event. At first, the tone is mainly comic. A grandfather volunteers to sing "Ave Maria" in exchange for some cigars. The director rehearses actors to appear in a crowd scene calling for a miracle. An uncle fluffs his lines in a prepared speech. But the tone grows more serious and then reaches a pitch of hysteria. A mother appears with her baby and prays at the tree to the Virgin to make her baby well. The children arrive and lead the crowd on a chase through the field. A cold rain falls and begins to explode the lights. People rip at the tree of the Virgin in hopes of obtaining a holy relic. An old woman calls out that someone, presumably her husband, has died. The sequence ends with the funeral at dawn for the dead man. Here Fellini goes one step beyond destroying the facade of the spectacle. He shows the duped victims.

Marcello is both the viewer's guide to the events of the movie and a character in his own right. He is a man from the provinces who has become experienced in the ways of the city. He is attracted to the beautiful and wealthy Maddelena and her sophisticated friends, and, as an aspiring writer, he is attracted to the intellectual Steiner and his circle. Maddelena takes him in her white convertible to the apartment of a prostitute where they make love. She meets him later at a party given by aristocrats and leads him to a whisper gallery. While Marcello tells her of his love, Maddelena allows another man to make love to her as she listens to Marcello's words, out of sight at her end of the gallery. As she explains forthrightly, she has too many possibilities and will not make a single choice. She goes from one sensation to another. Moreover, she is a representative of her set. We see at the party that the other aristocrats behave as Maddelena does. Steiner appeals to Marcello because he seems to have built a rational sanctuary for himself with his books, his children, and his artistic wife, a sanctuary from which he can view and understand the hurly-burly of life. But in fact, Steiner has fled from life. He records sounds from nature on his tape recorder in order to listen in the safety of his study, and he intellectualizes his children's responses to life. Moreover, with his terrible lucidity, Steiner knows what's wrong with what he does and warns Marcello against his kind of life. "The most awful life is better than a sheltered one, in a world where everything is in its place," Steiner tells Marcello. When Steiner commits suicide, Marcello is shocked as deeply as is possible for him. Marcello gives up his own plans for serious writing, and, at an orgy in the home of a movie producer, Marcello announces he has become a publicity agent. By tracing Marcello's relations with Maddelena and with Steiner, Fellini is able to criticize the worlds Maddelena and Steiner move in.

The institution of the provincial family is criticized also in La Dolce Vita. When Marcello's father comes to visit his son in Rome, Marcello hopes he will at last get to know the man who was gone from home so much on sales trips when Marcello was a boy. The father maneuvers his son into an evening at a club the father had visited many years in the past. The father flirts with a dancer, goes home with her, and suffers a slight heart attack. He departs from Rome the next morning. Marcello achieves nothing more than a jovial, superficial relationship with his father. Marcello's mistress, Emma, behaves like a wife. More precisely, she behaves like a parody of the Southern Italian wife. (Emma comes from Calabria.) She is jealous and possessive. She carries food for Marcello to the field of the miracle. She phones Marcello at the press conference with Sylvia. And she takes an overdose of sleeping pills when Marcello spends the night away from home. Marcello tells her: "I'm afraid of you! Of your selfishness, of the poverty of your ideals!... You talk of nothing but the kitchen and the bedroom. Do you understand that a man who accepts a life like that is through?... I don't believe in this aggressive, sticky, maternal love of yours." But Marcello never does give up the relationship with Emma. Although he leaves her several times, he always returns. To be sure, the failure of the father-son and of the husband-wife relationships are as much Marcello's fault as the faults of his father and Emma. But Fellini's wish is not so much to affix blame as to show failures in the relationships.

At the ending of the movie, Marcello encounters a beautiful and innocent adolescent girl he had met earlier. She calls to him on the beach, from the other side of an inlet. Not able to hear what she is saying, he shrugs and leaves her. He rejoins a group of revelers who have been inspecting a strange and monstrous sea creature that fishermen have dragged onto the beach. The ending recalls the final scene in I Vitelloni, where Moraldo, the serious vitellone who wishes to break away, leaves behind a young boy with whom he equates his own youth and sets out by train for the city. (Parts of La Dolce Vita were based on Moraldo in the City, an unrealized sequel to I Vitelloni.) In I Vitelloni, Moraldo has no idea what he will encounter in the city. Marcello, on the other hand, has a rather good idea of what to expect when he turns and walks away from the figure of adolescent hopefulness. The city of Maddelena, Steiner, Sylvia, the revelers, and the paparazzi.

Fellini achieved a succès de scandale with La Dolce Vita. The movie made for Fellini something of a reputation as a P.T. Barnum among film directors. It had huge box office receipts in Italy and abroad. Critical reaction in Italy was almost the opposite of the reaction to La Strada. Marxist critics praised the film as an attack on the decadence of the aristocrats and the bourgeoisie. The Osservatore, the Vatican newspaper, denounced the film, and the Centro cattolico cinematografico classified it as "unsuitable for all." At the premier in Milan, a man spat on Fellini and told him, "You are dragging Italy through the mud." Objections were made by some Catholics and conservatives to the representation of the Church, to the depiction of the casual or sadistic attitudes of the characters toward sex, and to an attitude of despair in the film. Debate took place in the Italian Parliament as to whether or not the film should be withdrawn from circulation or cut. It was decided, however, that no official action would be taken. The controversy, of course, aided greatly the movie's box office appeal.

Partly in answer to the debate about the censorship of La Dolce Vita, Fellini made his episode The Temptations of Doctor Antonio in the anthology film Boccaccio '70 in 1962. (Other directors who contributed segments to the export print were Luchino Visconti and Vittorio De Sica.) Fellini's short film is a satiric comedy about the efforts of a prude to censor the depiction of Anita Ekberg in a low-cut gown, on a billboard outside his apartment. The episode is remarkably free of rancor. Fellini defeats the efforts of the prude as much by the air of good humor in the film as by the prude's foolish excesses.

* * *

8½ (1963) and Juliet of the Spirits (1965) are two works of interior drama. Fellini has summed up 8½ as a "film in which parts of the past and imaginary events are superimposed upon the present," and the same assertion could be made about Juliet of the Spirits. Both works move freely from the present events to memories and to fantasies, in order to reveal totally the inner life of their protagonists. Perhaps the greatest strength of the two films is the ease with which they conduct us through three different spheres of reality. We can literally see the workings of the minds of the two protagonists as we watch elements of the past merge with those of the present to form anxiety dreams or wish-fulfillment fantasies. Fellini treats both his protagonists at crisis points in their lives when both are extremely vulnerable. Guido, the director hero of $8\frac{1}{2}$, wishes to make an autobiographical film that will give an honest representation of his life. He finds himself confused about the important values and emotional pulls in his life, and he finds himself creatively blocked in his ability to make his film, while his producer and crew stand by impatiently waiting to turn the cameras. Juliet, the house-wife of <u>Juliet of the Spirits</u>, undergoes also a crisis of self-definition when she discovers her husband's infidelity and sees her marriage crumble. Hesitantly, she tries to break free from inhibitions stemming from her religious upbringing and the social definition of the role of the wife impressed on her by her family.

Certainly, the quests for self-definition and liberation have become major themes for Fellini. He has said: "I have struggled to free myself--always from the past, from the education laid upon me as a child. That is what I'm seeking, though through different characters and with changing tempo and images." These themes of self-definition and liberation seem to run counter to his themes of self-sacrifice and of the need for communication of Fellini's trilogy of loneliness. Rather than a reaction against the earlier themes, though, Fellini probably intends his films on self-definition and liberation to be work done at the other end of the spectrum of human experience. In both $8\frac{1}{2}$ and <u>Juliet of the Spirits</u>, the protagonists feel at the end a sense of release and happiness through fuller self-acceptance. Critics Isabella Conti and Albert Benderson have used Jung's term "individuation" to sum up the sense of psychic wholeness that Guido achieves, and this conception could be applied also to Juliet's development.

$8\frac{1}{2}$ abounds in situations and images of confinement and escape. The film opens with Guido's anxiety dream of suffocating in his car caught in a traffic jam in a tunnel. In his imagination, he soars free and hovers in the air above a beach. He discovers a cord attached to his leg, and two men on the beach involved in his film project pull him back down into the sea. Images of confinement continue in the sequences in the lobby, at the night club, in the dining room, and in the audition theater where the producer, the French actress, agents, and reporters keep after Guido. This pattern culminates in the frightening sequence of the press conference at the base of the rocket launching pad. Faces of reporters loom at the camera, and Guido's producer threatens, "If you don't make this film, I'll ruin you." Anxiety is increased in the film through Fellini's use of audial effects such as the buzzing telephone and "Ride of the Valkyries." Apparently, Guido intends his movie to treat an escape. The hero of Guido's movie will lead away from earth a group of people to make a new start. Pace, the producer, explains: "The scene begins with a panoramic view of the earth completely destroyed by nuclear war. [The rocket] is the modern Noah's Ark.... The survivors of all mankind seek shelter on a new planet." At the opening of <u>Juliet of the Spirits</u>, the house of Juliet is taken over by guests brought by her husband. She is threatened on the beach by a group of fantasy figures of invading Turks. She tries to flee, but finds herself unable to move quickly. Throughout the course of the movie she is assailed by phantoms of her imagination, until near the end they seem to control her house as the real life guests had done earlier. The main image of escape for her is the old circus biplane in which she imagines her grandfather flew off.

Liberation for Guido and Juliet, however, does not come from escape, but rather through self-acceptance. Although Guido would like to believe in only one value, represented by the dream figure of a girl in white, he is a man with diverse emotional pulls. In his memories of childhood, we can see these emotional wants beginning, and, in his adult fantasies and his adult life, we can see their continuation. His harem fantasy as an adult is an expansion of his experience as a child being bathed by warm, living nurses in the wine vat at the farm of his grandparents. His extra-marital affair with the simple, plump Carla is an extension of his sexual interest as a child in the leonine prostitute Saraghina who dances for him on the beach. (Both women are associated with the same musical theme hummed by a soprano voice. Guido makes up Carla's face to resemble the face of a prostitute. And the designs of the necklines of the clothes of the two women are similar.) Guido's relationship with his wife reflects something of his childhood relationship with his mother. He contrives situations where his wife must play the role of moral enforcer. His curiosity about the spirit world of Rossella, his wife's friend, is a retention of his excitement about the magical portrait at the farm of the grandparents. Guido achieves an exhilarating sense of a psychic wholeness when he gives up his pursuit of the ideal of the girl in white and accepts in her place a circle of diverse people from his past, present, and fantasy worlds. In an interview, Fellini has said about Guido at the conclusion of 8½: "He is at peace with himself at last--free to accept himself as he is, not as he wished he were or might have been."

In <u>Juliet of the Spirits</u>, at the outset, the heroine defines herself within an ideal of marriage. Juliet tells her neighbor Suzy about her attitude toward her husband, Giorgio: "He became all my world. My husband, my lover, my father, my friend, and my house. I didn't need anyone else." In the course of the movie, Juliet sees her marriage crumble. Giorgio forgets their anniversary. He says the name "Gabriella" in his sleep. Juliet catches him speaking in endearing terms late at night on the telephone. The private detective Juliet hires makes movies of Giorgio's liasons with his young mistress. And finally Giorgio leaves the house. As Juliet's world falls apart, she comes to recognize more and more the emotional longings she has restrained. At the end, she is prepared to accept the truth given her by a psychologist, "You long for your husband to go away. Without Giorgio you'd begin to breathe, to live," and to accept the psychologist's advice, "Be yourself spontaneously, without fighting your desires and passions."

Both $8\frac{1}{2}$ and <u>Juliet of the Spirits</u> are anti-clerical. The Church condemns the child Guido's sexual curiosity and presents him with an image of idealized beauty as a substitute. In the confessional, he is advised that the prostitute Saraghina is the Devil. For going to see her, Guido is shamed before his mother and the other students and made to kneel on kernels of corn as penance. When Guido as an adult consults the Cardinal in the park, the Cardinal merely questions him about his marriage and asks him to listen to the mournful sound of the Diomedes bird. In his fantasy of a meeting with the Cardinal in the steam baths, Guido sees the skeletal form of the Cardinal silhouetted behind a sheet. "Outside the church there is no salvation," the Cardinal tells him. The Church is at the very root of Juliet's sexual inhibitions. In her convent school play as a child, Juliet is given the role of a martyr who submits to self-sacrifice on a bed of flames to preserve her innocence and purity. Juliet's intensely religious, young friend Laura commits suicide for love. When Juliet nearly submits to the charms of the handsome, faunlike young man at Suzy's party, the image of Laura as the martyred saint appears to her and causes her to run off. Images of faceless, shrouded nuns haunt Juliet. Perhaps the most satiric stroke in the movie, however, is Fellini's device of having the prying detective disguise himself as a priest. In $8\frac{1}{2}$ and <u>Juliet of the Spirits</u>, Fellini's attack on the Church is directed primarily at its inhibiting and life-denying aspects.

$8\frac{1}{2}$ and <u>Juliet of the Spirits</u> are visually striking films. In $8\frac{1}{2}$, shot composition and camera movement are extremely effective. The film was the first feature-length movie in which Fellini worked with the cinematographer Gianni di Venanzo. (They had collaborated earlier on the episode <u>A Matrimonial Agency</u>.) Certainly this collaboration with di Venanzo contributed importantly to Fellini's development as a film artist. Almost each shot in $8\frac{1}{2}$ has a distinctive and strong impact. There is, for example, a strong sense of bizarre sterility in the almost whited-out shots of the lines of people at the spa waiting for water, or a sense of fearsomeness in the shots of the rocket tower lit by hundreds of spotlights on the ground (the tower is based on Brueghel's painting of "The Tower of Babel"), or a sense of weight in the deep-focus shot which shows la Saraghina's giant hips in the foreground, with the comparative speck of Guido's entire body in the far distance. The movie also contains elaborate dolly and tracking shots which put us subjectively in Guido's place as he stalks through his harem or through the steam baths on his way to visit the Cardinal.

In <u>Juliet of the Spirits</u>, color is the important element. Fellini had used color earlier in <u>The Temptations of Doctor Antonio</u> merely to conform with the other episodes of <u>Boccaccio '70</u>. In <u>Juliet of the Spirits</u>, however, he and di Venanzo attempt to exploit the possibilities of color. Fellini has said, "Color is a part not only of the language but also of the idea and the feeling of the dream. Colors in dreams are concepts...." In <u>Juliet of the Spirits</u>, color is often used to make a statement about the heroine. For instance, in one sequence Juliet in a dull white pajama suit and sampan hat is dominated totally by her mother and sisters in elaborate dresses and hats of pink, turquoise, and heliotrope in the midst of a brilliant green forest. Color also establishes mood. In Juliet's anxiety dream of the barges of the savage Turks, the sky and sea are a dirty green, and at Suzy's party where Juliet is sexually aroused, the color red is predominant in the gauzelike drapes, Suzy's ribbons, and Juliet's dress. Perhaps most important in a technical sense, though, is the seance which is lit by a single, internal light source. It is an effectively shadowy scene, and it demonstrated in 1965 that color could match black and white stock in reproducing shadows.

* * *

Fellini: A Director's Notebook (1968), The Clowns (1970), and Roma (1972) are subjective documentaries. The first two were made originally for television. Fellini appears on camera as himself in all three. The films are as much or more about his imagination and about the impact his subjects have on him as they are documentaries about motion-picture directing, clowns, and the city of Rome. In his essay "Why Clowns?" Fellini has remarked, "The only documentary that anyone can make is a documentary on himself." Fellini: A Director's Notebook is an account of the director's work methods as he moves away from a project he has scrapped, The Voyage of G. Mastorna, to the beginning of work on his new film, Fellini Satyricon. In particular, we see him tour the Colosseum, the Forum, the Appian Way, the subway diggings beneath the city, and a slaughter house, looking for material and ideas concerning the past of Rome, and most of all, we see him interviewing people whom he may wish to use in his film. In The Clowns, Fellini presents clowns from three different viewpoints: first, as they appeared to him as a child, overwhelming him with their energy and violence; second, as they seemed to him as a young man, stylized and controlled versions of village "grotesques," and third, as he considers them as a mature man in terms of the comic theory of the white, authoritarian clown versus the anarchistic, tramp clown known as the Augusto. Fellini attempts to discover what has happened to the clowns who have meant so much to him. He interviews former clowns and reconstructs their acts. With Roma, Fellini treats the city of Rome and its myths. Here, there are four points of view. He shows Rome as he feels it may have been in ancient times, as it seemed to him as a boy in the provinces, as it seemed to him as a young man in the 1930's newly arrived to test himself against the challenges and opportunities of the city, and as he finds it in contemporary times now that he has become middle-aged.

Running through all three documentaries is Fellini's fascination with grotesques. These are people who differ from the norm, either in terms of their physical characteristics or their mental and psychological attitudes or their behavior. In Notebook, Fellini moves among the street vendors, the homosexuals, and transvestites

who prowl the Colosseum at night; he screentests gypsies and enormous
butchers; and he interviews in his office a group of people who range
from the obese and gigantic to the small and thin. In The Clowns,
he presents us with a midget nun, with Giudizio the village idiot who
re-enacts war scenes in the street, with the pompous stationmaster
who brings a Fascist officer with him to gain the respect of school
children, with a wife who carts her drunken husband home in a wheelbarrow, and with a mutilated war veteran who sits on the beach with
a woman who recites Mussolini's speeches from memory. In Roma, the
young man newly arrived in Rome meets in his pension the mountainous
landlady in bed with "inflamed ovaries," her sunburnt son of twenty
or more who crawls into bed with her and assumes the fetal position,
a tiny grandmother who rocks in her chair in her room, a Chinaman who
cooks spaghetti in his room, and an old man who looks like Mussolini.
This group is extended by the assortment of people at the outdoor
restaurant where the young man eats, by the audience at the variety
hall he attends, and by the array of prostitutes that Fellini shows
us at the various brothels. (Much of the sense of challenge the
young man feels on coming to the city stems from the range of grotesques he meets.) Of the unusual people who seek him out in his office
in Notebook, Fellini says in the film, "I am very fond of all these
characters who are always chasing after me. They are all a little
mad, I know that. They say they need me, but in truth I need them
more. Their human qualities are rich, comic, and sometimes very
moving." In "The Purpose of the Grotesque in Fellini's Films,"
Harvey G. Cox, Jr., argues interestingly that Fellini is drawn to
grotesques as a means of recapturing a sense of "the mysterious, the
transcendent, and the holy." Grotesques, he states, are those people
who can't be contained in a conventional or neatly rational world.
They suggest another realm that is irrational, irregular, and fascin-
ating. While we may not want to accept Cox's premise that this
realm is "holy," we must surely accept his argument that grotesques
suggest to Fellini a "mysterious" dimension to life. Grotesques, of
course, appear in Fellini's early works. Giudizio has a role in I
Vitelloni. And Matilda, the huge, fleshy prostitute who hurls oaths
and taunts constantly at the other prostitutes in Nights of Cabiria,
can be considered an example. But it is in Fellini's later works
that grotesques appear most. In addition to the three documentaries,
Fellini Satyricon, Amarcord, and Casanova are works literally filled
with such characters. Grotesques are certainly one of the elements
in Fellini's films which the critics now term felliniesque.

Important in The Clowns and Roma are the themes of mutability,
age, and death. In both films, Fellini deals with things that were
important to him as a child and a young man. Both the clowns and
the city of Rome, however, have undergone changes which now alarm
the mature Fellini. Both films could be considered expressions of
this alarm. In The Clowns, Fellini poses the question, "Where are
the clowns of my childhood?" He is told by clowns, historian Tristan
Rémy, and even a taxi driver that clowns now no longer move people
as they used to. Fellini tries to recapture the clown acts of the

past by looking at old films and by interviewing former clowns. Neither method is successful. Particularly moving are Fellini's visits to the homes of retired clowns Bario and Père Loriot. Bario lives a kind of life in death, isolated in his house, looked after by his wife. He refuses to be interviewed. "I spent sixty years with the circus," he tells Fellini simply. "It was my whole life." The past tense is particularly significant in his statement. As Fellini withdraws from the house, Bario stands watching sadly from his second-floor window the retreat of this man who asked him to recall his past. Père Loriot tells Fellini that he tries to perform his act from time to time, but he concludes sadly, "In Rome, nobody laughed." In the final section of his film, Fellini stages the death scene of the tramp clown Augusto. The scene is replete with a grieving widow whose eyes spurt tears, a long comic will, and a lurching, veering funeral hearse. The body of Augusto keeps popping out of his coffin. At last, he escapes and soars into the air above the ring. His resurrection, or the resurrection of the clown spirit, is celebrated. The epilogue of the film makes the same statement, but in a more elegiac tone. A clown summons back his partner Fru-Fru from the dead by playing a solo on his trumpet that Fru-Fru answers on his. The two endings are assertions that the comic spirit of the clowns will continue.

Fellini's attitude in Roma seems less optimistic. In this film, he presents a splendid image of an ancient Roman villa sealed in the earth beneath Rome. The frescoes and the mosaics shine in their original, bright Mediterranean colors. The empty villa is the very essence of serenity. It is discovered by the crew digging a tunnel for the subway. As the crew penetrates the wall of the villa and lets in outside air, the colors begin to fade and the house begins to crumble. The picture of Rome in the 1930's which Fellini shows is not so idyllic. We are in the era of Fascism. But the pension where the hero lives, the restaurant where he eats, the vaudeville hall, and the brothels all teem with life and a certain raucous energy. These qualities are missing from Fellini's picture of the contemporary city. A sense of paralysis and a sense of violence predominate in the city of today. He depicts a traffic tie-up of the main highway around Rome, the Raccordo Anulare, caused by the wreck of a cattle truck and then a complete jam-up at the Colosseum, caused by a protest march by Marxists. At the "Festival of Ourselves" in Trastevere, in a sequence near the end of the film, police fall on a group of young, radical protesters, beat them, and lead them away, while diners in the outdoor restaurants applaud the police and laugh at the protesters. In the last sequence, helmeted motorcyclists, embodiments of speed and power, roar through streets deserted at night, claiming the city as theirs. Critic Stuart Rosenthal has wisely pointed out that Fellini carefully disassociates himself from the mocking diners in Trastevere and from the reactionaries who gather at the home of a princess and worship the dream return of Pope Pius XII. Fellini, in fact, praises the young hippies of the modern city for their candor in their attitudes toward sex, and he is tolerant, even gracious, to the student radicals who tell him his films lack social relevance. But finally, Fellini makes clear that these young people--for better or for worse--represent a world he can no longer feel part of. His city has changed, and it has grown strange to him. The themes of aging and of death became important ones in 8½ where Guido suffers the anxieties of middle age. From that point on, the themes of change, aging, and death have grown increasingly important to Fellini, particularly in Amarcord and Casanova, in addition to The Clowns and Roma.

In The Clowns, the historian Tristan Rémy expounds the idea that much of the comedy of clowns comes from the battle between the white clown and Augusto, the tramp clown. Fellini develops the idea further in his essay "Why Clowns?" It interests him greatly. The white clown, he says, "stands for elegance, grace, harmony, intelligence, lucidity." These attributes, the Augusto, or tramp clown, would feel drawn to, "if only they were not so priggishly displayed" by the white clown. The Augusto is "the child who dirties his pants, rebels against this perfection, gets drunk, rolls about on the floor and puts up an endless resistance." The battle between the two clowns is, then, "the struggle between the proud cult of reason...and the freedom of instinct." The two clowns are "teacher and child, mother and small son, even the angel with the flaming sword and the sinner." Finally, they are "two psychological aspects of man: one which aims upwards, the other which aims downwards; two divided, separated instincts." Fellini has applied the two categories to people in public life. Pasolini is "a white clown of the graceful, pretentious kind," and Antonioni is a "sad, silent, speechless" Augusto. Hitler is a white clown, and Mussolini an Augusto. Freud a white clown, and Jung an Augusto. Stuart Rosenthal has applied the categories to Fellini's characters and finds that they work well if one bears in mind that the characters can shift categories in different situations. The newlywed husband in The White Sheik is a white clown when he is with his wife, but is an Augusto when he is in the presence of his important relatives. Guido in 8½ is a white clown to his mistress Carla, but an Augusto to his wife Luisa. Rosenthal suggests that Gelsomina of La Strada most consistently stays in the role of the underdog Augusto, and that Zampano is most consistent in the role as the authoritarian and powerful white clown, albeit not a beautiful one.

* * *

Toby Dammit (1968), Fellini Satyricon (1969), and Casanova (1976) are Fellini's literary adaptations. All are "free" adaptations in the sense that Fellini has used his originals only as starting points for his own statements. Toby Dammit is based on Edgar Allan Poe's nineteenth-century short story "Never Bet the Devil Your Head." Fellini Satyricon is from Petronius Arbiter's first century A.D. satiric fragments on Roman life. And Casanova is from Giacomo Girolamo Casanova de Seingalt's eighteenth-century memoirs, History

of My Life. The last two films were high budget, costume dramas.
Fellini Satyricon is reputed to have cost $4,000,000 and to have re-
quired eighty-nine sets. Casanova, $10,000,000, and fifty-four sets.
The casts of both were enormous. They are Fellini's experiments with
spectacle on the grandest scale. In both, Fellini works to show a
society, Roman in one and eighteenth-century European in the other,
exactly on the razor's edge of collapse and change. This was something he had tried earlier in La Dolce Vita, but here in these later
works, the distance of history aids him. He is freer to reshape the
societies according to his imaginings. He is less restricted. All
three of the literary adaptations have about them an air of detach-
ment or disengagement. Fellini attacks his protagonists in Toby
Dammit and Casanova, and he observes the hero of Fellini Satyricon
with neutrality, at least until near the end of the film. There is
little or no autobiographical identification between Fellini and the
protagonists. But more importantly, there is little sympathy extended
to the protagonists. The cold, detached manner is not Fellini's
best. When he attacks or remains neutral, he tends to be reductive.

Comparing the Roman world of Petronius with the contemporary one,
Fellini underlines his interest in catching the world of antiquity at
its point of break up. He states: "In fact it seems we can find
disconcerting analogies between Roman society before the first arrival
of Christianity--a cynical society, impassive, corrupt and frenzied--
and society today.... Then as now we find ourselves confronting a
society at the height of its splendor but revealing already the signs
of progressive dissolution;... a society in which all beliefs--
religious, philosophical, ideological, and social--have crumbled, and
been displaced by a sick, wild, and impotent eclecticism." Fellini
was insistent on the dreamlike quality of the film. He told novelist
and critic Alberto Moravia, "Everything will be disconnected, frag-
mentary. And at the same time mysteriously homogeneous." There are
few devices of transition among the separate episodes, but certain
common denominators do run through many of them. The world of
Fellini Satyricon is a world of excess. The prime example of this is,
of course, the banquet of Trimalchio. The wealthy freedman parades
dish after dish, entertainment after entertainment, before his guests
and then has read to them a list of his holdings. But excess is evident too in the sheer number of sexual delights offered to the protagonist, Encolpius, in the house of prostitution at the beginning of
the film and in the Garden of Delights near the end of the film.
Further, Lichas of Taranto has been commissioned by the young Caesar
to roam the seas gathering objects and people of curiosity for
Caesar's amusement. The world of Fellini Satyricon is also a world
of death. The first sequence concerning Encolpius' loss of the boy
he loves to his rival Ascyltus ends with the collapse of the Insula
Felicles and the disastrous loss of life by many of the dwellers.
Trimalchio's feast ends with the mock funeral of the host. (The tone
here is partly lightened, however, by a tale told of a widow who
sacrifices the corpse of her husband to save the life of her new
lover.) The executions of the young Caesar and Lichas by the troops

of the new Caesar lead to the suicide of the Roman magistrate and his wife. The movie concludes with the heirs of the poet Eumolpus eating the body of the poet in order to collect their legacies. The impact of the gods and the myths is reduced. The albino hermaphrodite at the Temple of Ceres, reputed to be an oracle, is kidnapped by Encolpius, Ascyltus, and a robber, and the hermaphrodite dies. Encolpius is pushed into acting the role of Theseus in the labyrinth for the comic amusement of villagers in the South. Encolpius is moved by paintings he sees in an open-air gallery, and the guests at the banquet are moved by the performance of homeric actors, but the paintings and the dramatic performance are presented as vestiges of earlier cultures. The virtues of friendship and love are called into question. In the opening sequence, Ascyltus states, "Friendship lasts as long as it is useful." The actions of the boy Giton seem to bear out Ascyltus' words. Faced with a choice between Ascyltus and Encolpius, Giton chooses the more aggressive Ascyltus. Trimalchio turns on his avowed friend Eumolpus and has him beaten nearly to death when the poet accuses him of plagiarism. Trimalchio's wife, Fortunata, quarrels with her husband over Trimalchio's interest in a young boy. The battle of wills between the old magician and the sorceress Oenothea stems from Oenothea's sexual humiliation of the old man. However, Fellini does allow his Roman world some moments of touching rapport. Ascyltus does come to the aid of his rival Encolpius when the latter is attacked by the robber after the death of the hermaphrodite. The two students, Ascyltus and Encolpius, do share the affections of the slave girl in the villa of the suicides, and Ascyltus and Encolpius end that episode caressing each other. Lichas sings tenderly to Encolpius on the ship after their mock marriage. And the wife of the Roman magistrate joins her husband in suicide, in a near reversal of the tale of the widow told at Trimalchio's feast. These moments of rapport deepen and complicate Fellini's portrait of the Roman era. For the most part, though, relationships are founded on power and expediency.

Alberto Moravia has pointed out that Fellini's treatment of various European courts and societies in Casanova may be as interesting as, or more interesting than, his portrait of Casanova, the seducer. Moravia argues that Fellini shows these societies in their last decadent stages. This idea is supported by the fact that the final sequences of the film, at the Castle of Dux in Bohemia, take place after the French Revolution, when the ostentatious, court clothes and manners of Casanova are grotesquely anacronistic to the young people of the new era. In the first half of the film, there is a decadence about the worlds of Venice, Paris, and Parma, but it is a stylized decadence. The French Ambassador to Venice watches through a peep hole as Casanova makes love to a nun. Madame D'Urfé in Paris invites Casanova to make her pregnant so that she may "transfer her soul" to a male child. And at Parma, the wealthy DuBois acts out a ritualized drama where he devours a handsome young man. In the second half of the movie, in London, Rome, and Wurttemberg, the facades of stylized manners fall away. In London, Casanova sees grotesque slides of female genitalia projected on the walls of a strange amusement grotto inside a wooden whale. At Rome, in the house of the English Ambassador to the Vatican, Casanova witnesses a drunken race and participates in a contest pitting his sexual prowess against that of a coachman. At Wurttemberg, he finds a court world gone mad. Guests play a large bank of organs which cover an entire wall, and they create a deafening cacaphony.

In Toby Dammit, Fellini attacks his protagonist as an actor who has sold out his craft. Toby is an English Shakespearean actor who has agreed to come to Rome to make a Catholic western in exchange for a Ferrari sportscar. He confesses that he is an alcoholic. The story owes as much to the Faust myth as it does to the Poe story. Toby seems to have promised his soul to the Devil in exchange for ease and status. (The Poe story is an amusing sketch of a young person who uses once too often the figure of speech "to bet the Devil one's head" and is decapitated while doing a pidgeon-wing over a stile on a covered bridge.) Interestingly, the Devil in Toby Dammit is portrayed as a pretty blond girl, not unlike the girl from Umbria who is an image of innocence to Marcello in La Dolce Vita. Toby drives his Ferrari across the collapsed span of a bridge to reach this girl and is beheaded by a safety cable intended to block off the bridge. It is Fellini's irony that the apparition of the Devil seems far less threatening than the sea of real faces around Toby—the reporters at Fiumicino Airport, the TV interviewer, and the people who come up to him at the awards banquet. Fellini seems deliberately to curtail sympathy for Toby. He presents Toby only after he has sold out. Filled with self-loathing, Toby is antagonistic to everyone he meets, and badly frightened; he drinks more and more. Fellini establishes no basis for us to care about Toby's fate, unless it be the very depth of his self-destructive urge and our conviction, brought by us to the film, that no one should have to know such self-loathing.

Fellini's antagonism for Casanova is well documented in interviews. He told Leo Janos of Time that Casanova "is all shop front, a public figure striking attitudes...in short, a braggart Fascist," and he told Melton S. Davis of Oui, "I see him a sort of shadow of myself, of all Italians. He is a super vitellone, a do-nothing who avoids responsibility and lives in the comfortable conviction that everything is supposed to come from on high.... I see him as a courtesan, a big cumbersome, prancing man who stinks of sweat and face powder, with the arrogance of the barracks and the church— someone who always has to be right." Fellini pictures Casanova as a lover who moves from woman to woman like a mechanical man, each time hoping to find some illusory, transcendent value or some practical solution for his financial needs, and each time failing. In the sex act, Casanova is usually photographed from below, with his straining face looking directly into the camera. He pumps up and down like a man doing push-ups. The mechanicalness of his actions is mirrored by the mechanical bird he places nearby. The bird too spins and pumps up and down at a regular rhythm. The Italian critic Valerio

Riva has observed that at the end of many sex acts Casanova is shot lying spent and exhausted in a shadow, while his partner is in the light and usually contented and lively. Casanova's last love appropriately is a mechanical doll. A waltz with her on the frozen canals of Venice is the final image nurtured by Casanova as the film ends. The most striking visual images of the film are images of stasis or death. In addition to the image of the dance on the ice, the shots of the gigantic head of the goddess of Venice sinking beneath the canal and the shots of the chandeliers in the Dresden theater sinking to the floor and being extinguished by workmen with fans are among Fellini's most evocative. Few critics quarrel with Fellini's depiction of Casanova in his round of love affairs as a mechanical man. Many, however, do quarrel with Fellini's decision not to offer other views of the man in addition. The single view of Casanova, they maintain, is reductive, and worse, it is repetitive and joyless. Casanova's memoirs reveal a man with more sides. They reveal a man who lived by his wits—a man who engineered a break out from the prison of Venice and who constructed the national lottery in France. With his love for con artists and vitelloni, Fellini could have treated this side of Casanova. The attack on the film has merit. And it can be extended. If Fellini were to have created Casanova as a man of some wit and daring about whom we could care more, his loss of self in the endless cycle of seductions would be more moving than it is.

In his preface to the screenplay of Fellini Satyricon, Fellini has described Encolpius and Ascyltus as "two hippy students, like any of those hanging around today in Piazza di Spagna, or in Paris, Amsterdam or London, moving on from adventure to adventure, even the most gruesome, without the least remorse, with all the natural innocence and splendid vitality of two young animals.... They live from day to day, taking problems as they come, their life interests alarmingly confined to the elementaries: they eat, make love, stick together, bed down anywhere.... They are drop-outs from every system, and recognize no obligations, duties or restrictions." For the most part, Fellini's generalization holds true. Although Encolpius resents losing his loved one Giton, he seems strangely unmoved by the beating administered to his benefactor Eumolpus at the banquet and unconcerned about his crime of kidnapping the hermaphrodite. For much of the film, Encolpius is filmed from a distance as another exhibit in the society on the verge of dissolution. Stuart Rosenthal has noted that the tracking camera which records the walk of Encolpius and Giton through Suburra moves sometimes with them, sometimes behind or in front of them. "They are," Rosenthal says, "as much a part of the landscape as the drunks, whores and herb sellers." We look at them as we look at the other people in the street who vie for our attention. However, at the end of the film, Encolpius is the figure who breaks away from the Roman world and sets out for new lands and new possibilities. As if in preparation for this decision, Encolpius undergoes an experience analogous to the rites of passage. Humiliated in the labyrinth, in terms of his cowardice before the minotaur

and his sexual failure with Ariadne, Encolpius regains sexual prowess
and self-esteem when he makes love to the earth goddess Oenothea.
The effect is a deepening of Encolpius' character. After his trial,
he is capable of sorrow at the death of his rival and friend Ascyltus,
and he is capable of understanding and rejecting the greed of the
heirs who devour the body of Eumolpus. It is as if a child became an
adult.

* * *

Amarcord (1973) is probably Fellini's most mature work because of
the broadness of his outlook. The movie is a study of a provincial
town, based on Rimini. It is a treatment of the world of Fellini's
past. Fellini pours into it all the affection and humor he used in
earlier accounts in I Vitelloni, 8½, The Clowns, and Roma, and he
brings to bear also the penetrating sense of criticism predominant in
those later works just discussed. Much of what is in Amarcord was
latent in I Vitelloni, but in Amarcord, the major elements of provincial life are more directly faced. Certainly, Amarcord is Fellini's
most "open" work. It is filled with interesting secondary characters
and with episodes that are stories in themselves. Originally, Fellini
considered using the title The Man Profaned and announced that the
film would be about a person totally conditioned by false learning.
Something of that initial plan remains. But in its final form,
Amarcord is a movie about adolescence. As he had done in La Dolce
Vita, Fellini Satyricon, and more arguably, Casanova, Fellini balances
a broad, general picture with a particularized portrait of an individual: the town and the boy Titta. What they have in common is an
adolescent outlook on life. Fellini celebrates the capacities of
the townspeople to wonder, to dream, to play, and to fantasize--
positive capacities inexperienced people may bring to experience. He
celebrates the energy of the townspeople and their sense of group
membership. At the same time, however, he makes clear the reverse
side of these characteristics: credulity, the capacity for cruel
tricks, the impracticality and waste of yearning for impossible goals,
and provincial narrowness. Fellini feels that the adolescent state
of mind of the provincials was the basis for their Fascism. In a
letter to Gian Luigi Rondi, published in Cinema (Quebec), Fellini
states: "I consider Fascism as a kind of degeneration to a historical
level comparable to the stage of an individual--that of adolescence--
which corrupts itself and can proliferate monstrously, without
succeeding to evolve and to become adult. Also Fascism and adolescence are certainly representations of our most concealed complexes,
expressions of a confused and repressed psychic state which is,
therefore, stupidly aggressive."

Amarcord begins gently and comically. Light clusters of seeds
float through the village. We meet the townspeople at an evening
celebration of spring where the Witch of Winter is burnt on a pyre.
Titta's uncle, il Pataca [the Bad Penny], sets fire to the pyre while
Guidizio, the town idiot, is on top of it, and the idiot scrambles

and falls to safety. Titta sets off a firecracker. Il Pataca starts the game of jumping the embers. "Greased Lightning" roars through the square on his motorcycle. The townspeople have created and participated in a spectacle. Their games reflect their high spirits. The same is true of the evening passeggiata up and down the main street some days later. Titta and his friends follow the town vamp, Gradisca. Il Pataca looks over the telegram received from a rich Swedish woman by il Pataca's friend White Feather. The Fascist party leader flirts with Gradisca. Most of the people watch with awe and interest as the new group of prostitutes are paraded through town in a carriage. Again, the people make their own spectacle.

Three institutions are presented early in the film: the school, the church, and the family. All are treated comically. The first two are shown to be repressive, but not to the extent that they inhibit the boys. In fact, the contrary seems true. To the science teacher's question about a pendulum made of string and a lead sphere, Ciccio answers that the device looks like one of the balls of an elephant. In Greek class, Ovo turns the pronunciation of the Greek word Emarpszamen into a series of verbal raspberries. In math class, Gilgliozzi pisses through a tube of cardboard and deposits a puddle of urine near Candela who has been working at the blackboard with the teacher. At confession in church, Don Balosa asks Titta if he "touches" himself and tells him that when he masturbates, St. Luigi cries. But the sequence gives way to a series of Titta's sexual fantasies and fumbling experiences and ends with the boys masturbating in an automobile, quarreling over who has the right to fantasize about Aldina Cordini, the beautiful, haughty girl in school. Titta's family is almost a parody of the Italian provincial family. The father is fiery, iconoclastic, and autocratic. The mother has pretensions of manners, but can stage a theatrical scene of hysteria when she is upset. There is an earthy grandfather who pats the maid's posterior and farts ceremoniously. Il Pataca is the brother-in-law overindulged by his sister and despised for not working by Titta's father. In a dinner table scene, the father chases Titta for pissing from the balcony of the theater; the mother locks herself in the bathroom; the father pulls the tablecloth and dishes from the table; and il Pataca calmly eats his meal.

A serious note of criticism begins to emerge near the middle of the work when the town holds its rally on April 21st to honor the founding of Rome. The Fascist Party Secretary comes to town, and he is escorted through the main street by the townspeople. A gigantic, representation of Mussolini's face, made of flowers, is raised above the assembled group in the square. The raising of the head has a shocking effect on us, for we see the townspeople respond as enthusiastically to this totalitarian image as they did earlier to the burning of the Witch of Winter. They can see no difference. Both fulfill their love for group spectacle. Then Fellini eases the shock. He presents the comic fantasy of Ciccio that the flowered face of il Duce marries him to Aldina while the townspeople watch.

But again Fellini shocks us when Titta's father, an anarchist, is
arrested later that night for the trick of playing the Communist
anthem on a gramaphone from the church steeple. (The father suspects
il Pataca turned him in.) The Fascists force him to recant and feed
him castor oil. He returns home covered with excrement. Stuart
Rosenthal has pointed out that these cruel tricks are adult, sadistic
versions of the pranks the boys of the town play.

One of the major set pieces of the movie is the sequence about
the oceanliner Rex. The ship's route on its maiden voyage brings it
near the town. The townspeople climb into boats and go out from the
harbor to watch it pass by. The event fills the people with wonder.
Titta's father, the foreman of a construction gang, expresses amazement at the design of the universe, and Gradisca talks about her
hopes of finding a lasting love. Their statements are naive, but
heartfelt, inspired by the idea of the dream ship which they will see.
We admire the townspeople's capacity to hope and wonder. But this
scene, coming as it does after the Fascist rally, evokes reminders of
the dangerous side of the townspeople's credulity. The sequence is
rich in resonances.

The Rex itself is a stylized model, and the sea that the townspeople row on is made up of a wetted, plastic sheet. Fellini makes
his artifice obvious. This insistence on revealing his own artifice
to us is an extension of his earlier insistence on showing us the
workings behind the scenes of staged performances by characters in
his movies. In his later films, Fellini reminds us increasingly that
he himself is an illusionist. In Juliet of the Spirits, the heroine
walks from the beach through a forest of plastic vines and flowers.
The greens and yellows are too bright to be real. And if we look
closely, we can see a metal stand that is an artificial tree. In
Fellini Satyricon, the tilled field where Encolpius and Eumolpus sleep
is obviously studio made, with the furrows painted perfectly to run
to the vanishing point on the horizon. In Casanova, the hero rows
on a plastic canal in Venice, and he makes love without removing his
underwear, in the straight up-and-down push-up motion mentioned
earlier. Probably Fellini has gone too far with the device of making
obvious his artifice in Casanova. The artifice becomes a major means
to comment on the artificiality of Casanova's world, but it is an
easy means which loses its force through repetition. In Amarcord, the
artifice seems a secondary means, which supports the idea of the
artificiality of the dreams of the townspeople through tone. When the
townspeople row out toward the Rex, they are large in the frame, and
the plastic sea is shown around them as secondary interest. When
Casanova rows on the canal, he is a small figure in the background,
and the plastic waves loom huge in the foreground. The difference in
subtlety is all important.

Fellini's treatment of Titta's family grows more serious as the
movie progresses. The sequence concerning Uncle Teo is an important
part of this development. Teo lives in a mental institution and his
behavior is erratic. At one moment, he may function normally and be

42

attentive to what happens around him, but at another moment, he may withdraw and act strangely. The family takes him on an outing to the country. Teo climbs a tree and shouts that he wants a woman. (The tree is artificial.) Teo hurls stones at the various males who try to climb the tree to get him down. At last a midget nun arrives from the asylum. She orders Teo from the tree and leads him off with no fuss. The sequence is a variation of the clown routine where the midget clown easily lifts the weight that the strongman clown has huffed and puffed unsuccessfully over. Here the midget nun accomplishes the task which was impossible for the self-assured males. More than this, though, Teo's stubbornness in remaining in the tree so long and calling for a woman so many times is a measure of his loneliness. Teo injects a note of sadness into Fellini's presentation of the family. This sadness is intensified at the end when Titta's mother dies. Prior to her death, Titta has been unable or unwilling to consider the seriousness of her illness. On a visit to her at the hospital, he complains about life in their house without her presence to protect him from tantrums of the father. His concern is self-centered. Her death comes as a painful surprise to him. After the funeral, Titta returns to the house with his father and brother and prowls the corridors aware for the first time of the fact of death.

Fellini's treatment of the town vamp, Gradisca, also grows more somber as the film progresses. She is an object of sexual fantasy for Titta. He moves close to her in the movie theater and puts his hand on her leg for a moment before retreating in confusion when she asks if he has lost something. He tries to follow her in the labyrinth of paths through the snow, and he tries to protect her during a snowball fight. He fantasizes that she is in the racing car with him when he wins the <u>Thousand Miles</u>. As Stuart Rosenthal has shown, Gradisca is also an object of sexual fantasy for the entire town. The lawyer tells how she got her name which means "Please do." He recounts that she spent the night with a prince in order to win for the town financial help for the completion of work on the seashore promenade. We watch as she undresses for the prince, gets under the covers wearing her jaunty red beret, and tells the prince, "Please do." Gradisca herself dreams of finding a lover like Gary Cooper. She tries to touch the uniformed Fascist Party Secretary when he comes to the town on April 21st. But when she marries at age thirty in the final sequence of the movie, it is to a plump, bald-headed policeman. He is neither prince nor Gary Cooper. All that remains of a dream mate for the town vamp is the gaudy uniform of the policeman. Her marriage marks the end of a fantasy.

<u>Amarcord</u> starts in spring and ends in spring. It goes through the seasons of summer, fall, and winter. Its cyclical pattern emphasizes the ideas of growth and change. Its form argues against the idea of stasis. Fellini shows the need for growth beyond adolescence. Many critics have argued that <u>Amarcord</u> is an attack on provincial life frozen at a level of adolescence. Most of Fellini's pronouncements tend to reinforce this attitude. But we must acknowledge, as

other critics have done, Fellini's celebration of the festive energy of the people, their group sense, their openness to wonder, and the creativeness in their fantasies and their play. The celebration must be weighed against the criticism of the provincials, and the criticism against the celebration. Amarcord is a film of mature, broad outlook.

Acknowledgment of Major Sources:

Geneviève Agel, Les Chemins de Fellini (Paris: Editions du cerf, 1956), 195 pp.

Suzanne Budgen, Fellini (London: BFI, 1966), 128 pp.

Federico Fellini, "Fellini dit Amarcord," Cinema (Quebec), 4, No. 1 (1974), 43-44.

Alberto Moravia, "Il seduttor scortese," L'espresso, 22, No. 52 (26 December 1976), 90-91.

Edward Murray, Fellini the Artist (New York: Ungar Publishing, 1976), 256 pp.

Valerio Riva, "Casanova, in arte Pinocchio," L'espresso, 22, No. 22 (30 May 1976), 90-105.

Stuart Rosenthal, The Cinema of Federico Fellini (New York and London: A. S. Barnes and Tantivy Press, 1976), 190 pp.

Gilbert Salachas, Federico Fellini: An Investigation into His Films and Philosophy, translated by Rosalie Siegel (New York: Crown Publishers, 1969), 224 pp.

The Films: Synopsis, Credits and Notes

1   LUCI DEL VARIETÀ [VARIETY LIGHTS] (1950)

The film begins with shots of a variety company performing in the theater of a provincial town. We see the last parts of an evening performance. Checco, the group's light comedian, comes on stage to sing a comic song. He is a small man in his forties, with a toothbrush mustache. The audience applauds his song vigorously. We see in the audience Liliana, a pretty girl in her twenties. She shouts, "Bravo." The performance ends with all members of the cast on stage, singing about the lure and the illusion of variety lights. The troupe includes Melina, a light comedienne, Valeria, a plump soloist, Kali, a magician, Adelmo, the suave master of ceremonies and the director of the troupe, and five female dancers.

Backstage, Adelmo learns that the evening's receipts have been impounded by the local hotel owner. Adelmo argues furiously. The hotel owner, however, insists that a bill of two year's standing must be paid. Checco enters into the argument, demanding to receive his salary. He and Adelmo nearly come to blows. Liliana, seeking the director, approaches the hotel owner who rebuffs her.

At the railroad station, Checco suggests to Melina that they will have to withdraw money from their savings account. Melina retorts that there will be no need for such a thing, and she gives Checco an aspirin. The troupe grumbles over the loss of the evening's receipts. Liliana arrives at the station.

On board the train, Liliana approaches Checco. Melina is asleep on the seat next to Checco. Liliana asks Checco if he is the manager, tells him of the dance contests she has won, and lifts her skirt to show him her legs. Checco leads her to the next car. When he reaches out to take her in his arms, however, Liliana puts him off.

The next morning at a railroad station outside of town, the business manager discovers to his dismay that the theater owner has not arranged transportation for the troupe into town. The driver of a carriage will not transport them unless they pay in advance. With a good deal of grumbling the troupe sets out on foot. Checco argues with Melina again about the savings account. She informs him that forty-nine thousand and eight hundred lire of the fifty thousand in the account were deposited by her and that she wishes to keep the money to buy a delicatessen store for them in ten years. Then Liliana drives up in the carriage and invites the troupe to join her for the ride into town.

In the theater, Liliana remarks that she has spoken to the "director," Checco, about a place in the chorus line. The troupe reacts angrily. They do not want to share their receipts with anyone else. Adelmo is incensed that Checco has passed himself off as the director. At that moment, the theater owner arrives. He is shocked that the troupe is as small as it is. He includes Liliana in his head count. Liliana declares herself a member of the troupe.

Evening at the theater. The show begins with a song by Adelmo. Backstage, Checco helps Liliana put on a pair of slacks which she claims are too tight. The next act begins. It consists of a song by Valeria about Hawaii, with the six girls, including Liliana, dancing behind Valeria. Suddenly Liliana's slacks rip and fall down. She continues to dance in her black underwear, and the largely male audience applauds and cheers. They continue their cheering after the number ends. Kali attempts a magic act, and Checco and Melina begin a Spanish dance, but the crowd calls for Liliana. At last, the theater owner tells the orchestra to play "El Muchacho," and Liliana returns to sing and dance. There follows a brief montage. We see a sign on the theater announcing a repeat performance, and then we see Liliana on stage again, in a grass skirt this time, singing "El Muchacho."

Backstage come three well-dressed, middle-aged men. Renzo, the chief speaker of the three, invites Liliana to his country manor for dinner. When she hesitates, he indicates that she may bring along a friend. Adelmo seizes the opportunity and tells Renzo that the whole troupe accepts his offer. On foot, the group sets off for the manor. Renzo and Liliana in the lead, with Checco trailing after them. The march is a long one, and the troupe complains. Renzo sings "Figaro."

Inside Renzo's house, a banquet is served. Afterward, Kali plays the piano, and some couples dance. Renzo dances Liliana off to the side of the living room and presents her with a string of pearls. Checco interrupts the dance and announces that the troupe must leave. Renzo, however, offers to let the troupe stay the night at his manor, and the party continues. Angrily, Checco dances with Liliana.

Later that night in a bedroom, we see Melina and Liliana. As Liliana slips under the covers of the bed, Melina announces that she will sleep elsewhere. She leaves the room and seeks out Checco in the living room. Melina tries to attract Checco's interest, but they hear Renzo's door open, and Checco rushes to Liliana's room. He finds Renzo inside and pulls him outside

46

the room again. The two men argue loudly, awaking the other
sleepers. In anger, Renzo orders the troupe from his house.
They trudge back to town. Checco proudly holds Liliana's head
on his shoulder, while Melina watches the two of them from
behind.

It is a bright morning in a piazza in Rome. Checco and
Liliana enter a cafe. Checco introduces Liliana to a producer
and states that he and Liliana are working as a team now. The
producer puts them off.

A scene unfolds in which we move by cross-cutting back and
forth between Liliana's pension and Checco's. They talk on
the phone. In her pension we can see the landlady sewing
Liliana's evening dress. In his, we see the landlord clutching
Checco's dress pants. Checco arranges to take Liliana to a
night club where they can meet theater people. The landlord
refuses to return Checco's pants until he pays his rent.
Checco, however, grabs the pants away and tells the landlord
to weep.

At the night club, Checco and Liliana are shown to a table.
To Checco's horror, Liliana orders lobster and champagne. A
floor show begins. Two actors appear. One is dressed like a
parrot. The "parrot" points to Checco in his evening dress
and expresses fear in the presence of a "penguin." The audience laughs at Checco. After the act ends, Checco spots a
producer named Parmisani and bounds over to his table. Meanwhile, Conti, an associate of Parmisani, spots Liliana and
introduces himself. Checco returns to the table. Conti
invites the two of them to join his party of friends as they
move to another night club. Checco is delayed in paying his
bill. Outside, he finds the group, including Liliana, already
in cars. They pull away without him. One member of the group
shouts the name of the "Florida" night club at him.

Without money to pay for a cab, Checco goes on foot to the
"Florida." When he arrives, he learns that the group has left
for another night club. Checco wanders the streets. He encounters Adelmo. His former director tells Checco to go back
to Melina. He tells Checco that Liliana is using him. They
part angrily.

Outside of Liliana's pension, Checco waits. She returns
at dawn. Checco demands to go to her room with her and then
is shocked when she agrees calmly. He slaps her and starts to
move away. She calls him back and soothes him. She tells him
that they will find success. He declares he will put together
his own company.

In a cafe frequented by theater people, Checco explains his
ideas to Kali and Valeria. Melina and the business manager of
the old troupe watch from a separate table. When Checco explains that there will be no guaranteed wages, the two performers lose interest. Checco and Valeria argue. Liliana enters.
She shows Checco a new dress she has bought and a hat she got
for him.

At night in front of his pension, Checco discovers that he is locked out. He meets Johnny, an American negro with a trumpet. Johnny leads him to Moema, a gypsy woman who sings. Checco is enthused. He promises both a part in his show. Johnny then leads him to the apartment of an American cowboy who is a sharpshooter. Checco takes Johnny and the cowboy to Liliana's pension. It is early morning by now. Liliana is not pleased to see them. She states that she did not get home until five in the morning. She wants to move to a new hotel. She says that she has had an offer from another source which she has turned down. Checco promises to find the money soon for his company.

Backstage of a theater, Checco seeks out Melina. He plays on her pity. He tells her that the chance to start his own troupe is one he has always been looking for. She gives him the money in the savings account.

In a rehearsal hall, Checco's female choreographer drills a group of dancers. She calls their attempts horrible. Checco and Liliana arrive. He proudly introduces Liliana to the group and shows her a poster that he has prepared. She asks for top billing.

A few days later at the rehearsal hall, Checco introduces a theater manager to the group. The manager has come to watch and judge the troupe. Checco frets that Liliana has not arrived. Outside, we see Liliana talking with Conti. She comes in alone, however, and breaks the news that she has signed a contract with Parmisani. She tells Checco that Conti will pay a "penalty" for taking her from Checco's show. Proudly Checco spurns the offer. After she leaves, Checco breaks down.

In an elegant theater, we see Liliana perform. She is one of two dancers flanking an older female star who sings. It is Liliana, however, whom the audience responds to, and the star gives her an angry glare.

At the railway station in Rome. Conti and Liliana walk toward the Milan express. She has the accoutrements of a star--a fur coat and a lapdog. She boards the train and then sees Checco from the window. He tells her that he has put together an excellent show, with a Viennese ballet. After her train leaves, however, he walks to a third-class car on a train to the mezzogiorno. Inside, he joins his previous troupe. He sits with Melina. Later that evening, a pretty young girl enters the train car and takes a seat. When Melina goes to get some coffee, Checco strikes up a conversation with the young girl. He asks if she is an actress and tells her that he is an impresario.

[This summary is based on the screenplay published in Fellini's Early Screenplays. New York: Grossman, 1971, and on viewings of the film several years previous to the preparation of this volume. JCS]

Credits

Producers:	Alberto Lattuada and Federico Fellini (Capitolium Film)
Directors:	Lattuada and Fellini
Screenplay:	Lattuada, Fellini, Ennio Flaiano, Tullio Pinelli, based on a story by Fellini
Photography:	Otello Martelli
Sets:	Aldo Buzzi
Music:	Felice Lattuada
Editor:	Mario Bonotti
Cast:	Peppino De Filippo (Checco Dalmonte), Carla del Poggio (Liliana), Giulietta Masina (Melina Amour), John Kitzmiller (Johnny, the trumpet player), Folco Lulli (Conti, Liliana's lover), Franca Valeri (the designer), Carlo Romano (Renzo, the lawyer), Silvio Bagolini (the journalist), Dante Maggio (Remo, the comedian), Giulio Cali (Edison Will), Gina Mascetti (Valeria Del Sole), Checco Durante (theater owner), Joe Faletta (Bill), Enrico Piergentili (business manager), Mario De Angelis (the maestro), Fanny Marchio (the soubrette), Giacomo Furia (the duke), Vania Orico (the gypsy singer), Nando Bruno, Il Duo Bonucci-Caprioli.

Filmed in Rome and Capranica in the summer of 1950.

Distribution:	Contemporary Films
Running Time:	93 minutes
Released:	Italy: 1950
	U.S.: May 6, 1965 (NYC)
Note:	The division of labor between Fellini and Lattuada has never been clear on this film which marks Fellini's transition from screenwriter to director. Solmi claims that "Fellini was mainly concerned with the acting and Lattuada was in charge of the technical side," but several critics are more generous, calling it true Fellini from start to finish. This film also marks the first screenwriting collaboration of Fellini, Pinelli, and Flaiano which continued through Juliet of the Spirits (1965).

2   LO SCEICCO BIANCO [THE WHITE SHEIK] (1952)

The movie begins with shots of a train approaching Rome.
Inside the train, we see Ivan, a man in his thirties with a
small mustache and bulging eyes, watching the approach through
the window. On the platform, Ivan calls Wanda who appears at
the train window and passes out their luggage to Ivan. She is
a young woman in her twenties, dressed in brand-new clothes.
They ride in a carriage to the Hotel Tre Fiori. It is apparent
that they are honeymooners from the provinces.

In the lobby of the hotel, Ivan places a phone call to his
uncle. Meanwhile Wanda is led by the impatient bellboy to the
room. When Ivan turns from the phone to put Wanda on the line,
he is surprised to find her gone. In the room, Wanda asks
directions of the bellboy for Via XXIV Maggio. When he leaves,
she takes from her suitcase a sheaf of letters and a small
cardboard tube. The letters fall. She gathers them up quickly
and puts them in her pocketbook. She hides the tube in the
sleeve of her dress just before Ivan enters the room. He is
angry that she was not by the phone to greet his important
uncle. However, he goes on to announce their schedule. The
uncle has arranged an audience with the Pope at eleven that
morning. Then there will be dinner with the relatives and
sight-seeing in Rome. Wanda looks upset by the tightness of
the scheduling. When the maid comes, Wanda requests that a
hot bath be prepared. Ivan consults his schedule and agrees
that there will be time for a bath. While Ivan naps, Wanda
leaves the room, ostensibly to go to the bath. Underneath
her bathrobe, however, she is completely dressed. She dis-
cards the robe in the bathroom and leaves the hotel.

She makes her way to the offices of the romance _fumetti_ on
Via XXIV Maggio. (_Fumetti_ are photographed stories similar
to comic strips.) She asks to see Fernando Rivoli, the actor
who plays the White Sheik. She is told that he is not in the
building. Before she can leave, however, Marilena, the female
editor of the story strip, arrives and invites Wanda to her
office. They discuss the _fumetti_, and Wanda tells Marilena
how much she loves to dream romantic dreams. Wanda explains
that she has written to the White Sheik and signed herself
"Impassioned Doll." She has brought a sketch of the White
Sheik which she wants to present to Fernando. A Bedouin
appears suddenly at the door and asks for the day's script.
With some advice from Wanda, Marilena writes down the lines.
She tells the Bedouin to take Wanda to Fernando.

At the hotel, Ivan is awakened from his nap by a pounding
on the door. A Black priest who doesn't speak Italian tries
to tell him that the bath is overflowing. Ivan finds one of
Wanda's letters which she failed to pick up and discovers that
she has left the hotel. On the bellboy's advice, Ivan heads
for Via XXIV Maggio.

Outside the *fumetti* offices, Wanda watches the actors, her idols, climb into a truck which will carry them to the shooting location. The group includes Oscar, the cruel Bedouin, and Felga, the jewel of the harem. Wanda is told by the Bedouin who is leading her to climb into the truck.

On a street in Rome, Ivan reads a section of the letter that he found. In the letter, the White Sheik invites the Impassioned Doll to visit him when she comes to Rome. As Ivan stands astounded in the middle of the street, a parade of soldiers approaches. Ivan is swept along by the crowd accompanying the parade. Later, back at the hotel, Ivan finds his relatives waiting for him. The group includes the uncle and the aunt, Cousin Rita and her fiancé, and a young nephew. The uncle is anxious to set off for the audience with the Pope which he has arranged. Ivan leads them out of the hotel, but the relatives stop him. They ask where Wanda is. While Ivan explains that Wanda is ill, the aunt returns to the hotel. Ivan races after her. He must dash up the steps to catch the aunt who is already ascending in the elevator. During the chase, Ivan kicks over a bucket which bounces down several flights of stairs. He does manage to head off the aunt, and they descend together in the elevator. Ivan asks if they may see the Pope the next day, and he arranges to meet his relatives for lunch.

In the pine woods by the Fregene beach. The *fumetti* group is on location. Wanda is worried about how she can return to Rome. She goes off from the group to look for a telephone. She hears singing. She looks up and sees the White Sheik high in the air on a swing. He blows a kiss to her. He hops off the swing, and Wanda goes to him with the cardboard tube in her hands. Fernando looks at the sketch. He recalls the letters from Impassioned Doll. He takes a long look at Wanda and then gallantly leads her off to a snack bar nearby. A middle-aged man, Mambroni, drives up to the snack bar. His car radio plays soft music. Fernando takes Wanda in his arms and dances with her. Wanda closes her eyes and hums.

Later, on location, Felga does a belly dance. Mambroni in shorts and baseball cap watches her. The director begins to organize the shooting. He explains the story line to the actors. Oscar, the cruel Bedouin, will lead a raid on the White Sheik and the Harem of Mystery. Wanda now appears, dressed as a slave girl. Fernando oversees the final touches of her make-up. A Bedouin takes her in his arms. Fernando mounts a white steed, with some misgivings, and prepares to cross swords with Oscar. The director orders Mambroni out of the scene. Wanda must be told to stop smiling.

At a restaurant in Rome, Ivan is on the telephone. He talks to the bellboy at the Tre Fiori. As the conversation begins, Cousin Rita approaches, and Ivan pretends that he is talking with Wanda, much to the confusion of the bellboy. We shift by cross-cutting back and forth between the restaurant and the hotel. The sequence ends at the table in the restaurant. Ivan explains to his uncle that Wanda cannot come to the theater with them. He tries to recite a sonnet that he has composed about Wanda, but he falls into tears.

Lunch break on location. Mambroni offers Felga a cigarette. Fernando and Wanda are near the sea. He lifts Wanda into a small sailboat, and they put out to sea, despite the angry cries of the director. Fernando tries to kiss Wanda. She tests that she is not free. He admits that he too is married, but he claims he was tricked into the marriage by a woman who drugged him. Wanda melts with pity. Fernando leans to kiss her, but is struck a mighty thump on the head by the ship's boom.

At the opera, Ivan and his relatives are in the balcony for a performance of <u>Don Giovanni</u>. Ivan excuses himself and goes to a phone in the lobby. He learns from the desk clerk at the Tre Fiori that Wanda has not returned.

At the police station, Ivan is shown into an inspector's office. Ivan is extremely nervous. He tries to discuss Wanda's disappearance without involving his name. The inspector takes from him the letter to the Impassioned Doll from the White Sheik. Ivan plays with the inkwell on the desk, gets ink on his fingers, and unknowingly rubs the finger on his face. The inspector now demands Ivan's name, tries to humor him, and leaves the room to call for a psychiatrist. Ivan overhears what the inspector says to the policeman in the adjoining room, and Ivan flees from the building. In the courtyard, he is swept along, for the second time in the day, by a marching column of men, this time policemen.

The end of the day on the beach. A motorboat tows in the sailboat. Waiting on shore are the actors, the angry director and a huge woman who is Fernando's wife. The director tells Fernando that he is fired. The wife attacks Wanda. In turn, Wanda accuses the wife of drugging Fernando. The wife flies into an even greater rage.

Later. The truck is ready to depart. The director calls for the Impassioned Doll through his megaphone, but Wanda is nowhere to be found. Fernando and his wife, almost reconciled, depart on a motor scooter. Mambroni, still in his shorts, claims that the actors have taken his suit. He is driven off by the director. At last, the truck leaves without Wanda. We discover her in the woods. She meets an animal keeper for the group who tells her that the truck has left.

In a carriage, Ivan and his relatives drive to the hotel. Ivan promises that Wanda and he will be ready to meet the Pope at eleven the next morning. Inside the hotel, Ivan learns that Wanda has not returned.

Later that night in a deserted square, Ivan walks in a daze. He is crying. Two prostitutes come upon him. One is short; the other big. The short one, Cabiria, comforts Ivan. He shows them photographs of Wanda and tells them that Wanda has left him. Cabiria spots a flame swallower on his way home and induces him to perform in the square. The big prostitute leads Ivan off to a hotel room.

Mambroni's car pulls up near the Hotel Tre Fiori. Wanda is in the car with him. She is wearing her coat over her slave costume. She rejects Mambroni's advances and leaves the car. She is, however, afraid to enter the hotel, and so she goes to a pharmacy and telephones the desk clerk. She leaves an incoherent message for Ivan in which she mentions dishonor which she has brought to his name.

Dawn at the Tiber. Wanda tries to commit suicide. She leaps into the river, but lands near the shore in water only a few inches deep. A man emerges from the cabin of his boat and shouts at her. Later, we see an ambulance speeding through the streets.

At the hotel, Ivan enters. The clerk hands him his message. Before he can read it, his relatives who have been waiting approach him. Ivan tells his uncle that he wants to speak to him. The uncle waits. The telephone rings. Ivan is summoned to the phone. He listens closely to the voice on the other end, hangs up, and passes out. The relatives begin to carry him to his room, but Ivan revives and sends them off to the Vatican with frantic promises to join them at eleven. Inside the room, alone, Ivan grabs up a bundle of clothes. Rushing outside, he hails a cab and rides to a mental hospital.

At the hospital, Ivan runs to the room where Wanda is waiting. When they see each other, they break into sobs. Then Ivan recovers sufficiently to tell Wanda to get dressed in the clothes he has brought.

At St. Peter's Cathedral. The bells are tolling eleven. Ivan's relatives wait impatiently. A taxi speeds up. Ivan and Wanda emerge and greet the relatives. All file toward the church. Wanda tells Ivan that she is still pure. He whispers that he too is still pure. Wanda tells Ivan that he is now her White Sheik. He notices that her gaze has wandered off. He is jealous, until he realizes that her gaze is directed at an angel high atop the colonnade. The uncle urges them to walk faster. They mount the steps to the doors of the basilica.

[This summary is based on the screenplay published in Fellini's <u>Early Screenplays</u>. New York: Grossman, 1971, and on viewings of the film several years previous to the preparation of this volume. JCS]

<u>Credits</u>

Producer:	Luigi Rovere (PDC-OFI, Rome)
Director:	Federico Fellini
Screenplay:	Fellini, Ennio Flaiano, Tullio Pinelli, based on a story by Michelangelo Antonioni, Fellini, and Pinelli.
Photography:	Arturo Gallea

Cameraman:	Antonio Belviso
Photographer:	Osvaldo Civirani
Sets:	Raffaelo Tolfo
Music:	Nino Rota
Music Director:	Fernando Previtali
Sound:	Armando Grilli, Walfredo Traversari
Editor:	Rolando Benedetti
Assistant Director:	Stefano Ubezio
Make-up:	Franco
Production Manager:	Enzo Provenzale
Cast:	Alberto Sordi (Fernando Rivoli, the White Sheik), Brunella Bovo (Wanda Giardino Cavalli), Leopoldo Trieste (Ivan Cavalli), Giulietta Masina (Cabiria), Lilia Landi (Felga), Ernesto Almirante (Director), Fanny Marchio (Merilena Vellardi), Gina Mascetti (the Sheik's wife), Enzo Maggio, Jole Silvani, Anna Primula, Nino Billi, Armando Libianchi, Ugo Attanasio, Elettra Zago, Giulio Moreschi, Pierro Antonucci, Poldino.

Filmed in Rome and
Fregene, October through
December, 1951.

Distribution:	Contemporary Films
Running Time:	86 minutes
Released:	Italy: First showing at Venice Film Festival, Spring of 1952. U.S.: April 25, 1956 (NYC)

3 I VITELLONI [THE YOUNG AND THE PASSIONATE or THE WASTRELS]
   (1953)

   The movie begins with a shot of a deserted square in a provincial town late at night. Five people come into the square
singing, their arms linked. They are the vitelloni, young men
approaching thirty who have not taken on jobs.
   Suddenly we are in the midst of the "Miss Siren Contest"
on the terrace of a seaside cafe. The narrator introduces the
five vitelloni separately. Riccardo, who sings, is the master
of ceremonies. Alberto, with an innocent, baby face, is in
the act of trying to borrow a cigarette. Leopoldo, the group
poet, wears huge, horn-rimmed glasses. Moraldo, the youngest
and most serious of the group, is watching the lightning of
an approaching storm with great wonder. Fausto, a handsome
young man, is described as the group's "spiritual leader."
We see him on a path near the terrace with a young woman.
She asks him pointedly about his relationship with Sandra,
Moraldo's sister, and leaves him. On the terrace, Riccardo

announces that Sandra has won the contest. A movie star from Rome, Lilia Rondi, pins the victory sash on her. Sandra tries to speak in the microphone, but at that moment the storm arrives and forces the group to take shelter inside. In the crush of the crowd, Sandra faints. A doctor is summoned to examine her. Fausto watches the events and turns pale. He leaves the cafe. Moraldo stares after him.

At Fausto's house, Fausto begins to pack a suitcase hastily. His father eyes him suspiciously. Fausto tells him he is leaving town to take a job. Moraldo arrives, and the father leaves the two young men alone in Fausto's room. Moraldo announces that Sandra is pregnant. Fausto declares he will leave town to find a job and will return for Sandra when he has a position. In the hall, Fausto is stopped by his father, who orders him to stay and marry the girl he has gotten pregnant. Fausto opens the front door and discovers Riccardo, Leopoldo, and Alberto outside. They break into laughter at him.

Inside a church, we witness the marriage of Sandra and Fausto. Later, we see the group at the train station. The couple boards a train for Rome. Sandra's parents snub Fausto's father and announce that the couple will live with them until they can set up house for themselves. Alberto, angered by such behavior, invites Fausto's father for a drink. The father quietly declines and goes home with his small daughter.

We see Alberto, Riccardo, Leopoldo, and Moraldo in a cafe at night. On their way home, they taunt a middle-aged prostitute. In a brief montage, we follow each of the four after they separate. Alberto bids goodnight to his mother who has waited up for him and to his older sister who is typing in her room. Riccardo surveys his waistline in a bathroom mirror. Leopoldo sits down at his desk to work on his play, doodles for a moment, goes to the window, and calls to the maid in the house next door. Outside, Moraldo takes a seat in a deserted square. He listens to a train whistle. A young boy appears wearing a railroadman's cap. The boy is on his way to his job at the train station. Moraldo asks him if he is happy, and the boy shrugs goodnaturedly.

The next day. Alberto makes his way through town to the office where his sister works. She is tired from the typing that she did the night before. Alberto borrows money from her. From outside, Riccardo shouts to him. The vitelloni have found a sure thing at the racetrack. The sister shakes her head and goes back to work.

A Sunday on the beach. Alberto, Riccardo, Leopoldo, and Moraldo contemplate the sea. Alberto spots a dog and runs off to play with him. The dog, however, returns to his master who is with a woman behind some bathhouses. As Alberto approaches, he sees that the woman is his sister. She comes to him and asks him not to tell their mother what he has seen.

In the sister's room later that night, Alberto argues with his sister. The man she is meeting is married, even though separated from his wife. Alberto warns his sister not to make their mother cry.

Outside a cafe some days later, the four friends are surprised by the return of Fausto and Sandra. Fausto has brought back a phonograph from Rome. He plays a mambo and demonstrates a step for Alberto. Fausto sports a thin mustache. Sandra tells Moraldo that she is happy.

At a shop for religious items, Sandra's father introduces Fausto to the shopowner. Fausto is urged to begin work at once. He meets Giulia, the shopowner's wife. She is a woman in her forties, still attractive. Later, the other vitelloni look in the store window. Alberto, Riccardo, and Leopoldo want to mock Fausto, but Moraldo leads them away.

Sandra comes to the town's center to meet Fausto. She encounters two female "friends" who remark on the suddenness of the wedding. At last, she meets Fausto, and they go to a movie together. In the movie, Fausto lights a cigarette for a woman sitting on his side away from Sandra, and he rubs knees with the woman. When she leaves, Fausto excuses himself to Sandra and follows the woman. At her door, he kisses her and tries to arrange an appointment. When Fausto returns to the theater, he finds the movie over and Sandra waiting outside. She cries. She is afraid, she tells Fausto. He promises to stay beside her always.

A brief montage. Riccardo trims a new mustache. Alberto checks the length of new sideburns. Fausto now appears with his mustache shaved off. And Leopoldo has a goatee.

The day of Carnival. A parade passes in the street. Alberto, Riccardo, and Leopoldo are gathered in Alberto's room. Riccardo is dressed as a musketeer, and Leopoldo as a Chinese mandarin. Alberto is in the process of dressing as a woman. Alberto charges into his mother's room, looking for a woman's hat. He finds his mother and his sister in the midst of an emotional, strained conversation. The mother sends him off to look in a trunk.

Inside a dance hall filled with streamers and papier-maché figures, a large group of people dance. Riccardo and Alberto are present. Fausto arrives with Sandra, and they dance. Riccardo tries to lure a girl away to the basement, and Leopoldo tries to lure one to the upstairs. At the refreshment table, Leopoldo meets the maid from next door. He is embarrassed and slights her. Moraldo arrives and dances with his sister. Giulia approaches with a group, and slightly tipsy, she throws confetti at Fausto. He surveys her lowcut dress and asks her to dance. Somewhat flustered, she declines.

Later that night, the band plays "Yes, Sir, That's My Baby" at a violent pace. Then during a final trumpet solo, we see Alberto dancing slowly with a huge papier-maché head. Riccardo has gotten his girl off to a deserted part of the building and is kissing her. Leopoldo dances with the maid. Slowly Alberto makes his way from the hall dragging the papier-maché head behind him.

Outside the hall, Moraldo helps Alberto on his way home. Alberto says that the vitelloni are all nobodies. He dreams of taking a boat to Brazil. At Alberto's house, we discover the sister waiting. She explains that she is leaving home and climbs into the car of her lover after a brief good-bye. Dazed Alberto enters his house. His mother is crying. He comforts her by saying he will find a job. She asks if he has prospects. He answers no, and he falls asleep slumped in an armchair.

The next morning in the storeroom of the shop for religious items, Fausto drops a box of candles. Giulia helps him pick up the candles. He throws confetti at her. She leaves hurriedly. Later when the husband is out of the shop, Fausto approaches her again and kisses her. She slaps him. The owner enters the shop and observes a frosty silence between the two of them. At closing time, the owner invites Fausto to the apartment upstairs. He tells Fausto that the day is the owner's fifteenth wedding anniversary with Giulia. He offers Fausto a drink, tells Fausto he loves his wife, and then fires Fausto.

At the cafe that evening, Fausto tells Moraldo that he has been fired because he would not return the advances of the wife of the shopowner. He talks Moraldo into returning to the shop where the two young men steal a statue of an angel.

The next morning, the two young men try to sell the statue. Giudizio, the town fool, helps them by transporting the statue in his wheelbarrow. A nun at a convent and a monk at a monastery refuse to buy the statue. That night they leave the statue in Giudizio's shack by the beach. The next morning, Giudizio takes the statue outside and sits in awe of it.

At the dinner table at Moraldo's house, the father enters and explodes in anger. He knows about the theft. He chases Moraldo and accuses Fausto. Fausto blusters that his father-in-law has believed a pack of lies and leaves the table. Moraldo explains later to Sandra that Fausto was fired for refusing the advances of the wife of his boss. She leads Fausto back into the house.

Some months later, we see Sandra's parents and relatives, Moraldo, Fausto, and Sandra gathered around a new baby. Then we see Sandra at the house of Fausto's father with the baby.

At night in a deserted square, Moraldo sits with the boy from the railroad station. They look at the stars and talk.

At the theater, the five vitelloni are gathered. The narrator tells us that the visiting actor, Sergio Natali, has read Leopoldo's play and has promised to speak with Leopoldo after the show. We watch the actor recite a sentimental speech. There follows a patriotic finale with chorus girls dressed as soldiers and a female singer dressed as the spirit of Italy. Backstage, Leopoldo flatters Natali, and Natali, in turn, flatters Leopoldo.

At a cafe, Leopoldo reads his play to Natali while the actor eats. The other four vitelloni look on. The singer and the chorus girls enter and take another table. Later, we find Leopoldo still reading to Natali, but the four vitelloni have shifted to the other table. Fausto and the female singer dance together. Natali leads Leopoldo from the cafe.

Outside, Natali promises to perform Leopoldo's play in two months in Milan. Delighted, Leopoldo wants to finish reading the third act to Natali that night. Natali leads Leopoldo to the beach. Leopoldo protests that the beach is too dark for reading. Natali turns a faded, leering smile to him. Leopoldo runs off.

In another part of town, Fausto emerges from the singer's bedroom. Moraldo waits for him at the square. Moraldo mentions Sandra's name as a reproach and tells Fausto to wipe off the lipstick on his face.

In the bedroom of Fausto and Sandra. Sandra lies awake in the dark. She sees Fausto enter and wipe at his face in front of the mirror. She cries, and Fausto tries to comfort her. Early the next morning, Sandra takes the baby and leaves the house.

At a square of the city, Leopoldo and Fausto await the arrival of Riccardo and Alberto in the car of Riccardo's father. Sandra has not returned. Riccardo suggests that she may have gone to the home of the wetnurse. En route, Leopoldo leaves the car to urinate behind a tree. Alberto throws a clod of dirt at the tree. Riccardo and Alberto argue over a bird call they hear. Fausto runs ahead of the group. He discovers that Sandra is not at the home of the wetnurse, and his anxiety deepens. The other three young men walk up to the house, and Riccardo explains that the car won't start. Fausto sets off for town on a bicycle. The others accept an offer to stay for lunch with the wetnurse.

Inside the home of Sandra's parents, Fausto encounters the maid who tells him that the parents and the police are searching at the beach. Frantic, he runs off to the beach. There he encounters the lady from the movie theater, but shuns her overtures. He finds the beach deserted and returns to the home of his in-laws. He meets Moraldo and speaks of suicide. Moraldo tells Fausto that he is too cowardly for suicide. In a daze, Fausto goes to the shop of religious items and cries in front of the shopowner.

Riccardo, Leopoldo, and Alberto are seen driving back to town. They pass a group of workers repairing the road. Alberto gives them an obscene gesture. Fifty yards down the road, however, the car stalls and rolls to a stop. Alberto and Riccardo panic and run off. Leopoldo urges the workers to chase the other two. He yells that he is a socialist. At last, he too has to make a run for it.

Back in town, Fausto's young sister is in the streets looking for her brother. She spots him with the shopowner and leads them both to the home of Fausto's father. Sandra, the sister explains, has spent the day there. In the sitting room, the father administers a beating to Fausto with his belt. Forced to wait outside the sitting room, Sandra appears worried about the turn of events. The shopowner, however, appears pleased. At last, Sandra bursts into the sitting room and comforts Fausto. Later, however, as they walk to the home of her parents, she warns him if he betrays her again, it will be she who administers the beating.

Near dawn at the railroad station, Moraldo says goodbye to the young boy who works there. Moraldo can't tell the boy where he is going, only that he is leaving. He boards the train. As the train leaves, Moraldo looks at the town for a last time. We see inter-cuts of Leopoldo asleep with a book, Riccardo hugging a pillow in his sleep, Alberto on his back in bed snoring, and Fausto and Sandra in bed with the baby between them. Moraldo looks back down the tracks. We see the little boy walking in the other direction toward the station, balancing playfully on one of the rails.

Credits

Producer:	Lorenzo Pegoraro (An Italo-French co-production by Peg Films and Cité Films)
Director:	Federico Fellini
Screenplay:	Fellini, Ennio Flaiano, Tullio Pinelli
Photography:	Otello Martelli, Luciano Trasatti, Carlo Carlini
Cameramen:	Roberto Girardo, Franco Villa
Sets:	Mario Chiari
Music:	Nino Rota
Conductor:	Franco Ferrara
Editor:	Rolando Benedetti
Production Director:	Luigi Giacosi
Production Inspector:	Danilo Fallani
Production Secretary:	Ugo Benvenuti
Cast:	Franco Interlenghi (Moraldo), Franco Fabrizi (Fausto), Alberto Sordi (Alberto), Leopoldo Trieste (Leopoldo), Riccardo Fellini (Riccardo), Eleonora Ruffo (Sandra), Lida Baarowa (Giulia, Michele's wife), Carlo Romano (Michele), Arlette Sauvage (woman in the cinema), Maja Nipora (actress), Jean Brochard (Fausto's father), Claude Farère (Alberto's sister), Enrico Viarisio (Sandra's father), Paola Borboni (Sandra's mother), Vira Salenti, Achille Majeroni,

Silvio Bagolini, Franca Gandolfi,
Gondrano Trucchi, Guido Marturi,
Giovanna Galli, Milvia Chianelli.

Filmed in Viterbo, Ostia,
and Florence from Decem-
ber, 1952 until spring,
1953.
Distribution: API Productions
Running Time: 104 minutes
Released: Italy: First shown at 1953 Venice
                                 Film Festival
                                 U.S.: October 23, 1956 (NYC)
Note: The title, which many prospective
                                 producers and distributors fought
                                 unsuccessfully to change, literally
                                 means large, overgrown calves and
                                 is used in northern Italian dialects
                                 for loafers or ne'er-do-wells. It
                                 was the first of Fellini's films to
                                 receive distribution in Europe out-
                                 side of Italy.

4   UN'AGENZIA MATRIMONIALE [A MATRIMONIAL AGENCY, sometimes called
     LOVE CHEERFULLY ARRANGED] (1953). A sketch from the film AMORE
     IN CITTÀ [LOVE IN THE CITY], overall direction by Cesare
     Zavattini.

     The film opens with shots of a magazine. As the pages are
turned and the camera picks out pictures of people, a narrator
says that this episode will examine the phenomenon of an agency
which arranges marriages. He states that although many people
are unaware of the practice, it is still very common for marriages to be arranged. He says that a reporter was sent out
to look into this and find out what actually happens.
     The narration now switches to the voice of the reporter.
He says that he found an ad in a newspaper and found the agency
in an old building in Rome. While he speaks we are shown the
building. It is a large, old stone building with dirty hallways which wind in and out. He asks some of the residents for
directions to the agency, but no one knows of it. As he walks
down the hallways the camera tracks along peeking in on various occupants involved in their daily tasks. A little girl
says she can show him to "the agency." She leads the way and
is joined by five other small children. They disappear down
one of the labyrinthine corridors leaving the reporter by himself. He continues to search and the children reappear at
the end of one of the halls. He finds a small room crowded
with people. A middle-aged man reading a newspaper tells him
that this is the agency but he must wait his turn. The reporter asks for the proprietor, and the man tells him that he

is in charge. He brags to the reporter about the success of his agency and explains some of the procedures.

The reporter is taken to the receptionist. In the voice-over narration he says that he realized that he had to come up with a story. So he says that he told them he was a doctor who had a patient with an unusual problem. His patient was a young, wealthy man who was desparate for a wife but suffered from a strange "moon-madness" which turned him into a werewolf. The receptionist is not bothered by this at all and assures him that a bride can be found. She shows him a picture book containing photographs of some of the women who are available. The owner enters, cutting the edges of a piece of paper, and tells the reporter that his patient's problem is not that serious. He says that he has arranged marriage for all sorts of clients with physical and emotional handicaps.

One night the reporter is awakened in his apartment by the phone. The receptionist tells him that she has found a girl for his patient, and they arrange a meeting.

The reporter drives up to an outdoor cafe and is greeted by the receptionist. She takes him aside and tells him that she has not told the girl about his friend's sickness, thinking that they should meet first. She calls the girl (Rosanna) and introduces her to the reporter. The girl is young, blond, and very quiet. The receptionist suggests that the two young people take a drive. She prods Rosanna to get into the car and admonishes her to act like a lady and mind her manners.

As they are driving along, the reporter asks Rosanna what she has been told about his patient. She says only that he is rich. He tells her of the "moon-madness," but she is not frightened. Instead she is sympathetic and asks only if his patient is a kind person. The reporter insists on the sickness, but she remains willing.

He stops the car in the country and they get out. He offers her a cigarette. She explains that she doesn't smoke but takes it anyway for her brothers. She tells him that she is from a large family of two boys and seven girls of which she is the oldest. They sit in the grass next to the road. The reporter asks her why she would want to marry his friend. She says that she is all alone. She had tried to run away from the city and return to the family's original home in the provinces, but was unsuccessful. She did not even get out of Rome and was all alone and hungry when she saw the agency's ad in the paper. She wonders if she couldn't come to like his patient. The reporter has obviously been touched by her sad story and tries to discourage her. They get back into the car and drive back to the city.

As we see them driving in the city the reporter, in voice-over, explains that he tried to think of something encouraging to say to her, but he realized that her immediate problems were too pressing. "So I said nothing. When we parted, I wished her luck." And we see her getting out of the car in the city. She walks away, and the car drives off.

Credits

Producers:	Cesare Zavattini, Renato Ghione, Marco Ferreri (Faro Film)
Director:	Federico Fellini
Screenplay:	Fellini, Tullio Pinelli
Photography:	Gianni di Venanzo
Sets:	Gianni Polidori
Music:	Mario Nascimbene
Editor:	Eraldo Da Roma
Cast:	Antonio Cifariello and nonprofessional actors from the Centro sperimentale di cinematografia in Rome.

Filmed in Rome.

Distribution:	Italian Films Export
Running Time:	18 minutes
Released:	Italy: 1953
	U.S.: March 28, 1955 (NYC)
Note:	Fellini's sketch is one of six in this episodic film which was conceived by Cesare Zavattini as a semi-documentary examination of everyday events. The other episodes are: Dino Risi's PARADISO PER QUATTRO ORE [FOUR HOURS OF PARADISE]; Michelangelo Antonioni's SUICIDIO TENTATO [ATTEMPTED SUICIDE]; Alberto Lattuada's GLI ITALIANI SI VOLTANO [ITALIANS TURN ROUND]; Francesco Maselli and Cesare Zavattini's STORIA DI CATERINA RIGOGLIOSO [THE STORY OF CATERINA RIGOGLIOSO]; and Carlo Lizzani's L'AMORE CHE SI PAGA [LOVE AT A PRICE]. Lizzani's episode was cut from prints meant for foreign distribution. According to Fellini, his fantastic tale of the search for a bride for a victim of lycanthropy was accepted by Zavattini as proof that fact is stranger than fiction.

5   LA STRADA [THE ROAD] (1954)

The movie begins with a young woman walking along the seashore. Children run to her calling, "Gelsomina," and she follows them back to her house. There she finds her mother talking with a very rough looking man, Zampano. The mother tells Gelsomina that her sister, Rosa, who had been travelling

with Zampano as his assistant, has died; and she offers
Gelsomina to Zampano as a replacement. Zampano gives the older
woman some money and walks toward his vehicle with Gelsomina
following. The vehicle is an odd amalgamation of a motorcycle
and a trailer. The mother seems to change her mind, but
Gelsomina kisses her brothers and sisters and leaves.

Zampano is performing his daring feat of strength for a
crowd in a small village. He wraps a chain around his chest,
fastens it with a metal clasp, and, after warning those who
are frightened at the sight of blood, successfully breaks the
hook. Gelsomina applauds approvingly along with the crowd.

Later at their camp, Zampano takes some old clothes from
his trailer and tries them on the young woman. He then takes
out a trumpet and plays a tune. Next, he places a small snare
drum around Gelsomina's neck. He plays a roll and snaps,
"Zampano is here!" Gelsomina tries unsuccessfully to imitate
him. Zampano makes a switch from a branch and proceeds to
beat Gelsomina as she continues to try to learn her speech.
That night Gelsomina sits in front of the camp fire chanting a
strange, sad cadence. Zampano orders her into the trailer.
For the first time he asks her name. Later, we see her gazing
at him as he sleeps. Then she cries.

Again, Zampano is performing his stunt, only this time to
the accompaniment of Gelsomina's drum. He announces a new
comedy act which he will perform with his "wife." Zampano,
dressed as a clown, pretends to be a hunter. Gelsomina, in a
similar costume, pretends to be a duck, and her mimickry delights the crowd.

That night the two are eating at a local <u>trattoria</u>. Zampano
spots a woman in the restaurant, and his interest is piqued.
He introduces Gelsomina as his "assistant," and brags about his
strength. Gelsomina watches this and laughs along with the
other woman as if she understood the courting game that is being played. They all leave the restaurant together, but when
they get to the vehicle, Zampano tells Gelsomina she must stay,
and he drives off with the other woman. Gelsomina is left on
the street alone. A dissolve to Gelsomina sitting on the curb
later that night. A horse silently plods by. A dissolve to
the same scene the next morning. Some of the local residents
offer Gelsomina food, but she refuses. When one of them tells
her she can find the motorcycle at the edge of town, she jumps
up and hurries off.

At the vehicle, she tries to wake Zampano who is sleeping
on the ground nearby. When she fails to awaken him, she thinks
he must be dead, and she cries. Zampano finally awakens, and
Gelsomina tells him that she has been busy planting tomatoes.
On the road Gelsomina questions Zampano about his relationship with her sister, Rosa. She asks if Zampano slept with
her and with other women. He tells her to be quiet and says
disgustedly: "Tomatoes! I think you have tomatoes for
brains!"

The next scene is a wedding reception. A large crowd is assembled around an outdoor table, eating, drinking, talking, and singing. Gelsomina dances. Delighted by her, some children lead her to an attic room. There in bed is a deformed child, Oswaldo, who stares blankly at Gelsomina. She is transfixed by his gaze. The children urge her to entertain him. She begins a dance, smiles, and approaches the bed. At that moment, a nun who looks after the child, rushes in and chases Gelsomina and the others away. Downstairs Zampano is eating a large plate of pasta with a woman of the house. Gelsomina tries to tell Zampano of the child in the attic, but he is not interested. The woman propositions Zampano with an offer of some of her husband's old suits. Gelsomina winks at Zampano, then realizes what is taking place, and is sad. The woman and Zampano leave together.

Later that night, Zampano is proudly trying on his new suits in a barn. Gelsomina is obviously very hurt. She tries in vain to recall for Zampano the good times they have had together. She asks him to teach her to play the trumpet. As Zampano falls asleep, Gelsomina tries to tell him that she is going home. She walks out of the barn, throws the clothes Zampano has given her into the trailer, retrieves her old clothes and shoes, and walks away.

Gelsomina is walking on the road, alone, and she stops to rest. She picks up a bug, examines it, and blows it away. Suddenly a three-piece band marches by. Gelsomina falls into step and dances down the road with them.

The scene shifts suddenly to a crowded religious procession which is winding its way through the streets of a town. There are priests, altar boys, and townspeople carrying large religious statues. Gelsomina is trapped and afraid, but she stands in awe as a picture of the Blessed Virgin Mary is carried past her.

That night the square is crowded with people, and all of them are intently watching a tightrope walker high above the street. An assistant announces over a loud-speaker: "Ladies and gentlemen--the Fool!" The Fool is the young tightrope walker who wears a pair of angel's wings on his back. He fakes a fall and swings safely from the wire.

Much later that night, Gelsomina is in the square which is now almost deserted. She marches around like a little soldier. A man approaches her, but another stops him: "Leave her alone. She's crazy." Zampano's motorcycle thunders into the square, and he tells her to get into the trailer.

Gelsomina is awakened by the sound of a donkey. She gets out of the trailer to discover that Fool she is in a circus. She wanders into a tent and finds the Fool playing a sad tune on his violin. Zampano calls her over and introduces her to the manager of the circus troupe. They join up, and the manager's wife tells her that they are in Rome. Zampano and the owner go into the tent where the Fool is playing, and the Fool begins to taunt Zampano.

The circus is performing that night. The Fool joins the crowd. Zampano, "the man with the lungs of steel," begins his act. While he is giving his opening pitch, the Fool mockingly applauds. As Zampano nears the conclusion of his act, the Fool yells out, "Zampano, you are wanted on the telephone." Zampano is enraged and chases the Fool, but is unable to catch him. Later that night Zampano is washing up, and Gelsomina questions him about the Fool. She hears the violin and sees the Fool, but when she approaches him he bids her to return to Zampano.

In the morning, the Fool is rehearsing. Gelsomina looks on. He gives her a trombone and teaches her how to march. The owner of the circus is impressed with the possibilities of a new act and says that he will ask Zampano if she can perform with the Fool. But when Zampano happens onto the scene, he grabs her horn and says, "She works with nobody but me." An argument breaks out between Zampano, the owner of the circus, and the Fool. Furiously, Zampano chases the Fool who runs into a small cafe and hides in the back room. Zampano, wielding a knife, tries to break down the door, but he is stopped by the police. Back at the circus the owner says that both Zampano and the Fool have been taken to the police station.

At night the Fool returns to the circus and begins to talk with Gelsomina. He gently mocks her appearance and tells her that she looks like an artichoke. Quite suddenly he tells her that he will soon die. He asks her why she teamed up with Zampano. Gelsomina tells him of her brothers and sisters at home and of her feelings of uselessness. The Fool speculates that perhaps Zampano will not let Gelsomina go because he loves her. Perhaps it is her purpose in life to provide comfort for Zampano. The Fool then picks up a small stone and says: "Everything in this world is useful for something. Even this little stone has a purpose, because if this pebble is useless, then so are the stars." Gelsomina is elated. She grabs the pebble, and her face lights up with a smile. She, then, tells the Fool that he is no longer welcome in the circus, and she asks him what he meant earlier about dying. He responds that in his profession he could die very suddenly and no one would care. The Fool puts Gelsomina in the back of Zampano's vehicle and drives her to the police station. He gives her a necklace as a souvenir and walks away singing, "Gelsomina, Gelsomina." Zampano emerges from the station to find Gelsomina waiting for him. She tells him that she will stay with him.

Zampano and Gelsomina are on the road again and Zampano stops along the sea shore. Gelsomina can barely control her happiness as she runs to the water. She asks Zampano to point out the direction of her home, but then she says that now her home is with Zampano.

They are travelling and have another rider, a young nun, with them. They take her to her convent, and she secures permission for them to stay in the granary for the night. She brings them supper, and Gelsomina plays on the trumpet the sad theme which has been repeated throughout the film. Zampano chops some wood for the nun. Gelsomina and the nun discuss their lifestyles, and the nun concludes, "You follow your husband, and I follow mine." That night Gelsomina asks Zampano why he keeps her; she inquires if he would be sorry if she died; she talks about marriage; and she tells him about the usefulness of the stone. He calls her a fool. While she continues to talk, Zampano falls asleep. Gelsomina takes up her trumpet and begins to play softly. Later she awakens and finds Zampano trying to break into the chapel to steal the sacred vessels. When she refuses to help, he beats her. The next morning as they prepare to leave, Gelsomina and the young nun are talking. It is obvious that Gelsomina is distressed, and the nun tries to convince her to stay at the convent. Gelsomina refuses the offer, jumps into the trailer, and waves and cries as Zampano drives off.

Zampano stops the motorcycle in the road. Ahead of him is the Fool who is trying to repair a flat tire on his car. Zampano, wanting revenge for past wrongs, begins a fight with him. The larger man brutally beats the Fool until the Fool hits his head on the car. Zampano walks away thinking the injury is not a serious one, but the Fool stumbles into a field and collapses. Gelsomina begins to cry and runs to him saying, "He's hurt." Zampano tries to revive the Fool, but it becomes clear to him that the Fool is dead. Zampano panics. He drags the body away from the road and throws it under a bridge. He pushes the car off the bridge, and it breaks into flame, giving the appearance of an accident.

Zampano is performing his act to a very small crowd. Gelsomina wanders in a daze. She fails to respond to Zampano's instructions as she repeats, "The Fool is hurt."

Later outside of town, Zampano stops the motorcycle. Gelsomina gets out of the vehicle and begins to wander off, obviously in a state of shock. Zampano is very worried. He stops her and asks if she would like to be taken back to her mother. That night she will not eat.

A morning. Gelsomina seems better. Zampano is puzzled by her new attitude, but thankful that she is more like herself. He offers to make her some soup, but she says she will fix it. Zampano tells her that she hasn't moved for two weeks. He tries to apologize for the Fool's death, saying it was only an accident. Gelsomina doesn't seem to hear him and says that now they can go on. Suddenly she begins to cry and mumble about the Fool, but she stops herself. Zampano tells her that he will take her home. She says, however, that she must stay with him. She lies down in the sun and whispers that she should stay with Zampano as the Fool had instructed her. She falls asleep.

Later while Gelsomina is still sleeping, Zampano quietly removes blankets from the back of the cycle. He carries them over to where she is sleeping and leaves them. He packs up his own belongings quickly. He stops, picks out Gelsomina's trumpet from the trailer, and leaves it by her side. He pushes the motorcycle down the road until he is a safe distance from Gelsomina, and then he starts it up and drives away.

A circus parade makes its way through a small town. Zampano, greyed, much older, and now with another woman, leaves to take a walk. As he walks down the road, he hears someone singing the sad song Gelsomina always played. For a moment he doesn't react, almost as if he were in a dream. He sees a young girl hanging clothes on a line. She is singing the song. He anxiously asks her where she learned it, and she tells him that it is a song that a strange girl used to play on a small trumpet four or five years ago. She says that the strange girl hardly spoke and that she is now dead. She asks Zampano if he had known the girl, and she tells him that the mayor could inform him where the strange girl was buried.

Later, Zampano is back at the circus performing his act. He delivers his warning to the audience, but his former enthusiasm is no longer in his voice. He merely walks through the routine.

That night Zampano is drunk in a local cafe. He begins a fight with the other patrons and is thrown out. He continues to attack any object he can get his hands on. He stumbles down to the seashore, drops in the sand, and stares silently at the water and the sky. Zampano begins to cry and to claw at the sand. The camera cranes back showing Zampano on the shore as we hear Gelsomina's theme.

Credits

Producers:	Carlo Ponti, Dino De Laurentiis
Director:	Federico Fellini
Screenplay:	Fellini, Tullio Pinelli, Ennio Flaiano
Photography:	Otello Martelli
Cameraman:	Roberto Girardi
Sets:	Mario Ravesco
Costumes:	M. Marinari
Artistic Collaborators:	Brunello Rondi, Paolo Nuzzi
Music:	Nino Rota
Conductor:	Franco Ferrara
Editor:	Leo Cattozzo
Assistant Editor:	Lina Caterini
Assistant Director:	Moraldo Rossi
Sound:	A. Calpini
Script:	Narciso Vicari
Director of Production:	Luigi Giacosi
Production Assistants:	Danilo Fallani, Giorgio Morra, Angelo Cittadini
Special Effects:	E. Trani

Set Photographer: A. Piatti

Cast: Giulietta Masina (Gelsomina),
Anthony Quinn (Zampano), Richard
Basehart (the Fool), Aldo Silvani
(Colombaini), Marcella Rovena (the
widow), Lidia Venturini (the nun).

Filmed in Viterbo,
Ovindoli, Bagnoregio, and
various small towns in
Central and Southern
Italy from December, 1953
to May, 1954.

Distribution: Trans-Lux

Running Time: 107 minutes

Released: Italy: First shown September 11,
1954 at the Venice Film Festival
U.S.: July 16, 1956 (NYC)

Note: Although the script was written in
1951, Fellini could not find a producer willing to finance the film
for two years. This film was an
overwhelming international success
(it ran in New York for more than
three years), and it received the
Academy Award for Best Foreign
Film in 1956.

6   IL BIDONE [THE SWINDLE] (1955)

The movie opens with a shot of "Baron" Vargas sitting on a
hill in the countryside surrounded by empty fields. A car
approaches from the far distance below him. He hails the car.
From it emerge his accomplices: Roberto, a tall, blond man in
a chauffeur's uniform; Augusto, a heavyset man in his late
forties; and Picasso, a younger man and an apparently innocent
type. Roberto puts a Vatican license plate on the car.
Augusto disguises himself as a prelate. Picasso is already
dressed as a priest. Vargas gives them a map and explains
where to find the farm of those who are to be swindled.
Roberto notes that Augusto is getting old and "scared."

At the farm of two sisters, the men pull off their swindle.
Augusto as the prelate tells the sisters that a criminal has
murdered his cohort and buried the cohort with their loot on
the property of the sisters. According to the terms of the
deathbed will of the criminal, the treasure will go to the
sisters, with the exception of whatever is necessary to pay
for masses for the criminal's salvation. All follow the map
to a spot in a field. Roberto digs for awhile and then gives
up. One of the sisters continues the digging eagerly. It is
she who discovers the bones and then the treasure box. Back

at the farmhouse, Augusto springs his trick. The sisters must pay for five hundred masses at one thousand lire each, or the treasure of six million lire will be given to the poor. The sisters disappear into town. The three swindlers must wait, unsure their swindle has worked. At last the sisters return, with the necessary money, and the swindlers drive off. Gay music is heard on the soundtrack.

At the Piazza del Popolo in Rome, Picasso says goodbye to Roberto and Augusto. He goes to his apartment and greets his wife, Iris, and daughter, Silvana. He takes them out for dinner, gives them gifts, and eventually turns his money over to Iris. He lies that he and his partners have earned the money as salesmen. All are happy.

At a cabaret, Augusto and Roberto enter. Augusto buys cigarettes for the band and champagne for Roberto and himself. Roberto spies an older woman surrounded by younger men. He breaks through the ring and invites her to dance. Augusto strikes up a conversation with an English girl who dances at the cabaret. Roberto makes a date for the next day with the older woman, as Augusto watches the English girl dance.

Daylight at a cafe. Augusto tries to sell his "wife's watch" for fifteen thousand lire to an older man. Roberto enters and begs Augusto to sell it to him. But the older man is in the rackets himself and can't be fooled. He buys drinks for Augusto and Roberto and leaves. Roberto chides Augusto. The gay music of the first sequence is repeated here.

In a poor section of Rome, the car of the swindlers pulls up. Picasso gets out and asks for various citizens. He announces that the assignment of public housing is to begin. At this point, Augusto as the important government official steps in. The citizens on his list may have their apartment assignment if they pay the first month's rent. They set up headquarters in a hut and accept the money which the anxious crowd brings them.

On New Year's Eve in the Piazza Navona of Rome, Augusto and Picasso walk. Picasso is charmed by soap bubbles blown by a street vendor and buys a bubble pipe. Both jump aside as a big white Buick convertible bears down on them. Inside is Augusto's friend, Rinaldo. He is obviously successful. Beside him is a sullen brunette woman in a mink coat. She is Luciana. Rinaldo knocks her forward to admit Augusto and Picasso to the back seat. He invites both of them to his party and then knocks Luciana forward again so they can leave the car.

Augusto, Picasso, and Iris enter Rinaldo's apartment as the party is in full swing. Iris worries that she is not dressed as elegantly as the other women who wear strapless evening gowns. A crowd is gathered around a girl who is being talked into stripping. Rinaldo takes the girl into the bathroom, only to be brought out again by Luciana's pounding on the door. A man with a lampshade wanders through the scene.

Picasso tries to pass off a painting he has done to Rinaldo as a real "De Pisis," but is rebuffed. In the midst of the attempt, Roberto who is also a guest tries to flatter Rinaldo and is rebuffed too. Then Augusto tries to interest Rinaldo in a partnership in the Texas Club, but to no avail. The party reaches a crescendo at midnight. A guest is dangled over the edge of the veranda many stories above the ground. Roberto spots an expensive cigarette case on a chair and slips it into his pocket. Picasso dances happily with his wife, and a man with a fur wrap on his head dances with a rose. In a bedroom, Rinaldo with the girl who was ready to strip tells Augusto he is too old for petty larceny. Then Rinaldo is called away by Luciana to confront Roberto. Rinaldo forces Roberto to pretend the theft was a joke and return the cigarette case.

In the street outside, Augusto angrily berates Roberto, and Iris demands to know from Picasso what business he does with two such men. The street is littered with confetti.

Daylight, later. Roberto picks up Augusto and Picasso with a car. He has a number of cheap coats in the car. They have been cleaned and sewn to look good. Augusto is hailed by his daughter and promises to call her. It has been two years since they have seen each other. Outside of Rome, Roberto cons an old gas station attendant into giving him gasoline and loaning him some spending money in exchange for the "security" of an "expensive coat." Augusto repeats the trick on a young boy at a second gas station. The gay theme is played throughout the episodes outside of Rome.

At a small town where a carnival has been set up. Picasso becomes drunk that night and runs through the streets. He comes to a deserted merry-go-round and offers to buy the others rides. Augusto and Roberto argue. Augusto says flatly that Roberto will never get out of the rackets to become a singer as he brags he will, and Roberto taunts Augusto about his age. Augusto sobers up Picasso by putting his head under a pump. Picasso says he is worried that Iris will leave him. Augusto tells Picasso to say "million." He tells Picasso that he can't say it properly because he doesn't think in big enough terms. Augusto also tells Picasso that a swindler needs to be alone. Picasso decides to leave the group and go back to Iris. "How do you keep it up at your age?" Picasso asks Augusto.

At an outdoor restaurant, Augusto eats with his daughter. Patricia wants to go on with her studies, but worries about expenses. She could work on a part-time basis, if she could put up a guarantee of three hundred thousand lire. Father and daughter go to a movie. As they settle into their seats, Augusto promises his daughter he will get the necessary money for her. At the intermission, however, Augusto is spotted by a man to whom he sold false Terramycin. The man assails Augusto in the back of the theater, the man's friend brings a policeman, and Patricia sees her father taken off to a police station. Later that night, she sees him emerge with handcuffs on and be transported to another jail.

At a later date, Augusto leaves prison and returns to his cafe. He asks for Roberto, but learns from Riccardo, Roberto's friend, that Roberto has left town. Augusto asks for "Baron" Vargas.

The buried treasure swindle begins again, this time with Riccardo as the chauffeur and a stranger as the priest-secretary. The family being swindled has a crippled daughter, Susanna. Augusto plays his role as the prelate as if he were walking in his sleep. The farmer turns over to him three hundred fifty thousand lire he had been saving to improve the farm for his daughters. He wants, he explains, to provide for his daughters, especially Susanna. Before Augusto can leave, the wife asks him to console Susanna. He speaks to her briefly and is surprised to find she worries more about her parents than about herself. He tells her that she already has a great deal more than many others have.

Later, some distance away, the swindlers stop their car and rejoin Vargas. Augusto announces that he gave back the swindled money to Susanna. The swindlers try to search him, and he resists. He runs off, but hit by a rock thrown by one of the others, he falls and injures his back on a boulder. The swindlers search him. "My daughter," he cries. They find the money in his shoe and go off, leaving him to die.

Painfully, Augusto climbs a hill. Apparently his back is broken. He moves his hands and knees. As he nears the roadside, he sees two women and three children. The audience hears again, as voice-over narration, Augusto's conversation with Patricia, in which he promises to find her the money she needs. The women and children pass by Augusto without seeing him. "I'll go with you," he tries to tell them. Then, prostrate on the ground, his arms spread, Augusto dies.

[This synopsis is based on the English language version.]

Credits

Producer:	Titanus for Mario de Vecchi Films; an Italo-French co-production of Titanus and S.G.C.
Director:	Federico Fellini
Screenplay:	Fellini, Ennio Flaiano, Tullio Pinelli
Photography:	Otello Martelli
Cameramen:	Roberto Gerardi, Arturo Zavattini
Set Photographer:	G. B. Poletto
Artistic Collaborator:	Brunello Rondi
Sets and Costumes:	Dario Cecchi
Decorator:	Massimiliano Capriccioli
Music:	Nino Rota
Conductor:	Franco Ferrara
Sound:	Giovanni Rossi

Editors:	Mario Serandrei, Giuseppe Vari
Editing Secretary:	Nada Delle Piane
Assistant Directors:	Dominique Delouche, Paolo Nuzzi
Director's Aides:	Moraldo Rossi, Narciso Vicario
Make-up:	Eligio Trani
Hair Stylist:	Fiamma Rocchetti
Production Director:	Giuseppe Colizzi
Production Inspector:	Antonio Negri
Production Secretary:	Manolo Bolognini
Administrative Secretary:	Ezio Rodi
Cast:	Broderick Crawford (Augusto), Richard Basehart (Picasso), Franco Fabrizi (Roberto), Giulietta Masina (Iris), Giacomo Gabrielli (Vargas), Alberto de Amicis (Rinaldo), Lorella de Luca (Patricia), Irene Cefaro (Marisa), Sue Ellen Blake (Anna), Xenia Valderi (Luciana), Maria Zanoli (Stella Fiorina), Lucietta Muratori, Riccardo Garrone, Paul Grenter.

Filmed in Marino, Rome, and Cerveteri during the summer of 1955.

Distribution:	Astor
Running Time:	92 minutes
Released:	Italy: September 10, 1955 at Venice Film Festival
	U.S.: November 19, 1964 (NYC)
Note:	Following <u>La Strada</u>, Fellini planned a sequel to <u>I Vitelloni</u> entitled <u>Moraldo in citta</u>. A screenplay was written, but it was abandoned in favor of <u>Il Bidone</u>. It has been reported by Solmi and others that the original cast of <u>Il Bidone</u> was to have included Humphrey Bogart and Pierre Fresnay.

7 LE NOTTI DI CABIRIA [NIGHTS OF CABIRIA] (1956)

The movie opens with a long shot of a field on the outskirts of Rome near the Tiber. Cabiria runs playfully away from her lover, Giorgio, to the edge of the river, where she swings her pocketbook happily and calls to him. Cabiria is short. She wears a zebra striped dress, and her hair is arranged in a ponytail. Giorgio wears dark clothes and sunglasses. He looks around to be sure no one is watching. He grabs Cabiria's purse, pushes her into the Tiber, and runs off. From the river, Cabiria calls for help and calls to Giorgio.

A young boy, wearing an Indian feather in his hair, emerges from the undergrowth and takes up the cry. A man leaves a work site and runs along the bank shouting. The current carries Cabiria downstream. Three boys perched along the shore swim to her and pull her to the bank. Two farmers carry Cabiria by her feet and hold her upside down. When they set her down, she regains consciousness and cries out, "Where is Giorgio?" She gets to her feet and runs in various directions. A boy brings her one of her shoes. She snatches it angrily. Then she faints. As the men try to help her, she wriggles furiously from their grasp and heads for her home. The boys tell the men that she lives on the Ostia Road behind the gasoline tanks and that she is "one of them."

In a barren field near Ostia, we see small cinderblock houses, a jungle-gym made of pipes, and a swayback horse. Cabiria makes her way to her little house. She finds her door locked. "Has Giorgio come?" Cabiria calls to her friend Wanda, a big, round woman who is washing clothes in a tub nearby. Cabiria tells Wanda that she fell into the river and that Giorgio ran off frightened. Cabiria scrambles into her house through a window and then emerges through the door wearing a gaudy kimona to put her wet dress out to dry in the sun. To Wanda, she says only, "If you see Giorgio, tell him I'm in here."

Later that night in Cabiria's house, Wanda tries to comfort Cabiria. Wanda is now dressed in her uniform as a prostitute, with big loop earrings, a tight skirt, and a wide belt. She urges Cabiria to report Giorgio to the police. After Wanda leaves, Cabiria sits on the doorstep and says to herself, "And what if I died?" The thought frightens her. She takes a hen from a crate by the house and strokes the hen for comfort. Then a thought seizes her. She throws the hen up in the air, rushes inside her house, gathers up all of Giorgio's clothes, takes them outside, and throws them on a bonfire. She sees the full moon and throws a rock at it.

Night. A close-up of the pacing legs of a prostitute. She is Marissa, a young blond. The location is the Passeggiata Archeologica outside Rome. A group of prostitutes and their pimps are assembled, waiting for customers to drive up. One prostitute, Matilda, an amazon of a woman in a leopard-spotted blouse, stands off alone against a wall of the ruins. She boasts that she is a lady and different from the others. She admires her shadow on the wall. "Like Moby Dick," she proclaims. The rest of the group is gathered around a new Fiat 600 which Marissa has just bought. Her pimp, Amleto, has assumed control of it and sits behind the wheel.

Cabiria arrives. Her outfit as a prostitute is comic. She wears a zebra-striped blouse, black skirt, a scruffy fur jacket, and bobbysox. She carries a collapsed umbrella. Cabiria admires the car. She comments, however, that she would have chosen a different shade. A mambo comes on the car radio, and

Cabiria does a spirited dance. Matilda taunts Cabiria about the loss of Giorgio. Furiously, the small Cabiria hurls herself at the amazon. Wanda drags her away and puts her in the car with Amleto and Marissa.

Riding in the car, Cabiria asks to be driven to the fashionable Via Veneto. Amleto offers to take Cabiria under his protection along with Marissa. Cabiria turns him down and leaves the car.

Two tall, fashionable prostitutes glide down the Via Veneto. One wears a circular hat balanced squarely on her head. They move apart, and Cabiria passes between them, walking up the street in the opposite direction. One of the tall prostitutes looks down at her.

Later Cabiria crosses a street. A car honks and barely misses her. She gestures angrily at it. Then finding herself alone, she dances her mambo. A portly doorman appears from the Kit-Kat nightclub and stares at her unbelievingly. He gestures her away, but she stands her ground. Then from the nightclub rushes out Jessy, a young woman in a fur coat, followed by a handsome actor in a white dinner jacket. Jessy climbs into a convertible parked at the curb and demands the key. The couple argue, and at last Jessy leaves the car and walks off. The eyes of the handsome actor fall on Cabiria. "Get in," he orders her. The actor and Cabiria drive off.

Outside the nightclub Piccadilly, the actor pulls to a halt and orders Cabiria out of the car. She flares up angrily at him, but he makes his way to the door of the nightclub and invites her to follow. Mollified, Cabiria enters the nightclub after the actor.

On the dancefloor inside we see two briefly-clad black women doing an exotic dance. The actor enters and goes to the bar. In the foyer, an attendant demands Cabiria's umbrella and points the way through curtains to the interior. Cabiria gets tangled in the curtains, then spots the actor, and swaggers over to him. A young man, perhaps a press agent, approaches them and introduces a starlet to the actor. The starlet invites the actor to her table, but he avoids her by dancing with Cabiria. After a few moments, Cabiria breaks away from him into her spirited mambo. When the music stops, the actor announces that they are leaving.

In the convertible, Cabiria jumps up and shouts triumphantly at the two tall prostitutes of the Via Veneto whom she has spotted. The car roars off, however, jerking her back in her seat.

Shots of the car entering an estate, its horn sounding. A butler greets the actor and Cabiria at the door of the villa. The actor orders supper for two and gives instructions for the butler to tell Jessy he is asleep if she calls. The actor asks Cabiria her name and laughs when he hears the name of an empress. Cabiria hurries to follow the actor. We see her climb up a long flight of stairs, sputtering, and we track with her down a hallway as she looks at exotic birds in a glass-enclosed aviary.

In the bedroom, the actor opens chiming, mirrored closet doors to get his robe. He "reclines" on a couch and puts Beethoven's Fifth Symphony on a record player. Cabiria sits primly on an oversized ottoman. As the music reaches a climax, the butler wheels in supper. Cabiria tells the actor that she loved his last picture--"the one in costume with all the trimmings." She touches him as if to make sure he is real. Then she bursts into tears. "Who is going to believe it?" she wails. The actor signs a photograph, testifying that Cabiria was in his villa alone with him. The telephone rings. The butler has phoned to warn the actor that Jessy has arrived and is on her way to his room.

Quickly, the actor ushers Cabiria into the bathroom and locks the door, promising to get rid of Jessy in a hurry. The girlfriend enters the bedroom, takes off her fur coat, asks for a drink, and then breaks down in tears. Through the key-hole, Cabiria watches the couple make up. She discovers a dog in the bathroom, cuddles him, and sinks to the floor with the dog in her arms. Morning. Cabiria awakens. The actor unlocks the bathroom door and leads her past the sleeping Jessy and out of the bedroom. Silhouetted through his glass door, we see him pay Cabiria for her night's work despite her attempts to refuse. With difficulty, Cabiria finds her way to the foyer. She bumps into a clear glass door and gives it an elo-quent gesture with her hand.

Night on the Passeggiata Archeologica. It is raining, Cabiria and Wanda share an umbrella. The other prostitutes tease Cabiria about her night with the actor. Amleto's uncle, a crippled man on crutches, arrives. Amleto explains that the uncle looks forward to the upcoming celebration at the Church of the Madonna of Divine Love in the hope that he will be cured by a miracle. The prostitutes debate whether they will attend. A group of pilgrims walk by reciting the Rosary and singing hymns. Cabiria begins to follow them. A truck, how-ever, pulls up behind her, and the driver hails her. She gets in his cab.

A shot of a loud speaker mounted on the tower of the Church of the Madonna of Divine Love. The sound of chimes. The Fiat 600 with the crippled uncle, Almeto, and Marissa pulls up. Cabiria and Wanda emerge from another car and join the crowd. Cabiria buys a candle, but she expresses skepticism about the celebration. She stares at a person carried to the church on a stretcher. Wanda and Cabiria light their candles and advance to the church. Almeto helps his uncle along. Cabiria stares at canes, crutches, and braces left in the church as offerings to the Virgin. The crowd begins to chant a litany. Cabiria joins in the singing. She relights her candle, which had gone out, from the candle of another person. "Feel how my heart is beating," she tells Wanda. The uncle asks Almeto, "Will I be granted my prayers?" Cabiria kisses the step before the shrine and prays to the Madonna, "Help me change my life." At Almeto's urging, the uncle throws away his crutches. He crumples to the ground.

A littered field outside the church. A picnic is in session. Cabiria sits apart from her group with her back to them. She gulps down a drink Wanda offers her and then kicks away a soccer ball that has rolled near her. "We haven't changed," she says bitterly. She taunts some pilgrims off in a field, "Looking for snails?" Then she runs to a bus and slumps to the ground against it. She stares at some pilgrims and wipes her head sadly.

Night. Cabiria in her raincoat appraises the entrance of a theater. She buys a ticket and enters. Inside, a magician finishes a trick and calls for volunteers for his next piece of entertainment. A group of men go to the stage. The magician sets the men to work rowing a make-believe boat. After dismissing the men, he calls Cabiria to the center of the stage. He doffs his hat and reveals a set of rubber horns on his head. The magician offers to find Cabiria a husband, someone rich and handsome. Cabiria retorts, "I don't need anything. I've got plenty of money. The house I live in belongs to me!" The magician hypnotizes her and introduces her to an imaginary person, Oscar. The magician puts a garland on her head. Cabiria thinks that she is in a garden with Oscar. She picks imaginary flowers. "Take Oscar's arm," prompts the magician. Then we hear "The Merry Widow Waltz," and Cabiria dances gracefully with her imaginary partner. "You should have met me when I was eighteen. I had long, very long, beautiful black hair," she says. "You really love me?" she asks. "Tell me, it's really true? Don't try to deceive me." The magician brings her from her trance, and as the audience hoots at Cabiria, he calls for the curtain.

Cabiria peers out the rear door of the theater. A cleaning lady tells her the crowd is gone, and Cabiria walks outside. A neatly dressed stranger steps out of the shadows, and very politely he invites Cabiria for a drink. At a table outside a small cafe, this man tells Cabiria that he was moved by her in the theater. He introduces himself as a civil servant, and then tells her his name is Oscar. He arranges to meet Cabiria at Rome's Terminal Station the next day.

At the station, Oscar appears in the crowd and looks around. His shirt collar is open now, and he has a toothpick in his mouth. Cabiria sees him from the place where she has chosen to wait. She starts to walk away, but Oscar catches up to her and gives her flowers.

Night on the Passeggiata Archeologica. While the prostitutes eat from Cabiria's box of candy, she tells them about Oscar. "What is he after?" asks Wanda. Cabiria answers: "I don't know...but as long as he pays...." The police raid the

prostitutes. Matilda urges them to arrest the others. Cabiria
hides behind a bush. We see her frightened face.

Day. Cabiria's train arrives at the Pyramid Station.
Oscar meets her, and they walk on the Aventine Hill. He talks
of his childhood in general terms.

In her house, Cabiria listens to music on the radio. She
goes outside for a stroll and meets a Franciscan brother on
the road. He asks for money for St. Anthony and then inquires
if Cabiria is in a state of grace. "Whoever lives in God's
grace is happy," he tells her. "Boys and girls should marry,"
he adds, and then tells her his name is Brother Giovanni.

At night in the rain, Cabiria stands beneath her umbrella
on the Passeggiata Archeologica and smiles dreamily. A driver
hails her, but she does not respond.

During the day in Rome, Oscar and Cabiria walk. She tells
him that this meeting must be their last. Oscar, however,
proposes marriage. Cabiria whistles. "You don't know who I
am," she tells him. But Oscar insists. "We two are alone,"
he says. "We must be together. We need each other."

Cabiria runs across a field shouting Wanda's name. Wanda
comes to the window of her house, and Cabiria tells her that
she and Oscar will marry and buy a shop in the country.
Cabiria announces that she will sell her house.

At the Franciscan monastery. Cabiria tells the priest that
she wants to confess to Brother Giovanni. The priest states
that Brother Giovanni is away. Furthermore, he says that
Brother Giovanni is a lay brother and cannot hear confession.
Cabiria leaves disappointed.

Cabiria and Wanda pack Cabiria's possessions in her house.
Cabiria puts on a hat and a short plaid cape, and goes to the
door. A new family is waiting to take possession. Cabiria
gives her key to them, and she and Wanda walk to the busstop.
In tears they embrace. We see a shot of Wanda from Cabiria's
point of view on the back of the bus. Wanda grows small as
the bus moves away.

High-angle long shot of the lake at Castelgandolfo. Cabiria
and Oscar are seated at a terrace cafe. Oscar wears dark
glasses. The bill arrives, and Oscar insists that he will pay
it. Cabiria holds a huge wad of money. "My dowry," she calls
it. Cabiria explains that it is the money from the sale of
her house and from her savings account. Oscar invites Cabiria
for a walk.

In a woods, Oscar leads Cabiria by the hand. They kiss.
She picks flowers and playfully puts her hat on his head.
"Let's go and see the sunset on the cliff," he suggests.

At a promontory above the lake, Cabiria muses, "There is
justice. Some moment for each of us to be happy." Then she
looks at the water. "Can you swim?" Oscar asks. She begins
to tell him about her near drowning, but notices his agitation.
We see an extreme close-up of his eyes. "The money," she
cries and extends her purse toward him. "Throw me in," she

begs. "I don't want to live." She sinks to the ground. Oscar grabs the purse and runs off. Cabiria gets up slowly and begins to walk through the woods.

Evening. Cabiria walks from the woods onto a road. A group of young people are moving along the road, and gradually they overtake her. They wear party hats. One boy plays a guitar, and another a harmonica. "We lost our way," calls a girl, riding slowly on a Vespa with her boyfriend. A young girl looks directly into the camera and says, "Good evening." A close-up of Cabiria's face. A dark tear is painted in the corner of her eye. Another close-up of Cabiria's face as she looks into the camera and begins to smile.

Credits

Producer:	Dino De Laurentiis
Director:	Federico Fellini
Screenplay:	Fellini, Ennio Flaiano, Tullio Pinelli
Additional Dialogue:	Pier Paolo Pasolini
Photography:	Aldo Tonti, Otello Martelli
Sets and Costumes:	Piero Gherardi
Music:	Nino Rota
Conductor:	Franco Ferrara
Sound:	Roy Mangano
Editor:	Leo Cattozzo
Assistant Directors:	Moraldo Rossi, Dominique Delouche
Production Inspector:	Emimmo Salvi
Production Secretary:	Nando Bolognini
Production Director:	Luigi De Laurentiis
Editing Secretary:	Narciso Vicario
Cast:	Giulietta Masina (Cabiria), Amedeo Nazzari (the actor), Francois Perier (Oscar), Franca Marzi (Wanda), Dorian Gray (Jessy), Aldo Silvani (the hypnotist), Franco Fabrizi (Giorgio), Mario Passante (crippled uncle), Ennio Girolami, Christian Tassou.

Filmed in Rome during the summer and autumn of 1956.	
Distribution:	Lopert
Running Time:	110 minutes
Released:	Italy: First shown at Cannes Film Festival in March, 1957, but distribution in Italy did not begin until October, 1957. U.S.: October 28, 1957 (NYC)
Note:	According to Solmi, this film went through eleven producers before it

was completed. Masina had appeared
briefly as the prostitute Cabiria
in <u>The White Sheik</u> (1952). A scene
of "the man with the sack" who
roams the slums of the city which
was cut from the final version of
this film appears in <u>Fellini: A
Director's Notebook</u> (1969). <u>Nights
of Cabiria</u> won the Academy Award
for best Foreign Film in 1957. It
was made into the American musical
comedy for the stage <u>Sweet Charity</u>
in 1965.

8   LA DOLCE VITA (1960)

In the opening shots, we see two helicopters flying above
the San Felice aqueduct, approaching Rome. Suspended from the
first helicopter by a cable is a statue of Christ with his arms
outstretched in blessing. He is being transported to the Pope.
In the second helicopter is Marcello, a journalist in his
thirties, who is covering the event. With him is the photographer Paparazzo, a younger man. On the roof of an apartment
building, four young women sunbathing in bikinis wave at the
statue of Christ. The second helicopter circles back over the
roof. Marcello and Paparazzo try to call to the young women
in an unsuccessful attempt to get their phone numbers. Then
this helicopter moves off to rejoin the other. The first carries the statue over St. Peter's Square. The statue seems to
bless the crowd below.

A jump cut. We see suddenly the Siamese mask of a dancer.
The camera is moved back to reveal that we are in a Roman
night club. Marcello is gathering information about the dinner
of the Prince. He sends Paparazzo to take a photograph of the
Prince. One of the customers of the club warns Marcello to
stay out of private affairs. At this time, Maddalena, an
aristocratic young heiress wearing sunglasses, walks to the
bar. When she raises her glasses to look around, we can see
that she has a black eye. Marcello greets her, and they leave
the night club together.

Outside, the freelance photographers crowd around Maddalena.
Quickly she and Marcello get into her Cadillac convertible,
and she drives off. In a deserted piazza in another part of
Rome, Maddalena stops the car and gets out. She tells Marcello
she wants to escape Rome. She finds her life boring. Only
when she makes love, does she find an interesting "tension" in
her life. A prostitute hails Marcello, and Maddalena invites
her for a ride. They drive the prostitute to her apartment in
an outlying district of Rome. They cross through a flooded
basement hallway on a walk of planks to get into the apartment.

Maddalena and Marcello make love in the prostitute's bedroom and then depart the next morning after paying the prostitute handsomely.

The apartment of Marcello. Emma, a dark-haired woman in her twenties, cries in pain. She tries to telephone, but the receiver falls from her hand. She attempts to walk to the door and slips down to the floor. Next, we see Marcello drive up to his apartment building in his sports car. We follow him into the apartment where he discovers Emma on the floor. In the bathroom, Marcello finds an empty container of pills. He carries Emma from the apartment and drives her swiftly to the hospital.

Inside the hospital, Marcello waits in the hall. He is approached by a reporter friend, but asks the newspaperman to leave him alone. After having been admitted to the emergency room, Marcello kneels beside Emma's examination table and kisses her hand. In the hall again, Marcello places a phone call. We shift to a shot of Maddalena asleep on her bed. Her phone rings, but she does not hear it.

At Ciampino Airport, a crowd of reporters and photographers gathers for the arrival of the curvaceous Swedish movie star from Hollywood, Sylvia Rank. She comes down the steps from the airplane, blowing kisses to the reporters. Her producer presents her with a pizza. Marcello, who is part of the group, looks on. Later in his sports car, Marcello and a photographer follow Sylvia's cavalcade into Rome.

In a hotel suite, Sylvia grants an interview to members of the press. (She sleeps in "only two drops of French perfume." Her "happiest day" was "a night.") Marcello is called to the telephone to speak with the jealous Emma. Sylvia's fiancé, Robert, arrives. He is an actor and an athletic man. He has had a little too much to drink. Sylvia angrily asks why he did not meet her at the airport. Marcello promises the producer that he will arrange publicity for Sylvia at important locations.

At St. Peter's Cathedral, Sylvia dressed in the style of a cleric is climbing the steps in the dome. She is followed by an entourage including Marcello and photographers. Only Sylvia and Marcello, however, finish the climb to the balcony. Sylvia turns to Marcello and looks into his eyes, but the romantic spell is broken when her clerical hat blows off. For a moment, the hat appears to cover the city.

In a night club inside the Baths of Caracalla, Marcello dances with Sylvia to the music of "Arrivederci, Roma." He tells her that she is the "first woman on the first day of creation..., the mother, the sister, the lover, the friend..., the home." It is not clear, however, whether she understands his Italian. Robert is at the table with others of the group. He sketches. Suddenly, Frankie Stout, a dancer with a satyr's beard, arrives and calls to Sylvia. They dance a rousing cha-cha together. She kicks off her shoes. A thin, bespectacled waiter in a toga returns the shoes to Robert. A rock-and-roll singer does a number which ends unceremoniously when he falls off the stage. Sylvia then leads a dance among the tables to the song "Patricia." At the end of the dance, Robert insults Frankie and then Sylvia. She leaves, and Marcello follows her, carrying her shoes. Marcello guides her through the group of photographers outside the night club and drives her off in his car.

Marcello stops his car in the countryside. He leans to kiss Sylvia, but she hears the howl of a dog and howls back at the dog, setting off a chain of howls from other dogs. Later, in the city, Marcello phones a friend to get a key to a studio, but finds only the friend's mother at home, and he phones the house of Maddalena only to learn she is playing cards with her father. Shortly after Marcello finishes his calls, Sylvia finds a stray kitten in the streets. She sends Marcello for milk. While he is gone, she wanders to the Fountain of Trevi and wades into it. Marcello discovers her there and follows her into the fountain. He holds her in his arms, but before he can kiss her, the fountain stops spouting and the mood of the moment is lost.

Outside Sylvia's hotel, the photographers wait, and Robert sleeps in his car. When Marcello and Sylvia return, the photographers wake Robert. He slaps Sylvia and knocks down Marcello, while the photographers take pictures.

Marcello, on a fashion assignment, leaves the photographer and model and goes into a church. Inside he finds his friend Steiner, a grave, intellectual man. Steiner has come to the church to pick up a Sanskrit grammar. He asks Marcello how his book is coming along, embarrassing Marcello. Steiner invites Marcello to visit his home, and then Steiner plays a Bach fugue on the church's organ.

Marcello, Emma, and Paparazzo drive out of Rome to find the field where two children have claimed to have seen the Madonna. On the ride, Emma "mothers" Marcello, giving him an egg and a banana and telling him to chew carefully. At the field of the miracle, TV crews are setting up equipment, and a crowd is beginning to gather. The family of the children are shown to us inside the police compound. The mother and father quarrel over money, and the grandfather sings "Ave Maria" for the photographers. Marcello interviews a priest who knows the children and doubts their vision. Emma listens to a tape of the children's voices and argues with a woman about the need of people to believe. A mother brings a sick child to the tree where the vision is supposed to have taken place. Marcello takes notes on her. Emma is visibly moved by the woman's situation.

At night, an enormous crowd has formed. Marcello climbs a scaffold. He tells Emma not to follow him. She wanders away and prays for a return of his love. The two children arrive. A cold rain begins. It shatters the hot TV lights.

Suddenly, the little girl cries that she sees the Madonna.
The children run. The crowd surges after them. The girl tells
the crowd that the Madonna wants a church built on the field.
The uncle takes the children away. People in the crowd begin
tearing at the tree in the field. Emma is one of them.
Marcello pulls her away, while Paparazzo takes pictures of her.
An old woman appears and cries, "He's dead." The sequence ends
with the priest saying a prayer over the body of the man who
has died.

An evening at Steiner's apartment. Anna, Steiner's wife,
looks into the camera and welcomes us as if we were Marcello
and Emma. A group of intellectuals is assembled. One guest
speaks of the appeal of the Oriental woman who has remained
close to nature. Marcello talks with a woman poetess he
admires. She tells Marcello not to choose between literature
and journalism, rather to stay open to possibilities. She
describes Steiner as a Gothic steeple. Steiner responds sadly
that he feels very small. The guests listen to Steiner's tape
of sounds from nature. The noises on the tape wake Steiner's
young children, and they come briefly into the livingroom.
Emma expresses much interest in them. She tells Marcello that
one day they will have a home and family as the Steiners do.
Her remark irritates Marcello. Yet, Marcello speaks enviously
to Steiner about the qualities of a sanctuary which Steiner's
home seems to provide. Steiner answers that any life, even a
miserable one, is preferable to one in which everything is
ordered. He offers to help Marcello find a job which would
provide more free time for serious writing. The two men go
into the children's bedroom to look at the children who are
now asleep again. Steiner talks of his fear that behind the
apparent peace of the present time lurks the menace of atomic
destruction.

Bright morning at an outdoor restaurant in Fregene.
Marcello's typewriter is on one of the tables. The jukebox
plays "Patricia." Marcello speaks on the telephone with Emma.
He refuses to tell her where he is and slams down the receiver.
Marcello takes his seat at the typewriter and tries to work.
The waitress Paola, a young girl of about fourteen, moves
among the tables humming. She tells Marcello that she is from
Umbria, misses her home town, wishes to become a typist, and
plans to leave her present job after Christmas. Marcello
looks at her face and calls her an Umbrian angel. She plays
"Patricia" again on the jukebox. Marcello gives up trying to
work and calls Emma back on the telephone.

At night on Via Veneto. Marcello discovers his father waiting at one of the sidewalk tables. The father is middle-aged,
heavy, and jovial. He gives Marcello a letter from Marcello's
mother. The father suggests an evening at the Kit-Kat Club.
Paparazzo is invited along by Marcello.

Jump cut to a shot of a whip being handled by a clown.
Girls are dressed as tigers. We are in the Kit-Kat Club, and

a circus routine is in progress. Marcello, his father, and Paparazzo take a table. The father recalls a visit he made to the night club in 1922. A new act begins. A chorus line of girls carrying balloons files past the table. One of the girls, Fanny, who is French, knows Marcello and speaks to him. Marcello's father and Fanny exchange gallant compliments, and Marcello asks her to come to the table after her act. The girls exit leaving their balloons behind them. The father orders champagne, and it is delivered by Fanny who joins the group of men. A clown blowing a mournful tune on a trumpet enters the room. He walks across the dance floor, and the balloons follow him out of the room. Marcello's father shows Fanny a parlor trick with a coin, and she shows him one with the table napkins. A waltz strikes up, and the father leads Fanny to the dance floor. Marcello tells Paparazzo that when he (Marcello) was young, he rarely saw his father who was a travelling salesman. He tells about the loneliness of his mother.

Outside the night club. Fanny has invited the father and the others to her apartment. Fanny and the father leave first in her car, despite Marcello's misgivings. Marcello, Paparazzo, and two chorus girls drive off in Marcello's car. Later, Marcello's car arrives at the area of Fanny's apartment. One of the chorus girls complains that Marcello has taken an inordinate amount of time driving around. Fanny runs down the street to the group, crying that the father is ill and needs drops from the drugstore.

Marcello rushes into the apartment to find his father sitting quietly by the window. Apparently he has had a mild heart attack. He avoids looking at Marcello. He says that he wishes to take the 5:30 train home. Marcello tries to persuade him to rest for a day at Marcello's apartment. "We never see each other," Marcello says sadly. A taxi arrives outside, and we watch from Fanny's window as Marcello escorts his father to the cab.

On the Via Veneto in the evening. Marcello meets a young Swedish girl he has known previously. She arranges for him to ride along with a group of aristocrats to a party given by her fiancé's family, in their castle in Bassano di Sutri.

In the castle, Marcello meets the aristocrats and Jane, an American artist with silver-streaked hair. Also present at the party is Maddalena. She leads Marcello to a gallery of whispers. He takes a seat in the center of the gallery, and she moves to a fountain out of his view. She whispers to him that she is torn between the desire to love him and be a faithful wife to him and the desire to amuse herself as a whore. She has lost the power of choosing. He professes his love for her. While Marcello is talking, however, one of the aristocrats approaches Maddalena and kisses her. When Marcello searches for her, he finds that she is gone. He walks then to the old villa with the aristocrats and participates in a seance. In the dark, a woman leads him away from the group. It is Jane. He makes love to her. The next morning, as the group walks in the garden, Jane introduces Marcello to her son. The matriarch of the aristocratic family appears and leads the family off to church.

On a highway in the outskirts of Rome. Marcello has parked his car. He argues with Emma. She denounces his infidelity and accuses him of being incapable of love. He, in turn, denounces her kind of maternal love as stifling. He drives off, leaving her by the side of the road. In the morning, he returns and picks her up again in his car. We see them next asleep together in Marcello's apartment. The phone rings. Marcello answers it. His face becomes grim.

A crowd of police, newspapermen, and photographers are gathered outside Steiner's apartment building. Marcello makes his way through the crowd. One of the press group says that Steiner shot his two children and then killed himself. Inside the apartment detectives are investigating. Marcello sees Steiner's corpse. The detectives play Steiner's tapes and question Marcello. In the bedroom, Marcello sees the body of Steiner's little boy. Shaken, Marcello walks out onto the terrace. Later he volunteers to go to the bus stop with the commissioner to point out Anna Steiner to him when she returns. At the bus stop, the photographers swarm around Mrs. Steiner. She is confused at first and then alarmed. The commissioner guides her into a police car.

Jump cut to the headlights of two cars at night, racing to a villa in Fregene. A group including business people, artists, show business people, and Marcello break into a villa and begin a celebration of the annulment of the marriage of Nadia, one of the group. Two transvestites dance. Marcello announces that he has given up journalism and literature and that he is now a publicity agent. Nadia does a striptease to the song "Patricia." As she finishes, Riccardo, the owner of the villa and a movie producer, arrives. He is upset to find a window broken and wants the group to leave. Marcello, now drunk and cynical, berates the others. He rides on the back of a woman, and when she collapses, he pours water on her and pastes pillow feathers on her wet skin. As the group departs, Marcello scatters feathers in the air.

On the beach in the morning, the group inspects a huge sea creature brought ashore by fishermen. The strange creature seems to stare at the group as its members stare at him. Marcello wanders away. He sees Paola, the young waitress, calling to him from the other side of an inlet. The wind carries her voice away. He cannot hear what she says. He turns to rejoin his group. The movie ends with a close-up of Paola's tenderly smiling face.

Credits

Producer:	Giuseppe Amato (Riama Film, Rome-- Pathé Consortium Cinéma, Paris).
Director:	Federico Fellini
Screenplay:	Fellini, Tullio Pinelli, Ennio Flaiano, Brunello Rondi, from a story by Fellini, Pinelli, and Flaiano.
Photography:	Otello Martelli
Cameramen:	Arturo Zavattini, Ennio Guarnieri
Art Director:	Piero Gherardi
Assistant Art Directors:	Giorgio Giovannini, Lucia Mirisola, Vito Anzalone
Artistic Collaborator:	Brunello Rondi
Music:	Nino Rota
Conductor:	Franco Ferrara, with the assistance of I Campanino, Adriano Celentano
Sound:	Agostino Moretti
Editor:	Leo Cattozzo
Assistant Directors:	Guidarino Guidi, Paolo Nuzi, Dominique Delouche
Director's Aides:	Giancarlo Romani, Gianfranco Mingozzi, Lilli Veenman
Make-up:	Otello Fava
Hairdresser:	Renata Magnanti
Script-girl:	Isa Mari
Production Directors:	Manlio M. Moretti, Nello Meniconi
Production Inspector:	Alessandro Von Norman
Production Secretaries:	Mario Basile, Mario De Biase, Osvaldo De Micheli
Executive Producer:	Franco Magli
Cast:	Marcello Mastroianni (Marcello Rubini), Walter Santesso (Paparazzo), Giulio Paradisi (first photographer), Enzo Cerusico (second photographer), Enzo Doria (third photographer), Anouk Aimée (Maddalena), Adriana Moneta (prostitute), Anna Maria Salerno (second prostitute), Yvonne Fourneaux (Emma), Anita Ekberg (Sylvia), Harriet White (Edna, Sylvia's secretary), Carlo Di Maggio (Toto Scalise, the producer), Francesco Luzi (the radio announcer), Francesco Consalvo (Scalise's assistant), Guglielmo Leoncini (Scalise's secretary), Lex Barker (Robert, Sylvia's fiancé), Alan Dijon (Frankie Stout), Adriano Celetano (the rock-and-roll singer),

Giacomo Gabrielli (Maddalena's
father), Alain Cuny (Steiner),
Valeria Ciangottini (Paola), Alfredo
Rizzo (television director), Rina
Franchetti (mother of the lying
children), Aurelio Nardi (uncle of
the lying children), Giovanna and
Massimo (the lying children),
Marianna Leib (Emma's companion at
the miracle), Renée Longarini (Mrs.
Steiner), Annibale Ninchi (Marcello's
father), Vittorio Manfrino (manager
of the Kit-Kat Club), Polidor (the
clown), Magali Noel (Fanny), Lily
Granado (Lucy), Gloria Jones
(Gloria), Nello Meniconi (irate man
on the Via Veneto), Massimo Busetti
(the gossip), Nico Otzak (sophis-
ticated prostitute on the Via
Veneto), Audrey McDonald (Sonia),
Ferdinando Brofferio (Maddalena's
lover), Prince Vadim Wolkonsky
(Prince Mascalchi), Giulio Questi
(Don Giulio Mascalchi), Eugenio
Ruspoli (Don Eugenio Mascalchi),
Ivenda Dobrzensky (Don Giovanni
Mascalchi), Juan Antequera (the
Spanish nobleman), Rosemary Rennel
Rodd (the English medium), Doris
Pignatelli (the woman in the white
shawl), Ida Galli (the debutante of
the year), Maria Marigliano (Massi-
milla), Giulio Girola (the police
commissioner), Paolo Fadda (the
vice-commissioner), Giuseppe
Addobbati (the doctor), Nadia Gray
(Nadia), Mino Doro (Nadia's lover),
Antonio Jacono and Carlo Musto (the
transvestites), Tito Buzzo (the
muscleman), Sandra Lee (the Spoleto
ballerina), Jacques Sernas (the
matinee idol), Leontine van Strein
(his mistress), Leo Coleman (the
black dancer), Laura Betti (Laura),
Daniela Calvino (Daniela), Riccardo
Garrone (Riccardo, the owner of the
house), Cesare Miceli Picardi,
Donatella Esparmer, Maria Pia Sera-
fini, Oscar Ghiglia, Gino Marturano,
Thomas Torres, Carlo Mariotti,
Leonardo Botta, Sandy von Norman,

Tiziano Cortini, Henry Thody, Donatella Della Nora, Maite Morand, Donato Castellaneta, John Francis Lane, Concetta Ragusa, François Dieudonne, Mario Mallamo, Nadia Balabine, Umberto Felici, Maurizio Guelfi, Gondrano Trucchi, Gio Staiano, Paolo Labia, Gianfranco Mingozzi, Alex Messoyedoff, Iris Tree, Leonida Repaci, Anna Salvatore, Letzia Spadini, Margherita Russo, Winie Vagliani, Desmond O'Grady, Mario De Grenet, Franco Rossellini, Loretta Ramaciotti, Cristina dei conti Paolozzi, Elisabetta Cini, Maria Teresa Wolodimeroff, Carlo Kechler, Brunoro Serego Alighieri, Nani Colombo, Vando Tres, Franco Giacobini, Giuliana Lo Jodice, Federika Andre, Giancarlo Romani, Christine Denise, Decimo Cristiani, Umberto Orsini, Sandra Tesi, Renato Mambor, Mario Conocchia, Enrico Glori, Lucia Vasilico, Franca Passutt.

Filmed in Rome, the Odescalchi Palace in Bassano di Sutri (Fregene), and in the studios of Cinecittà from March 16 to August 27, 1959.	
Distribution:	Astor
Running Time:	180 minutes
Released:	Italy: First shown in Rome to a group of critics and intellectuals in November of 1959 and released for public showing in February, 1960.
	U.S.: April 19, 1961 (NYC)
Note:	Some of the scenes in this film were originally written for <u>Moraldo in città</u>, Fellini's unrealized sequel to <u>I Vitelloni</u>. Awarded Gold Palm at Cannes, 1960.

9 LE TENTAZIONI DEL DOTTOR ANTONIO [THE TEMPTATIONS OF DOCTOR ANTONIO] (1962)

A sketch from the film <u>Boccaccio '70</u>, a scherzo in four acts conceived by Cesare Zavattini.

The film opens with a sequence depicting springtime activities in Rome's ultramodern E.U.R. (Esposizione universale di Roma) section. It is Sunday, and church bells ring. People sit in the sidewalk cafes and move about in the streets. A couple kisses inside a car. School girls on a tour pass through and stop to watch a group of bicycle racers. In a vacant lot, some workmen are putting up an advertisement on a giant billboard. As we watch, we listen to the voice-over narration of Cupid. He complains that he is being prosecuted by a certain censorious individual, Dr. Mazzuolo, a small, middle-aged man in a dark suit with glasses and a carefully trimmed mustache. He introduces Mazzuolo to us first by a series of still photographs and then by a series of short scenes (Mazzuolo interrupting lovers in parked cars, slapping a woman in tight-fitting clothes at a resort, and calling a halt to a dance in a variety hall).

A church in the E.U.R. district. We discover Mazzuolo taking the collection. After the mass, the people leave the church, and Mazzuolo follows slowly behind. Outside, the workmen have finished pasting up their sign. It shows Anita Ekberg in a tight-fitting, low-cut evening gown, reclining on a couch and holding a glass of milk. The advertisement reads, "Drink more milk." Shocked, Mazzuolo stares at the advertisement. Then he rushes up to the workmen and asks them if they intend to leave in public view a sign which is immoral. One of the workmen tries to placate Mazzuolo by telling him that the police have approved the sign. The workmen drive off, and Mazzuolo trudges to his apartment building across the square. The doorman makes an appreciative remark about the billboard, and Mazzuolo retorts angrily.

While drying himself after a shower in his bathroom, Mazzuolo looks at the billboard from his window. Anita seems to look back at him. He closes the window quickly. At the dinner table with his spinster sister, Mazzuolo sees the billboard again as the curtains blow aside in the opened window. He closes the window angrily, but his sister finds the room too warm and asks the maid to open it again. Mazzuolo chokes momentarily on his food.

In Mazzuolo's study. On the wall hangs a picture of St. George slaying the dragon. We see Mazzuolo making a phone call. He explains to the party on the other end that he wants to invoke the law which prohibits obscene publications. He is told that he must speak to another party.

On his balcony, Mazzuolo stares at the billboard. He makes a decision and rushes off. We see him next at the home of a government official. He has interrupted a dinner party, and the official is not pleased with his presence. Mazzuolo leads the official to a window and shows him the poster. Mazzuolo complains of the escalation of obscenity. The official appears interested in the poster. A maid in a short skirt announces dinner to the official who tries to ease Mazzuolo out the door.

He outdoes Mazzuolo's complaints by expressing alarm at a picture of a naked foot beneath a dress in a magazine picture.

Outside, Mazzuolo makes his way past the billboard. He arrives at a church. The sexton leads him to the secretary of the Monsignor. Later we see Mazzuolo and the secretary climb out of a car in front of the poster. Mazzuolo tries to argue that the poster has a corruptive influence on the people of the district, but his argument is undercut by the fact that the square is deserted at the moment.

In his apartment, Mazzuolo watches with binoculars the reactions of passers-by to the poster. His sister calls him. But he runs from the room.

Mazzuolo, in the square, is now seen throwing bottles of ink at the poster. A crowd gathers. A police car arrives. Mazzuolo announces to the police that he wishes to create a scandal and that he is a defender of moral values.

During the early evening, the workmen are pasting strips of paper over the picture of Anita Ekberg on the billboard. Mazzuolo observes their work from his balcony. He smiles. "We've won," he calls inside to his sister. A distant roll of thunder is heard.

That night, in his study, Mazzuolo dictates into his tape recorder a speech on morality in movies. More thunder can be heard. When Mazzuolo runs his tape back, he accidentally comes to a section of a love song he has recorded. He snaps the machine off. Outside, a heavy rain has begun. Mazzuolo looks out the window and discovers that the rain is washing off the sheets of paper covering the poster. The image of Anita Ekberg gradually returns to view. She seems this time, however, to be alive. She moves her head and looks directly at Mazzuolo. He steps away and then returns to the window for another look. He discovers that she has turned her back to him. Mazzuolo fetches his umbrella and leaves the apartment.

Outside, Mazzuolo stands quaking in front of the poster. The giant figure of the woman turns and looms over Mazzuolo. She asks him why he persecutes her when she just lies in the poster like a big cloud. Fighting down his terror, Mazzuolo tries an ironic laugh. The woman echoes his laughter, but her laughter is much louder and frightens Mazzuolo. He calls her a corrupter of morals. She begins to cry, her enormous tears falling around him. He opens his umbrella. She asks how should she appear in order to be decorous. She tries to cover one area of exposed flesh, only to reveal more elsewhere. One of her giant shoes falls off nearly smashing Mazzuolo. The woman lowers her leg out of the sign, searching with it for her shoe. Her skirt falls over Mazzuolo. Suddenly, she runs off laughing through the E.U.R. district. "I dress like I want to," she shouts. Mazzuolo runs after her, calling her shameless. She disappears around a corner and then pokes her head back out, frightening Mazzuolo. "You don't even know what a woman is," she taunts. She runs off, and he pursues. "You're still sixteen years old," she shouts. "I'll drive you away," he yells back. The woman now begins to undress before Mazzuolo. He seizes an umbrella pole from a cafe table and waves it like a spear. Suddenly, he is dressed in armour, with a plumed helmet. "Stop, demon," he cries. He hurls his lance.

Mazzuolo is discovered in his suit clothes now beneath the poster. A pole vibrates in the poster. It pierces the heart of the woman. The night darkens. Two processions of hooded monks approach, followed by eight pairs of black horses. Mazzuolo tries suddenly to pull out the pole from the poster figure, but he can't reach it.

Morning. An ambulance approaches the E.U.R. square. A crowd has gathered. They stare at Mazzuolo who is standing on top of the billboard. His sister weeps in the crowd. Firemen raise a ladder to him and help him down. He stares blankly at his sister and then enters the ambulance. Anita Ekberg's eyes in the poster seem to be on him. As the ambulance pulls away, we see on the roof a laughing Cupid.

[This summary is based on the screenplay published in Federico Fellini: Three Screenplays (New York: Orion Press, 1970), coupled with viewings of the film several years before publication of this edition.]

Credits

Producer:	Carlo Ponti (Cineriz)
Director:	Federico Fellini
Screenplay:	Fellini, Ennio Flaiano, Tullio Pinelli, with the collaboration of Brunello Rondi and Goffredo Parise
Photography:	Otello Martelli (Eastmancolor)
Art Direction:	Piero Zuffi
Music:	Nino Rota
Editor:	Leo Cattozzo
Cast:	Peppino De Filippo (Dr. Antonio Mazzuolo), Anita Ekberg (Anita), Antonio Acqua (government official), Donatella Della Nora (Mazzuolo's sister), Eleanora Maggi (Cupid), Giacomo Furia, Alberto Sorrentino, Monique Berger, Mario Passante, Silvio Bagolino.

Filmed in Rome during the summer of 1961.

Distribution:	Avco-Embassy Pictures
Running Time:	70 minutes (approximately)
Released:	Italy: February 22, 1962 U.S.: June 26, 1962 (NYC)

Note:

Fellini's "scherzo" is the second of four in another collaborative effort conceived by Cesare Zavattini. The film represents Fellini's reaction to the harsh criticism which La Dolce Vita received from the Catholic press, especially Fr. Enrico Baragli's articles in La civiltà cattolica (12 September 1960 and 15 October 1960). This is Fellini's first color film.

10   OTTO E MEZZO [8½] (1963)

8½ begins with an anxiety dream of Guido, a forty-three year old movie director. In his dream, Guido is stuck in his car in a traffic jam in an underground tunnel. He claws at the windows. Motorists and bus passengers stare impassively. Guido manages to open a window and climb to the roof of the car. Then he soars up into the air above a beach. A horseman rides along the beach and stops near a prone man holding a kite string. (The horseman becomes known to us later as the manager of the actress Claudia, and the prone man as her press agent.) A high-angle helicopter shot reveals that Guido's leg is tied to the cord held by the prone man. Guido is pulled down into the sea.

Guido wakes from his dream in a bedroom at a fashionable health spa. He has come to the spa for a rest as he tries to revise his screenplay for an autobiographical film. Various members of his staff have come with him. In the bedroom, a doctor examines him. Daumier, a writer-collaborator, enters. He does not like what he has seen so far of Guido's screenplay. Guido goes into the bathroom and stares at his face in a mirror. A telephone buzzes. We hear Wagner's "Ride of the Valkyries."

A pan around the terrace of the spa in dazzling, noon light. We can now identify the source of the music we have heard as an orchestra playing for guests on the terrace. Most of the guests are older people. They wear 1930's clothes. Guido is waiting in line for water from the fountain. The music shifts to Rossini's overture to The Barber of Seville and then stops. Guido sees a vision of a young, beautiful girl in white who offers him a glass of mineral water. The music resumes as the vision ends. The girl in white is replaced by an older, perspiring attendant. Daumier appears and gives Guido some notes on the screenplay. Suddenly, Guido discovers an old friend, Mario Mezzabotta. This friend introduces Gloria, his young, pseudo-intellectual fiancée. Guido moves off and reads Daumier's notes which criticize the figure of the girl in white in the screenplay.

At the railroad station, Guido meets his mistress, Carla. She is a rounded, buxom woman who walks with a bounce. She is overdressed for the summer weather with a fur hat, collar, and muff. Guido explains that he has reserved a room for her in a small hotel near his.

In Carla's hotel. Carla washes her hands. In the background can be heard the voice of a soprano humming. Carla joins Guido at a dining table and chatters about her husband.

Carla's head is silhoutted against her bedroom window. She is wrapped in a towel. Guido makes up her face as if she were a prostitute and asks her to re-enter the room. She does as he asks, but re-enters giggling. The hotel owner saw her in the hall. Then she undoes the towel around her and advances to Guido in the bed.

Later in bed, Carla reads a comic book while Guido dreams. We see his dream. His mother enters the room as if she were polishing a window. Dressed in a school uniform, Guido follows her. He meets his father in a cemetary. The father complains about the size of his coffin. Pace, Guido's producer, and Conocchia, his production manager, arrive and complain about Guido as a director. Guido helps his father into a grave. He kisses his mother goodbye, but as he pulls back he discovers before him his wife, Luisa.

Guido walks down a corridor of his hotel humming and kicking out his feet. In an elevator, he rides with a Cardinal, a priest, and a male secretary.

In the lobby, Guido is approached by various people involved in his film. The manager of the actress Claudia wants to see the screenplay. An insecure French actress asks about her role. Guido sees a beautiful, mature woman walk across the lobby. Cesarino, an assistant, presents three candidates for the role of the father. Pace and his girlfriend arrive, and the producer gives Guido a watch as a gift.

Night at an outdoor club at the spa. Elderly people dance. Then the music speeds up, and Mezzabotta attempts to dance the twist with Gloria. From his table with his associates, Guido watches. Carla enters and sits alone. Pace and Conocchia discuss costs. Mezzabotta and Gloria come to the table, and Guido and Mezzabotta discuss the latter's relationship with the young girl.

On stage, the magician Maurice announces the mindreader Maya. With Maurice's assistance, Maya identifies objects while she is blindfolded. Maurice approaches Guido's group. Gloria screams for him to go away. Maurice and Guido recognize each other as old friends. Maya reads Guido's mind. "ASA NISI MASA," Maya writes on her blackboard. (The phrase is a magic-formula word, transformed from <u>anima</u>, or spirit.)

We see the interior of the farmhouse of Guido's parents, and we hear the voice of a soprano humming. Guido as a child is scooped up by his nurse and bathed in a huge wine vat along with his young cousins. Afterward, the nurse carries him bundled in a sheet to the children's bedroom. One of the cousins tells Guido that the magic phrase "ASA NISI MASA" can make the eyes in a portrait on the wall reveal where a treasure is hidden.

The hotel lobby. Guido sees the beautiful, mature woman again. The French actress tries to engage Guido's attention. Guido returns a telephone call to his wife and invites her to the spa.

Guido enters a production room set up by his staff at the hotel. Behind a partition, he discovers that Cesarino has hidden two girls. One of them says that the other feels Guido cannot make a good love story. In a corridor, on the way to his bedroom, Guido meets Conocchia. The production manager complains that Guido doesn't tell him what to do. Losing his temper, Guido calls Conocchia an "old fool."

Guido enters his room. "A crisis of inspiration?" he wonders to himself. The girl in white comes into the room and turns down his bedcovers. "It's time to get rid of symbols, the call of innocence, escape," Guido says. Then he muses about the girl in white: "It could be like this. In town there is a museum, and you are the daughter of the custodian. You grew up among images of ancient beauty...." The girl looks through the screenplay on Guido's table and laughs. Then she goes to his bed. "I came never to go away," she whispers. "I want to make order. I want to make cleanness." The telephone buzzes. Guido answers. Carla tells him that she is sick.

Carla's hotel room. She has a fever and asks Guido to stay with her. He stretches out on the bed and asks himself, "What am I going to say to the Cardinal tomorrow?"

Guido walks on the grounds of the spa with the priest and the Cardinal's secretary. He explains to them: "My protagonist has had a Catholic education that causes him some complexes, some needs that cannot be suppressed. A leader of the church appears to him as a depository of a truth which he can accept no longer, but which fascinates him nevertheless." The group reaches the Cardinal who is seated in the open air. The Cardinal asks Guido about his marriage and then directs his attention to the call of a Diomedes bird. Guido catches sight of a heavy peasant woman in black, and the sight triggers a memory.

A schoolyard. A group of students play soccer. Guido as a young boy is with them. Someone of the group calls to him: "Let's go see Saraghina."

A huge prostitute in black sweater and skirt emerges from the pillbox on the beach where she lives. Guido gives her money. Saraghina opens her sweater somewhat, raises her skirt, and dances a spirited rumba for the group of young onlookers. The music we hear is the theme previously hummed by the soprano voice. Toward the end of her performance, Saraghina dances with Guido. Suddenly, priests arrive from school, and after a chase (in fast-motion), they seize Guido.

The school. Guido is judged by the priests. His mother is present. She appears to cry into her handkerchief, but she keeps one dry eye on the priests. Guido is made to wear a dunce cap and a sign with the word "shame" on it into the classroom. He is forced to kneel on kernels of corn. Later, he goes to confession, passing decayed relics of a saint. At confession, Guido is told that Saraghina is the Devil. After confession, Guido kneels before a statue of the Virgin. Dissolve to Saraghina's pillbox. Guido returns, and he sees Saraghina sitting on a chair and humming the theme of the soprano voice. He kneels and waves his hat to Saraghina.

The hotel dining room. Guido is seated with colleagues and reporters. Daumier criticizes Guido's planned treatment of the Saraghina episode. He calls for a more intellectual analysis of the impact of the Church on Italian life.

A band plays in a large hall. Men and women wrapped in towels descend steps to the steambaths. Guido is among them. The voice of a Swedish airline hostess from Guido's past announces that the Cardinal will see Guido. The camera cranes down to a casement window which opens. In the room beyond the window is the Cardinal preparing for a mud bath. His skinny form can be seen silhouetted behind a sheet. He tells Guido that there is no salvation outside the Church. The camera pulls back out of the window. We hear the song "Blue Moon."

As the music continues, we see people strolling on the main street of the resort town. Guido encounters his wife, Luisa, in the crowd.

In a cafe, Guido and Luisa dance. Also in the group are Luisa's sister Tina, Enrico who has a crush on Luisa, and Luisa's friend Rossella. Pace joins the group and invites them to the rocket-launching tower built for Guido's film. As the group reaches the cars, Luisa becomes strangely quiet.

At the launching tower, Pace explains how the rocket launch will be used in Guido's film. He states: "The scene begins with a panoramic view of the earth completely destroyed by nuclear war. This is the modern Noah's Ark that offers an escape from the atomic blast. The survivors of all mankind seek shelter on a new planet." Guido and Rossella talk while the others climb the tower. She tells him that Luisa wishes he were different than he is.

The bedroom of Guido and Luisa. Luisa charges Guido with lying and infidelity. They argue bitterly.

Morning in an open air cafe. Guido, Luisa, and Rossella eat breakfast. Carla comes to the cafe. Guido hides behind his newspaper. Luisa announces that she caught sight of Carla the night before. Guido denies his affair with Carla. "Is it possible," asks Luisa bitterly, "that true and false are both the same to you?" Guido smiles, puts his feet on the table, and has a fantasy. Carla sings the soprano's theme. Luisa goes to her and the two women glide arm and arm toward Guido.

The Films: Synopsis, Credits and Notes

In the farmhouse of Guido's grandparents is gathered a harem of women from Guido's life. Guido enters from a snowy outdoors and hands out gifts to the women. A black woman dances a version of Saraghina's rumba for him. Guido is bathed in the wine vat and then wrapped in a sheet by the women. Jacqueline Bonbon, the first "artiste" in Guido's life, complains about the age regulation which banishes her to the upstairs. Led by the French actress and by Saraghina, the women protest against the rules. "Ride of the Valkyries" springs up. Like an animal trainer, Guido uses a long whip to drive back the women and to tame them. Meanwhile, Luisa prepares dinner. Jacqueline is allowed to give a final dance. The group sits down to dinner. Luisa kneels to scrub the floor.

Guido sits in an auditorium. To Luisa several rows away, Guido says softly, "If only you could have some more patience, Luisa. But maybe you cannot go on any more." Behind Guido, Daumier criticizes the film project, and, in fantasy, Guido has him hung. On a screen in the auditorium are shown actresses auditioning for the parts of Carla and Luisa. Pace calls for Guido to choose. The real Luisa is hurt by the screen portrayal of her and leaves the auditorium. Guido follows. "What can you teach other people?" she snaps at him. "You're not even honest with the woman who shares your life." Guido returns to the theater. The acresss Claudia has arrived. She is identical to the girl in white of Guido's fantasies, with the difference that she wears a black dress. They go to Claudia's car.

As Claudia drives, Guido asks her, "Would you be able to leave everything and start your life all over again? Would you be able to choose one thing, only one thing and be faithful to it, make it the reason for your life?" The protagonist of his movie, Guido explains, "wants to take everything, grasp everything. He changes route everyday; he is afraid he might lose the right one; and he is dying. He is bleeding to death." Guido, then, describes Claudia's role as the girl in white in the film. "There is no doubt that she is his salvation," Guido states. They come to a square in an old village. In a window of a building is the girl in white. She carries an oil lamp out into the square and places it on a table. Then she vanishes.

Guido and Claudia get out of the car. Claudia asks why the protagonist refuses the salvation offered by the girl in white. "Because he can no longer believe," answers Guido. "Because he doesn't know how to love," returns Claudia. "Because, above all, I don't want to tell another false story," says Guido. Finally, he tells Claudia that there will be no part for her in the film. Suddenly, Pace's car speeds into the square. The producer announces a press conference at the launching tower the next day.

Daylight. Guido is partially led and partially dragged to the conference area by his assistants. He is beseiged by reporters. We hear again "Ride of the Valkyries." Guido sits at a glass-topped table. Reflected in the top is Luisa in a wedding gown. Pace urges Guido to talk to the reporters. Guido slips beneath the table. He withdraws a gun from his coat. The film shifts to a shot of Guido's mother who spreads her arms and runs forward. A close-up of Guido. The gunshot.

Evening at the launching tower. Guido tells some workmen to dismantle everything. He and Daumier enter a car. Daumier congratulates Guido on terminating the project. "Why add disorder to disorder?" Daumier says. Then, at the window of the car appears Maurice, the magician. "We're ready to begin," he states. The girl in white reappears. Then we see nurses from the farmhouse, Saraghina, Guido's parents, Carla, Rossella, and Luisa, all dressed in white. They walk into a circus ring. "What is this sudden joy? I do accept you. I do love you," says Guido. He gets out of the car and goes to the ring. "This confusion in me no longer frightens me," he states. To Luisa, he says, "Life is a holiday. Let us live it together. Accept me as I am. Only then will we discover each other." She responds, "I'm not sure that's true. But I can try, if you'll help me."

A line composed of four clowns and Guido as a young boy enters the ring playing circus music on instruments. A curtain opens and people descend from the tower. They are dressed normally, and they intermix with the characters in white. With a bullhorn, Guido attempts to direct the group. But, of their own accord, the people climb up on the rim of the circus ring and begin to move in a circle. Guido leads Luisa into the circle, joins hands with the others, and moves with them.

Night. Most of the group drifts away, leaving only the band of four clowns and Guido as a boy. The clowns, then, march off. The young boy plays his flute in a single spotlight. Finally, he, too, marches from the ring.

Credits

Producer:	Angelo Rizzoli (An Italo-French co-production by Cineriz and Francinex); presented in the U.S. by Joseph E. Levine for Embassy Pictures.
Director:	Federico Fellini
Screenplay:	Fellini, Ennio Flaiano, Tullio Pinelli, Brunello Rondi, based on a story by Fellini and Flaiano
Photography:	Gianni di Venanzo
Cameraman:	Pasquale De Santis
Assistant Cameraman:	Tazio Secchiaroli
Art Director:	Piero Gherardi
Assistant Art Director:	Luciano Ricceri

Scenery and Wardrobe Assistants:	Vito Anzalone, Orietta Nasalli Rocca, Alba Rivaioli, Clara Poggi, Renata Magnanti, Eugenia Filippo
Music:	Nino Rota
Sound:	Mario Faraoni, Alberto Bartolomei
Editor:	Leo Cattozzo
Assistant Directors:	Guidarino Guidi, Lina Wertmuller
Director's Aides:	Giulio Paradisi, Francesco Aluigi
Script Girl:	Mirella Gamacchio
Artistic Collaborator:	Brunello Rondi
Production Supervisor:	Clemente Fracassi
Production Director:	Nello Meniconi
Assistant Production Director:	Alessandro von Normann
Assistant Editor:	Adriana Olasio
Production Assistants:	Angelo Jacono, Albino Morandin, Mario Basili
Make-up:	Otello Fava
Hairstyles:	Renata Magnanti
Still Photography:	Paul Ronald
Cast:	Marcello Mastroianni (Guido Anselmi), Anouk Aimée (Luisa Anselmi), Sandra Milo (Carla), Claudia Cardinale (Claudia), Rossella Falk (Rossella), Madeleine Lebeau (actress), Caterina Boratto (the fashionable woman), Barbara Steele (Gloria Morin), Mario Pisu (Mario Mezzabota), Guido Alberti (Pace, the producer), Mario Conocchia (Conocchia), Jean Rougeul (the writer Daumier), Edra Gale (La Saraghina), Ian Dallas (Maurice, the magician), Annibale Ninchi (Guido's father), Giuditta Rissone (Guido's mother), Tito Masini (the Cardinal), Alfredo de la Feld and Sebastiano de Leandro (the Cardinal's assistants), Georgia Simmons (Guido's grandmother), Maria Raimondi and Marisa Colomber (the nurses), Palma Mangini (the old country relative), Roberta Valli (the little girl at the farmhouse), Riccardo Guglielmi (Guido as a farm boy), Marco Gemini (Guido as a schoolboy), Yvonne Casadei (Jacquelin Bonbon), Elisabetta Catalano (Luisa's sister), Rossella Como (Luisa's friend), Mark Herron (Luisa's admirer), Francesco

Rigamonti (Enrico), Eva Gioia and
Dina De Santis (the two girls on
the bed), Cesarino Miceli Picardi
(Cesarino, the production super-
visor), Bruno Agostini (Bruno
Agostini, the production director),
Hazel Rogers (the Black dancer),
Hedy Vessel (Edith, the model),
John Stacy (the accountant), Olimpia
Cavalli (Miss Olympia, as Carla in
the screen tests), Maria Antonietta
Beluzzi (La Saraghina in some screen
tests), Roberto Nicolosi and Luciana
Sanseverino (the spa doctors),
Eugene Walter (the American journal-
ist), Gilda Dahlberg (his wife),
Annie Gorassini (Pace's girl friend),
Mary Indovino (Maya), Nadine Sanders
(the airline hostess), Matilde
Calnan (a friend of Luisa's; also
an old journalist), Elisabetta Cini
(the Cardinal in screen tests),
Polidor [Ferdinand Guillaume]
(clown in the parade), Neil Robinson
(the agent), Mino Doro (Claudia's
agent), Mario Tarchetti (Claudia's
press representative), Maria
Tedeschi (college dean), Guilio
Paradisi, Valentina Lang, Annarosa
Lattuada, Agnese Bonfani, Flaminia
Torlonia, Anna Carimini, Maria
Wertmuller, Edward Fleming Moller,
Prince Vadim Wolkonsky, Grazia
Fransnelli, Gideon Bachmann, John
Francis Lane, Deena Boyer.

Filmed at the Titanus-
Appia Studios and in the
Esposizione universale
di Roma (EUR) district
in Rome, Filacciano,
and Ostia, between May
and October, 1962.
Distribution:
Running Time:
Released:

Note:

Avco-Embassy
135 minutes
Italy: February, 1963
U.S.: June 25, 1963 (NYC)
Fellini originally shot an ending
that took place in the dining car
of a train. He replaced it with
the current ending which had been
conceived as a "preview" for the

98

film. Winner of two Academy Awards
as Best Foreign Language Film and
Best Achievement in Costume Design
(to Piero Gherardi); Best Foreign
Language Film by the New York Film
Critics, 1963; Grand Prize at 1963
Moscow Film Festival; seven silver
ribbons in Italy.

11 GIULIETTA DEGLI SPIRITI [JULIET OF THE SPIRITS] (1965)

The camera dollies through the shrubbery to discover
Juliet's neat, white house. It is located in Fregene near the
Tyrrhenian Sea, with a forest of tall pines around it. Inside, Juliet dresses for her wedding anniversary that evening.
Her two maids, Elisabetta and Teresina, make preparations. A
horn sounds outside. Juliet turns off the electric switches
lights some candles, and waits expectantly. Giorgio, her
husband, enters. "What's the matter? The current is off?"
he asks. He has forgotten the occasion, and he has brought
home a group of friends from his public relations office.

The guests troop into the house. They include, among
others, the following: the beautiful and flighty Val who has
brought Juliet wind chimes; Dolores, a sculptress; her male
model; Genius, a medium; and a middle-aged lawyer who has a
crush on Juliet. Retreating to the bathroom, Juliet tells her
reflection in the mirror, "Now don't be stupid and start crying." Val and Genius join her, and Genius tests Juliet's
psychic vibrations with a pendulum. Giorgio apologizes to
Juliet, picks her up in his arms, and begins to dance with her.

Later in the evening, Genius organizes a seance. Some of
the guests gather around a table. A knock is heard. Genius
identifies the spirit as Iris. This spirit delivers the message: "Love for everybody." A new spirit knocks. It is
Olaf. The telephone rings. The male model answers, but finds
no one on the line. Olaf, then, raps out a message to Juliet:
"Who do you think you are? You're nothing to anybody. Nobody
needs you." Juliet faints.

The next morning, we find Juliet asleep in her bedroom.
The room is drenched in white. The noise of a departing car
wakens Juliet. Elisabetta calls in that Giorgio has left.
Juliet looks out into the garden and sees the strange sight
of the gardener wading through and cleaning the lily pond.
Juliet, then, goes to a back door and discovers Teresina em-
bracing a male friend at the fence. Juliet sits at her dressing table and muses, "Love for everybody."

Outside the house in the garden, Elisabetta sets down the
table used for the seance beneath the wind chimes brought by
Val. Juliet goes to the table and touches it. A knock is
heard. Juliet jumps back.

A ball rolls along the beach by the sea. Juliet's two nieces chase it. Juliet is with a group of friends. She wears a white pajama suit and a white sampan hat. A doctor in the group discusses her visions with her. Juliet closes her eyes and has for a moment a vision of a beautiful circus performer on a swing. The doctor advises exercise and lovemaking. Suddenly a barge approaches. It is the entourage of Suzy, the mistress of a rich industrialist. Suzy lives in the neighboring villa. She wears a bright yellow bikini, with a high yellow hat and a tentlike yellow veil.

Juliet closes her eyes and has another vision, this time an extended one. A man seems to be pulling a rope from the sea. (Later we learn that he is Lynx-eyes, a private detective Juliet will hire.) Behind him the sky appears a dirty green. He gives his rope to Juliet, and she pulls it. Slowly there comes into view a barge and a raft. On the raft are two standing, sway-back horses and a dead horse on his back. The mouth of the barge opens to reveal a group of half-naked prisoners. Juliet calls for the doctor. He can be seen far off down the beach. Another craft appears. It is manned by armed Turks. Juliet tries to make her way toward the doctor, but she has great difficulty in moving. The roar of a jet plane awakens Juliet.

Suzy sends Juliet a basket of fruit. Juliet nods her thanks. Suzy throws off her hat and veil and runs to the sea.

The camera tracks with Juliet as she and her group walk through the forest. The foliage is a beautiful yellow. Juliet's sister Adele arrives. She is the mother of the two nieces, and she is pregnant. Adele wears a light pink dress. Next appears Juliet's actress sister, Sylva. She wears a turquoise dress, and she recites a romantic poem in French. And finally, Juliet's mother arrives. She wears a heliotrope cape. The mother and the two sisters are very tall and very beautiful. They dominate the tiny figure of Juliet. As the sisters walk to their cars, they question Juliet about Giorgio. Defensively, Juliet tells them that he has been working hard and that they plan to take a vacation together soon. The mother looks at Juliet and tells her to wear make-up.

At home, Juliet and the two maids watch a model on television perform eye movement exercises. Giorgio enters and sits on the couch with Juliet. She starts to tell him of her vision on the beach, but breaks off and dismisses the subject.

That night in bed, Giorgio says the name "Gabriella" twice in his sleep. Juliet asks who Gabriella is, but Giorgio sleeps on. The next morning at breakfast, Juliet puts the question to Giorgio again. He stalls, denies knowing any Gabriella, and leaves the house hastily. The telephone rings. Teresina answers it, but finds no one on the line.

In the garden, Juliet and the maids sit stringing garlands of peppers. Juliet recalls to herself that Giorgio once promised he would never lie to her. Val arrives and invites Juliet to come with her to visit Bhishma, a half-male and half-female seer.

That evening, in the midst of a thunderstorm, Juliet and Val enter the lobby of the Plaza Hotel. The electricity has gone off. A bell boy with a flashlight leads the women upstairs. They meet a friend, Elena. The lights come on. Juliet sees a wedding dinner and stops to watch.

In a meeting room, Bhishma sits behind a long table. A male assistant holds aloft an apple and asks members of the audience to define it. Then the assistant plays a tape of Bhishma's explanation that the object is both an apple and the spirit of Buddha. Next, an American painter in the audience is given a sword and invited to act out a parable of Lao-Tze with a female assistant. Bhishma is discovered asleep by his physician and is carried from the room.

Juliet enters Bhishma's chamber to ask advice. The walls and the furniture are red plush. Bhishma advises Juliet on how to behave during love-making. "Your husband is your god," says Bhishma. Juliet tells Bhishma her fear that her husband has another woman. Bhishma goes into a trance. A female spirit, perhaps Iris, speaks through Bhishma. "Women all want to be sirens, but don't know their trade," the spirit says. Another spirit, perhaps Olaf, battles for control of Bhishma. Juliet sees visions of Iris as a circus performer on a swing, on a plumed horse, and on the bed in the chamber. As Juliet leaves, Bhishma or a voice speaking through Bhishma tells her that she will find something new and beautiful that evening. "Sangria," the voice says, "it quenches every thirst in those who drink it and even the thirst which is unconfessed."

On the car ride home, Juliet tells her friends that Iris resembles a woman of the circus who ran away with her grandfather. We see the remembered episode. The circus woman swings gently on a low trapeze. She wears white tights, a high white hat, and a veil. Juliet as a young girl sits with her mother, sisters, and grandfather behind a gauze curtain. Later, Juliet and the grandfather encounter the circus woman. The grandfather kisses the hand of the circus performer. Juliet, then, watches some animals (the parts are played by men) and sees the approach of a circus biplane. The grandfather and the circus woman fly off in the biplane, pursued on the ground by the superintendent of the school where the grandfather taught and by Juliet's mother and sisters. Juliet explains to the friends in her car that her mother never forgave the grandfather. We see Juliet's mental picture of her mother dressed as if for a ball and a vision of the grandfather who winks.

Later that evening, Juliet enters her garden and encounters José, a handsome Spanish guest Giorgio has brought home. José mixes a pitcher of sangria for Juliet and repeats the words Bhishma had said earlier.

After the evening meal, José demonstrates the bullfighter's
art for Juliet. She attempts to imitate José, but Giorgio
plays the role of the bull and frightens her. When Giorgio
leaves the room, José kisses Juliet's hand and speaks of the
harmony of the evening in her house. Later, Giorgio and Juliet
look at Suzy in her window through a telescope José has
brought them.

In the bedroom, Giorgio puts plugs in his ears and a sleeping mask over his eyes. Juliet listens to José walking in his
room.

Later that night, Juliet discovers Giorgio's half of the
bed empty. She goes downstairs and overhears Giorgio whisper-
ing endearments to someone on the phone. Giorgio tells Juliet
that he was calling his wake-up service.

Adele and Juliet approach the office of the Eagle Detective
Service. In the elevator, Juliet expresses reservations.
Adele, however, will not let her sister back out of the appointment. In an upper hall, they find the detective Lynx-eyes hid-
ing in a doorway, disguised as a priest. He leads the women
to his office. A psychologist assistant analyzes Giorgio from
a photograph. The assistant describes Giorgio as a placid,
self-indulgent man. Lynx-eyes asks Juliet if she is certain
she wants to investigate. Juliet sees a vision of the school
superintendent as the Lord of Justice. She answers that she
does want the investigation.

At the gate of her garden, Juliet catches sight of José
walking in the garden. She does not enter. She continues to
the studio of Dolores. There she watches Dolores work. The
studio is filled with gigantic statues of nudes. "I want to
restore God's physicality," claims Dolores. Juliet recalls
that she used to think God was behind a small door over the
stage in her convent school. We see Juliet's memory of her
participation in a religious play on the stage. The role which
the child Juliet plays is that of a saint martyred on a bed of
flames by the ancient Romans. Laura, a childhood friend, asks
Juliet to tell her everything she discovers about God. Juliet
is strapped on a grill over artificial flames and then by
means of a cranking device raised toward the door above the
stage. At this point, however, Juliet's grandfather comes
forward from the audience to stop the pageant. "What are you
teaching? What are you doing to these innocents?" he cries.

In her garden the following day, Juliet discovers a cat who
belongs to Suzy and decides to return the cat. Inside Suzy's
villa, Juliet meets her neighbor. Suzy wears a low-backed
white gown with an artificial butterfly on her back. Workmen
are re-doing the living room, and the house is filled with
Suzy's friends and family. Suzy takes Juliet on a tour of the
villa. In one of the bedrooms is a young girl who has
attempted suicide. Juliet states that her friend Laura committed suicide for love at age fifteen. Finally, Suzy shows
Juliet the bedroom where Suzy and her industrialist friend

make love. The room has a mirror on the ceiling and a chute to a swimming pool. Also there is a bouquet of irises on a table. A spirit voice tells Juliet to do as Suzy advises. Suzy plunges down the slide to the pool, but Juliet won't follow.

Suzy and Juliet move through the forest with bicycles. They go up to Suzy's tree house in a basket elevator. Suzy sunbathes. Juliet talks about her marriage. Giorgio was her first love. "He became all my world," she says. With a mirror, Suzy attracts the attention of two young men. Juliet departs.

At home, Juliet receives a telephone call from the Eagle Detective Service. She goes to the agency. Lynx-eyes and his assistant show her films and slides of Giorgio on various romantic outings with a twenty-four year old model, Gabriella Olsen. Tears appear in Juliet's eyes. As she rises stiff-backed to leave, she casts a shadow on the movie screen.

Wearing a bright red dress, Juliet enters a party in Suzy's villa. Suzy introduces her to the guests. Suzy wears a yellow gown, with black wings. The predominant color in the living room is red. A mock brothel scene is staged by the guests. Juliet is introduced to Suzy's stepson, a handsome young man. Suzy sends the two of them to the bedroom with the mirror and the pool. Juliet reclines on the bed. At this point, however, she sees a vision of Laura as the martyred saint, and Juliet flees from the bedroom.

A party is in progress during an afternoon on the lawn of Juliet's house. Dr. Miller, a female psychologist, is trying to involve the guests in psycho-drama. Juliet is in her bedroom. She is hallucinating. She sees a bare-breasted woman in her closet. An image of the martyred saint appears to her and makes lascivious gestures. From her window, Juliet sees a transparently veiled woman. Giorgio comes for Juliet and leads her out among the guests. Val tries to draw her into the psycho-drama. Dr. Miller explains that psycho-drama involves acting out one's most painful moment. "Can you really help me?" Juliet asks. Juliet sees more hallucinations: the martyred saint, shrouded nuns, a naked Venus against a shell background, Saint Simon on his column, and a naked woman entwined by a snake. José dances with Juliet. "I want you to live completely," he tells her. Juliet notices cars pulling away and stops dancing.

Juliet and Dr. Miller walk in the forest. "Be yourself spontaneously, without fighting your desires and passions," advises Dr. Miller. They stretch out on the ground of pine needles. Dr. Miller suggests that Juliet may long for her husband to leave her. She says: "Without Giorgio, you'd begin to breathe, to live. You'd become yourself. You think you're afraid. You fear only one thing. You're afraid of being happy."

Juliet enters the apartment of Gabriella Olsen. The maid explains that Gabriella is not home at the moment and that she is planning a vacation trip. While Juliet is waiting, Gabriella telephones the apartment. Briefly, she speaks with Juliet, but refuses to meet Juliet face-to-face.

Returning to her home, Juliet finds Giorgio packing. Juliet prepares dinner for him. At first, Giorgio tells Juliet that he must go away for reasons of health, but then he drops his pretense and admits a "friendship" with a "person." He is in a "moment of confusion," he tells Juliet. Juliet sees a vision of her introducing Giorgio to her family and one of Giorgio and her asleep together in bed. Giorgio says goodbye.

Alone in the house, Juliet sees threatening figures. The armed Turks from the sea craft begin to set up camp. Lynx-eyes and his assistant are with them. Juliet sees Laura's reflection in a pond. Laura urges her to commit suicide. More phantoms appear. Suzy's basket elevator descends from the second story. The hearse of Laura passes outside. In the air, Juliet sees her grandfather's biplane. "I can't get down," the grandfather laments.

Juliet flees to her bedroom. Her mother appears in the room dressed in her ball gown. "Mama, help me," begs Juliet. Juliet hears crying and sees a small door like the one above the convent stage. The mother forbids Juliet to open the door. Juliet tells her mother that she no longer fears the mother. The door opens. Beyond it, Juliet sees herself as a child strapped on the grill of flames. Juliet releases the child.

The frightening phantoms withdraw from the house. The biplane of the grandfather lands on the lawn. The grandfather tells Juliet: "You don't need me anymore. I'm your invention, too."

Juliet walks outside her gate. The sun is shining. There is a breeze. She smiles. Then she starts back to the house. A spirit voice, however, calls her. "Who are you?" she asks. "True friends," the voice answers. "Listen to us." Juliet walks into the pine forest.

<u>Credits</u>

Producer:	Angelo Rizzoli (Federiz)
Director:	Federico Fellini
Screenplay:	Fellini, Tullio Pinelli, Ennio Flaiano, Brunello Rondi, from a story by Fellini and Pinelli
Photography:	Gianni di Venanzo (Technicolor and Totalscope)
Cameraman:	Pasquale de Santis
Art Director:	Piero Gherardi
Music:	Nino Rota
Editor:	Ruggero Mastroianni

Assistants to the Director:	Francesco Aluigi, Liliana Betti, Rosaria Zavoli
Make-up:	Otello Fava, Eligio Trani
Production Manager:	Clemente Fracassi
Directors of Production:	Mario Basili, Alessandro von Normann
Production Inspector:	Walter Benelli
Cast:	Guilietta Masina (Juliet), Alba Cancellieri (Juliet as a child), Mario Pisu (Giorgio, the husband), Caterina Boratto (Juliet's mother), Luisa Della Noce and Sylva Koscina (Juliet's sisters), Rosella di Sepio and Sabrina Gigli (the granddaughters), Lou Gilbert (the grandfather), Valentina Cortese (Valentina), Silvana Jachino (Dolores), Elena Fondra (Elena), José de Vilallonga (the Spanish gentleman), Cesarina Miceli Picardi (a friend of the husband), Milena Vucotich and Elisabetta Gray (Juliet's maids), Sandra Milo (Suzy, the neighbor; Iris, the apparition; Fanny, the dancer), Irina Alexeieva (the grandmother in Suzy's coterie), Alessandra Mannoukine (the mother), Gilberto Galvan (the chauffeur), Seyna Seyn (the masseuse), Yvonne Casadei, Hildegarde Golez, Dina de Santis (the maids), Edoardo Torricella (the Russian teacher), Dany Paris (the desperate friend), Raffaele Guida (the oriental lover), Fred Williams (the Arabian Prince), Alberto Plebani (Lynx-Eyes), Federico Valli, Remo Risalti, Grillo Rufino (his agents), Waleska Gert (Bhishma), Asoka Rubener, Suiata Rubener, Walter Harrison (Bhishma's assistants), Felice Fulchignoni (Don Raffaele), Anne Francine (the psychoanalyst), Mario Conocchia (the lawyer), Fredrich Ledebur (the Headmaster), Genius (the medium), Massimo Sarchielli (Valentina's lover), Giorgio Ardisson, Bob Edwards, Nadir Moretti (Dolores' models).
Distribution:	Rizzoli Film

Running Time: 137 minutes
Released: Italy: October 1965
                     U.S.: November 3, 1965 (NYC)

12   TOBY DAMMIT/IL NE FAUT JAMAIS PARIER SA TÊTE AVEC LE DIABLE
      [NEVER BET THE DEVIL YOUR HEAD] (1968)

An Episode in HISTOIRES EXTRAORDINAIRES/TRE PASSI NEL DELIRIO
[SPIRITS OF THE DEAD/TALES OF MYSTERY].

The movie opens with a shot of clouds. The English actor
Toby Dammit is on an airplane bound for Rome. He muses to himself that the trip seems predestined.

At Fiumicino Airport, Toby walks through the lobby. The
dollying camera replaces him, and, from his point of view, we
see a female announcer on a TV set, a group of nuns by the
gate, some Moslems prostrating themselves in a departure area,
a black girl who looks up from a fountain in surprise, and a
man in a wheelchair. A group of photographers crowd around
Toby, snapping pictures of him. He hurls his briefcase at
them and rushes to the escalator. Riding up the escalator,
he turns and tries to apologize to the group below. The lights
frightened him, he explains. Then at the top of the escalator,
he seems to see something or someone. "Why did you come
here?" he asks.

A few minutes later, on the upper level, Toby meets a
priest who identifies himself as a representative of a film
production company. This man introduces two young men as the
film's directors, another man as a secretary, and a woman as
a translator.

In a car approaching Rome, the priest talks to Toby about
the film he has agreed to make. It will be the first Catholic
Western, a movie about Christ. The two directors describe how
the film will represent the crisis of modern society. Toby
reminds the priest that the production company has promised
him a new Ferrari sportscar for taking the part in the film.
As the car stops for a traffic light, two gypsies come up to
the car and begin to read fortunes. However, when one looks
at Toby's palm, he withdraws at once. "No, no good," he says.

We are at the airport again. Toby's mind returns to the
vision he had at the top of the escalator. A large white
rubber ball bounces toward him. He bends to retrieve it and
finds a ten-year-old, blond girl before him. She is a strange
apparition, thin with feverish eyes. She wears a nineteenth-
century child's dress. She looks at Toby as if she knows him,
then snatches the ball from him, and disappears. "But you
promised to leave me alone," he says.

Back in the car, we see Toby pale and shaken. He takes a
drink from his silver flask.

Inside a television studio. Most of the studio is dark and deserted, but in one brightly lit corner a program is being televised. A young woman is presenting Toby Dammit to the television audience. "He has come to Rome to act in a film on the myth of redemption," she explains. Toby is hostile. He has come to Rome for a Ferrari, he corrects the interviewer. He tells her that he takes drugs when he wants to return to normal and that he hates the public. She asks if he believes in God, and he answers, "No." "The Devil?" she asks. "Yes," he answers. "What does he look like?" Toby explains, "I'm English, not Catholic. The Devil is cheerful, agile." Toby describes the Devil as a young, blond girl. Suddenly, the girl appears before him.

A night club. Toby is seated at a table, drinking. Other guests also are drinking. There is a stage with microphones and an L-shaped table. It is an awards banquet. The master of ceremonies announces the Tenth Annual Italian Oscar Presentation. Well-wishers come up to Toby and try to speak to him. He is, however, very drunk. A mother tries to introduce her daughter. One of the officials tells Toby that he will be expected to recite some Shakespeare when he goes on stage. Fashions are modelled. Toby's double rides up on a horse and puts a cowboy hat on him. A female star poses with him. Toby wants more to drink. The PR man tells him not to drink any more and seats him near the stage. A woman approaches Toby. She strokes his hair and promises to care for him. She promises that he will have no more need to run and that they will have a perfect life together. Toby rests his head on her shoulder and dozes. The music of "Ruby" is heard. The woman touches Toby's hand and leaves.

Toby is called to the stage. The M.C. calls him a great actor. Photographers snap pictures of him. He staggers to the stage, swinging at the cameras. He receives his award. A hush falls over the audience. Toby begins to recite the "Tomorrow and tomorrow and tomorrow" speech from Macbeth. He breaks off. He denies that he is a great actor. He might have been, he tells the audience. He confesses that he hasn't worked in a year and that his last director called him a drunk. "What do you want from me?" he asks. Seized with the urge to escape, Toby runs to the street and zooms off in his Ferrari sportscar.

Toby drives in a frenzy through streets. The camera often replaces him, and we see from his point of view. He goes down a street with workers on it. Then he comes to a highway. Ahead there looms in his lights a cardboard cut-out of a waiter, an advertisement for a restaurant. The cardboard waiter seems to hail him. He stops. He is alone. He cries out in a moan. He starts to drive again, but must stop soon for some sheep in the road. He asks a man the route to Rome. The man doesn't understand him and gives no answer. Driving on, Toby discovers another, different cardboard waiter. He comes to the dead end of a street. At last, he sees a well-lit street and follows it to its end. He gets out and washes his face in a well. A bell sounds. Toby resumes driving. A fog sets in. Toby passes by some road barriers and slams to a halt. "The bridge has collapsed," calls out a man. "Take another route." Out of his car, Toby bangs on an oil drum and then kicks it. He sees the end of the bridge in the fog. The blond girl with the ball is on the bridge, on the far side. Toby gets into his car and backs up. We see the vision of the girl. Toby smiles and then laughs. He drives forward.

A shot of a cable stretched across the end of the bridge. Blood drips from it. The girl's ball bounces. The girl smiles. She picks up Toby's head.

Credits

Producer:	Raymond Eger for Les Films Marceau-Cocinor-PEA
Director:	Federico Fellini
Screenplay:	Fellini, Bernardino Zapponi, from a story by Edgar Allan Poe "Never Bet the Devil Your Head."
Photography:	Giuseppe Rotunno
Music:	Nino Rota
Art Director:	Fabrizio Clerici
Sets and Costumes:	Piero Tosi
Special Effects:	Joseph Nathanson
Editor:	Ruggero Mastroianni
Production Assistant:	Tomaso Jagune
Cast:	Terence Stamp (Toby Dammit), Salvo Randone (the priest), Fabrizio Angeli (1st director), Ernesto Colli (2nd director), Marina Yaru (child), Anna Tonietti, Aleardo Ward, Paul Cooper, Polidor, Rick Boyd, Antonia Pietrosi.
Distribution:	American International Pictures
Running Time:	40 minutes (overall time of the complete film is 117 minutes)
Released:	France: June 10, 1968 Italy: September 1968 U.S.: September 3, 1969 (NYC)
Note:	Other episodes in this anthology film are Louis Malle's William Wilson and Roger Vadim's Metzengerstein.

13 BLOCK-NOTES DI UN REGISTA [FELLINI: A DIRECTOR'S NOTEBOOK]
    (1969)

The film opens with a shot of a desolate square in a field
overgrown with weeds. In voice-over, Fellini tells us that
the square is part of a set for his aborted film The Voyage of
G. Mastorna. He talks about the film and then converses with
some hippies who are camping on the abandoned set. They tell
him of their new definition of relationships between people,
without "ownership." One recites a poem about the useless city
of Mastorna. The set darkens. A storm. A plane approaches,
the plane of G. Mastorna himself. Mastorna with his 'cello
walks from the plane toward the city.

Cinecittà. Daytime. Fellini takes us on a tour of the studio, accompanied by his secretary, Marina Boratto. They chat
with technicians along the way and then visit a building which
Fellini explains is a graveyard for old sets and props. Fellini
shows us sketches for The Voyage of G. Mastorna.

The Colosseum. Night. In voice-over, Fellini tells us we
are on a voyage different from the one in the Mastorna film,
a voyage in time. Shots of the Colosseum. A narrator explains
to us that Fellini likes to make jaunts at night through the
city to gather ideas for his films. Here he is doing research
for his next film, Fellini Satyricon. On camera now, Fellini
interviews various night people in the Colosseum--street-
vendors, homosexuals, and transvestites.

An interview with Giulietta Masina. She tells an interviewer about the curious Roman phenomenon, the man with the
sack who tours the poor sections of Rome performing various
charitable acts. The scene shifts. We see the man with the
sack. In voice-over, Masina explains that we are looking at a
sequence cut from Nights of Cabiria. In the sequence, as we
watch, Cabiria follows the man with the sack on his rounds and
tries to get to know him.

The Roman Forum. In voice-over, Fellini says that he will
now take us on a tour of another Rome, the ancient Rome of his
youthful film-viewing days. We shift to the interior of a
movie theater in a provincial town of the 1930's. The audience is watching a silent movie of Romans in togas. The
characters are dissipated. A fat emperor, a scheming empress,
and an orgy. The film-within-the-film ends with the emperor's
assassination by his wife.

Night. An automobile heading toward the Appian Way.
Fellini is inside the car with his secretary, Marina, his collaborator, Bernardino Zapponi, a clairvoyant, Professor Genius,
and some others. They tell us they are going to a Roman cemetary to establish contact with some ancient Romans. They
arrive. Genius goes into a trance. He detects bones in the
walls. He holds Marina for inspiration and then goes back in
his mind to the time of the Roman republic.

In the Rome subway. Fellini is with a professor of archaeology. They discuss various archaeological phenomena discovered in the subway. They board a train. As they ride, specters appear along the tracks. Nervously, Fellini and the professor get off the train at the next stop.

Appian Way. Daytime. In voice-over, Marina says that we will once again visit the Appian Way with Fellini, this time to see some living specters. Now we discover prostitutes sitting among graves. They speak together in various dialects. Suddenly, they are transformed into ancient Roman prostitutes speaking Latin. A truck drives up. The drivers get out and are transformed into Roman legionnaires. They leap on the prostitutes. An orgy takes place. The drivers return to their trucks and drive off.

Porto San Sebastiano. Daytime. A camera car approaches the villa of Marcello Mastroianni. In voice-over, Fellini says that we will pay the actor an impromptu visit.

The garden of the villa. Mastroianni is in the middle of an interview with American newswomen and a photographic session. He models various kinds of fashions and deals with inane questions. A tourist bus drives by. Fellini looks on all this from a little distance and says that he must use Mastroianni for the role of Mastorna if he takes up again The Voyage of G. Mastorna.

A flashback to a sound stage at Cinecittà. Fellini is shooting the screen test of Mastroianni for the film. We see Mastorna playing his 'cello in a dressing room. Out of his role, Mastroianni tells Fellini that Fellini is frightened of the project.

Piazzale Mattatoio. Early morning. In voice-over, the narrator announces that Fellini has come to an edifice constructed at the time of Pius IX in a location which might still capture the ferocity and cruelty of ancient Rome. Shots of the building. It is a slaughter house. The camera dollies through empty rooms and a long corridor. Occasional shrieks of unseen animals are heard. The camera enters a room with strange devices apparently for torture. A yellow light. A room where pigs are being slaughtered. From this, the camera passes to a gallery of busts of ancient Romans. Outside the building, we discover two custodians with whips. The narrator explains that Fellini is interviewing typical Romans. People come up to Fellini and talk with him. They are from all walks of life-- mechanics, butchers, and gypsies. Some of them do improvisations, performing as gladiators and emperors. Screen tests are shot. Caterina Boratto, the actress, visits the set to see Marina. She assumes the role of an empress and turns thumbs down. One would-be actor is slightly wounded. Fade-out as the narrator states that Fellini feels that the faces of these people make them the right ones to choose for Fellini Satyricon.

Fellini's office. The narrator says that Fellini is again in the process of interviewing would-be actors for Fellini Satyricon. Fellini is seated at his desk, just off camera.

Various people enter to be interviewed: musicians, intellectuals, young girls, and matrons. Somehow a salesman slips in
and tries to sell Fellini a painting. Fellini is curt and
business-like with everybody. However, in voice-over narration, he tells us that he feels strong affection for these
people: "I am very fond of all these characters who are always
chasing after me. They are all a little mad, I know that.
They say they need me, but in truth I need them more. Their
human qualities are rich, comic, and sometimes very moving."
The sequence ends with the appearance of a giant who has come
to see Fellini.

A sound stage. Fellini is seen filming a screen test with
English actor Martin Potter. Cameras, technicians, and secre-
taries are reflected in the mirror of a make-up table.
Fellini is preoccupied with his directing. <u>Fellini Satyricon</u>
is coming to life. Credits appear over this scene, as music
from <u>8½</u> is heard on the sound track. Fade-out.

<u>Credits</u>

Producer:	Peter Goldfarb (for NBC-TV with the cooperation of the Productions International Corporation)
Director:	Federico Fellini
Screenplay:	Fellini, Bernardino Zapponi
Music:	Nino Rota
Photography:	Pasquale De Santis
Editor:	Ruggero Mastroianni
Production Manager:	Lamberto Pippia
Assistant Directors:	Maurizio Mein, Liliana Betti
Production Secretary:	Norma Giacchero
Assistant Editor:	Adriana Olasio
Series Unit Manager:	Joseph Nash
Dialogue Director:	Christopher Cruise
English Dialogue:	Eugene Walter
Cast:	Fellini, Giulietta Masina, Marcello Mastroianni, Caterina Boratto, Marina Boratto, David Maumsell, Professor Genius, Bernardino Zapponi, Pasquale De Santis.
Distribution:	NBC-TV
Running Time:	54 minutes
Released:	U.S.: April 11, 1969 on NBC-TV
Note:	This television documentary begins on the set of <u>The Voyage of G. Mastorna</u>, a film which Fellini abandoned in favor of <u>Toby Dammit</u>. It documents Fellini's casting of <u>Fellini Satyricon</u> and contains a short scene from <u>The Nights of Cabiria</u> which was cut from the final version of that film.

14   FELLINI SATYRICON (1969)

Against the background of an exterior wall stands Encolpius, a blond young man. He is distraught. He tells us that he has escaped the arena and that he has stained his hands with blood, only to wind up penniless and alone. Encolpius lays the blame for his condition on Ascyltus, his former companion. He complains that Giton, a young boy whom Encolpius loves, has gone off with Ascyltus. Encolpius vows to find Giton. He enters the baths and searches among the various groups in the various rooms. He calls for Ascyltus. We discover Ascyltus before Encolpius does. He is a dark young man, and he is crawling on the floor of the baths. He tells us that he took Giton away while Encolpius was sleeping. "Friendship lasts as long as it is useful," he explains. After a night of love, he has sold Giton to a famous actor. Ascyltus, at last, answers Encolpius' call. The two young men fight savagely. Encolpius gets from Ascyltus the confession that he has sold Giton to Vernacchio.

The interior of the theater of Vernacchio. A standing, chattering crowd watches as Vernacchio performs. He is a large man, and he wears a strange mask and a tail. He seems to catch and eat a fly to the delight of the crowd. He farts, and his tail flies up. Next, he stages a show. A man is shoved on-stage and is punished by having his hand cut off. A boy dressed as Caesar appears and orders the arm restored. Vernacchio's helpers fit a golden hand onto the end of the man's arm. The audience applauds. When Vernacchio begins the next show, which involves the young Giton dressed as Eros with a bow and arrows, Encolpius rushes to the stage. He demands Giton's return. Vernacchio mocks Encolpius and pushes him off his feet. One of the crowd offers to buy Giton. Encolpius is menaced by Vernacchio's helpers. At this point, a Roman magistrate strides forward and orders Vernacchio to return the young slave to Encolpius. He mentions that Vernacchio is already in poor standing with Caesar because of a previous satire.

Encolpius and Giton are in the streets of the Suburra of Rome. They embrace and kiss. Encolpius professes his love. They walk through a street on which there are houses of prostitution. Suddenly they catch sight of the Roman magistrate beckoning to them, and they rush into one of the houses of prostitution to avoid him. They see a childless couple praying, various prostitutes, and citizens arriving secretly by raft from the underground sewer. Eventually Encolpius and Giton depart by another exit. They make their way to the Insula Felicles, a tall structure approximating an apartment building. Inside Encolpius' cubicle they embrace. Later that night, Ascyltus enters the cubicle. Encolpius and Ascyltus agree to divide their possessions and to separate. Given his choice, Giton decides to go with Ascyltus. After Giton and Ascyltus leave, Encolpius contemplates suicide. At this point, however, he hears a loud rumble and feels a vibration. The building begins to collapse. The dwellers flee. We watch the collapse of the giant structure.

In an open gallery for paintings, Encolpius meets the poet Eumolpus. The poet complains that Rome has fallen to crass concerns and that its society neglects the arts. There will be no more masterpieces such as Encolpius and he are viewing, he predicts sadly. Eumolpus, then, leads Encolpius to the country estate of Trimalchio, a wealthy freedman. Eumolpus promises Encolpius a feast. He explains that Trimalchio likes to lay false claim to being a poet and therefore enjoys Eumolpus' presence at his feasts. Eumolpus and Encolpius bathe in one of the pools. Trimalchio, carried on a litter, makes a grand entrance, and the bathers greet him. He is an old, heavy-set man with a face composed of folds and pouches, but he displays a certain vigor in his words and movements.

At the dining hall of Trimalchio, the guests take their places. Trimalchio and his wife, Fortunata, are at the head table. Eumolpus and Encolpius are seated at a table to one side. Trimalchio blesses his three household gods, Good Business, Good Luck, and Good Profit. Tryphaena, a regal woman, catches sight of Encolpius. She smiles at him and kisses her tabletop. Trimalchio comments at some length on the state of his bowels. At this point, servants bring in a roast pig on a platter. Trimalchio feigns anger. He says that the pig could not have been cleaned properly. He commands that the cook be whipped. The cook calls for mercy. Trimalchio orders the cook to cut into the pig. The cook slits the pig and pulls out triumphantly a string of sausages. The guests applaud Trimalchio's staged trick. Encolpius laughs and is immediately chastised by an older freedman who interprets Encolpius' laughter as condescension. Four actors stage a short play about Diomedes, Ganymede, Helen, and Ajax. Afterward a cook dressed as Ajax slaughters a calf. Eumolpus declaims a poem in Latin. The guests jeer him. Trimalchio offers some lines, and he is applauded. Fortunata does a tempestuous dance. Eventually, Trimalchio joins her dance and embraces her.

Later that night, Trimalchio listens to a reading of the accounts of his farms. Habinnas and his wife Scintilla arrive. Habinnas has been building Trimalchio's tomb. Scintilla and Fortunata kiss. Trimalchio fondles and kisses a young boy. Fortunata rages at him, and Trimalchio berates her. Then Trimalchio takes up a little skeleton and delivers a poem on the transitoriness of life. Eumolpus accuses him of plagiarism. At Trimalchio's orders, Eumolpus is taken away and beaten by the servants.

At Trimalchio's tomb, Trimalchio climbs into his coffin. The servants weep as if he were dead. Fortunata and Scintilla wander off and kiss each other. An old man tells the story of the widow of Ephesus.

113

We see a funeral procession at a cemetery. In a tomb, a
widow laments her husband's death. In another section of the
cemetery, a young guard begins watch over a hanged criminal.
Later, the soldier goes to the tomb of the widow. He consoles
her, and they make love. Outside, relatives cut down and
carry off the criminal. The soldier discovers the gallows
empty, and he prepares to commit suicide. The widow stops him
and offers her husband's body as a substitute to put on the
gallows.

Outside Trimalchio's estate, Encolpius finds Eumolpus in a
field. Encolpius falls asleep, while Eumolpus speaks of legacies he will leave behind if he dies.

As Encolpius awakens, he sees Giton and Ascyltus looking
down at him. They are, however, in chains. Encolpius, too,
is seized. Tryphaena is transporting a group of captives to
the ship of Lichas of Taranto. Encolpius explains in voice-
over narration that it is the task of Lichas and Tryphaena to
comb the seas, looking for things of interest for Caesar. On
board the ship, Lichas challenges Encolpius to a wrestling
match and defeats him. During the wrestling, however, he becomes enamoured of Encolpius. Lichas decides to marry
Encolpius. He has Tryphaena perform a mock marriage ceremony.
Ascyltus laughs at the proceedings. When the ceremony ends,
Lichas leads Encolpius solemnly below. In voice-over narration,
Encolpius tells us that Lichas granted freedom to Ascyltus,
Giton, and him because of the mockmarriage. We see scenes of
Lichas singing to Encolpius and scenes of a sagging, lugubri-
ous whale being captured.

We shift to the pleasure boat of the young Caesar. A big
ship looms up to challenge Caesar's small craft. A crew of
men discover the young Caesar ashore on a small island. They
encircle him, while he takes his own life with a sword.

Back on Lichas' boat, the same group of men who overthrew
Caesar have seized control. The officer informs Lichas that
he must give up his ship to the new Caesar. Lichas rushes
forward to attack him. The officer, however, decapitates
Lichas. At the end of the scene, we watch the head of Lichas
sinking in the sea.

The march of the new Caesar to Rome. The soldiers wear
torn uniforms, and many are wounded. Caged animals and slaves
are also a part of the procession.

Day in a lovely villa. Two boys and a girl play in the
garden. A wagon behind the villa is being loaded by slaves.
Inside the villa, the master is in the process of setting free
his slaves. A notice of confiscation, he tells them, will
come on the next day. The master and his wife take leave of
the children next. The wagons move off. The master and his
wife remain behind. In the garden, the master cuts his wrists
and stretches out on a divan. He looks at his wife tenderly.
The scene grows dark.

At night, Encolpius and Ascyltus approach the villa. They discover the dead bodies of the master and his wife. Fearfully, they push on into the villa. They find a young, black slave girl who has stayed behind. They chase her, catch her, and make love to her. Encolpius and Ascyltus caress each other. In the morning, they awaken to find Roman soldiers burning the master's body on a funeral pyre.

In a desert, the two young men happen upon a wagon. Screams and moans come from a woman inside the wagon. The servants explain that the woman has been cursed to desire a man every hour. They encourage Ascyltus to go to her. The woman's husband will reward him. Ascyltus climbs into the wagon and begins to make love to the woman. Outside, a servant tells Encolpius of the Hermaphrodite in the Temple of Ceres, who is an oracle.

The interior of the Temple of Ceres. The young, albino Hermaphrodite is gently sponged by his old protector. Various people gather to consult the strange creature. Among the group are Encolpius, Ascyltus, and a tall, older man. Later that night, the old protector is killed by Encolpius. Ascyltus picks up the Hermaphrodite.

During the day. Encolpius, Ascyltus, and the older man are transporting the Hermaphrodite through the desert by means of a mule-drawn cart. The Hermaphrodite appears to be suffering. Encolpius reports that the Hermaphrodite needs water. He makes an unsuccessful attempt to find water. During the night, the Hemaphrodite dies. In a rage, the older man attacks Encolpius. Ascyltus comes to Encolpius' aid, and, after a violent battle, the two young men kill the older man.

In a labyrinth of an amphitheater, Encolpius is pushed forward by a group of citizens who urge him to play the role of Theseus. He moves through the labyrinth until he comes to a man wearing a mask of a bull. This minotaur easily defeats Encolpius in battle. Encolpius begs mercy. The official of the town, then, explains to him that he has participated in a festival in honor of the god of laughter. Encolpius has provided the citizens with much laughter, and he may claim his prize. Encolpius approaches a woman representing Ariadne in the center of the amphitheater. He takes her in his arms, but finds himself unable to have an erection. Ariadne kicks him away in disdain. The audience jeers. Encolpius looks up and sees Ascyltus standing near him. Ascyltus laughs at Encolpius. Then he indicates to Encolpius the poet Eumolpus borne on a litter by slaves.

As Encolpius and Ascyltus walk by his litter, Eumolpus explains that he has gained power and wealth in the town. He will take Encolpius to the Garden of Delights to help him recover his potency. Inside the Garden, prostitutes throng to Eumolpus. The poet turns Encolpius over to the master of the Garden. The master presents a whiplike tree branch to one of the girls. She and others whip Encolpius. Ascyltus frolics with some of the girls on a swing. Later, while others sleep, we find the disconsolate Encolpius wide awake. Eumolpus bids him goodbye, but invites him on a journey to Africa in the near future.

The master tells Encolpius that Encolpius has been cursed by the sorceress Oenothea. He narrates her story while we see the events take place. A very ugly magician once fell in love with Oenothea, a tall, striking black girl. She invited him to come to her house at night and promised to lower a basket for him. On the appointed night, when the magician climbed into the basket, Oenothea had him hoisted part of the way to her window and then left him suspended in mid-air until morning. In revenge, the magician took away fire from the town and informed the townspeople they could light their torches only from a source between Oenothea's legs. Now Oenothea holds a magic power over the town in a revenge of her own. The master advises Encolpius that he may find Oenothea in the marshes.

We see a small skiff making its way among the marshes. On board are Encolpius, Ascyltus, and a boatman. Ascyltus displays a bag of money that Encolpius may use to pay Oenothea. The boatman stares at the bag. On an island, Encolpius enters a labyrinthine dwelling. Inside, an old woman gives Encolpius a cup to drink from. After drinking down the liquid, Encolpius sees Oenothea as tall, slim black girl. She smiles. Through the window, Encolpius makes out Ascyltus and the boatman in the midst of a furious battle. Then Oenothea appears to Encolpius as a huge, forceful, mature, black woman. Encolpius stands in awe of her. Finally, he goes to her and makes love to her.

Encolpius and Ascyltus make their way through the marshes. Ascyltus pales, falls behind Encolpius, stumbles, sinks to the ground, and dies. (The last several shots are in slow-motion.) Encolpius returns and discovers the fatal wound in Ascyltus' side, inflicted probably by the boatman. He strokes the hand of the dead Ascyltus. Encolpius walks dejectedly on the beach.

Later, Encolpius comes to the ship of Eumolpus. He learns from the captain that Eumolpus has died. The captain reads Eumolpus' will to a group of heirs. They are left his possessions on the condition that they eat his body. At first the heirs refuse the condition of the will, but then gradually they change their minds. Invited by the captain, Encolpius sets sail on Eumolpus' ship in search of further adventures. The film images become patterns in frescoes on ruins standing by the edge of the sea. We move out of the world of antiquity.

Credits

Producer:	Alberto Grimaldi (PEA, Rome)
Director:	Federico Fellini
Screenplay:	Fellini and Bernardino Zapponi, freely adapted from the book by Petronius Arbiter.

Photography:	Giuseppe Rotunno
Cameraman:	Giuseppe Maccari
Sets and Costumes:	Danilo Donati
Art Directors:	Luigi Scaccianoce, Giorgio Giovannini
Music:	Nino Rota, Ilhan Mimaroglu, Tod Dockstader, Andrew Rudin
Editor:	Ruggero Mastroianni
Assistant Director:	Maurizio Mein
Director's Aides:	Liliana Betti, Lia Consalvo
Script Girl:	Norma Giacchero
Assistant Scene Designers:	Dante Ferretti, Carlo Agate
Assistant Costume Designers:	Franco Antomelli, Renzo Bronchi, Dafne Cirrocchi
Still Photographer:	Mimmo Cattarinich
Assistant to Film Editor:	Adriana Olasio
Production Supervisor:	Enzo Provenzale
Production Manager:	Roberto Cocco
Production Assistants:	Lamberto Pippia, Gilberto Scarpellini, Fernando Rossi
Production Secretary:	Michele Pesce
Linguistic Adviser (Latin):	Luca Canali
Scene Painters:	Italo Tommassi, Sante Barelli, Carlo Rissone, Paulo Mugnai
Boom Operator:	Alberto Moretti
Sound Mixer:	Oscar De Arcangelis
Make-up:	Rino Carboni
Hair Stylist:	Luciano Vito
Special Effects:	Adriano Pischiutta
Electricians:	Rodolfo Bramucci, Alvardo Romagnoli
Stage Hands:	Salvatore Mazzini, Domenico Mattei
Property Man:	Raffaele Vincenti
Script Editor:	Enzo Ocone
Cast:	Martin Potter (Encolpius), Hiram Keller (Ascyltus), Max Born (Giton), Fanfulla (Vernacchio), Salvo Randone (Eumolpus), Mario Romagnoli (Trimalchio), Magali Noel (Fortunata), Giuseppe San Vitale (Habinnas), Alain Cuny (Lichas), Capucine (Tryphaena), Lucia Bose (the suicide's wife), Joseph Wheeler (the suicide), Hylette Adolphe (the slave girl), Tanya Lopert (the emperor), Luigi Montefiore (the minotaur), Marcello Bifolco (the proconsul), Elisa Mainardi (Ariadne), Donyale Luna (Oenothea), Carlo Giordana (the

captain of Eumolpus' ship), Gordon
Mitchell (the thief), Genius
[Eugenio Mastropietro] (Cinedo, the
freedman), Danica La Loggia
(Scintilla), Antonia Pietrosi
(widow of Ephesus), Wolfgang
Hillinger (soldier at Ephesus'
tomb), Elio Gigante (master of
Garden of Delights), Sibilla Sedat
(nymphomaniac), Lorenzo Piani (her
husband), Luigi Zerbinati (her
slave, the storyteller), Vittorio
Vittori (notary).

Distribution:	United Artists
Running Time:	127 minutes
Released:	Italy: First shown at 1969 Venice Film Festival
	U.S.: March 11, 1970 (NYC)

15   I CLOWNS [THE CLOWNS] (1970)

The film begins with a reminiscence by Fellini of his first
experience of witnessing a circus. He shows a little boy
waking up in the night and watching from his window as the
circus comes to town. The boy goes to the tent and watches
the practice. Gradually the circus comes to life. We see,
with the boy, the startling and frightening side of the
clowns' routines. We see a clown with a hatchet in his head.
We see a gigantic female wrestler defeat a male and then take
on a woman from the audience. A fakir is buried. A huge
clown on stilts towers over the proceedings. The performance
so overwhelms the boy that he cries and has to be taken home.

In the second section, Fellini develops the idea that
clowns, for him as a young man, seemed to summarize and turn
into controlled form the antics of village grotesques. Such
antics comprise the second section. Fellini shows us a man
who makes obscene gestures, a midget nun, a wife who takes her
husband home in a wheelbarrow, and Giudizio, the village idiot,
who reenacts war scenes. We see an episode concerning a pompous station-master who cannot command respect from the schoolboys on the train and so brings a Fascist officer to stand
beside him. In an episode in a poolroom, a beautiful, exotic
blonde woman draws the attention of all the young men (including the one who represents Fellini). After she leaves,
Giudizio, the idiot, vows he would make love to her...for as
little as five lire.

During a third section, Fellini appears on camera in the
process of dictating material to his secretary. "Where are
the clowns of my childhood?" he asks. On a visit to a modern
circus, we see clowns squirting each other, and we see Anita

Ekberg on a visit of her own admiring the tigers. Finally we
are told the story of Jim Gillion, the legendary Augusto or
tramp clown, who left a hospital to see Footit and Chocolate's
famous clown act and died during the performance. This section ushers in the documentary style of the fourth section.

The fourth section takes place in Paris. At a restaurant
in Les Halles, Fellini discusses the subject of clowns with
some clowns and with a historian of the art of clowns, Tristan
Rémy. Rémy expounds the theory that there are two types of
clowns, the white clown and the tramp clown Augusto. The white
clown is authoritarian and attempts (with few successes) to
control the tramp clown. The costumes of the white clown are
elegant. Fellini presents a fashion show of their costumes.

A visit to the <u>Cirque d'Hiver</u> allows Fellini to catch a
glimpse of Baptiste, a psychiatrist turned clown, and Chaplin's
daughter Victoria in rehearsal. Briefly, Fellini interviews
Jan Hucke, Rivel, Pierre Etaix, and Pierre Fratellini. He re-
creates the performances which the Fratellini family put on in
asylums and hospitals. He further interviews Père Loriot and
Mrs. Bario. (Bario himself won't talk to Fellini, but can't
forget the circus and watches wistfully from his window as
Fellini leaves.) Tristan Rémy tells Fellini that Rhum was the
best of the Augusto clowns. Women, however, did not like Rhum,
and as a result he drank a great deal. Fellini tracks down an
8mm. print of Rhum, but finds it lifeless and disappointing.

The final section of the film is the funeral for the Augusto
figure. Fellini laments that there seems no room in the
sophisticated modern world for the anarchist spirit of Augusto.
The comic figure of a sobbing widow is produced in the circus
ring. A very long, comic will is read. An attempt to photograph the assembled mourners fails. Clown workers appear.
They hit their thumbs with hammers and each other with planks.
A critic who asks the meaning of the goings-on has a bucket
thrown over his head. And, then, the same thing happens to
Fellini. A huge funeral hearse careens into the ring. There
is an attempt to stuff the corpse of Augusto into a coffin, but
the corpse keeps falling out. At last all is in order, and the
hearse resumes movement. But then a fire breaks out. A fire
company of clowns arrives. The hearse opens. And Augusto soars
into the air above the madness. Then the lights go out. The
excitement ends. When the lights return, the circus is empty,
except for one clown. The clown recalls his act with his partner Fru-Fru. Fru-Fru would pretend to be dead, and the clown
would call to him to come back. The clown then plays a mournful passage from "Ebbtide" on his trumpet. It is answered by
Fru-Fru. The two advance to meet each other and leave the ring
side by side.

Credits
Producers: Elio Scardamaglia, Ugo Guerra (RAI--
                                  O.R.T.F., Bavaria Film and Compagnia
                                  Leone Cinematografica Coproduction)

Director:	Federico Fellini
Screenplay:	Fellini, Bernardino Zapponi
Photography:	Dario Di Palma (Technicolor)
Cameraman:	Blasco Giurato
Costumes:	Danilo Donati
Set Decorator:	Renzo Gronchi
Music:	Nino Rota
Conductor:	Carlo Savina
Editor:	Ruggero Mastroianni
Assistant Director:	Maurizio Mein
Director's Aide:	Liliana Betti
Assistant to the Editor:	Adriana Olasio
Production Manager:	Lamberto Pippia
Production Secretary:	Norma Giacchero
Make-up:	Rino Carboni
Hair Stylist:	Paolo Franceschi
Mixing:	Alberto Bartolomei
Cast:	The Italian Clowns: Billi, Scotti, Fanfulla, Rizzo, Pistoni, Furia, Sbarra, Carini, Terzo, Vingelli, Fumagalli, Zerbinati, Reder, Valentini, Merli, The 4 Colombaioni, The Martana, Maggio, Janigro, Maunsel, Peverello, Sorrentino, Valdemaro, Bevilacqua. The Troupe: Fellini, Maya Morin, Lina Alberti, Alvaro Vitali, Gasparino. The French Clowns: Alex, Bario, Père Loriot, Ludo, Charlie Rivel, Maiss, Nino. And with: Pierre Etaix, Victor Fratellini, Annie Fratellini, Baptiste, Tristan Rémy, Liana Orfei, Rinaldo Orfei, Nando Orfei, Franco Migliorini (the animal trainer), Anita Ekberg, Victoria Chaplin.
Distribution:	Levitt-Pickman
Running Time:	92 minutes
Released:	Italy: December 25, 1970 on TV U.S.: June 14, 1971 (NYC)

16 ROMA [FELLINI ROMA/FELLINI'S ROMA] (1972)

Over the initial credits, the voice of the director says: "Ladies and gentlemen, good evening. The film you are about to see does not have a story in the traditional sense, with a neat plot and characters that you can follow from the beginning to the end. This picture tells another kind of a story, the story of a city. Here I have attempted a portrait of Rome.

When I was very small and still had never seen her, since I lived in a little provincial town in the north of Italy, Rome for me was only a mixture of strange, contradictory images."

The first episode takes place in the past, during the rise of Fascism, and treats the impressions of Rome formed from afar by the narrator as a schoolboy in the North. The first impression the narrator can remember is that of a mysterious stone marker which reads, "Roma, 340 Km." Later, the schoolboys are led to the Rubicon by their teacher who declaims with great drama in his voice on Caesar's crossing. He leads the boys across "to Rome." In the center of the village, we are shown a statue of Caesar, with half his face missing. "Old half-head" is joked about by a villager. In the theater, we see a dramatization of Brutus' stabbing of Caesar. Stories of the Empire are presented in school. We witness a slide showing of Roman art and architecture, which ends abruptly when a "nudie picture," slipped in, doubtless, by a schoolboy, appears on the screen. A family dinner is interrupted with the Pope's blessing and the ringing of the bells of St. Peter's come on the radio. At the movies, the family of the narrator scrambles for seats to watch a story of the Empire, involving gladiators. The father sits open-mouthed; the mother cries. A newsreel shows Fascist youth. In the movie-house, the sexy wife of the dentist is pointed out to us by the narrator. We next see her making love in a car outside. Some villagers watch. She, then, seems to be transformed into a Roman empress. At the end of the segment, the boy of the family watches the train from Rome arrive and dreams of Rome.

The second segment, also in the past, at the beginning of WWII, describes the arrival in Rome of the narrator as a young man. He is dressed in a brand new white suit and he intends to become a journalist. At the station he is recognized as a young man from the provinces by a "salesman" who offers to sell him a lighter, some English cloth goods, and/or a room with a French girl in it. The young man arrives at the pension run by the Palletta family where he will stay. The maid introduces him to the family and other residents. The sequence of the introductions is, in fact, a portrait gallery of character types. The young man meets the following: the mountainous mother of the Palletta family, in bed with inflamed ovaries; her lazy sunburned son, who at the end of the sequence crawls into bed with his mother to be comforted and assumes the fetal position; a Chinaman who cooks spaghetti in his room; a tiny grandmother rocking in a chair in her room; a woman washing her hair in the kitchen; the actor who previously played Caesar in the young man's village and now tries to impress him with his movie credentials; a number of old men, one of whom looks like Mussolini; and a vast horde of small children. This portrait gallery continues in the next sequence. The young man takes a meal at a sidewalk restaurant on the Via Albalonga. The hostess, proud of her handsome customer, leads the young

man through the tables to find just the right spot for him.
Finally, she seats him with a Roman family of four. The daughter chews gum and sticks her tongue out goodnaturedly to greet
him. The mother complains of heartburn. The camera dollies
among the tables and then tracks with a streetsinger. A
haughty young woman in a disdainful pose is shown on her balcony above the commotion. She is called down by her lover, who
is wearing his hairnet. All eat with gusto. The "countess"
comes down and her lover puts his arm around her and calls her
a "big shit." At the table of the narrator, the mother tells
him she never eats snails, as he is doing, at a restaurant.
Finally we see the street after the eaters have gone. We can
make out the shadows of dogs eating scraps of food and the
flashes of the welder's torch of a man repairing the trolley
line. The last shots show a shepherd driving his sheep through
the deserted city and a prostitute among ancient ruins imper-
iously looking over the city.

The third segment is in the present time. It describes the
entry into Rome by Fellini and his camera crew and a typical
day of shooting. Fellini appears as himself in this segment.
The first sequence takes place on the Raccordo Anulare, the
superhighway skirting Rome. The toll collector is upset. He
does not approve of the line-up for the day's soccer match between Rome and Naples. Fellini's crew travels in a station-
wagon and a truck with a camera crane on it. A Roman truck
driver calls them "bums" as a greeting. Prostitutes, female
and male, ply their trade on the side of the highway. A rider-
less white horse and men with handcarts mingle in the traffic.
The rain begins to fall, and traffic moves slowly. People in
a bus from Naples with a team banner throw firecrackers and
receive jeers from a Roman in a Fiat. The camera crew films
it all. A dog in the back of a truck barks at a dog in an elegant sedan. A man holding up a gilt mirror on the back of a
truck, for a moment, appears to be flying in the reflected sky.
Tanks roll along. Night falls, and lights come on. The crew
fire flares into the air so they can photograph. Motorcycle
police pass the two vehicles to take charge at an accident on
the road ahead. We see that a truck carrying cattle has
crashed. The highway is strewn with carcasses, and the truck
is in flames. The two vehicles pass, only to get caught in a
traffic jam. We see occupants of other cars talking and ges-
turing behind their closed windows, but cannot hear their words.
Gradually we can make out that the cause of the jam up is a
protest march by Marxists. The sequence ends with shots of a
giant traffic jam in the street beside the Colosseum.

The second sequence of this section opens in daylight with
a crane shot of a strange, crosslike tree. The crew is on
location at the Villa Borghese. A bus of English-speaking
ladies arrive. They scurry to photograph each other. A smiling gigolo approaches and offers to photograph one of the

ladies. She poses for him. A Roman citizen tells Fellini to show the best side of Rome in his movie. Some Marxist young people criticize the film for its lack of political statement.

The fourth segment returns us to a small, variety theater as it was at the beginning of WWII. The first act features a chorus line of girls dressed in a vaguely Spanish way. The music resembles Ravel's "Bolero" at a slow tempo. Into the theater march two young men. One wears sunglasses which he raises to get a better look at the girls. They join a friend in an undershirt. A belly-dancer moves on stage. Someone moves closer for a better look and is insulted. A comedian comes on stage to do pantomines and is shouted down. He retorts he wants to make a living. The young man with the sunglasses leads a mock exodus. We see, at this point, that the narrator as a young man is in the audience. Three men made up as Oliver Hardy, Charlie Chaplin, and Ben Turpin try to sing, but receive a loud raspberry from the young man with sunglasses. A mother puts a child in the aisle to piss and is scolded by those behind her. A boy throws an object at a sleeping man. Then the M.C. announces amateur hour. Out comes a short, young electrician to imitate Fred Astaire. The young man in the undershirt hurls a dead cat on the stage. The dancing electrician throws it back with the taunt, "Is this your dinner?" and the audience applauds his spirit. The next attraction is the Kent Trio who sing harmony like the Andrews sisters. They sing the "Donkey Serenade." A man apparently injured in the war is helped inside. The show is stopped at this point for the announcement that the allied invasion of Sicily is being met strongly by Italian and German forces. "The cowardly attack," the announcer says, "will be repulsed for the glory of our land and il Duce." The show resumes. Girls in sailor suits dance on the deck of a mock battleship. The air-raid alert sounds, and the people move to the shelter. There the narrator as a young man meets an "artiste." She is German, and her husband is in Russia. She invites the young man home with her, but before they can leave, they witness a woman running toward them, screaming that a house has been bombed. A man runs to her and then runs on into the area she has come from. An ambulance, its siren on, moves in the same direction.

The fifth segment, in the present, shows the camera crew going down beneath Rome into excavations for a subway. The engineer explains to the crew that the excavation must proceed cautiously because of the archaeological artifacts that exist in the subsoil. Amusingly, the crew seems to ride through a tunnel of documents when the engineer explains about the administrative red-tape connected with the project, and we see a frightened couple react to the shaking of their bedroom when the car passes in the tunnel beneath them. The car passes a necropolis. When the crew arrives at the end of the tunnel, they find excavation stopped, because a hollow spot has been detected ahead. The excavators punch through a wall into a villa strangely preserved below ground. We cross-cut between

123

the drill outside the wall cutting in and the art objects inside which seem to wait quietly for the break-in. After the
drill makes an opening, members of the crew explore the house
with their flashlights. They see bright frescoes and statues
two thousand years old. As they watch, the frescoes fade,
destroyed by the air from outside.

The sixth segment begins in the present, but soon moves
back to the past of the narrator's early years in Rome. The
crew photographs the young hippies on the Spanish Steps, and
the narrator remarks on their sexual openness. This leads him
to recall the inhibitions of his generation. "We had to hide
to make love...," he says. "It was so difficult to make love.
So one went to the whorehouse. There were brothels of all
types, hidden away in the narrow streets of the old quarter....
It was furtive, haunted, sinful, and everywhere the sound of
bells followed us." The first brothel we visit is a working
class one. The camera positions us behind a crowd of men in a
tiled corridor. Only above the heads of them can we make out
the girls coming down the steps. One member of the crowd keeps
jumping up in the air to see the girls. Next we enter a
slightly more spacious brothel. There is a wooden rail sepa-
rating the men from the women on display. Again the camera
places us among the men. The women walk up and down in front
of the crowd, entreating or challenging the potential customers.
Then the camera moves us to the other side of the barrier for
a better look at the parade of the women. The brothel closes,
and the women sit to rest. Next, we see a "luxury" brothel.
The narrator as a young man is present, with a friend who gig-
gles. The women descend in an elevator to the ornate waiting
room where the men are. These prostitutes too, however, parade
before the men. Descending in the elevator by herself, a beautiful, dark-haired prostitute arrives. The young man stares
at her, but she is quickly chosen by an army officer. Sometimes, the narrator tells us, important personages ascend
secretly to the upper floors to make their choices in private.
He speculates on who such people were. The young man relates
that sometimes he went to the brothel in the early morning when
he could have the beautiful one. We see him in her room as
she dresses. He asks her many questions about her life and
invites her out.

The seventh section appears to begin in the present, but it
moves quickly to fantasy. The narrator takes us to the palace
of an aged princess, "the prisoner of a world that doesn't
exist anymore." We tour the palace, looking at portraits.
There appears a Cardinal suddenly who is welcomed as if to a
party. Other guests, some from the past, come forward. The
Cardinal greets members of the princess' family. All sit, and
the Cardinal accepts a glass of crème de menthe. A fashion
show is presented to the guests. Down the runway, come two
nuns in black satin outfits designed for novices, two nuns with
immaculate white, turtle dove headdress, and two little sisters

of the temptations in Purgatory. The announcer calls next for
sports models. Two priests on rollerskates come out. "You
get there faster," the announcer tells us. Two country priests
on little bicycles move by. Then three models for sacristans.
New materials for ecclesiastical ornament are displayed. Robes
with nobody in them march through. A matyred saint appears to
model her veil. A procession of Popes is followed by a float
of skeletons. The audience rises. Scenery descends from the
flies. And at the center of a shining, artificial sun appears
a Pope who resembles Pius XII.

The final segment takes place in Rome of the present era.
The narrator takes us first to the "Festa De Noantri" (The
Festival of Ourselves) in Trastevere on the left bank of the
Tiber, the artists' quarter. The camera dollies among the
crowd. The camera crew comes across Gore Vidal. He explains
that he lives in Rome because it is the city of illusion. As
the world ends through overpopulation, he chooses to live in
Rome to watch the end of the last illusion. Soldiers arrive
to drive off a gathering of young hippies who are singing by a
fountain near the restaurants. "They are the dregs of society!"
shouts one diner about the hippies. We switch from the battle
of soldiers and hippies to a prize fight staged in a ring
mounted in the street. The winner is carried through the
streets. Eventually the crowd thins out. The crew follows
actress Anna Magnani to her home. The narrator tells her that
she sums up Rome for him, "Rome seen as vestal virgin and she-
wolf, an aristocrat and a tramp, a somber buffoon." He wishes
to ask her a question, but she sends him away. "I'm sorry. I
don't trust you. Ciao, go to sleep," she tells him. The
movie concludes with a sequence of helmeted motorcyclists,
like night demons, speeding through the deserted streets and
squares.

Credits

Producer:	Turi Vasile (An Italo-French co-production for Ultra Film and Les Productions Artistes Associés)
Director:	Federico Fellini
Screenplay:	Fellini, Bernardino Zapponi
Photography:	Giuseppe Rotunno (Technicolor)
Cameramen:	Giuseppe Maccari, Piero Servo, Roberto Aristarco, Michele Picciaredda
Art Director:	Danilo Donati
Assistant Art Directors:	Giorgio Giovannini, Ferdinando Giovannoni
Assistant Set and Costume Designers:	Romano Massara, Rita Giacchero
Set Painter:	Italo Tomassi
Music:	Nino Rota
Conductor:	Carlo Savina

Editor:	Ruggero Mastroianni
Assistant Editor:	Adriana Olasio
Assistant Director:	Maurizio Mein
Director's Aides:	Paolo Pietrangeli, Tonino Antonucci
Production Supervisor:	Danilo Marciani
Production Manager:	Lamberto Pippia
Production Inspectors:	Allessandro Gori, Fernando Rossi, Allessandro Sarti
Script-girl:	Norma Giacchero
Special Effects:	Adriano Pischiutta
Frescoes and Portraits:	Rinaldo - Antonello - Giuliano - Geleng
Make-up:	Rino Carboni
Hair Stylist:	Amalia Paoletti
Dialogue Secretary:	Marie-Claude Francine Decroix
Set Photographer:	G. B. Poletto
Mixing:	Renato Cadueri
Choreography:	Gino Landi
Post-synchronization:	Mario Maldesi
Cast:	Peter Gonzales (Fellini as a young man), Fiona Florence, Britta Barnes, Pia De Doses, Marne Maitland, Renato Giovannoli, Elisa Mainardi, Paule Rout, Galliano Sbarra, Paola Natale, Marcelle-Ginette Bron, Mario Del Vago, Alfredo Adami, Stefano Mauore, Alberto Sordi, Marcello Mastroianni, Gore Vidal, Anna Magnani.
Filmed on location in Rome and in the studios of Cinecittà.	
Distribution:	United Artists
Running Time:	113 minutes
Distribution:	Italy: March, 1972
	U.S.: October 15, 1972 (NYC)

17   AMARCORD [I REMEMBER] (1974)

The movie begins in spring. We are in a small, provincial seaside town in the mid-1930's. Clusters of seeds float through the air. They fly past the home of Titta, the protagonist of the film, who is a boy of about fourteen.

That night the townspeople turn out for a celebration of spring. People bring pieces of wood to burn in fires called forgarazze. In the main piazza, Giudizio, the village fool, stands on top of a pyre, arranging wood. An effigy of the Witch of Winter is brought to the pyre. Gradisca, the town vamp, lights a torch, and the master of ceremonies applies it to the pyre. Titta's uncle, il Pataca (The Bad Penny), takes

away the ladder from the pyre, forcing Giudizio to scramble
and fall to safety. The people circle the fire. A group of
boys threaten to throw into the flames a pretty and retarded
girl, Volpina. She squirms like a wild animal and escapes.
Il Pataca begins a game of jumping over embers. "Greased
Lightning," a motorcyclist, roars through the square, making
people leap out of his way. Later when the square is nearly
deserted, a scholarly man known as the Lawyer advances to the
camera and begins to lecture us on the history of the town.
From the darkness, an unseen adversary launches a series of
raspberries at the Lawyer.

In the courtyard of the school, an official photograph of
Titta's class is being taken. Ciccio, a pudgy boy with a
cherubic face, calls to the pretty and haughty Aldina Cordini
who ignores him. Gigliozzi, a tall, thin boy, puts a frog up
to the face of a chubby girl in front of him. At last, the
photograph is taken.

Science class. The teacher holds up a stone on a string.
"What is it?" he asks. Ciccio responds, "The ball of an elephant." "A pendulum," announces the teacher.

History class. Titta is at the desk of the teacher, answer-
ing questions. The teacher is smoking. He tries to keep a
long ash on the tip of his cigarette. Titta misses a question
and bangs the teacher's desk in anger. The ash falls from the
teacher's cigarette.

Italian class. The teacher recites verses, spraying the
students in the first several rows with saliva.

Philosophy class. The teacher mimes the ideas he discusses.
He crawls behind a wardrobe to illustrate the loss of one's
self in an intellectual abyss.

Religion class. The priest Don Balosa discusses the Holy
Trinity. He closes his eyes as he speaks, and one by one the
students slip out of the room.

Art history. The teacher is a genteel, elderly woman. She
pours coffee from a thermos, munches a biscuit, and lectures
on Giotto. Titta raises his hand and announces that Bobo has
farted. Bobo, a fat boy in glasses, denies the charge.

Math class. Miss Leonardis, a tall woman with large breasts,
who wears a tight sweater, stands at the blackboard with a well
groomed student named Candela. She tries to get him to solve
a problem. With the help of friends, Gigliozzi pieces together
sections of rolled up maps. He pisses through this long "pipe-
line" and leaves a puddle of urine near Candela for Miss
Leonardis to discover.

Greek class. The teacher tries to get the student Ovo to
pronounce the word emarpzamen. Ovo's attempts sound like
raspberries.

Titta, Ovo, and Ciccio smoke in the restroom and look out
the window toward the seashore. On the jetty, "Greased Lightning" drives his motorcycle. Further down the beach, Volpina

127

walks about, calling her cat. She looks around, lifts up her
dress, squats down, and urinates in the sand.

Volpina approaches a house under construction on the sand.
The foreman of the bricklayers is Titta's father. He shooes
Volpina away. A bricklayer recites a poem on the irony that
the bricklayer's family has no house of its own. Titta's
father preaches the virtues of hard work and patience.

The family meal in the kitchen of Titta's house. The grandfather touches the maid on the buttocks. The mother serves il
Pataca, her brother, solicitously. She herself refuses to eat.
The father loses patience with her. The maid announces to the
father that Mr. Biondi is at the door. Il Pataca juggles some
table objects to amuse Oliva, Titta's younger brother. The
father returns to the table, asks Titta about his activities
at the movies on the previous night, and then makes a lunge
for his son. A chase ensues that takes father and son outside
the house. Scandalized, the mother calls her husband back.
He explains that Titta pissed from the balcony of the movie
theater onto Biondi's hat. The mother defends Titta and then
storms off to lock herself in the lavatory. The father rips
the table cloth and dishes from the table.

During an evening on the main street, the townspeople stroll
and shop. Titta and his friends follow Gradisca as she walks,
her hips swinging bouncily, with her sisters. She, in turn,
smiles at Gerarca, the Fascist Party Leader, and stops at the
movie theater to ask the manager when the next Gary Cooper
film will arrive. (The manager dresses and trims his mustache
to look like Ronald Coleman.) A carriage passes down the
street. Seated in it are Madam Dora and the new prostitutes
she has brought to town. Later we see the street nearly deserted. Suddenly, "Greased Lightning" drives down it with an
earsplitting roar. Still later, in front of the palace of
Count Lovignano, we discover a sewer worker descending through
a manhole into the sewer line to search for a ring lost by the
Countess. The Count and the Countess watch from their window.

At church, Don Balosa hears Titta's confession. He asks
Titta about masturbation. We see figures of Titta's fantasy:
the huge tobacco shop woman with enormous breasts; the math
teacher in her tight sweater; and statuesque peasant women
slowly mounting their bicycles outside of church. Titta recounts stories about Volpina and Gradisca. We see the stories.
In the first, Titta helps Volpina pump up a bicycle tire and
she leans toward him to kiss him. In the second, Titta shifts
closer and closer to Gradisca in a sparsely occupied movie
house. At last, he moves into the seat next to her and puts
his hand on her thigh, "Looking for something?" she asks, star-
ing at his hand. Don Balosa tells Titta his penance. Gigliozzi, Ciccio, and Candela follow Titta to confession. Later
we see these three and another boy masturbating in a car in a
garage. The car bounces up and down, and its headlights
flicker.

In the square in front of the railroad station, various Fascist groups are assembled. The day is April 21, the celebration day for the founding of Rome. Titta is present as a member of the youth group Avantguardisti, and il Pataca as a member of the Fascist militia. Gradisca, the Lawyer, and the headmaster of the school are seen in the crowd. Gerarca welcomes to town a federal official of the Fascist Party. This official leads the people in a trot to the ceremony in the main square.

At Titta's house, the father discovers that he has been locked in by his wife. She undoes his black, anarchist ribbon from his neck.

The various Fascist youth groups perform exercises on the main square. Suddenly, a giant head of Mussolini, formed from flowers, is erected. The people salute it. Ciccio who is among the Avantguardisti fantasizes that Aldina Cordini and he march toward the giant head to be married.

That night Gerarca and the federal official are in the Commerical Cafe. Il Pataca and his friends are playing billards. The lights go out. The socialist anthem, the "International," played on a violin can be heard. The group traces the sound to the bell tower of the church, and they make out an old phonograph up in the tower. A Fascist shoots down the machine.

At Fascist Party Headquarters, Titta's father is led in as a prisoner. He is questioned by Gerarca about the incident of the phonograph, and he is forced to drink castor oil.

Titta's mother meets her husband in the street and leads him home. Inside the house, she rinses excrement from him in a wooden tub. Titta enters. "Papa, you smell," he gasps out. The father goes to the foot of the stairs and shouts in the direction of il Pataca's room that there is a betrayer in the house.

On the terrace of the Grand Hotel, the Lawyer explains that the hotel is the seat of love in the town. To illustrate, he tells how Gradisca got her name, which means "Please do," at the Grand Hotel. We see the story unfold. Gradisca approaches the hotel in an expensive car with a local political official. He urges her to win for the town the favor of the prince she will meet. The prince may help them finance the completion of their seaside promenade. Gradisca sweeps through the lobby of the hotel and enters the prince's room. As she undresses, she assumes various cheesecake poses. The prince pours a glass of champagne. Then we discover Gradisca in bed, wearing only a jaunty, red beret. "Please do," she says to the prince.

Seated on a divan in the hotel, with a drink in his hand, the Lawyer launches into another story. This one concerns Pinwheel, the peanut vendor. Again we see the story the Lawyer presents. A bus full of the concubines of an emir arrives. Pinwheel drives his peanut wagon up to the hotel and watches. Later that night, the concubines throw out sheets for Pinwheel to climb up. We see him inside the hotel playing a recorder

129

to the women who rise up around him. In voice-over narration, the Lawyer tells us Pinwheel's claim to have made love twenty-eight times that night.

Couples dance on the terrace of the hotel in the evening. Hidden behind some plants, Titta and his friends watch. "White Feather," a handsome man with a streak of white in his hair, establishes eye contact with two American women, perhaps mother and daughter, and invites the older one to dance. Il Pataca leads off a young woman to the beach. The Lawyer joins a Scandinavian woman and tries to tell her about the poets Leopardi and Dante. Il Pataca returns from the beach and confides to a friend that the lady granted him "posterior intimacy." Slowly the lights fade.

In a horse drawn cart, Titta's family picks up Uncle Teo from an insane asylum and takes him for an outing at a farm leased out by Titta's father. Teo shows them his pocketful of stones. He leaves the cart to urinate, but forgets to undo his fly. At the farm, Titta's family and the family of the farmer eat outdoors. Teo climbs a high, solitary tree and cries out, "I want a woman." He hurls stones at the various males who try to climb up to get him. At last, a midget nun arrives from the asylum, leads him down from the tree, and returns him to the asylum.

A day in summer. The people go to the beach and enter water craft. The oceanliner Rex is going to pass the town on its maiden voyage, and the townspeople wish to get a close look. Gradisca and her sisters go out on a paddle craft with Ronald Coleman. Il Pataca swims out. As night falls, Titta's father looks up from his small boat and marvels at how the stars are suspended in the heavens. Gradisca tells of her longing to marry the right man. The Rex arrives. At first, it terrifies the people, for it seems to come straight at them. But, when they realize it will pass at a distance, they stare enchanted at the shape which glitters with lights.

A foggy morning in autumn near Titta's house. The grandfather is outside. He becomes terrified when, for a moment, he can't find his way back to the house. Oliva leaves for school and is frightened by shapes he sees in the fog.

On a grey, damp day, leaves swirl on the terrace of the Grand Hotel which is closed for the season. Titta and his friends dance with imaginary partners. "Where are you, my love?" sighs Titta.

A banner on the main street announces the <u>Thousand Miles</u> auto race which will pass through town. Crowds line the sides of the street. Titta and Ciccio are in the crowd. Ciccio calls to Aldina who is sitting in a window, but she spurns him. Titta fantasizes that he wins the race and drives off with Gradisca. Ciccio fantasizes that he wins the race and gives Aldina an obscene gesture. The night ends with il Pataca's discovery of the ear of a dog hit by one of the racing cars.

Another evening. Titta passes by the tobacco shop. The
iron shutter is pulled halfway down. Titta ducks under. He
wishes to buy a cigarette. The tobacconist is the huge, buxom
woman of Titta's fantasies at confession. He offers to help
her move a heavy sack. She tells him that he isn't strong
enough. To demonstrate his strength, Titta lifts her up again
and again. Excited by the physical intimacy, the tobacconist
takes her breasts from her sweater and plunges them into Titta's
face. Confused and overwhelmed, Titta sputters that he can't
breathe. The tobacconist pulls away, gives Titta his cigarette,
and orders him to leave.

Titta is in bed with a fever. His mother comforts him.
She tells him about her husband's courtship of her and about
their elopement. Titta, however, is wrapped up in a love
affair of his own and speaks of going away to Africa to punish
the girl who has mistreated him.

An evening in winter. Giudizio runs into the movie theater
and summons the audience outside to see a snowfall. (Snow is
rare on the Adriatic coast where the town of <u>Amarcord</u> is
located.) All over town, people watch the snow come down. A
man sets up a trap for sparrows with crumbs in the snow.

Day on the main square. Paths have been shoveled through
the snow. The banks of snow are very high. The Lawyer announces to us that the snowfall was a record one. He is hit
by a snowball. Gradisca's head can be seen as she walks
through the maze of paths, wearing her red beret. Titta spies
her and tries unsuccessfully to follow her. Don Balosa encounters Titta and asks, in a serious tone, about his mother's
health. Titta replies that she is still in the hospital.

Titta and his father visit the mother in the hospital.
Titta half-jokes and half-complains about his father's discipline at home.

Outside the Commerce Cafe, il Pataca engages Gradisca in a
snowball fight. Titta rushes to her aid, but she hits him in
the face accidently with a snowball intended for another assail-
ant. The battle is interrupted by the flight of the Count's
peacock overhead. The bird lands and spreads its magnificent
tail to the delight of all those who have gathered to watch it.

At Titta's house early in a spring morning, Titta leaves
his room and discovers the house filling up with relatives. A
young cousin announces that her aunt is dead. Titta rushes to
his parents' bedroom, now empty, and locks himself in the room.

In church, Don Balosa presides over the funeral service of
Titta's mother. Il Pataca faints during the service and must
be carried home. Then the funeral procession makes its way to
the cemetery. Finally, Titta and Oliva return to the house
together. Titta sees his father sitting along at the kitchen
table. Titta goes to the beach and stares at the sea. He
catches a cluster of seeds blowing in the spring air.

Gradisca's wedding dinner in an open field under a structure
of straw mats. Gradisca sits at a long table with her husband,

a bald, chubby police officer. Ronald Coleman makes a toast.
Don Balosa blesses the couple. Gradisca cries. The photographer begins to take pictures. A short burst of rain drives
the group under the mats. As the rain stops, Gradisca prepares to leave. Titta is a bit drunk. He announces that he
wants to go home. He runs after some carriages which are pulling away. Gradisca and her husband go to a car, and she
throws her bouquet. The couple drives away. Those who have
remained in the field call goodbye.

Credits

Producer:	Franco Cristaldi (An Italo-French co-production for F.C. Productions, Rome, and P.E.C.F., Paris)
Director:	Federico Fellini
Screenplay:	Fellini, Tonino Guerra
Photography:	Giuseppe Rotunno (Panavision, Technicolor)
Cameramen:	Giuseppe Maccari, Massimo di Venanzo, Roberto Aristarco
Art Director:	Danilo Donati
Music:	Nino Rota
Conductor:	Carlo Savina
Sound:	Oscar De Arcangelis
Post-synchronization:	Mario Maldesi
Editor:	Ruggero Mastroianni
Assistant Directors:	Maurizio Mein, Liliana Betti, Nestore Baratella, Gerald Morin
Script-girl:	Norma Giacchero
Production Manager:	Lamberto Pippia
Production Supervisors:	Alessandro Gori, Gilberto Scarpellini
Special Effects:	Adriano Pischiutta
Animation:	Rino Carboni
Make-up:	Amalia Paoletti
Cast:	Bruno Zanin (Titta), Pupella Maggio (Titta's mother), Armando Brancia (Titta's father), Giuseppe Lanigro (Titta's grandfather), Magali Noel (Gradisca), Stefano Proietti (Oliva), Nando Orfei (il Pataca), Carla Mora (the maid), Ciccio Ingrassia (Uncle Teo), Luigi Rossi (the Lawyer), Maria Antonietta Beluzzi (the tobacconist), Josiane Tanzilli (Volpina), Gennaro Ombra (Pinwheel), Gianfilippo Carcano (Don Balosa), Aristide Caporale (Giud- izio), Ferrucio Brembilia (the Fascist leader), Antonio Faa' Di Bruno (Count Lovignano), Gianfranco Marrocco (Count Poltavo), Alvaro

Vitali (Naso), Bruno Scagnetti
(Ovo), Bruno Lenzi (Gigliozzi),
Fernando de Felice (Ciccio), Fran-
cesco Vona (Candela), Donatella
Gambini (Aldina Cordini), Franco
Magno (Zeus, the school principal),
Mauro Misul (the philosophy teacher),
Armando Villella (Fighetta), Dina
Adorni (the math teacher), Francesco
Maselli (the physics teacher), Mario
Silvestri (the Italian teacher),
Fides Stagni (the history teacher),
Marcello Bonini Alos (the gym
teacher), Domemco Pertica (the
blind man), Fausto Signoretti (the
coachman), Fredo Pistoni (Colonia),
Mario Liberati (the proprietor of
the Fulgor), Mario Nebolini (the
secretary of city hall), Vincenzo
Caldarola (the begger), Fiorella
Magalotti and Marina Trovalusci
(Gradisca's sisters), Milo Mario
(the photographer), Antonio Spac-
catini (the Federal Officer),
Bruno Bartocci (Gradisca's bride-
groom), Marco Laurentino, Riccardo
Satta, Carmela Eusepi, Clemente
Baccherini, Mario Del Vago, Marcello
Di Falco.

Distribution:	American International Pictures
Running Time:	127 minutes
Released:	Italy: February 18, 1974
	U.S.: September 19, 1974 (NYC)

18   IL CASANOVA [CASANOVA] (1976)

The film opens on a festive carnival in Venice. A large
crowd of Venetians in richly brocaded and grotesque costumes
lines the canal. Music and fireworks fill the air. The crowd
begins to recite a poem, "Venice, Our Queen," as a very large
sculpted head of a goddess is lifted from the canal. They suc-
ceed in hoisting the head half-way out of the water and then
the support poles collapse, and it sinks back into the canal.
A hooded figure is handed a note. The person lowers the hood
and is revealed to be Casanova. The note comes from a secret
admirer, a nun, who would like to arrange an assignation with
Casanova that evening on the island of San Bartolo.

That night, Casanova arrives on the island and sees the nun
by an old castle. They enter and she leads him down a hallway
decorated with Oriental, erotic murals. They enter a large

bed-chamber, and the nun tells Casanova that their lovemaking
will be observed by the French Ambassador who is spying on
them through the eye of a fish which decorates one wall.
Casanova shows her a gilded, mechanical bird which he sets on
a table. In the manner of a music box, it plays music, and
the bird spins and flaps its wings. She undresses under
Casanova's loose gown, and they begin their very stylized love-
making. They end up under the eye of the fish. Their intercourse takes on aspects of a highly choreographed wrestling
match. Casanova, shot from below, appears to be a man posses-
sed by the mechanics of intercourse. He pumps up and down as
if doing push-ups. Following orgasm, Casanova is congratulated
by the Ambassador for "a truly admirable piece of work."
Casanova acknowledges the compliment and introduces himself as
an intellectual and inventor who could be of service to the
French government. He asks the Ambassador for letters of
introduction to the Court, but the Ambassador has gone.

Casanova is rowing a boat on a canal during a violent storm.
The scene calls attention to the billowing sheets of black
plastic which make up the "canal." A large gondola appears
and one of the occupants informs Casanova of his arrest by the
Inquisition.

In court Casanova is accused of Black Magic and is found
guilty. Quickly, he is led to his cell in a dank and muddy
dungeon of the Piombi Prison. As he sits dejectedly, he muses
in voice-over narration about "the pleasant days."

In flashback, we see a number of women sewing in a shop.
Casanova speaks to one of the women, a very pale young girl
named Anna Maria. A well-dressed woman arrives, and Casanova
follows her to a back room. They sit down to a meal. The
woman complains of a very disobedient man while she eats vorac-
iously. She begs for mortification, and Casanova whips her
across the buttocks.

When Casanova goes back into the sewing room, he finds Anna
Maria dancing on a make-shift stage. They dance together to
the accompaniment of a harpsichord while the other women look
on. Anna Maria faints. An old doctor promptly arrives and
bleeds her. She awakens, and Casanova voices his love for her.

Sometime later, Casanova is startled from sleep. He goes
out into a courtyard and sees Anna Maria. "You're so pale, I
thought you were Diana become mortal," he tells her. She
faints again. Casanova begins to make love to her, but is
interrupted by the doctor who bleeds her. She revives, but
faints again. Casanova carries her into the villa and begins
to have intercourse with her. Again he is shot from below as
he pumps up and down.

Casanova is rowing a gondola. He sings to Anna Maria who
sits quietly and smiles.

Back in prison, Casanova, carrying the box which contains
his mechanical bird, is escaping. We see him crawling over

the roof while he says, in voice-over, that the escape was a masterpiece of planning, "favored, of course, by fortune."

Casanova is seated at a small banquet in the home of Madame D'Urfé in Paris. He is surrounded by an odd assortment of aristocrats, clerics, magicians, and mediums. He engages a priest in a philosophical discussion concerning the soul of a woman. Casanova's wit carries the day, and he wins the argument. The elderly Madame D'Urfé stares at Casanova, and their gazes meet.

Madame D'Urfé leaves the banquet, and Casanova follows her to her bed-chamber. It is decorated with various magical and alchemical objects and symbols. She asks him for the secret of the philosopher's stone, but she says he does not possess such knowledge. She asks for his assistance in her "Great Work." She dreams of being transformed into a man by passing her soul into a child. She wants Casanova to impregnate her so that the process can be initiated. Casanova begins to cry. She shows him a chest of money which will be his when the "Great Work" is completed.

Later that night, Casanova is riding in a carriage. He is singing joyfully about Paris. The carriage swerves to avoid hitting a cleric, and it overturns. Casanova confronts the man only to find that he is his brother. Casanova meets the woman, Marcolina, who is travelling with his brother. They engage in a furious bout of intercourse in Casanova's room while the brother is locked out. Casanova tells her that he needs her assistance in an intrigue with Madame D'Urfé.

In Madame D'Urfé's chambers, Casanova and Marcolina are chanting gibberish while the older woman bathes. Following Casanova's instructions, Marcolina lifts Madame D'Urfé from the bath and carries her to Casanova who is wearing a large flaming headdress. He carries her to the bed as a swish pan reveals the gilded bird. Casanova has intercourse with the old woman, aided by Marcolina who stands on the other side of the room and gives him "encouragement" by wiggling her buttocks. The mechanical bird whirls furiously. Again, Casanova is photographed from below as he pushes up and down.

In voice-over narration, Casanova says that he will tell how he met "the love of my life." We see Casanova intervening in a quarrel between an innkeeper and a tenant. The tenant, a Hungarian soldier, is being evicted for sneaking a woman into the hotel disguised as a man.

In a carriage with the soldier and the young woman, Henriette, Casanova, in voice-over, is musing about the identity of this mysterious couple. He talks with the soldier in Latin. The Hungarian says he knows nothing about the girl and gives her to Casanova to protect.

Casanova and Henriette attend a banquet at a villa in Parma. The host, DuBois, is a hunchback. The guests include many French and Spanish aristocrats. Casanova is discoursing on man's subjugation of women. He says that most men are tyrannical, but one must suffer at the hands of a woman in order to know her. DuBois takes exception to this. The entertainment begins. Two castrati, dressed in white, come out onto the stage. DuBois, in an androgynous costume, dances and sings with them. A beautiful male dancer begins to perform. He and DuBois begin a ritualized love dance with DuBois seemingly destroying and devouring the young man. The servants laugh, the French guests applaud, and the Spanish are appalled. Casanova voices displeasure with the homosexual theme of the dance. Henriette begins to play a beautiful, sad song on the 'cello. Casanova begins to cry and goes out into the sculpted gardens. A large, mysterious man arrives, and Henriette stops her song. Later that night Casanova pledges his love to Henriette. As they begin to make love, the gilded bird starts up.

The next morning, Casanova awakens alone in bed. DuBois is present and informs him that Henriette has left with the mysterious man from the party. DuBois warns Casanova not to look for her, but Casanova vows to search her out regardless of any consequences, saying, "She is the only woman I will ever love."

An older Casanova rides in a coach with a woman and her daughter. The setting is London. The mother is in a heated argument with Casanova about the fact that Casanova's sexual prowess is failing. She also says that he owes her money. She draws a pistol, takes some of Casanova's belongings, and throws him out of the carriage. The carriage drives off and Casanova angrily throws and kicks his bags around a deserted street. He talks to himself, saying that he is getting older and the possibility of impotence is more than he can take. On a bridge overlooking the Thames, he contemplates suicide. He throws his hat into the water, picks up a rock, and begins to walk into the river. As he is preparing to dash his head against the rock, he sees a giantess with two dwarves walking on the shore. He calls to them but they cannot hear him. They leave, and Casanova follows them.

Casanova finds himself at a carnival. In contrast to the Venetian carnival, this fair is dirty and dingy. A barker stands in front of a huge wooden whale. He is exhorting the men to enter and discover the mysteries of Mouna. A long line of dirty, crippled men enter the whale's mouth. Casanova joins the line. Inside the walls are covered by a series of magic lantern "slides" of female genitalia. The pictures become grotesque images.

Casanova enters a dingy pub. Inside the giantess is arm wrestling with any man who will challenge her. The men taunt Casanova into a test of his strength. He asks her to let him win, but she easily defeats him.

Casanova follows the giantess and her two dwarves to a large cage-like arena. One of the dwarves tells Casanova that here the giantess fights against men who challenge her strength.

136

As Casanova watches, the scene is transformed into one of her contests in which she defeats all of her challengers.

Casanova goes to the tent of the giantess. He peers in from outside as the dwarves undress the giantess and she gets into a large tub to bathe. The dwarves get in also, and they listen as she sings softly. Casanova sleeps outside. In the morning, they have gone.

A brief scene in the Vatican. Casanova kisses the hand of the Pope. The Pope caresses Casanova's head.

Casanova is attending a drunken banquet in the opulent villa in Rome of Lord Talou, English Ambassador to the Vatican. A grotesque race is in progress, and wine and food are being thrown about. A prince challenges Casanova's sexual prowess. A contest is proposed between Casanova and a peasant coachman to determine which one is the better man. They each choose a partner from among the assembled guests and the contest begins. Casanova's partner remains passive throughout the ordeal. Again, Casanova is shot from below as he moves up and down. Casanova is victorious and is carried triumphantly around the room, while the loser's partner continues to exhort her fatigued lover.

Casanova is in Bern at the home of a famous entomologist, Dr. Moebius. He is having a discussion with the doctor's two young daughters on science, philosophy, and psychic phenomena. Casanova passes out. The two women perform an acupuncture-like experiment on him. He is revived and feels better than ever. Casanova tries to seduce one of them, Isabella. He speaks in funereal images, and she comments on his language.

Casanova enters an inn in Dresden where he has arranged to meet Isabella. An actress introduces herself to Casanova as a former acquaintance. She introduces him to a hunchbacked girl, and Casanova asks for a room.

Casanova, the young, hunchbacked woman and the former acquaintance are in a large bed-closet in the center of a room at the inn. They begin to make love furiously. The entire closet begins to rock. The large shadow of the gilded bird covers one wall. Others join in the orgy, and soon they are all moving in one rhythm.

Casanova attends a performance of <u>Orpheus and Eurydice</u> staged by the troupe he has been cavorting with. Following the performance, the theater empties, but Casanova remains. He watches as the chandeliers are lowered, and men with large fans extinguish the candles. Someone calls to Casanova from one of the boxes. The voice chastises him as a scoundrel. Casanova recognizes the voice as that of his mother. He tells her about one of his inventions, but she is unimpressed. He carries her out to a carriage, and she drives away.

In voice-over narration, Casanova describes the next setting as the court at Wurttemberg. Another banquet is in progress, but the people are very shabbily dressed. Casanova is trying to sell himself and his inventions to a prince, but no one will

listen to him. They are being entertained by a large bank of
organs which cover an entire wall. The noise is deafening.
The prince has an invention of his own to show Casanova. A
lifesize mechanical woman is brought in. Casanova is amused.

Later that night, Casanova returns to the banquet room and
finds the mechanical doll. She rises and walks away from him.
He follows her, and they begin to dance. He dances her to a
bed, and he has sexual intercourse with the doll.

An aged Casanova is eating in the servants' quarters of a
castle in Bohemia. The others in the room are screaming and
carousing, but Casanova, like a spoiled child, is complaining
about his food. The others taunt him as he demands macaroni.

Casanova protests to the master of the house that he is
being vilely mistreated by the others. He takes the Count into
the latrine to show him that a drawing of Casanova has been
affixed to the wall with excrement.

The Count and his friends are having a party in the castle.
Casanova, dressed in all of his finery, hobbles down a long
staircase and joins the gathering. He is asked to perform,
and he responds by reciting a poem by Ariosto. The guests
laugh at his flowery gestures and his recitation. Casanova
bows and ascends the stairs. Up in his room, Casanova begins
to recall a dream of Venice.

In fantasy, a young Casanova walks on the frozen canals
of Venice. The head of the goddess peers up at him through
the ice. Many of his former lovers come to him and run off.
The mechanical doll appears. She takes his hand, and they
dance. A cut to the red eyes of the old Casanova in extreme
close-up. Then, again in fantasy, Casanova and the doll dance
on the frozen canal.

Credits

Producer:	Alberto Grimaldi (Universal)
Director:	Federico Fellini
Screenplay:	Fellini, Bernardino Zapponi
Poetry in Venetian Dialect:	Andrea Zanzotto
Additional Verse:	Tonino Guerra, Antonio Amurri, Carl Walken
Photography:	Giuseppe Rotunno
Set Design and Costumes:	Danilo Donati
Editor:	Ruggero Mastroianni
Music:	Nino Rota
Conductor:	Carlo Savina
Post-Production Coordinator:	Enzo Ocone
Set Designers:	Giantito Burchiellaro, Giorgio Giovannini
Assistant:	Antonello Geleng
Building Supervisor:	Italo Tomassi
Painters:	Rinaldo and Giuliano Geleng

Frescoes:	Mario Fallani
Magic Lantern Designer:	Roland Topor
Set Decorator:	Emilio D'Andria
Assistants to the Producer:	Alessandro von Normann, Mario di Biase
Production Supervisor:	Giorgio Morra
Production Manager:	Lamberto Pippia
Assistant Director:	Maurizio Mein
Assistants to the Director:	Liliana Betti, Gerald Morin, Anita Sanders
Production Secretary:	Norma Giacchero
English Dialogue Directors:	Frank Dunlop, Christopher Cruise
Casting:	Paola Rolli
Costume Assistants:	Gloria Mussetta, Raimonda Gaetani, Rita Giacchero
Sculptures:	Giovanni Gianese
Special Effects:	Adriano Pischiutta
Make-up:	Rino Carboni
Donald Sutherland's Make-up:	Giannetto De Rossi, Fabrizio Sforza
Hair Stylist:	Gabriella Borzelli
Choreographer:	Gino Landi
Dialogue Consultant:	Anthony Burgess
English Translation:	Christopher Cruise
Continuity:	Norma Giacchero
Assistant Production Managers:	Gilberto Scarpellini, Alessandro Gori, Fernando Rossi
Assistant Editors:	Adriana Olasio, Marcello Olasio, Ugo De Rossi
Costuming:	Tirelli, Farani
Jewelry:	Nino Lembo
Footwear:	L.C.P., S.R.L.
Wigs:	Rocchetti-Carboni
The Italian Voice of Casanova:	Luigi Proietti
Sound Mixer:	Fausto Ancillai
Dubbing Assistant:	Camilla Trinchieri
Dubbing:	C.V.D.
Dubbing/Music Mixing:	International Recording (Rome)
Music Coordination:	Eureka-C.A.M.
Glass Harp:	Bruno Hoffman
Publicity:	Nico Naldini
Assistant:	Tilde Corsi
Still Photographer:	Pierluigi Praturion
Cast:	Donald Sutherland (Giacomo Casanova), Margareth Clementi (Maddalena), Clarissa Mary Roll (Anna Maria),

Daniela Gatti (Giselda), Cicely
Browne (Madame D'Urfé), Clara
Algranti (Marcolina), Daniel Emil-
fork Berenstein (DuBois), Tina
Aumont (Henriette), Sandra Elaine
Allen (giantess), John Karlsen (Lord
Talou), Hans van den Hoek (Prince
del Brando), Olimpia Carlisi
(Isabella), Dudley Sutton (Duke of
Wurttemberg), Reggie Nalder
(Faulkircher), Luigi Zerbinati (the
Pope), Adele Angela Lojodice (mech-
anical doll), Carmen Scarpitta
(Madame Charpillon), Silvana
Fusacchia (Silvana), Marie Marquez
(Casanova's mother), Angelica Hansen
(the hunchback), Marika Rivera
(Astrodi), Veronica Nava (Romana),
Carli Buchanan (aristocratic woman),
Mario Gagliardo (Righetto, the
coachman), Mariano Brancaccio (the
ballet dancer).

Filmed at Cinecittà
Studios, Rome, from
July 21, 1975 to May 11,
1976.
Distribution:
Running Time:
Released:

Universal
165 minutes
Italy: December 1976
U.S.: February 11, 1977 (NYC)

Writings about Federico Fellini

1950

19   ANON. "Le luci del varietà." Oggi, 6, No. 47 (23 November),
      20–21.
         A picture spread of eight stills from Variety Lights.

20   MIDA, MASSIMO. "Lattuada e Fellini fra le luci del varietà."
      Cinema (nuova serie), 4, No. 47 (1 October), 171–173.
      Illustrated.
         A review of Variety Lights. Mida finds the film a suc-
      cessful blend of the neorealistic taste for realistic
      detail and the traditional Italian love for spectacle.
      [This issue of Cinema (nuova serie) could not be located
      in the U.S.A. A copy was found, however, in the library
      of the Centro sperimentale di cinematografia in Rome. JCS]

1951

21   ARISTARCO, GUIDO. "Luci del varietà." Cinema (nuova serie),
      5, No. 55 (1 February), 49–50, and rear cover. Illustrated.
         A review of Variety Lights by Italy's leading Marxist
      critic of film. Aristarco finds the movie successful
      despite an illogical ending. He praises the emphasis on
      psychological situations. [This issue of Cinema (nuova
      serie) could not be located in the U.S.A. A copy was found,
      however, in the library of the Centro sperimentale di
      cinematografia in Rome. JCS]

22   DI GIAMMATTEO, FERNALDO. "Le luci del varietà." Bianco e
      nero, 12, No. 4 (April), 69–71. Credits.
         Review of Variety Lights. Di Giammatteo states that
      Lattuada has achieved a new feeling for little people, and
      Di Giammatteo attributes part of this new understanding to
      Lattuada's collaboration with Fellini.

1952

23 ARISTARCO, GUIDO. "Lo sceicco bianco." Cinema nuovo, 1,
        No. 1 (15 December), 26.
            A brief review of The White Sheik. Aristarco identifies
        Fellini as a unique, new director of importance, but goes
        on to say that the film has a disequilibrium of tone and an
        excessive reliance on parody and farce.

24 BRUNO, EDOARDO. "I film della mostra." Filmcritica, No. 17
        (October), pp. 97-112. Illustrated.
            In this article on the Venice Film Festival, Bruno dis-
        misses The White Sheik in one sentence as unworthy of
        discussion.

25 CASTELLO, GIULIO CESARE. "Lo sceicco bianco." Cinema (nuova
        serie), 8, Nos. 99-100 (15-31 December), 335-37. Illus-
        trated. Brief credits.
            A review of The White Sheik. Castello identifies in the
        movie a new cinematic departure in the mixture of fantasy
        and reality. Castello also comments on Fellini's tendency
        to pause too long over situations he loves. [This issue
        of Cinema (nuova serie) could not be located in the U.S.A.
        A copy was found, however, in the library of the Centro
        sperimentale di cinematografia in Rome. JCS]

26 GHELLI, NINO. "Lo sceicco bianco." Bianco e nero, 13,
        Nos. 9-10 (September-October), 44-47.
            An attacking review of The White Sheik. Ghelli finds
        the movie sadly lacking in firm, consistent direction. He
        deplores the emphasis on spectacle and on cliché
        observations.

27 MIDA, MASSIMO. "Fellini, 'Diogene' del cinema." Cinema
        (nuova serie), 8, No. 95 (1 October), 163-65. Illustrated.
            A review of The White Sheik. Mida comments on Fellini's
        extension of neorealism to include more than social be-
        havior. Mida argues that Fellini explores the inner work-
        ings of his characters. [This issue of Cinema (nuova serie)
        could not be located in the U.S.A. A copy was found, how-
        ever, in the library of the Centro sperimentale di cinema-
        tografia in Rome. JCS]

28 SOLMI, ANGELO. "Il mondo dei fumetti rivelato dal cinema."
        Oggi, 8, No. 15 (10 April), 37.
            A favorable review of The White Sheik. Solmi praises it
        especially as a satire on the fumetti and comments with
        particular enthusiasm on the night scenes of deserted Rome.

1953

29   BERGER, RUDI. "I vitelloni." Filmcritica, No. 28 (September), pp. 130-31.

In this review, Berger praises I Vitelloni as a great step forward in Fellini's artistic development and commends him for treating a difficult and even unpleasant subject with skill and insight.

30   CASTELLO, GIULIO CESARE. "Troppi leoni al lido." Cinema (nuova serie), 9, No. 116 (31 August), 94-113. Illustrated.

In this general article on the Venice Film Festival of 1953, Castello praises I Vitelloni as a fine satirical commentary on social mores and identifies Fellini as new director of importance. [This issue of Cinema (nuova serie) could not be located in the U.S.A. A copy was found, however, in the library of the Centro sperimentale di cinematografia in Rome. JCS]

31   FELLINI, FEDERICO. "Strada sabarrata: via libera ai vitelloni." Cinema nuovo, 1, No. 2 (1 January), 19. Illustrated.

Gracefully written essay by Fellini about the making of I Vitelloni. He says that he turned to the project when he was unable to begin work on La Strada. He thought of the project as a joke he would play on his friends in Rimini. While making the film, he testifies that he found himself falling back into the ways of a vitellone.

32   GHELLI, NINO. "L'amore in città." Bianco e nero, 14, No. 12 (December), 63-66. Credits.

An attacking review of Love in the City. Ghelli finds the film as a whole full of gimmicks. He states that the episode directed by Fellini is the best, because it is the most human.

33   _____. "Venezia 53." Bianco e nero, 14, No. 10 (October), 3-31. Illustrated.

Article on the Venice Film Festival in which Ghelli surveys many of the films shown, including I Vitelloni. This film, he finds superior to Fellini's previous offering, The White Sheik. He states that the depiction of provincial life is rich in humane observations and biting satire. Fellini's incapacity to condemn the vitelloni for their weaknesses, however, leads him to an ending which is too conventional.

34   KOVAL, FRANCIS. "Venice 1953." Films in Review, 4, No. 8 (October), 387-88.

Report on the showing of I Vitelloni at the Venice Film Festival.

35   MARTINI, STELIO. "Gelsomina e Zampano sulla strada di Fellini."
     Cinema nuovo, 2, No. 22 (1 November), 274-75. Illustrated.
          An article providing background information on La Strada
     before its filming. In interview, Fellini discusses his
     conceptions of the characters of Gelsomina and Zampano.

36   SOLMI, ANGELO. "Arrivano i vitelloni capitanati da Fellini."
     Oggi, 9, No. 40 (1 October), 40-41.
          A positive review of Fellini's I Vitelloni. Solmi draws
     on interview material in which the director acknowledges
     and discusses the autobiographical elements in the movie.

37   VICE. "I vitelloni." Cinema nuovo, 2, No. 20 (1 October), 220.
          A generally favorable review of I Vitelloni. The critic
     commends the director for his story idea and the results he
     gets from his actors, but questions the film's lapses into
     superficial good spirits where the subject matter demands
     more thoughtful treatment.

                              1954

*38 AGEL, GENEVIÈVE. Federico Fellini. Brussels: Club du livre
     de cinéma, 213 pp.
          [No copy of this book could be found in the U.S.A. It
     is listed, however, by the British Film Institute in
     London. JCS]

39   ARISTARCO, GUIDO. "La strada." Cinema nuovo, 3, No. 46 (10
     November), 311-12.
          The Marxist critic discusses Fellini's art, with La
     Strada serving as his chief source. He finds at the center
     of Fellini's work a conception of individual isolation.

40   BENEDETTI, BENEDETTO. "Moraldo in città incontra se stesso."
     Cinema nuovo, 3, No. 41 (15 August), 94-96. Illustrated.
          Benedetti discusses Fellini's proposed film Moraldo
     in Città. Benedetti states that the film will be a contin-
     uation of the life of Moraldo from I Vitelloni. This
     character closely resembles Fellini himself, but Moraldo's
     story, argues Benedetti, could be the tale of any young man
     from a small town in Italy who goes to Rome. Moraldo will
     be a humble, naive hero. He thinks that to face the world
     he needs only to have faith in himself. He will experience
     many of the elements which Fellini did in his early days in
     Rome including a squalid rented room, meager meals, ragged
     clothes, and loneliness. He will learn that no experience,
     no matter how trivial, is wasted. Benedetti's article con-
     tains a good deal of biographical information. [Moraldo in
     Città was never made, but Fellini returned to parts of it
     for sections of La Dolce Vita and Roma. JCS]

41 BRUNO, EDOARDO. "Noi donne, Amore in città, etc." Filmcritica,
      No. 32 (January), pp. 50-51.
        A brief review in which Bruno attacks Love in the City
      and some other films for the fragmentary nature which robs
      them of substance.

42 _____. "La strada." Filmcritica, Nos. 39-40 (August-
      September), pp. 128-30.
        In this review, Bruno suggests that La Strada is another
      example of Fellini's crepuscolarismo. Bruno acknowledges
      the poetic value of Fellini's vision with its emphasis on
      immediacy and nostalgia and with its preoccupation with
      provincial life. But Bruno is critical of Fellini for his
      narrow, personal view of reality and his disregard for
      characterization. (Crepuscolarismo refers to a "twilight"
      mood produced by certain Italian poets in the early
      twentieth century.)

43 CAVICCHIOLI, LUIGI. "Per merito di Pallina smise d'essere
      vitellone." Oggi, 10, No. 30 (29 July), 26-28. Illustrated.
        A highly romantic biographical essay on Fellini, empha-
      sizing how the love of a good woman (Giulietta Masina)
      changed his life for the better.

44 "D., G." "Hanno eletto Caterina." Cinema nuovo, 3, No. 28
      (1 February), 43-44. Illustrated.
        An article on the results of a poll taken at a public
      preview of Love in the City. The poll reveals that of the
      six portions of the film, Fellini's section ranked third in
      popularity. It won much praise from women viewers.

45 FABRINI, IVANO. "I vitelloni ci guardano." Cinema nuovo, 3,
      No. 41 (15 August), 96-97.
        In response to Fellini's announcement that his next film
      will be a sequel to I Vitelloni, entitled Moraldo in città,
      Cinema nuovo publishes an open letter to Fellini from a
      reader. This reader identifies himself as a "vitellone"
      and urges Fellini to continue the story begun in I Vitelloni.

46 FELLINI, FEDERICO. "In tre si chiacchiera." Cinema nuovo, 3,
      No. 39 (15 July), 13. Illustrated.
        In response to a series of questions, Fellini discusses
      the role of the screenplay in his approach to making his
      movies.

47 _____. "Ogni margine è bruciato." Cinema (nuova serie),
      No. 139 (10 August), p. 448. Illustrated.
        In this brief statement, Fellini describes his reactions
      after completion of the editing of La Strada. He states
      that his usual reaction is to feel disturbed by the differ-
      ences between his intentions and the finished movie. Such,

however, he announces joyfully, is not the case with La
Strada. This film, he finds, expresses his intentions
perfectly. [This issue of Cinema (nuova serie) could not
be located in the U.S.A. A copy was found, however, in the
library of the Centro sperimentale di cinematografia in
Rome. JCS]

48 FLAIANO, ENNIO. "Ho parlato male de La strada." Cinema
(nuova serie), No. 139 (10 August), p. 449.
    In this brief statement, Flaiano describes his work as a
collaborator on the screenplay of La Strada. He defines
his role as that of devil's advocate to Fellini and Tullio
Pinelli. [This issue of Cinema (nuova serie) could not be
located in the U.S.A. A copy was found, however, in the
library of the Centro sperimentale di cinematografia in
Rome. JCS]

49 GIACOSI, LUIGI. "Il film più faticoso in una carriera di
quarantare anni." Cinema (nuova serie), No. 139 (10
August), p. 458.
    A brief behind-the-scenes account of some aspects of the
production of La Strada. One of the things discussed is
the making of the scene with the tight-rope walker. Giacosi
served as production director on the project. [This issue
of Cinema (nuova serie) could not be located in the U.S.A.
A copy was found, however, in the library of the Centro
sperimentale di cinematografia in Rome. JCS]

50 KOVAL, FRANCIS. "Venice 1954." Films in Review, 5, No. 8
(October), 395-96.
    Report on the showing of La Strada at the Venice Film
Festival.

51 MARTIN, ANDRÉ. "Ce que tous fils à papa doit savoir." Cahiers
du Cinéma, No. 35 (May), pp. 48-50. Illustrated.
    A review of I Vitelloni. Martin announces his discovery
of Fellini as an authentic cinéaste. He marvels that the
film which won a Silver Lion at the Venice Film Festival
was scheduled for a poor time in Paris and almost over-
looked. He finds that Fellini treats an aspect of provincial life with an interesting mixture of fondness and
satire.

52 MASINA, GIULIETTA. "Gelsomina sente la vita degli alberi."
Cinema (nuova serie), No. 139 (10 August), pp. 450-51.
Illustrated.
    An interesting essay in which Masina discusses her con-
ception of the character of Gelsomina and describes some of
the attributes she tried to give to Gelsomina in her portrayal of the character. Masina stresses Gelsomina's need
to find contact with the people and things around her. She

comments that Gelsomina imitates people and things as a way of approaching nearer to them. Masina, also, discusses the Fool as a figure who externalizes many of the longings in Gelsomina. [This issue of Cinema (nuova serie) could not be located in the U.S.A. A copy was found, however, in the library of the Centro sperimentale di cinematografia in Rome. JCS]

53   MONTESANTI, FAUSTO. "Genesi segreta di Gelsomina e Zampano." Cinema (nuova serie), No. 139 (10 August), pp. 446-48. Illustrated.

In this article on La Strada, Montesanti summarizes an interview with Fellini and offers a critical reading of the movie. According to Fellini in this account, his first impulse to make a tale of lonely vagabond life came from his own experience travelling with a variety hall troupe of actors. An early plan of Fellini was to treat an errant knight in medieval Italy. This conception gave way eventually to the idea of a gypsy couple, based on two different gypsy couples Fellini had observed. In his reading of the movie, Montesanti emphasizes the couple's incapacity to communicate, and he compares the movie briefly with Broken Blossoms, Modern Times, and Brief Encounter. [This issue of Cinema (nuova serie) could not be located in the U.S.A. A copy was found, however, in the library of the Centro sperimentale di cinematografia in Rome. JCS]

54   MUCCHI, GABRIELE. "Dietro c'è sempre la macchina da pressa." Cinema nuovo, 3, No. 30 (1 March), 114-16.
A review of Love in the City. Mucchi discusses the pros and cons of realism in filmmaking and arrives at the "safe" conclusion that too much emphasis on realism can stiffle artistic creation. Mucchi considers Fellini's episode in the movie as the one with the most characteristics of a fable.

55   PINELLI, TULLIO. "Una diversità complementare." Cinema (nuova serie), No. 139 (10 August), p. 449. Illustrated.
In this short, interesting article, Pinelli describes his relationship as a collaborator with Fellini from the beginning up to and including their work together on La Strada. Pinelli remarks that he and Fellini arrived independently at similar story ideas for La Strada at virtually the same time. Also, he recounts how they worked out together the basic plot situation for The White Sheik. [This issue of Cinema (nuova serie) could not be located in the U.S.A. A copy was found, however, in the library of the Centro sperimentale di cinematografia in Rome. JCS]

56   RONDI, BRUNELLO. "Un regista che disegna gli attori con la
      matita." Cinema (nuova serie), No. 139 (10 August),
      pp. 452-53. Illustrated.
         Rondi discusses Fellini's traits as a director, and he
      comments on Fellini's intentions in La Strada. Rondi finds
      Fellini extremely attentive to the gestures and accents of
      his actors. He stresses the extreme importance of the mov-
      ing camera in Fellini's work, and he states that formal
      shot composition is of less importance to Fellini. In La
      Strada, Rondi declares, Fellini worked hard to avoid the
      twin dangers of literariness and picturesqueness. The film
      is for Rondi an almost existential statement about the
      solitude and the need for communication of beings without
      roots, goals, or a sense of equilibrium. He describes
      Fellini's anxiety about shooting the ending of the film.
      Rondi served as artistic collaborator on the film project.
      [This issue of Cinema (nuova serie) could not be located in
      the U.S.A. A copy was found, however, in the library of
      the Centro sperimentale di cinematografia in Rome. JCS]

57   ROSSI, MORALDO. "Fellini e il cavallo fantasma." Cinema
      (nuova serie), No. 139 (10 August), p. 454.
         In this brief article, Rossi recounts some behind-the-
      scenes details of production of La Strada. In particular,
      he describes an evening drive through the countryside out-
      side of Rome with Fellini in 1952 when Fellini explained
      his ideas about La Strada and looked for mixtures of the
      mysterious and the real in the countryside. (Fellini caught
      sight of a mysterious dappled horse which immediately dis-
      appeared from view and could not be found again.) And Rossi
      describes on-location work at the convent of Bagnoregio.
      Rossi served as assistant director on the project. [This
      issue of Cinema (nuova serie) could not be located in the
      U.S.A. A copy was found, however, in the library of the
      Centro sperimentale di cinematografia in Rome. JCS]

58   SOLMI, ANGELO. "Zampano e Gelsomina." Oggi, 10, No. 39
      (30 September), 38.
         An enthusiastic review of Fellini's La Strada. Solmi
      emphasizes the tragic failures of Zampano and Gelsomina to
      communicate with and support each other. Also Solmi de-
      fends the movie against charges by Marxist critics that
      Fellini has betrayed neorealism and retreated to mysticism.
      Solmi sees La Strada as an inevitable step forward in the
      development of neorealism.

59   TAILLEUR, ROGER and BERNARD CHARDÈRE. "Les Vitelloni."
      Positif, No. 11 (September-October), pp. 68-70. Brief
      credits.
         A review of I Vitelloni. The reviewers praise Fellini's
      editing of the episodes to form a mosaic of whims, small

acts and lives. The mosaic, they argue, has the quality of
subjective recollection. Only gradually, through the quiet
character of Moraldo, does the author's point of view
surface.

60 UBEZIO, STEFANO. "Federico Fellini crede ancora ai sentimenti."
    Cinema (nuova serie), No. 139 (10 August), pp. 443-45.
    Illustrated.
        An interesting overview of Fellini's career up to and
    including La Strada. Ubezio argues that Fellini is absorbed
    with themes, characters, and costumes from the period of
    his youth before World War I. He is instinctively, rather
    than intellectually, in revolt against the tendency to be-
    lieve in illusory ideals, which characterized the epoch.
    [This issue of Cinema (nuova serie) could not be located in
    the U.S.A. A copy was found, however, in the library of
    the Centro sperimentale di cinematografia in Rome. JCS]

                              1955

61 ANON. "New Names." Sight and Sound, 25, No. 3 (Winter), 120.
    Illustrated.
        A brief essay to introduce Fellini to British movie-goers.
    I Vitelloni is praised. La Strada and Il Bidone are called
    "uneasy" combinations of "poetry and melodrama."

62 ARISTARCO, GUIDO. "Cinéma italien." Cinéma 55, No. 3
    (January), pp. 15-22.
        The Italian Marxist critic surveys the year's production
    of films in Italy for the French journal. Aristarco attacks
    La Strada as literary and poetic as opposed to realistic,
    and individualistic and self-absorbed as opposed to socially
    programmatic. Aristarco praises Love in the City as the
    neorealism of Zavattini carried to its extreme. Fellini's
    episode, however, reveals Fellini's difficulty in treating
    the individual in his social environment.

63 AUBIER, DOMINIQUE. "Mythologie de La Strada." Cahiers du
    Cinéma, No. 49 (July), pp. 3-9. Illustrated.
        A pioneering article on the importance of religious and
    metaphysical elements in Fellini's works, especially La
    Strada. Aubier feels La Strada is strongly Franciscan. It
    is a modern version of The Flowers of St. Francis. Beyond
    that, it has a basis in man's primitive and specific need
    to push himself higher beyond himself to a level of meta-
    physical activity. Aubier traces Gelsomina's progression
    or ascension. Also Aubier discusses symbolic roles played
    by the Fool and by Zampano and comments on the functions of
    the circus, music, and the sea in Fellini's mythological
    world.

64 BASTIDE, FRANÇOIS-RÉGIS, JULIETTE CAPUTO, and CHRIS MARKER,
    eds. La Strada. Paris: Éditions du seuil, 119 pp.
    Illustrated. Filmography.
      This work contains the cutting continuity and dialogue
    of La Strada in slightly condensed form, numerous photo-
    graphs, reproductions of parts of the musical score, of
    sketches of Gelsomina by Fellini, and of early cartoons by
    Fellini, and a long interview with Giulietta Masina and
    Fellini. Masina discusses her early career, her conception
    of Gelsomina, her manner of playing certain scenes, Fellini's
    methods of directing, her makeup for the part, and the re-
    action of viewers to La Strada. Fellini tells the inter-
    viewer his favorite biographical tales--how he ran away
    with a circus at age twelve and how he began in show busi-
    ness by touring with a vaudeville troupe. (Both stories are
    questioned by biographer Angelo Solmi.) Of much interest
    is Fellini's discussion of scenes he cut from La Strada.
    Appended to the book is André Bazin's essay entitled "Si
    Zampano a une âme" which was published first as "La Strada"
    in Esprit, 23, No. 5 (May 1955), 847-51.

65 BAZIN, ANDRÉ. "La Strada." Esprit, 23, No. 5 (May), 847-51.
      Bazin's tribute to La Strada as a "phenomenology of the
    soul." He praises Fellini's use of the film medium to
    express his vision without sacrificing the medium's realis-
    tic base. The motorcycle caravan of Zampano, Bazin argues,
    is both mythic and real. Bazin argues against Italian
    Marxist critics who attack the work as not in the tradition
    of Zavattini's neorealism. Bazin calls for a broader defi-
    nition of neorealism. Reprinted as "Si Zampano a une âme"
    in La Strada. Eds. François-Régis Bastide, Juliette Caputo,
    and Chris Marker. Paris: Éditions du seuil, 1955.
    Pp. 115-17. And also reprinted as "La Strada." Qu'est-ce
    que le cinéma? 4. Collection 7e Art. Paris: Éditions du
    cerf, 1962. Pp. 122-28.

66 BENAYOUN, ROBERT. "La Strada, ou quand Fellini s'ouvre aux
    chimères." Positif, No. 13 (March-April), pp. 26-28.
      A highly laudatory review of La Strada. Benayoun states
    that Fellini has established himself head and shoulders
    above other Italian directors. He praises La Strada as a
    moving treatment of the conquering power of love, and he
    argues against a too explicitly Christian interpretation.

67 BRUNO, EDOARDO. "Il bidone." Filmcritica, No. 52 (September),
    pp. 341-42.
      A negative review of Il Bidone. Bruno acknowledges
    Fellini's skill in general in exploring themes of solitude
    and melancholy, but specifically in Il Bidone, Bruno crit-
    icizes Fellini's superficial characterizations and his
    trumped-up ending.

68 CHARDÈRE, BERNARD. "Propos un peu libres." Positif, Nos. 14–
    15 (November), pp. 129–30.
        A counter statement to the praise of La Strada by other
    French critics. Chardère finds the intellectual pretensions
    of the film suspect. The ideas expressed in the film are
    vague and confused.

69 CHEVALLIER, JEAN. "Le Cinéma ne peut se passer du réel."
    Image et Son, No. 82 (May), pp. 12–13. Illustrated.
        A balanced review of La Strada. Chevallier praises
    Fellini's ambition in attempting lyricism in the cinema and
    praises the humanity of the character of Gelsomina, but
    finally calls the movie less "authentic" than I Vitelloni.
    He objects that in the second half of the movie, the images
    and symbols intended to suggest a spiritual level are
    labored and forced. He objects strongly to the banality of
    the Fool's speech on the purpose of a pebble.

70 _____. "Le Sheik blanc." Image et Son, No. 84 (July), pp. 5
    & 9. Illustrated.
        A review of The White Sheik which Chevallier had seen at
    a private screening. (It had not been distributed in France
    at that time.) He tells his readers that the film is about
    "true romance" publications. He praises Fellini's comic
    exposé of the world of such publications, but at the same
    time he objects that the movie never rises above the level
    of comic incident. The influence wielded by such publica-
    tions, he thinks, is socially significant and deserves more
    serious examination and rebuttal.

71 FELLINI, FEDERICO. "Enquête sur Hollywood." Cahiers du
    Cinéma, No. 54 (Christmas), p. 77.
        Fellini responds to a questionnaire about the Hollywood
    system and American films. He describes the Hollywood sys-
    tem as repressive and states a fear that it is becoming a
    model for European cinema.

72 GHELLI, NINO. "Il bidone." Bianco e nero, 16, Nos. 9–10
    (September–October), 24–28. Brief credits.
        A review of Il Bidone after its presentation at the
    Venice Film Festival. Ghelli is critical of the film on
    two counts: the indecisive mixture of tragic and comic
    tones and the lack of character development.

73 KOVAL, FRANCIS. "Venice 1955." Films in Review, 6, No. 8
    (October), 381.
        A report on the showing of Il Bidone at the Venice Film
    Festival.

74 LAMBERT, GAVIN. "The Signs of Predicament." Sight and Sound,
    24, No. 3 (January–March), 150–51.

Lambert reviews "Italian Film Week" in London. He
laments the demise of neorealism in favor of commercialism.
Two of Fellini's films--I Vitelloni and La Strada--were
exhibited during the week, and Lambert praises I Vitelloni
over La Strada, since it concerns a "distinct social problem" which Fellini can treat in his "light, mordant and detached" manner. Of La Strada, he says the picturesque
episodes "reflect Fellini's desire to load his story with
atmosphere and symbols of profound meaning. But the 'meaning' isn't there."

75   L'HER, YVES. "La Strada." Télécine, Nos. 48-49 (May-June),
     pp. 1-18. Illustrated. Credits.
          An excellent informational "fiche" on La Strada. It con-
     tains the following: a plot summary; a brief biographical
     sketch of Fellini's discussions of the characters Zampano,
     Gelsomina, and the Fool; a consideration of the structure
     of the film; notes on the direction of the film; a critical
     overview; and interviews with Giulietta Masina and Fellini.
     L'Her sees the work as falling into three parts: (1) before
     the appearance of the Fool; (2) during the presence of the
     Fool; and (3) after the departure of the Fool. The Fool
     changes radically the relationship between Gelsomina and
     Zampano. Gelsomina receives a sense of worth from the Fool,
     and she, in turn, touches the conscience of Zampano. L'Her
     compares Fellini's Christian outlook with that of Paul
     Claudel. In the interview, Fellini speaks of his irritation
     with Italian critics who have attacked him for dealing with
     exceptional, rather than typical, characters. L'Her sug-
     gests that the character of the Fool is the one closest to
     Fellini (as Moraldo was in I Vitelloni), and Fellini agrees
     with L'Her. Giulietta Masina talks about Gelsomina. L'Her
     and Fellini look through some of the writing of Emmanuel
     Mounier and note correspondences between Mounier and Fellini.

76   MANGINI, CECILIA. "Le Cas Fellini." Cinéma 55, No. 3
     (January), pp. 23-35. Illustrated.
          Mangini reviews the split in Italian criticism over La
     Strada. The neorealists felt the film was regressive and
     evaded the confrontation of real social issues. The
     Catholics felt the film showed a deepening of Fellini's
     Christian sentiments. Along with other critics, Mangini
     insists on the importance of Fellini's past in his works.
     She offers a brief biographical sketch of Fellini. She
     discusses The White Sheik, I Vitelloni, and La Strada,
     emphasizing Fellini's use of material about the provinces.
     She argues that Fellini's themes deepen with each film.
     La Strada treats the inability of two people to communicate.

77   _____. "I due bidoni." Cinema nuovo, 4, No. 66 (10 September),
     174-75. Illustrated.

An interview with Tullio Pinelli, Fellini's co-writer, concerning their next film, Il Bidone. Pinelli explains that the movie will develop the theme of man's isolation and his incapacity to understand others.

78 MARRONCLE, JEANNINE. "Courrier du coeur." Téléciné, No. 52 (December), pp. 1-6. Illustrated. Credits.
An informational "fiche" on The White Sheik. It contains the following: a brief plot summary; notes on the direction of the film, the rhythm, the sound, the cinematography, and the acting; and critical discussion. Marroncle finds the movie a double-edged satire. Its targets are a reader of illustrated romance publications and a citizen rooted in conventional respectability. The emptiness of the life of each seems to Marroncle similar to the sense of emptiness in I Vitelloni and La Strada. Marroncle discusses at some length the need for forms of evasion by Fellini's two characters in The White Sheik.

79 MARTIN, ANDRÉ. "È arrivata La Strada." Cahiers du Cinéma, No. 45 (March), pp. 10-11. Illustrated. Brief credits.
A highly laudatory review of La Strada. Martin feels the movie places Fellini clearly among the ranks of the best directors of the period. He disagrees strongly with Italian Marxist critics who accuse Fellini of running from reality to an escapist world of his youth. On the contrary, Martin feels La Strada is a drama about "non-communication" and as such is a strong confrontation of human reality. Martin discusses at length the Franciscan aspects of the film.

80 _____. "Petit journal intime du cinéma." Cahiers du Cinéma, No. 49 (July), pp. 35-36. Illustrated.
After conversation with Giulietta Masina and Franco Fabrizzi about Il Bidone, Martin ponders a possible comparison between Fellini's movie and Forton's comic strip, Adventures des Pieds Nicklés.

81 MORAVIA, ALBERTO. "Fellini senza la sua ironia." L'espresso, 1, No. 3 (16 October), 11.
A review of Il Bidone, by the Italian novelist. Moravia argues that Fellini has failed to create a distance between himself and the despicable swindles of his protagonists, either by means of irony or moral judgment. Moravia resents being drawn into a kind of complicity with the swindlers who prey on poor people. [No copy of this review could be located in the U.S.A. A copy was found, however, in the archives of L'espresso in Rome. JCS]

82 RENZI, RENZO. "La crisi del quarto film." Cinema nuovo, 4, No. 70 (10 November), 327-28. Illustrated.

Renzi describes the long-awaited opening of Il Bidone
at the Venice Film Festival as a disaster. He analyzes
what he calls the "crisis of the fourth film" for contemporary Italian filmmakers. After early successes, many
directors fail approximately at the point of the fourth
film. Renzi asks why the Italian audiences exalt filmmakers
so much, so early, and then are so easily disillusioned
when the filmmakers falter.

83   RENZI, RENZO. "I problemi dell' indecisione." Cinema nuovo,
      4, No. 71 (25 November), 387-90. Illustrated.
          In this essay on Il Bidone, Renzi develops his ideas
      about characterization and morality in Fellini's films.
      Renzi speculates that there are no individual characteriza-
      tions in Fellini's films. All the characters reflect
      Fellini's own state of being. The morality of Fellini is
      frequently ambiguous because Fellini himself has not re-
      solved his own personal crisis.

84   SADOUL, GEORGES. "La mia posizione di fronte a Fellini."
      Cinema nuovo, 4, No. 71 (25 November), 385-87. Illustrated.
          Georges Sadoul, who readily confesses that he is not a
      strong admirer of Fellini and states that he prefers the
      methods of a director like Zavattini, acknowledges that
      there is a place for Fellini in contemporary cinema and
      even within the neorealistic movement. He goes on to illus-
      trate how Fellini's films can reflect real life to the
      average movie-goer. He covers the films from The White
      Sheik to Il Bidone.

85   SALACHAS, GILBERT. "Les Vitelloni." Téléciné, No. 51
      (October-November), pp. 1-8. Illustrated. Credits.
          An informational "fiche" on I Vitelloni. It contains
      the following: a brief plot summary; discussions of the
      characters; a section on the episodic structure and on the
      conception of the story idea; statements about the direct-
      ing, the editing and the sound; and a critical overview.
      Salachas praises the balance of comic scenes with more
      moving and serious ones, and he describes the theme as a
      double one, involving a meditation on the situation of the
      vitelloni as a social phenomenon and a depiction of the
      gradual rise of the character Moraldo.

                              1956

86   AGEL, GENEVIÈVE. Les Chemins de Fellini, suivi du Journal
      d'un bidoniste par Dominique Delouche. Collection 7e Art.
      Paris: Les Éditions du cerf, 195 pp. Illustrated. Brief
      credits.

An important, pioneering critical work on Fellini's movies through Il Bidone. Agel establishes or solidifies many of the critical attitudes that have become accepted now as orthodox. She finds three main influences running through Fellini's works: traditions of Italian cinema, both the epic or romantic cinema before WWII and the neorealist cinema after WWII; baroque qualities; and spirituality, with emphasis on Franciscan qualities and mysticism. Agel also discusses elements or symbols that Fellini uses over and over in his films: fire; the sea; a tree isolated in a field ("the lightning tree"); town squares; vast, open spaces; walls; festivals; and images of romantic dreams, such as boats, travelling companies, and circuses. All these combine in a style she calls "lyric realism." She analyzes Fellini's attitude toward the young bride's fantasies in The White Sheik and his attitude toward the adolescent qualities of the heroes in I Vitelloni. With La Strada, Agel discusses Gelsomina as a figure of spiritual redemption, and she discusses the surrealism in the style of the movie. She finds Il Bidone a work which sums up many of Fellini's previous concerns, and she discusses the movie as a descent into Hell with hope of redemption at the end. Agel concludes with some observations on the Christian nature of Fellini's work. Appended to the book is a brief interview with Fellini and Dominique Delouche's journal on the making of Il Bidone. A section of Agel's book has been translated into English by Rosalie Siegal in Gilbert Salachas' Federico Fellini. New York: Crown Publishers, 1969. Pp. 171-74.

87   AGEL, HENRI. "Une metaphysique de l'abîme." Cahiers du
      Cinéma, No. 58 (April), 34-36. Illustrated.
          In this article on Il Bidone, Agel discusses the Old
      Testament anguish he finds in Fellini's work. He compares
      Fellini briefly with Georges Rouault, and he considers the
      possibility of Augusto's redemption at the end of Il Bidone.

88   ANON. "Marty--Italian-Style." Newsweek, 48, No. 20 (12
      November), 130. Illustrated.
          Brief, favorable review of I Vitelloni. The reviewer
      states that the "meandering movie ... does not tell a story
      so much as take a long look at a human situation."

89   ANON. "The Strong Grow Weak." Newsweek, 48, No. 3 (16 July),
      84.
          A review of La Strada. The reviewer notes the long runs
      of the movie in London and Paris and expresses doubt that
      the movie will succeed as well in the U.S.A. He describes
      the movie as neorealistic and calls Giulietta Masina's per-
      formance "extraordinarily touching."

90   ANON. "Vitelloni." <u>Time</u>, 68, No. 19 (5 November), 110.
The reviewer compares <u>I Vitelloni</u> with <u>La Strada</u> and
prefers the former. <u>I Vitelloni</u> is "a murderous satire
curiously infused with tenderness for the thing it destroys."
He praises the "sharp observation of small-town life."

91   ARCHER, EUGENE. "Vitelloni." <u>Film Culture</u>, 2, No. 4, 24-25.
Laudatory review of <u>I Vitelloni</u>, in which Archer praises
the Chaplinesque mixture of comedy and pathos.

92   BENEDETTI, BENEDETTO. "Cabiria ospite del sultano." <u>Cinema
nuovo</u>, 5, No. 96, 332-33. Illustrated.
An article supplying background information on Fellini's
research for <u>Nights of Cabiria</u>, including his interviews
with prostitutes.

93   BORDE, RAYMOND. "<u>Il Bidone</u> (autre avis)." <u>Cinéma 56</u>, 2,
No. 11 (May), 79.
A brief mixed review of <u>Il Bidone</u>. Borde states that
there are two men in Fellini: a neorealist and a moralist.
The first fills Borde with enthusiasm; the second does not.

94   CASTELLO, GIULIO CESARE. <u>Il cinema neorealistico italiano</u>.
Milan: Edizioni radio italiana, pp. 55-61, & 71-76.
Castello's book on neorealism is the result of a radio
series he prepared for a general audience. He devotes a
chapter to Fellini and offers an appendix on <u>Il Bidone</u>.
Castello defines Fellini's kind of neorealism as bourgeois.
It is permeated by an autobiographical predilection for
certain environments and provincial attitudes. For
Castello, <u>Il Bidone</u> represents a middle road between
Fellini's tendency toward irony as seen in <u>I Vitelloni</u> and
his taste for pathos as observed in <u>La Strada</u>. <u>Il Bidone</u>
is, therefore, a very representative film.

95   CHARDÈRE, BERNARD. "Venice 1955: images et souvenirs."
<u>Positif</u>, 2, No. 16 (May), 56-61.
Chardère reviews the showing of <u>Il Bidone</u> at the Venice
Film Festival. He attacks the film's Christian existen-
tialism which, he finds, produces only sentimentality and
pathos.

96   CROWTHER, BOSLEY. "<u>I Vitelloni</u>." <u>New York Times</u> (24 October),
43. Illustrated. Brief credits.
A review which is balanced in tone. Crowther praises
Fellini's mixture "of gravity and burlesque in exposing
the sleazy involvements and the grotesque behavior" of the
parasitic sons of middle-class families. But he attacks
the movie's ending as utterly conventional.

97   _____. "The White Sheik." New York Times (26 April), 37.
      Illustrated. Brief credits.
           Crowther reviews the film in its American opening, four
      years after its Italian opening run. He comments that he
      will not offer an overall judgment on Fellini until he has
      seen more of his movies. This one, Crowther finds broad
      and ingenuous in the manner of a silent movie, but without
      the robust fun of a silent movie.

98   de LAUROT, EDOUARD. "La Strada--A Poem on Saintly Folly."
      Film Culture, 2, No. 1, 11-14.
           de Laurot declares that La Strada's Franciscan moral
      view is too simplistic for twentieth-century viewers, but
      he praises the movie's sustained lyric style. He discusses
      Fellini's use of "open" structure, ellipsis, and "thematic
      framing." The review is reprinted in Renaissance of the
      Film. Edited by Julius Bellone. London: Collier-
      Macmillan, 1970. Pp. 264-76.

99   DELOUCHE, DOMINIQUE. "Journal de Il Bidone." Cahiers du
      Cinéma, No. 57 (March), pp. 21-32.
           A printing of extracts from Delouche's Journal d'un
      bidoniste published in: Geneviève Agel's Les Chemins de
      Fellini, suivi du Journal d'un bidoniste par Dominique
      Delouche. Paris: Éditions du cerf, 1956. Pp. 97-159.
      Delouche's important interview with Fellini on June 17,
      1955, however, is given more space in Cahiers du Cinéma
      than in the book.

100   _____. Journal d'un bidoniste. Les Chemins de Fellini [By
      Geneviève Agel], suivi du Journal d'un bidoniste par
      Dominique Delouche. Collection 7e Art. Paris: Les
      Éditions du cerf, pp. 97-159. Illustrated.
           A day-by-day journal on the making of Il Bidone by the
      man who served as Fellini's assistant director. The journal
      covers the work done from the beginning of shooting through
      the final mixing. In addition, Delouche prints a scene cut
      from the movie involving Augusto and the dancer Maggie, an
      interview with "Lupaccio," the man who was the real model
      for Augusto, and an important interview with Fellini cover-
      ing such subjects as neorealism, Fellini's belief in
      Christianity, and his favorite artists and writers. Ex-
      tracts of the journal are reprinted in Delouche's "Journal
      de Il Bidone." Cahiers du Cinéma, No. 57 (March 1956),
      pp. 21-32.

101   LEFÈVRE, RAYMOND. "Peut-on parler du néo-surréalisme de
      Fellini?" Image et Son, No. 88 (January), pp. 14 & 16.
           An essay on The White Sheik and La Strada. Lefèvre de-
      fends both movies from the charge that they treat unusual
      situations and lack the qualities of realistic films. He

argues that both films raise the unusual to a state of surrealism. In La Strada, he discusses the horse passing
alone in the quiet street late at night, the procession of
three travelling musicians in the countryside empty except
for Gelsomina, and Gelsomina's visit to the sick, isolated
child, Oswald. On The White Sheik, Lefèvre notes that the
situations of the unusual lack the deep resonances of those
in La Strada, but he, nevertheless, cites some of the
scenes with the actors in the forest and the sequence of
the husband's late night encounter with the two prostitutes
and the fire-eater.

102   MARTIN, MARCEL. "Il Bidone." Cinéma 56, 2, No. 11 (May),
      75-78. Illustrated.
          An attacking review of Il Bidone. Martin's objections
      are twofold. He objects to the ending of the film where
      Augusto seems to have received grace, as having no impact
      on the world that lives on after Augusto's death. And he
      objects that Fellini's characters are too exceptional to
      have social relevance. He will not accept Fellini's claim
      that his characters are as real as the bicycle thieves of
      De Sica and Zavattini.

103   PROUSE, DEREK. "Il Bidone." Sight and Sound, 26, No. 3
      (Winter), 153-54.
          In this review of Il Bidone, Prouse singles out for
      praise the New Year's Eve party which he describes as a
      "gallery of human meanness." He expresses disappointment,
      however, that "goodness remains merely an abstraction" in
      the movie as a whole.

104   REICHLEY, JAMES. "The Beauty and the Beast." New Republic,
      135, No. 27 (31 December), 22.
          A favorable review of La Strada. Reichley compares the
      movie to The Petrified Forest, Citizen Kane, and Born
      Yesterday, all of which have in them a "natural" who
      represents "the simple verity in the hearts of ordinary
      people."

105   RENZI, RENZO. Federico Fellini. Parma: Guanda editore,
      63 pp. Illustrated. Filmography. Credits.
          A short critical biography of Fellini covering his
      career through Il Bidone (1955). Renzi's approach is to
      some extent psychoanalytical and to some extent Marxist.
      He stresses Fellini's middle class background and his
      bourgeois individualism. Much of Fellini's work, Renzi
      finds regressive. La Strada, for example, marks an extreme
      point in Fellini's pattern of wishing to return to infancy
      and to the mother from whom he felt excluded. Renzi iden-
      tifies the landscape of La Strada with Fellini's Gambettola
      and Gelsomina with Fellini's childhood sweetheart,

Bianchina Sorianis. Finally, the problem with Fellini, argues Renzi, is the conflict between his regressiveness and
his lyrical tendency, on the one hand, and his wish to make
moral statements, on the other hand. The book in expanded
form has been translated into French by P. L. Thirard.
Federico Fellini. Premier Plan No. 12. Lyons: S.E.R.D.O.C.,
1960.

106   SALACHAS, GILBERT. "Il Bidone." Télécine, No. 57 (May),
       pp. 1-12. Illustrated. Credits.
              An informational "fiche" on Il Bidone. It contains the
       following: a sequence outline; a brief summary of critical
       reaction to the movie; a comment on the episodic construc-
       tion of the movie; discussions of the characters; notes on
       the cinematography, the use of sound, and the acting; and
       a critical overview. Salachas feels the movie resists
       intellectual comprehension and requires the audience to
       respond emotionally to it. He discusses the curve of devel-
       opment of the three con men. And he considers the elements
       during Augusto's death which seem to indicate a possibility
       of grace for Augusto: the chiming of the village clock,
       the wind, and the family which passes.

107   SWADOS, HARVEY. "La Strada: Realism and the Comedy of
       Poverty." Yale French Studies, 17 (Summer), 38-43.
              Swados discusses La Strada as a neorealist movie that
       has in it the universality of the life of poverty pushed
       to its logical ends. He compares the miming of Giulietta
       Masina to that of Charlie Chaplin in that both give us
       immediate visual response to elements of the world seen by
       someone at the bottom.

108   WEILER, A.H. "La Strada." New York Times (17 July), p. 19.
       Brief credits.
              Laudatory review of La Strada. Weiler calls the film
       a tribute to Fellini and to Italian neorealism. He sees it
       as the picaresque story of an itinerant strong man and a
       simple-minded girl who is his foil and help-mate.

109   WILLING, DIANA. "La Strada." Films in Review, 7, No. 7
       (August-September), 351-52.
              Willing attacks La Strada as amateurish. The episodic
       nature of the film, she attributes to improvisation. She
       finds Fellini's use of the amorality of the feeble-minded
       girl inexcusable, and she is angered by the critical acclaim
       the movie has won.

110   _____. "Vitelloni." Films in Review, 7, No. 10 (December),
       527-28.
              Vitriolic attack on I Vitelloni as exemplifying the
       "incompetent and irresponsible mode" of neorealism.

111   YOUNG, VERNON. "La Strada: Cinematic Intersections." Hudson
      Review, 9, No. 3 (Autumn), 437-44.
            Young summarizes and comments on The White Sheik, I
      Vitelloni, and La Strada. His purpose is to introduce
      Fellini to the readers of Hudson Review. He particularly
      stresses the excellence of La Strada which he describes as
      "a rite of passage, a vision of perennially failing pig-man."

                              1957

*112   AGEL, GENEVIÈVE. Federico Fellini. Les Grands Createurs du
      Cinéma, No. 9, 14 pp. Illustrated. Filmography.
            [This work is cited in the Subject Catalogue of the hold-
      ings of the British Film Institute, but a copy could not be
      located in the U.S. JCS]

113   ALLOMBERT, GUY. "Le Dixième Festival de Cannes." Image et
      Son, No. 103 (June), pp. 15-16.
            Notice of Nights of Cabiria in the midst of a survey of
      films at the Cannes Film Festival. Allombert is scornful
      of another movie in praise of prostitutes and of another
      performance by Giulietta Masina with her same mannerisms.
      Fellini, he remarks ironically, has put in enough philo-
      sophical nuances to please both Georges Sadoul and François
      Truffaut.

114   ANON. "Cabiria." Newsweek, 50, No. 9 (4 November), 114-15.
            The reviewer compares Giulietta Masina to Chaplin as a
      tragicomedian. The reviewer prefers Nights of Cabiria to
      La Strada.

115   ANON. "Fellini, Federico." Current Biography 1957. New
      York: H. W. Wilson, pp. 184-86.
            Biographical sketch prompted by the award of an "Oscar"
      to La Strada in March 1957 as best foreign film. The essay
      lists Fellini's film credits and awards, the U.S. opening
      dates of his films, and the reviews of critics.

116   ANON. "Il mese." Bianco e nero, 18, No. 8 (August), i-v.
            Part of this monthly summary of film news is a brief
      section in which Fellini offers his ideas on the relation-
      ship between the producer and the director.

117   ANON. "Le notti di Cabiria." Cinema nuovo, 6, No. 106
      (1 May), 267.
            A report on Nights of Cabiria at the Cannes Film Festival.
      Fellini is quoted on how he came upon the idea for the movie
      and the character of Cabiria.

118   ARBOIS, JANICK. "L'Amore à la ville." Télécine, Nos. 70-71
       (November-December), pp. 7-8.
           An informational "fiche" on Love in the City after its
       release in France. Fellini's episode is described as the
       most elaborately fashioned of the five in the movie.
       Arbois feels that the heroine prefigures Gelsomina in La
       Strada. He notes also that the awakening of the conscience
       of the reporter through meeting the heroine is a theme now
       known to be typical in Fellini's works.

119   ARISTARCO, GUIDO. "Le notti di Cabiria." Cinema nuovo, 6,
       No. 118 (15 November), 263-65. Illustrated.
           A review of Nights of Cabiria. The Marxist critic feels
       this movie confirms the breach between Fellini and his
       audience. After a resumé of the tenets of neorealism,
       Aristarco traces Fellini's evolution away from realism into
       areas of subjectivity and autobiography. This tendency,
       Aristarco attributes to the poet Pascoli and the movement
       of the "Decadentismo."

120   _____. "Les Nuits de Cabiria." Cinéma 57, No. 18 (May),
       pp. 34-35. Illustrated.
           Review of Nights of Cabiria at its showing in the Cannes
       Film Festival. Aristarco remarks that Fellini wishes to
       contrast the human longings of Cabiria with the hard reality
       of the world in which she lives. As a Marxist critic,
       Aristarco points out, with some regret, the Franciscan
       basis of Fellini's treatment of Cabiria.

121   AUTERA, LEONARDO, ed. "Fellini e la critica." Bianco e nero,
       18, No. 6 (June), 31-40. Illustrated.
           An annotated bibliography of fifty-three critical works
       on Fellini. Mainly, these are works in Italian, but some
       works in French, German, and English are included.

122   AUTERA, LEONARDO. "Nascita di un personaggio." Bianco e nero,
       18, No. 6 (June), 24-30.
           An article in which Autera traces the evolution of the
       character of Cabiria. He argues that Fellini's conception
       of the little prostitute can be seen as early as 1947 in
       his idea for a Rossellini screenplay which was not used.
       He considers also the roles played by Giulietta Masina in
       The White Sheik and Il Bidone.

123   BAZIN, ANDRÉ. "Cabiria ou le voyage au bout du néo-réalisme."
       Cahiers du Cinéma, No. 76 (November), pp. 2-7. Illustrated.
       Brief credits.
           Bazin discusses Nights of Cabiria as a neorealist film.
       He defines neorealism to be not a specific ideology, but
       rather an emphasis on representational reality at the ex-
       pense of dramatic structure. Fellini goes to the

outer-limits of representational reality in depicting the
hidden accord which objects hold with their supernatural,
poetic or surreal counterparts. Fellini alters traditional
narrative by linking his episodes through analogy and echo
rather than through causality. Bazin discusses also the
last shot of Nights of Cabiria. The review is reprinted in
Qu'est-ce que le cinéma? 4. Collection 7ᵉ Art. Paris:
Éditions du cerf, 1962. Pp. 134-42. An English translation
of this essay appears as "Cabiria: The Voyage to the End
of Neorealism." What Is Cinema? II. Translated by Hugh
Gray. Berkeley, Los Angeles, London: University of California Press, 1971. Pp. 83-92.

124   BENAYOUN, ROBERT. "Deux doigts de Cannes, s'il vous plaît."
       Positif, 3, Nos. 25-26, 22-26.
           Harsh notice of Nights of Cabiria in the midst of an
       article on the Cannes Film Festival. Benayoun states that
       Fellini has become too intellectually self-conscious.

125   BIANCHI, PIETRO. "Federico Fellini." L'occhio del cinema.
       Milan: Garzanti, pp. 57-62.
           A brief chapter on Fellini in a book on directors, actors
       and genres of Italy, France, and the United States. Bianchi
       treats mainly Il Bidone and discusses reasons why it suc-
       ceeded in France and failed in Italy. Some mention also of
       La Strada, The White Sheik, and I Vitelloni.

126   BLUESTONE, GEORGE. "An Interview with Federico Fellini."
       Film Culture, 3, No. 3 (October), 3-4 & 21.
           Fellini discusses the following topics: censorship,
       neorealism, reasons why he could not film in America,
       Rossellini and Ingrid Bergman, and La Strada. He explains
       the success of La Strada in terms of its parable: "Every-
       one has a purpose in the universe; everyone, even the brute
       Zampano, needs someone to love." Audiences, he feels, need
       to be reassured on that simple truth.

127   BRUNO, EDOARDO. "Le notti di Cabiria." Filmcritica, 8, No. 71
       (October), 199-200.
           A laudatory review of Nights of Cabiria. Bruno feels
       that the film marks a maturing of Fellini in style and
       sensibility. Bruno praises especially Fellini's meticulous-
       ness in the depiction of Cabiria, even down to minute
       details of wardrobe.

128   CATTIVELLI, GIULIO. "L'ippogrifo di Fellini." Cinema nuovo,
       6, No. 108 (1 June), 332.
           A mixed review of Nights of Cabiria. Cattivelli de-
       scribes Fellini's penchant for autobiography as an artistic
       impasse and offers a concise list of the dominant themes
       of Fellini's movies up to Nights of Cabiria.

129 CAVICCHIOLI, LUIGI. "L'attrice che ci fa diventare buoni."
     Oggi, 13, No. 47 (21 November), 8-11. Illustrated.
     A biographical essay on Giulietta Masina, outlining her
     personal and professional background, as well as her meet-
     ing and subsequent marriage with Fellini.

130 CHEVALLIER, JEAN. "Les Nuits de Cabiria." Image et Son,
     No. 106 (November), pp. 14-15.
     A largely favorable review of Nights of Cabiria.
     Chevallier argues that in this movie as opposed to La
     Strada, Fellini avoids the exceptional and the symbolic
     and treats a more objectively observed social reality.
     Only at the ending where Cabiria finds happiness in resig-
     nation does Chevallier charge Fellini with trickery.

131 CHIARINI, LUIGI. Panorama del cinema contemporareo. Rome:
     Edizioni di Bianco e nero, pp. 139-48.
     In his survey of contemporary Italian cinema, Chiarini
     devotes a chapter to Fellini, covering La Strada, Il Bidone,
     and Nights of Cabiria. While acknowledging Fellini's
     genius, Chiarini is critical of certain tendencies. La
     Strada, he finds too symbolic and too deprived of humanity.
     Il Bidone is not instinctual enough. It does not express
     the artist's true sentiments. Chiarini argues that Nights
     of Cabiria is Fellini's best film to date because it
     expresses a good balance between sentiment and social
     commentary.

132 CORBIN, LOUISE. "Cabiria." Films in Review, 8, No. 10
     (December), 529.
     Vitriolic attack on Nights of Cabiria as a movie of "no
     consequence." The reviewer proclaims: "The talk about
     Masina's prostitute being equivalent to Chaplin's little
     tramp was started by Italian press agents."

133 CROWTHER, BOSLEY. "Cabiria." New York Times (29 October),
     34. Illustrated. Brief credits.
     A panning review of Nights of Cabiria. Crowther finds
     something elusive and insufficient about the character of
     Cabiria. Her "farcical mannerisms clash with the ugly
     realism of the theme."

134 DEL FRA, LINO. "A proposito di Fellini." Bianco e nero, 18,
     No. 6 (June), 1-21. Illustrated. Filmography. Brief
     credits.
     An essay on Fellini's evolution as a director up to and
     including Nights of Cabiria. In The White Sheik, Del Fra
     notes that the irregular camera movements create a sense of
     uneasiness. In La Strada, he finds Fellini's major concerns
     clearly delineated: the mythical figures of the diffident,
     crude, posturing Zampano, of the candid and simple

Gelsomina, and of the mercurial acrobat; la recherche du
temps perdu; love as an operative force; and the human
sense of community. In Il Bidone, Augusto resembles
Zampano, but Del Fra finds a sharp contrast between Il
Bidone and La Strada in the absence of a sense of community
in Il Bidone. Nights of Cabiria, Del Fra claims, is
Fellini's most mature work. Cabiria is a deepening of the
character of Gelsomina. Del Fra concludes that the decline
of neorealism will leave Fellini untouched.

135   DEL FRA, LINO. "Introduction and Commentary." Le notti di
      Cabiria di Federico Fellini. Rocca San Casciano: Cappelli
      editore, pp. 15-74 & 193-222. Illustrated.
           In this introduction and commentary, Del Fra essentially
      traces the growth of Nights of Cabiria from beginning to
      end. He describes Fellini's movement from La Strada to
      Nights of Cabiria. Del Fra feels that La Strada ended
      Fellini's interest in madness as a state of consciousness
      rich with insight. After La Strada, Fellini turned back to
      an idea he had as early as 1947, when he wanted to do a
      film for Anna Magnani. The idea was to do a film about
      prostitutes, stressing their naiveté, gullibility, and fas-
      cination with magic. Del Fra gives a detailed account of
      the research into prostitution undertaken by Fellini and
      his collaborators. He reports on problems with producers
      and discusses the stages of evolution of the screenplay.
      He comments on Fellini's method of directing, especially
      the amounts of film footage consumed in experimentation
      with scenes. He talks about the five, major musical themes
      in the film and discusses the character of Cabiria in the
      context of Fellini's work as a whole.

136   DELOUCHE, DOMINIQUE. "Ha cantato la Traviata." Cinema nuovo,
      6, No. 117 (1 November), 222-25. Illustrated.
           A diary of day-to-day shooting of Nights of Cabiria.
      Interesting for the details it supplies about the making of
      the film and about Fellini's style of directing. A French
      translation by Marie Rizzo appears as "Notes pour le journal
      de Cabiria." Cinéma 58, No. 24 (February 1958), pp. 44-51.

137   _____. "L'uomo dal sacco." Cinema nuovo, 6, No. 118 (15
      November), 262. Illustrated.
           In response to a reader's request, Delouche prints the
      dialogue and directions of the sequence about the man with
      the sack which was cut from Nights of Cabiria after its
      showing at the Cannes Film Festival.

138   FELLINI, FEDERICO. "A Personal Statement." Film, British
      Federation of Film Societies, 11 (January-February), 8-9.
      Illustrated.
           Fellini reviews his career up to Il Bidone. He states
      that many of his vital scenes take place on the seashore or

164

at night in deserted town squares. In his works, he balances moral ideas with personal statements (terrors of his
childhood, his complexes, and his experiences). The result
is "Personal Realism," as opposed to "Social Neorealism."

139   _____. "Prefazione." Cinemà e realtà by Brunello Rondi.
       Rome: Edizioni cinque lune, pp. 9-12.
       Fellini defines neorealism as a continuing state of
       virginity and searching.

140   FERRARA, GIUSEPPE. Il nuovo cinema italiano. Florence:
       Felice Le Monnier, pp. 304-309, 343-45 & 385.
       A survey of Italian film, concentrating on neorealism.
       In a brief section on Fellini, Ferrara comments that Fellini
       is too preoccupied with spiritual matters, at the expense
       of realism. Ferrara quotes a statement by Fellini on neo-
       realism in which Fellini identifies the main bond of the
       neorealists as a love for the "public man." This "public
       man" is man in his social, religious, and ethical relation-
       ships with other men.

141   GOW, GORDON. "The Quest for Realism." Films and Filming, 4,
       No. 3 (December), 13-15 & 30-31.
       An adaptation of a radio program Gow put together from
       tapes. He interviews six directors, including Fellini,
       and five actors on the subject of realism. Fellini con-
       tributes only briefly, offering a capsule definition of
       neorealism.

142   KNIGHT, ARTHUR. "The Noblest Roman of Them All." Saturday
       Review, 40 (9 November), 28-29.
       A review of Nights of Cabiria. Knight quotes Fellini's
       story of meeting the prostitute who was to serve as the
       model for Cabiria. Talking with the prostitutes of the
       Baths of Caracalla and those of the Via Veneto, Fellini
       found most of them "pathetically hungry for a real human
       relationship." This idea was "the springboard situation"
       for the film.

143   LABARTHE, ANDRÉ S. "Le Monde dans un chapeau." Cahiers du
       Cinéma, No. 67 (January), pp. 48-49. Brief credits.
       A review of Variety Lights. Labarthe discusses Fellini
       as a poet of the "marginal people"--the half-mad, thieves,
       bohemians, prostitutes, and show business people.

144   LANE, JOHN FRANCIS. "No Road Back." Films and Filming, 4,
       No. 1 (October), 10 & 32.
       Lane gives an overview of Fellini's career up to Nights
       of Cabiria and tries to explain his distrust of the success
       of La Strada. He argues that in La Strada Fellini takes
       seriously the "false magic" he was exposing in his first

three films. In <u>Nights of Cabiria</u>, Fellini "comes of age."
He exposes "false magic" again and now has his character
push through it to survive.

145 LAURA, ERNESTO. "Filmografia di Federico Fellini." <u>Bianco e
nero</u>, 18, No. 6 (June), 21-23.
   Filmography of Fellini's film work up to <u>Nights of Cabiria</u>.

146 LEFÈVRE, RAYMOND. "<u>Le Cheik blanc</u>." <u>Image et Son</u>, No. 102
(May), pp. I-VIII. Illustrated. Credits. Filmography.
   An informational "document" on <u>The White Sheik</u>. Lefèvre
includes a sequence outline, an essay on the cinematography,
and an essay on the dramatic content. Lefèvre expresses
his disappointment that Fellini did not choose to treat the
subject of "true romance" publications in a realistic manner. It is, he states, a subject of sociological concern.
Yet, his film is valuable, because Fellini at least underlines the absurdity of such publications. A second strand
of the movie is Fellini's mockery of familial conformity.
Lefèvre praises Fellini's handling of the parallel construction of his movie.

147 MARTIN, MARCEL. "<u>Les Nuits de Cabiria</u>." <u>Cinéma 57</u>, No. 22
(November), pp. 102-103.
   A review of <u>Nights of Cabiria</u>. Martin finds in the film
the traditional themes of Fellini, the search for spiritual
well-being and the need for human fraternity. Martin
objects to Fellini's all-consuming drive to illustrate a
thesis at the expense of his character's complexity. This
drive has become a tendency in Fellini's work beginning
with <u>La Strada</u>. It is, according to Martin, a tendency
toward the artificial and the exceptional.

148 MASINA, GIULIETTA. "Io e Cabiria." <u>Le notti di Cabiria di
Federico Fellini</u>. Edited by Lino Del Fra. Rocca San
Casciano: Cappelli editore, pp. 223-25.
   Masina comments on the character of Cabiria. She finds
Cabiria similar to Gelsomina in that both mask themselves.
A French translation by Marie Rizzo appears as "Cabiria et
moi." <u>Cinéma 58</u>, No. 24 (February), pp. 52-54.

149 MAURIAC, CLAUDE. "Federico Fellini." <u>Petite littérature du
cinéma</u>. Collection 7e Art. Paris: Editions du cerf,
pp. 87-94. Illustrated.
   In this history of the movies, Mauriac devotes a chapter
to Fellini as a film <u>auteur</u>. Mauriac discusses <u>Variety
Lights</u>, <u>La Strada</u>, and <u>Il Bidone</u>. He chides Fellini for
his obsession with ugliness, points out the quixotic aspect
of Checco, compares the inarticulateness of Gelsomina with
that of the characters played by Marlon Brando in <u>The Wild
One</u> and <u>On the Waterfront</u>, endorses the mixture of comedy
and tragedy in <u>Il Bidone</u>, and discusses Fellini's religious
beliefs.

150 MAYER, ANDREW C. "Films from Abroad – Progress and Poverty."
     <u>Quarterly Review of Film, Radio and Television</u>, 11, No. 3
     (Spring), 276-79.
          Review of foreign films, including <u>La Strada</u>. Mayer
     suggests that the movie is a modern-dress version of
     commedia dell'arte.

151 MORAVIA, ALBERTO. "Cabiria nipote di Fantine." <u>L'espresso</u>,
     3, No. 41 (13 October), 15.
          A favorable, if slightly condescending, review of <u>Nights</u>
     <u>of Cabiria</u>, by the Italian novelist. Moravia describes
     Cabiria, Fellini's good-hearted prostitute, as a literary
     descendent of Dostoyevski's Sonia and Hugo's Fantine.
     Cabiria survives the deceits practiced on her because of an
     incorrigible capacity for illusion and an automatism com-
     parable to that of an animal. Moravia is pleased that
     Fellini has put aside the "confused existentialism" of his
     previous film, <u>Il Bidone</u>, and has limited himself to a
     character and a milieu he can handle. Moravia praises
     Fellini's treatment of the "sub-life" existing on a humble
     and desperate level in and around Rome. [No copy of this
     review could be located in the U.S.A. A copy was found,
     however, in the archives of <u>L'espresso</u> in Rome. JCS]

152 MOULLET, LUC. "Biofilmographie de Federico Fellini." <u>Cahiers</u>
     <u>du Cinéma</u>, No. 68 (February), pp. 60-61.
          Filmography that covers Fellini's career up to <u>Nights of</u>
     <u>Cabiria</u>.

153 MURRAY, WILLIAM. "The Decline of Italian Realism." <u>New</u>
     <u>Leader</u>, 40, No. 5 (16 December), 26.
          A review of <u>Nights of Cabiria</u>. Murray calls Fellini the
     last Italian director of merit still trying to make films
     in the spirit of neorealism. He discusses and laments the
     ending of the movement. In Fellini's film, he describes
     the theme as the preservation of innocence in a world of
     corruption, and he praises the variety hall sequence.

154 PASOLINI, PIER PAOLO. "Nota su <u>Le notti</u>," in <u>Le notti di</u>
     <u>Cabiria di Federico Fellini</u>. Edited by Lino Del Fra.
     Rocca San Casciano: Cappelli editore, pp. 228-34.
          Pasolini views Fellini's <u>Nights of Cabiria</u> as an alarm-
     ing error. He objects to the mixture of fantasy and
     reality, the absence of historical reality, and Fellini's
     insistence on viewing the crisis of Cabiria as a meta-
     physical problem.

155 PINELLI, TULLIO. "Realtà favolosa." <u>Le notti di Cabiria di</u>
     <u>Federico Fellini</u>. Edited by Lino Del Fra. Rocca San
     Casciano: Cappelli editore, pp. 226-27.

An open letter to Del Fra by one of the co-writers of
the screenplay, after a private screening of Nights of
Cabiria. Pinelli describes his pleasure in watching the
consistent development of the character of Cabiria.

156 RANCHAL, MARCEL. "Deuxième Sexe urbain, recueil de nouvelles."
Positif, 3, No. 22 (March), 40-42.
A review of Love in the City. Ranchal argues that a
common theme of the separate episodes is the situation of
the woman in the city. Brief praise for Fellini's episode,
A Matrimonial Agency.

157 RENZI, RENZO. "Umori anarchici." Cinema nuovo, 6, No. 119
(1 December), 292-93. Illustrated.
A brief essay on the contemporary situation in Italian
filmmaking. Renzi describes Fellini as one who is trying
to combine tragicomedy with neorealism, or to make a collage
of fantasy and documentary.

158 RONDI, BRUNELLO. Cinema e realtà. Rome: Edizioni cinque
lune, pp. 203-13.
In his study of Italian cinema and reality, Rondi devotes a chapter to Fellini. He identifies Fellini with the
neorealistic movement while acknowledging that his methods
are not totally in keeping with the movement. According to
Rondi, Fellini is a neorealist for the following reasons:
(1) his tendency to deal with the negative aspects of
Italian life; (2) his preoccupation with provincial characters; (3) his exploration of man's need to communicate with
others; and (4) his feeling for the choral and epic nature
of man. Fellini, however, diverges from neorealism in his
heavy reliance on symbols and in his emphasis on human feelings rather than on social mores.

159 ROTHA, PAUL. "Il Bidone." Films and Filming, 3, No. 4
(January), 23. Illustrated. Brief credits.
A review of Il Bidone. Rotha describes Fellini as a
creator of "intangible half-worlds between realism and
fantasy" comparable to Jean Vigo. He praises Il Bidone and
I Vitelloni, but he attacks La Strada as "self-consciously
contrived" and attacks Giulietta Masina's performance in
La Strada as "artificial and shallow." The review is re-
printed in: Rotha on the Film. Fair Lawn, N.J.: Essential
Books, Inc., 1958. Pp. 195-97.

160 SALACHAS, GILBERT. "Les Feux du music-hall." Cinéma 57,
No. 14 (January), pp. 121-22. Illustrated.
A laudatory review of Variety Lights. Salachas describes
the film as an "overture" to Fellini's work. His basic
themes and characters are introduced to us. Salachas discusses especially Fellini's interest in artists in mediocre
troupes.

161   SOLMI, ANGELO. "Il film più sincero di un grande regista."
      <u>Oggi</u>, 13, No. 43 (24 October), 50-51. Illustrated.
          A positive review of <u>Nights of Cabiria</u> and of the per-
      formance of Giulietta Masina. The major element Solmi likes
      about the movie is Fellini's ability to find poetry and
      dignity in something as sordid as the life of a prostitute.

162   VISCONTI, LUCHINO. "È neorealismo <u>La strada</u>?" <u>Cinema nuovo</u>,
      6, No. 113 (1 September), 110.
          In answer to a reader's question, Visconti comments on
      <u>La Strada</u> that it is not neorealistic, but rather a depar-
      ture into a new film genre.

163   VOGEL, AMOS. "<u>Amore in Città</u>: Limits of Neorealism." <u>Film</u>
      <u>Culture</u>, 3, No. 2, 17-20.
          A review of <u>Love in the City</u>, including Fellini's episode,
      <u>A Matrimonial Agency</u>. Vogel argues that there is no such
      thing as a "neutral" image and that <u>Love in the City</u> proves
      that Zavattini's ideals cannot be taken to their limits.
      In the Fellini episode, Vogel singles out for attention the
      client's trek through the maze of the housing project.

                              1958

164   ANON. "Fellini parla del suo mestiere di regista." <u>Bianco e</u>
      <u>nero</u>, 19, No. 5 (May), iii-vi & back cover. Illustrated.
          An interview with Fellini at the <u>Centro sperimentale</u>
      <u>di cinematografia</u> in Rome after a retrospective of his
      films. Fellini discusses the following topics: his work
      with Roberto Rossellini, especially the Franciscan convent
      episode of <u>Paisan</u>; his methods of working with actors,
      especially Giulietta Masina; his intentions for the ending
      of <u>Nights of Cabiria</u>; his work with Nino Rota, Brunello
      Rondi, Ennio Flaiano, and Tullio Pinelli; and his intentions
      with the scene of the sick child shown to Gelsomina in <u>La</u>
      <u>Strada</u>. This interview was translated into French by Laura
      Dumoulin as "Mon Métier." <u>Cahiers du Cinéma</u>, No. 84 (June
      1958), pp. 14-21. And it was translated into English as
      "My Experiences as a Director." <u>International Film Annual</u>.
      No. 3. New York: Taplinger, 1959. Pp. 29-35.

165   ANON. "Mon Métier." Translated by Laura Dumoulin. <u>Cahiers</u>
      <u>du Cinéma</u>, No. 84 (June), pp. 14-21.
          Translation into French of an interview with Fellini at
      the <u>Centro sperimentale di cinematografia</u> in Rome and pub-
      lished first as "Fellini parla del suo mestiere di
      regista." <u>Bianco e nero</u>, 19, No. 5 (May, 1958), iii-vi
      & back cover. It was translated into English as "My Experi-
      ences as a Director." <u>International Film Annual</u>. No. 3.
      New York: Tapliner, 1959. Pp. 29-35.

166   ANON. "People Are Talking About...." Vogue, 131, No. 2 (15
       January), 56. Illustrated.
          Very brief note about the careers of Giulietta Masina
       and Federico Fellini to introduce them to the readership.

167   ANON. "Registi davanti alla TV." Cinema nuovo, 7, No. 134
       (July-August), 59-65.
          A questionnaire is put to six film directors about their
       attitudes toward television. Fellini responds that artistic
       creativity is impossible on television because of government
       controls. He concludes that the real role of the medium
       lies in the areas of news reporting and of interviews where
       spontaneity is important.

168   BAKER, PETER. "Le notti di Cabiria." Films and Filming, 4,
       No. 6 (March), 23. Illustrated. Brief credits.
          Laudatory review of Nights of Cabiria. Baker singles
       out for praise Giulietta Masina. He describes her perform-
       ance here as "Chaplinesque," whereas in La Strada he calls
       it "wooden."

169   CARPI, FABIO. Cinema italiano del dopoguerra. Milan: Schwarz
       editore, pp. 45-49, 249-51 & 277-78. Illustrated.
       Filmography.
          In this survey of Italian cinema after WWII, Carpi de-
       votes a chapter to Fellini. He raises a number of questions
       about Fellini's "impure poetry." Why, asks Carpi, does
       Fellini prefer to treat the abnormal rather than the normal
       and the profane rather than the religious? He calls
       Fellini's art decadent. At the end of the chapter, however,
       Carpi points to Nights of Cabiria as Fellini's masterpiece
       and hopes that it reveals a new, maturing judgment for the
       future.

170   DELOUCHE, DOMINIQUE. "Notes pour le journal de Cabiria."
       Translated by Marie Rizzo. Cinéma 58, No. 24 (February),
       pp. 44-51. Illustrated.
          A translation into French of Delouche's notes on the
       production of Nights of Cabiria, originally published as
       "Ha cantato la Traviata." Cinema nuovo, 6, No. 117 (1
       November 1957), 222-25.

171   FELLINI, FEDERICO. "Crisi e neorealismo." Bianco e nero, 19,
       No. 7 (July), 3-4.
          Fellini responds to a questionnaire about neorealism.
       He calls neorealism an energetic attempt to rewrite the
       grammar and syntax of film after World War II. He argues
       that filmmakers must push beyond neorealism, while taking
       it into account. He champions the work of directors who
       compose for the film medium, as the neorealists did, over
       the work of directors who "fish" in literary sources.

172 KERANS, JAMES. "Le notti di Cabiria." Film Quarterly, 12,
     No. 1 (Fall), 43-45. Illustrated.
          Laudatory review. Kerans states that the movie is a
     lyrical expansion of a germinal formula of trust and be-
     trayal. He comments on Cabiria's quality of being the one
     "called" or "singled out" as if imbued with grace.

173 LEFÈVRE, RAYMOND. "Regards sur l'oeuvre de Federico Fellini."
     Image et Son, No. 109 (February), pp. 4-8. Illustrated.
     Filmography.
          On the basis of Fellini's seven films from Variety
     Lights to Nights of Cabiria, Lefèvre attempts to set clear
     the major themes to be found in Fellini's work. He dis-
     cusses Fellini's treatments of show business or spectacle,
     of the decadent rich and the cupidinous poor, of loneliness,
     and of the worth of the human being in Christian or generally
     humanistic terms.

174 MASINA, GIULIETTA. "Cabiria et moi." Translated by Marie
     Rizzo. Cinéma 58, No. 24 (February), pp. 52-54.
     Illustrated.
          Translation into French of an article originally written
     in Italian by Masina as "Io e Cabiria." Le notti di Cabiria
     di Federico Fellini. Edited by Lino Del Fra. Rocca San
     Casciano: Cappelli editore, 1957. Pp. 223-25.

175 PENSOTTI, ANITA. "Via Veneto reciterà per Fellini." Oggi, 14,
     No. 46 (13 November), 26-28. Illustrated.
          This essay provides background information on La Dolce
     Vita compiled before filming began. Pensotti outlines
     Fellini's intention to make a luxurious, "baroque fresco"
     of a decadent society where all ideals including love of
     country and matrimony fall to pieces. A French translation
     appears as "La Via Veneto jouera pour Fellini." Cinéma 59,
     No. 34 (March 1959), pp. 84-87.

176 PHILIPPE, PIERRE. "Le Doight de Dieu est dans le champ."
     Cinéma 58, No. 24 (February), pp. 55-61. Illustrated.
          Philippe attacks and parodies the exegetical critics of
     Fellini, most notably Geneviève Agel and Dominique Delouche.
     Philippe makes clear his preference for Fellini's early
     works such as Variety Lights and I Vitelloni, as opposed
     to his more recent "moralizing" films such as Il Bidone
     and Nights of Cabiria.

177 POIX, GEORGES. "Les Nuits de Cabiria." Image et Son, No. 115
     (October), pp. II-XII. Illustrated. Credits. Filmography.
          A "document" on Nights of Cabiria, containing a brief
     biography, an extensive outline of the sequences, and an
     essay of critical analysis. Poix describes the structure
     of the movie as a series of discoveries: loneliness,
     derision, hope, the mysterious, and love of another. The

deepening of Cabiria's character is the main source of
unity. Poix notes various parallels in the five different
episodes. Futhermore, he discusses briefly the shot selection, the settings, and the use of sound and music.

178   ROTHA, PAUL. "Il Bidone." Rotha on the Film. Fair Lawn,
      N.J.: Essential Books, Inc., pp. 195-97.
         A reprinting of Rotha's review of Il Bidone published
      first in Films and Filming, 3, No. 4 (January 1957), 23.

179   SARRIS, ANDREW. "Nights of Cabiria." Film Culture, 4, No. 1
      (January), 18-21.
         An extended and thoughtful review of Nights of Cabiria.
      Sarris mentions Fellini's ironic reference in his title to
      D'Annunzio and the epic tradition of early Italian films.
      He goes on to discuss five events in the heroine's life,
      each related to the development of her character. He sees
      Cabiria and her fellow prostitutes as "another tribe in the
      confederation of wanderers and outcasts, wastrels and oppor-
      tunists, with whose irregular patterns of living Fellini
      has been concerned" in his previous films. For such charac-
      ters, "social theories are meaningless, since society itself
      seems to exist beyond the horizon." Personal relationships
      achieve exaggerated intensity, and mystiques of romantic
      illusion and religion become indispensable to the characters.
      Sarris also considers Fellini's realism. This review is
      collected in Sarris' Confessions of a Cultist: On Cinema
      1959-1969. New York: Simon and Schuster, 1970. Pp. 23-29.

180   THIRARD, PAUL-LOUIS. "Les Nuits blanches de Fellini."
      Positif, 3, No. 28 (April), 19-27. Filmography.
         A two-part article on Fellini. In the first part,
      Thirard sets clear Fellini's "spiritualism" by noting his
      deliberate turning away from opportunities to present
      rational, social programs in Il Bidone and Nights of Cabiria
      and by discussing his Franciscan leanings in La Strada. In
      the second part, Thirard argues that Nights of Cabiria is
      more pessimistic than other critics claim. Cabiria is with-
      out grace and suffers setbacks from the false worlds of
      materialist society, church miracles, and love.

181   THUILLIER, PIERRE and GILBERT SALACHAS. "Les Nuits de
      Cabiria." Téléciné, No. 72 (January-February), pp. 2-16.
      Illustrated. Credits.
         An informational "fiche" on Nights of Cabiria. It con-
      tains the following sections: a sequence outline; a dis-
      cussion of the episodic structure of the movie, with
      emphasis on the alternating rhythm of hope and deception;
      an essay on the character traits of Cabiria; notes on the
      direction and shooting, the sound track, and acting of
      Giulietta Masina; and a critical overview. Thuillier and

Salachas emphasize Cabiria's smile at the end of the movie
as an affirmation of her capacity to hope. They see the
movie as the search for an absolute in a world of doubt and
uncertainty. If Fellini has lost interest in the church,
he has, nevertheless, kept a strong belief in transcendency.

1959

182   ANON. "My Experiences as a Director." International Film
Annual. No. 3. New York: Taplinger, pp. 29-35.
        English translation of an interview with Fellini at the
Centro sperimentale di cinematografia in Rome in 1958. It
appeared first as "Fellini parla del suo mestiere di
regista." Bianco e nero, 19, No. 5 (May 1958), iii-vi
back cover. And it was translated into French by Laura
Dumoulin as "Mon Métier." Cahiers du Cinéma, No. 84 (June
1958), pp. 14-21.

183   BACHMANN, GIDEON. "Federico Fellini: An Interview," in
Film: Book I. Edited by Robert Hughes. New York: Grove
Press, pp. 97-105.
        An important early interview. Fellini talks about his
first years in Rome and his entry into movies. He defines
his idea of neorealism as "looking at reality with an
honest eye." He discusses what he considers his major
theme: "It's the terrible difficulty people have in talking to each other--the old problem of communication, the
desperate anguish to be with, the desire to have a real,
authentic relationship with another person." And finally
he describes the experience of editing his films.

184   BUACHE, FREDDY. "Misticismo di Fellini." Cinema nuovo, 8,
No. 140 (July-August), 291-92.
        Buache spells out in no uncertain terms why he dislikes
La Strada. Among his reasons are his antipathy for Fellini's
"mystical exaltations" when they substitute for authenticity
and his antipathy for the masochism of Fellini's
Christianity.

185   CAVICCHIOLI, LUIGI. "Ricostruita tale e quale la via Veneto
della Dolce vita." Oggi, 16, No. 25 (18 June), 32-34.
Illustrated.
        A lively interview with Fellini on La Dolce Vita, with
asides from Marcello Mastroianni. When asked how he would
classify La Dolce Vita in relation to his other films,
Fellini candidly admits that it is his most spectacular,
the one which will have the most general appeal to a wide
audience.

186 CELLI, TEODORO. "Il capello di paglia fa onore a Nino Rota."
     Oggi, 15, No. 16 (16 April), 50-51.
         A generous review of the musical score of I Vitelloni
     composed by Nino Rota.

187 FELLINI, FEDERICO. "My Sweet Life." Films and Filming, 5,
     No. 7 (April), 7. Illustrated.
         Fellini discusses his work-in-process, La Dolce Vita.
     He explains how the character of Marcello grew from the
     character of Moraldo in the projected movie Moraldo in città
     and talks about his problems with producers.

188 _____. "Temoignage à André Bazin." Cahiers du Cinéma, No. 91
     (January), p. 29.
         Fellini's eulogy of film critic André Bazin. He praises
     Bazin's intuitive ability to go directly to the heart of a
     work. He points out that Bazin was an excellent critic of
     Italian cinema.

189 FERRUZZA, ALFREDO. "Fellini cerca una ragazza col viso da
     miliardaria." Oggi, 15, No. 8 (10 February), 30-31.
     Illustrated.
         An anecdote describing Fellini's search for the ideal
     Milanese actress to cast in the role of Maddalena in La
     Dolce Vita.

190 HOVALD, PATRICE G. "Federico Fellini: l'arracheur de masques,"
     in Le Nèo-Réalisme italien. Collection 7e Art. Paris:
     Éditions du cerf, pp. 175-97. Illustrated.
         In this book on neorealism, Hovald tries to locate
     Fellini in the neorealistic movement. He compares Fellini
     to Rossellini, his teacher. Rossellini is in the classic
     style, and Fellini in the baroque. Brief critical analyses
     of Fellini's movies from Variety Lights to Nights of Cabiria.
     Hovald is especially interesting on the Franciscan quality
     of Gelsomina.

191 PENSOTTI, ANITA. "Inchiesta sulla dolce vita della capitale."
     Oggi, 15, No. 48 (26 November), 14-22; No. 49 (3 December),
     24-30; No. 50 (10 December), 44-48; No. 51 (17 December),
     34-39; No. 52 (24 December), 44-47. Illustrated.
         A five-part series on the night life in Rome, inspired
     as a parallel to La Dolce Vita. The first two parts con-
     cern Via Veneto. The photographs are especially interest-
     ing, because they are done in the rotogravure style Fellini
     wished to duplicate in his film. In the second part, there
     are two photospreads of scuffles between movie celebrities
     and press photographers which parallel Fellini's scene in
     La Dolce Vita.

192   _____. "La Via Veneto jouera pour Fellini." Cinéma 59,
       No. 34 (March), pp. 84-87. Illustrated.
            A translation into French and an editing of Pensotti's
       article in Italian on Fellini's use of the Via Veneto and
       his intentions in La Dolce Vita. See "Via Veneto recitera
       per Fellini," Oggi, 14, No. 46 (13 November 1958), 26-28.

193   SOLMI, ANGELO. "L'atto d'accusa di Fellini alla dolce vita di
       Roma." Oggi, 15, No. 48 (26 November), 23-24. Illustrated.
            A review of La Dolce Vita based on a preview of the film.
       Solmi finds the film engrossing despite its length. He
       points out ways in which the movie repeats many of the
       themes of Fellini's earlier movies, this time from a choral
       standpoint.

194   STANBROOK, ALAN. "The Hope of Fellini." Film, British Fed-
       eration of Film Societies, 19 (January-February), 17-20.
       Illustrated.
            A brief introductory essay on Fellini's films up to
       Nights of Cabiria (1956). Stanbrook stresses Fellini's
       Christian emphasis on hope and salvation in La Strada, Il
       Bidone, and Nights of Cabiria.

195   TOZZI, ROMANO. "Love in the City." Films in Review, 10,
       No. 6 (June-July), 358-59.
            A brief review. Tozzi remarks that the film was shown
       in a bawdy, Broadway theater as sexploitation. He labels
       Fellini's episode "downright absurd."

196   TRANCHANT, FRANCOIS. "L'Adolescent dans le cinéma italien."
       Image et Son, Nos. 122-23 (May-June), pp. 21-23.
            Tranchant surveys twelve Italian films on the subject of
       adolescence, released between 1948 and 1958. I Vitelloni
       is one of the films. He looks for attitudes toward the
       family, politics, religion, work, leisure pursuits, friend-
       ship, and love. Each topic, however, receives only brief
       treatment.

                              1960

197   AGEL, HENRI. "La Douceur de vivre." Études Cinematographiques,
       1, Nos. 3-4 (Summer), 217-19.
            Agel disagrees in the strongest of terms with the jury
       at Cannes and certain French critics who find Fellini to be
       a moralist in La Dolce Vita. The work for Agel is a clin-
       ical document on the obsessions of Fellini. Above all, it
       shows the impotence of a man to take charge of his life.
       The movie is a masochistic confession.

198   ANON. "La dolce vita, il film più geniale del cinema italiano."
      Oggi, 16, No. 6 (11 February), 32-35. Illustrated.
         A picture spread of thirteen still photographs from La
      Dolce Vita. There is no text, only captions explaining
      the context in which each still appears.

199   ANON. "Su La dolce vita la parola a Fellini." Bianco e nero,
      21, Nos. 1-2 (January-February), 2-18.
         An important interview with Fellini at the Centro speri-
      mentale di cinematografia after a special showing of La
      Dolce Vita. Also present are Marcello Mastroianni and
      Brunello Rondi. Questions by students and instructors
      cover a broad range from the technical to the philosophical.
      Some of the topics covered are Fellini's relationship with
      his actors, his use of Cinemascope, set design, musical
      scoring, the evolution of the screenplay, and his analysis
      of principal characters in the film. A long extract in
      English of parts of this interview is given in Susanne
      Budgen's Fellini. London: British Film Institute, 1966.
      Pp. 96-102.

200   ARISTARCO, GUIDO. "La dolce vita." Cinema nuovo, 9, No. 143
      (January-February), 39-44.
         The Marxist critic discusses La Dolce Vita as an example
      of irrationalism in contemporary Italian cinema. He com-
      pares Fellini's conception of religion with that of Kirke-
      gaard. Ultimately, he concludes on the basis of Zavattini's
      criteria that Fellini's movie is not revolutionary. It
      says nothing new.

201   ASTRE, GEORGES-ALBERT. "La Douceur de vivre." Études Cinema-
      tographiques, 1, Nos. 3-4 (Summer), 220-24.
         Astre's defense of La Dolce Vita. He finds it a work
      which treats the intolerable separation of appearance from
      reality. It is an indictment of existence lived as spec-
      tacle. He compares the form of the movie to Dos Passos'
      Manhattan Transfer.

202   BARAGLI, ENRICO, S.J. "Dopo La dolce vita I." Civiltà cat-
      tolica, 111, No. 3 (12 September), 602-17.
         First part of a two-part series on La Dolce Vita.
      Baragli discusses the film's reception by various critics,
      political groups, and sections of society. He considers,
      in addition, the religious symbols and verbal references to
      Christianity in the film. He feels that the use of such
      material is ambiguous and concludes that no positive
      religious meaning is to be found in the film.

203   _____. "Dopo La dolce vita II." Civiltà cattolica, 111, No. 4
      (15 October), 159-76.

Second part of a two-part series on La Dolce Vita. This essay is a passionate denunciation of the film on moral and religious grounds.

204   BENAYOUN, ROBERT. "Cannes 1960." Positif, No. 35 (July-August), pp. 29-36. Illustrated.
In a report on the Cannes Film Festival, Benayoun gives brief notice of La Dolce Vita. He praises the baroque style and picaresque narration as well suited to Fellini's vision of society, which is generous, but lucid.

205   BRUNO, EDOARDO. "La dolce vita." Filmcritica, No. 94 (February), pp. 160-63.
In this article on La Dolce Vita, Bruno begins with a point by point comparison between Fellini and Rossellini. He, then, lists elements of crepuscolarismo found in Fellini's works and concludes with comments on the treatment of religion in La Dolce Vita. (Crepuscolarismo refers to a "twilight" mood produced by certain Italian poets in the early twentieth century.)

206   CEDERNA, CAMILLA. "Confesso Fellini." L'espresso-mese, 1, No. 3 (July), 54-63 & 108-109. Illustrated.
An important, early biographical sketch of Fellini based on interview material. The sketch treats such things as Fellini's love for the circus, his alleged flight to the circus, his encounter with Saraghina on the beach, his attempts to gain attention as a child, his attraction for and resentment against religion as a young boy, his alleged flight with Bianchina Sorianis when he was fifteen, his career as a cartoonist for the editor Nerbini in Florence, his days in Rome as a young man, his friendship with the variety hall comedian Aldo Fabrizi, his marriage with Giulietta Masina, his film work with Rossellini, and his film career up to and including La Dolce Vita. [No copy of this essay could be found in the U.S.A. However, a copy was located in the office of L'espresso in Rome. JCS]

207   DELOUCHE, DOMINIQUE. "Cannes." Cinema nuovo, 9, No. 145 (May-June), 233-35.
On the occasion of the Cannes Film Festival, Delouche compares Fellini's La Dolce Vita with Antonioni's L'Avventura. Although both directors treat the crisis of consciousness in modern man, both have different approaches to their subject. Fellini treats the crisis by means of baroque, hallucinatory spectacle, while Antonioni deals with the crisis in terms of introspection.

208   _____. "Un Fellini Baroque." Études Cinematographiques, Nos. 1-2 (Spring), pp. 80-85.

The French director who worked as Fellini's assistant comments on the baroque quality of his films through La Dolce Vita. He remarks on his use of fantasy. Delouche comments that his visual compositions have a plurality of points of interest and illustrates his idea by relating how Fellini complicated a landscape in Nights of Cabiria. He deals also with Fellini's use of movement and his penchant for breaking cinematic rules to shock the audience.

209   DURGNAT, RAYMOND. "Lights of Variety." Films and Filming, 7, No. 3 (December), 33.
       A review of Variety Lights, released in England in 1960 to follow up the success of La Dolce Vita. Durgnat sees in it foreshadowings of Fellini's later work.

210   FELLINI, FEDERICO. "Federico Fellini." Edited by Roger Dardenne. La Table ronde, No. 149 (May), pp. 47-51.
       A printing of an autobiographical script by Fellini, broadcast on the radio as part of a series for Université Radiophonique Internationale. Fellini traces his career up to Nights of Cabiria (1956), emphasizing his relationship with Rossellini. Fellini discusses also his propensity for open endings.

211   FERRUZZA, ALFREDO. "La grande polemica sul film di Fellini." Oggi, 16, No. 8 (25 February), 15-17. Illustrated.
       An article on the controversy provoked by the release of La Dolce Vita, mainly regarding its morality or immorality. The author surveys the reactions of critics, different strata of society, religious groups, and various newspapers and periodicals.

212   GRANDI, LIBERO. "Filming La Dolce Vita in Black-and-White and Wide-Screen." American Cinematographer, 41, No. 4 (April), 234-35, 256 & 258. Illustrated.
       Grandi discusses cinematographer Otello Martelli's use of telephoto lenses in La Dolce Vita, his handling of greys in the dawn sequences, his photographing of exploding lights in the miracle scene, and his methods of lighting for Anita Ekberg and Marcello Mastroianni and for shots on the Via Veneto and at the airport.

213   GRENIER, CYNTHIA. "Three Adventurous Italians." Saturday Review, 43 (24 December), 46-47. Illustrated.
       A review of L'Avventura, Rocco and his Brothers, and La Dolce Vita. Grenier attacks La Dolce Vita on the grounds that the movie is sentimentalized and that it has too much "Sunday-school morality" in it.

214   KEZICH, TULLIO. "Fellini e altri," in La dolce vita di Federico Fellini. Bologna: Cappelli editore, pp. 11-127.

An excellent diary of Kezich's observations about the filming of La Dolce Vita. His notes cover not only the entire filming, but also preliminary preparations including financial details, casting and production problems, and screen tests. Kezich interviews Fellini and other principals involved in the film such as Nino Rota, Tullio Pinelli, and Marcello Mastroianni. Fellini comments on how he hopes the audience will respond to La Dolce Vita. Interestingly, Kezich discovers Fellini's plans to do a film on Casanova and another called Viaggio d'amore which resembles Amarcord.

215 LANE, JOHN FRANCIS. "Fellini Tells Why." Films and Filming, 6, No. 9 (June), 30. Illustrated.
    Transcript of a BBC interview with Fellini about the reaction in Italy to La Dolce Vita. Fellini parries more questions than he answers, but does speak directly to the issue of the role of the intellectual, Steiner, in the film.

216 LAUGIER, JEAN-LOUIS. "Il dolce Fellini." Cahiers du Cinéma, No. 109 (July), pp. 45-48. Illustrated. Brief credits.
    A review of La Dolce Vita. Laugier expresses his delight that Fellini has turned away from moral tales such as La Strada, Il Bidone, and Nights of Cabiria and turned back to the less moralistic style of Variety Lights and The White Sheik. Laugier calls La Dolce Vita a documentary in which situations and people are examined without a predetermined attitude.

217 LAURA, ERNESTO G. "La stagione delle mele d'oro." Bianco e nero, 21, Nos. 3-4 (March-April), 124-39.
    An article about the resurgence of Italian cinema (1959-60) after several arid years. Among the films discussed is Fellini's La Dolce Vita which Laura regards as the most important film of the year because of its perspective on the moral decadence of modern man. Laura traces Marcello's movement as a character from irony, to cynicism, to renunciation of his last moral standards.

218 LEFÈVRE, RAYMOND. "La Douceur de vivre." Image et Son, No. 134 (October), p. 14. Illustrated. Brief credits.
    Laudatory review of La Dolce Vita. Lefèvre expresses pleasure that Fellini has turned away from movies about exceptional and symbolic characters and has turned to this study of actual social problems. He describes the movie as a report on the disintegration of a world dominated by a corrupted aristocracy and by a Christian democracy which caricatures Christianity. He praises the sequence in the chateau of Bassano and the one about the false miracle. He laments that the French censor has cut a symbolic shot of Sylvia's cleric hat covering all of Rome.

219   MARDORE. "Essai sur La dolce vita." Positif, No. 35 (July-
       August), pp. 22-28.
            Mardore salutes La Dolce Vita as a film which marks the
       maturity of Fellini and mirrors the lethargy of post-war
       society. From a generally Marxist point of view, he praises
       Fellini for turning away from "poetic solutions, nebulous
       idealism, relief through grace, and other subterfuges de-
       signed to cloud and confuse his anguish." Fellini has
       returned to the clarity of I Vitelloni, but is after bigger
       game now--the emptiness and cowardliness of his contemporary
       society.

220   MORAVIA, ALBERTO. "Il satyricon di Fellini." L'espresso, 6,
       No. 7 (14 February), 23.
            A laudatory review of La Dolce Vita, by the Italian
       novelist. Prophetically, Moravia compares Fellini's movie
       with Petronius' Satyricon in terms of content and form.
       The decadent modern world treated by Fellini has the follow-
       ing aspects in common with Petronius' world of antiquity:
       sexual promiscuity, mysticism, boredom, cruelty, sterility,
       craving for unusual pleasures, cosmopolitanism, aesthetic-
       ism, and irrationalism. In terms of structure, Fellini
       uses an "open" form such as Petronius employed. Fellini is
       able to adapt his style to the needs of the different epi-
       sodes. He runs a gamut from caricature to neorealism. [No
       copy of this review could be located in the U.S.A. A copy
       was found, however, in the archives of L'espresso in Rome.
       JCS]

221   PASOLINI, PIER PAOLO. "L'irrazionalismo cattolico di Fellini."
       Filmcritica, No. 94 (February), pp. 80-84.
            A polemical article on Fellini and La Dolce Vita by the
       filmmaker and Marxist critic. Pasolini acknowledges that
       he found La Dolce Vita deeply moving, but as a political
       thinker, he criticizes and mistrusts Fellini's irrational
       tendencies and his Catholic ideology. He calls Fellini's
       art "neo-decadent." (His charges are answered by Brunello
       Rondi in "Dialettica de La dolce vita." Filmcritica, No. 94
       [February, 1960], pp. 85-87.)

222   PENSOTTI, ANITA. "La ragazzina innocente della dolce vita."
       Oggi, 16, No. 8 (25 February), 12-14. Illustrated.
            An interview with Valeria Ciangottini who plays Paola
       in La Dolce Vita. She relates how she was discovered for
       the part.

223   RENZI, RENZO. Federico Fellini. Premier Plan No. 12. Trans-
       lated by P. L. Thirard. Lyons: S.E.R.D.O.C., 48 pp.
       Illustrated. Filmography. Credits.
            A translation into French of Federico Fellini. Parma:
       Guanda editore, 1956. This version, however, is expanded

to include material on <u>Nights of Cabiria</u> and <u>La Dolce Vita</u>.
Renzi finds these two movies to be among Fellini's best,
for they are among his most realistic and his most socially
and politically enlightened. Yet, even in these films,
Renzi objects, Fellini tends to fall back to individual
solutions for his characters, rather than to push on for a
broader program of social change. Renzi includes interview
material with Fellini on <u>Nights of Cabiria</u> and <u>La Dolce</u>
<u>Vita</u>. A brief, but important section of the book has been
translated into English by Rosalie Siegel in Gilbert
Salachas' <u>Federico Fellini: An Investigation into His Films</u>
<u>and Philosophy</u>. New York: Crown Publishers, 1969.
Pp. 187-90.

224   RHODE, ERIC. "La Dolce Vita." <u>Sight and Sound</u>, 30, No. 1
(Winter), 34-35.
     A harsh review of <u>La Dolce Vita</u>. Rhode finds Fellini's
picture of the new bohemian life to be without an informing
point of view: "His characters remain the callow clichés
of the gossip column." He states: "We are asked to be
indignant at their scandalous behaviour and yet fully to
enjoy it." Rhode argues that Fellini's films have always
been, in the past, without sensuality--he has been drawn
often to androgynous characters--but here Fellini attempts
erotic love scenes and produces only cold abstractions of
them. Rhode suggests that the monster on the beach may be
a reference to the dead body of Wilma Montesi.

225   RONDI, BRUNELLO. "Dialettica de <u>La dolce vita</u>." <u>Filmcritica</u>,
No. 94 (February), pp. 85-87.
     As one of the co-writers of <u>La Dolce Vita</u>, Rondi states
that the purpose of the film was to examine the decadence
of the present age, reflected in the restlessness and disorder of society. He remarks that the film is retrospective
in that it comments on a situation from which we are emerg-
ing. He speaks of the liberating function of the film and
defends it against Pier Paolo Pasolini's charge of "neo-
decadence." (<u>See</u> Pasolini. "L'irrazionalismo cattolica di
Fellini." <u>Filmcritica</u>, No. 94 [February, 1960], p. 80-84.)

226   _____. "Nascita dello stile di Fellini." <u>Bianco e nero</u>, 21,
Nos. 10-11 (October-November), 62-81.
     A retrospective analysis of <u>Variety Lights</u>. In this
early film, Rondi feels he can identify many of the basic
elements to be found in Fellini's later films. The scenes
in the theater reveal a typical Fellini situation: life
portrayed as a mystery without real meaning either for the
actors or the audience. The young actress anticipates the
bride in <u>The White Sheik</u> and Gelsomina in <u>La Strada</u> for her
sense of separation from others and her preoccupation with
dreams. Other elements that will prove important are

Fellini's sense of the grotesque, his interest in magic,
his preoccupation with the past, and his tendency toward
misogyny. Rondi analyzes at some length the scene in the
train station. For Rondi, this scene sums up Fellini's
attitude toward provincial life with its emptiness, bore-
dom, and fatigue.

227   SALACHAS, GILBERT. "La Douceur de vivre." Télécine, No. 91
      (September–October), pp. 2–26. Illustrated. Brief credits.
         An informational "fiche" on La Dolce Vita. It contains
      a summary of the sequences, notes on the origin and growth
      of the film project, statements about the dramatic construc-
      tion, the set design and props, lighting, sound, mise en
      scène, character summaries, information about the selection
      of actors, and a concluding critical essay. Although
      Salachas feels that the movie is more than a film à clef,
      he offers information on references in it to Ava Gardner,
      Anita Ekberg, Marilyn Monroe, Wilma Montesi, and Cesare
      Pavese. Salachas argues that La Dolce Vita, like several
      earlier movies, treats the journey of a lost human being
      through a morally bankrupt world. He quotes Fellini on the
      film: "It is a journey through disgust which ends on a
      pale note of hope." Salachas discusses the vision of
      Fellini as apocalyptic. In the socially decadent world
      recorded in the film, the individuals adopt a passive
      stance. Salachas compares Fellini's view of vice and ennui
      with those of Charles Baudelaire.

228   SILVERMAN, DORE. "Cannes 1960." Films in Review, 11, No. 7
      (August–September), 420.
         A report on the showing of La Dolce Vita at the Cannes
      Film Festival.

229   SOLMI, ANGELO. "Ecco perchè La dolce vita è un'autentica
      opera d'arte." Oggi, 16, No. 7 (18 February), 50–52.
         A review of La Dolce Vita. Solmi discusses its literary
      importance, stressing themes, characterizations, symbols,
      and unity. He states that in La Dolce Vita Fellini has
      made a new departure in film structuring.

230   WEAVER, WILLIAM. "Letter from Italy." Nation, 190 (19 March),
      pp. 260–61.
         An interesting article describing the uproar in Italy
      caused by the release of La Dolce Vita. Weaver describes
      the situation in Milan where an elegant viewer cried, "You
      are dragging Italy in the mud," and spat on Fellini.
      Weaver outlines the division of the Roman press. The
      Vatican paper, L'osservatore romano called the film
      "obscene" and demanded its withdrawal. The left-wing
      papers, Paese sera and Unità, endorsed it with lengthy

editorials. Weaver also recounts how Romans had turned
out in numbers to watch the filming going on during the
summer preceding release.

1961

231   AGEL, HENRI. Le cinéma et le sacré. Collection 7e Art.
      Paris: Éditions du cerf, pp. 120-27.
      In this book on cinematic expressions of the sacred, Agel
      devotes a section to Fellini. Agel discusses La Strada,
      Il Bidone, Nights of Cabiria, and La Dolce Vita. He argues
      that a basic Christian theme in Fellini's work is the
      fecundity of crushed innocence. Along those lines, he dis-
      cusses Gelsomina, the paralytic girl in Il Bidone, and
      Cabiria. Agel attacks La Dolce Vita as a defeatist work.
      Throughout the essay, Agel compares Fellini with Robert
      Bresson.

232   ALPERT, HOLLIS. "Adventures of a Journalist." Saturday
      Review, 44, No. 15 (15 April), 33.
      A laudatory review of La Dolce Vita. Alpert describes
      the movie as a "parable of futility, a vista of spiritual
      decay" in which the hero is "able to penetrate fraud and
      yet is a dupe." Fellini infuses his subjects with "a pro-
      found feeling for the savor and anguish of life." This
      review is reprinted as the preface to the English language
      edition of Fellini's La Dolce Vita. New York: Ballantine
      Books, 1961. Np.

233   ANON. "Quattro domande sul cinema italiano." Cinema nuovo,
      10, No. 149 (January-February), 32-41; 10, No. 150 (March-
      April), 124-35; 10, No. 151 (May-June), 225-29; 10,
      No. 152, (July-August), 320-24.
      Cinema nuovo directs four questions about Italian
      cinema to leading novelists and critics. One of the ques-
      tions asks of the importance of La Dolce Vita, especially
      as compared to L'Avventura and Rocco and his Brothers.
      Respondents are Italo Calvino, Franco Fortini, Giansiro
      Ferrata, Giorgio Soavi, Domenico Tarizzo, Luigi Russo,
      Galvano della Volpe, Mario Alicata, Michele Prisco,
      Giuseppe Raimondi, Luciano Anceschi, Pier Paolo Pasolini,
      Mario Soldati, and Mario Spinella. Calvino discusses La
      Dolce Vita as a comedy of ideology and symbols. Ferrata
      calls it social commentary within the tradition of neo-
      realism. Pasolini, as a Marxist, calls the film "neo-
      decadent." Spinella finds it a chronicle of the Christian
      bourgeoisie presented more from a sentimental standpoint
      rather than from an intellectual one. He feels that the
      film provokes feelings as opposed to thoughts or actions.

234   BERGTAL, ERIC. "The Lonely Crowd in La Dolce Vita." America,
        106, No. 1 (7 October), 13-15.
            Bergtal considers La Dolce Vita from the point of view
        of a sociologist. Communication among the people of the
        movie, he demonstrates, never manages to penetrate "beneath
        the level of body-sex or beyond a stereotyped, status-
        conscious business of mere role-playing." The public
        "villain" is the press which directs attention only to the
        surfaces of life and reinforces the superficial outlooks of
        the individuals.

235   CORICH, NEVIO. "Le notti di Cabiria." Cineforum, Nos. 1-2
        (March-April), pp. 33-48. Illustrated. Brief credits.
        Filmography.
            A biographical profile of Fellini and a critical essay
        on Nights of Cabiria. Corich traces Fellini's career as a
        writer-director up to La Dolce Vita. He discusses the
        structure, the characters, the technical aspects, and the
        theme of Nights of Cabiria. Corich likens the film to La
        Strada and Il Bidone in theme. All three deal with the
        solitude of the individual. Cabiria's capacity to hope and
        to accept life, Corich finds, is the "grace" that is granted
        her.

236   CROWTHER, BOSLEY. "La Dolce Vita." New York Times (20 April),
        p. 30. Illustrated. Brief credits.
            In this review, Crowther praises the movie as "a bril-
        liantly graphic estimation of the whole swath of society in
        sad decay." He enjoys Fellini's eye for the grotesque
        incident or bizarre occurrence that "exposes a glaring
        irony." Such an occurrence is the transporting of the
        statue of Christ by helicopter over the sunbathers on the
        rooftop.

237   DUPREY, RICHARD A. "Bergman and Fellini, Explorers of the
        Modern Spirit." Catholic World, 194 (October), 13-20.
        Illustrated.
            This article deals with "film as an instrument of
        spiritual search," with the main works considered being
        Fellini's La Dolce Vita and Bergman's Seventh Seal and
        Virgin Spring. Bergman's vision is the more positive,
        especially in Virgin Spring where he treats the subject of
        grace. Fellini's vision is apocalyptic. He deals with
        seven days and nights of debauchery, following each with a
        cold, gray dawn of realization, but Fellini offers no
        solution that the main characters accept.

238   DURGNAT, RAYMOND. "La Dolce Vita." Films and Filming, 7,
        No. 4 (January), 31-32. Illustrated.
            In this laudatory review of La Dolce Vita, Durgnat com-
        pares Fellini to von Stroheim as a satirist "of cosmopolitan

high life, of the apparatus of glamour and the melancholy emptiness behind it." He finds Fellini a more compassionate satirist.

239 FELLINI, FEDERICO. "The Bitter Life--of Money." <u>Films and Filming</u>, 7, No. 4 (January), 13 & 38.
Fellini discusses his situation after the success of <u>La Dolce Vita</u>. He announces that his new company, Federiz, will be a gathering place for new directors and for discussions of the new ideas of his friends. He also discusses, with a mixture of amusement and horror, a trip to the United States during which a public relations man "layed on" a TV interview where Fellini was to demonstrate how to kiss a lady's hand. The essay is reprinted in <u>Film Makers on Film Making</u>. Edited by Harry M. Geduld. Bloomington and London: Indiana University Press, 1967. Pp. 191-94. And in <u>Fellini on Fellini</u>. Edited by Christian Strich. New York: Delacorte Press/Seymour Lawrence, 1976. Pp. 87-91.

240 FRANCHI, R. L. "<u>La Dolce Vita</u>." <u>Film Quarterly</u>, 14, No. 4 (Summer), 55-57. Illustrated.
An angry, attacking review. Franchi calls the film "the last great gasp of the <u>ancien garde</u>" and calls for Fellini to be more innovative. At the same time, he criticises the film's shallowness: "Marcello's salvation or damnation is a personal question and this film does not deal with the personal world of reality. It is too concerned with the public image of a corrupt society to penetrate into the subtle and dangerously basic reasons for that corruption."

241 HARCOURT, PETER. "<u>La Dolce Vita</u>." <u>Atlas</u>, 1, No. 2 (April), 65-70. Illustrated.
A reprinting of Harcourt's review published first in <u>Twentieth Century</u>, 169, No. 1007 (January 1961), 81-84.

242 _____. "Out and About: <u>La Dolce Vita</u>." <u>Twentieth Century</u>, 169, No. 1007 (January), 81-84.
A review of <u>La Dolce Vita</u>. Harcourt states that the movie concerns not individual characters and story as much as certain attitudes Fellini wishes to probe. Fellini reveals the shortcomings of intellectualism and worship of the flesh and offers as a comforting alternative the Umbrian angel, Paola, an indication of the continued existence of simple trust and hope. The review is reprinted in <u>Atlas</u>, 1, No. 2 (April 1961), 65-70.

243 HART, HENRY. "<u>La Dolce Vita</u>." <u>Films in Review</u>, 12, No. 6 (June-July), 352-54.
"Federico Fellini's new film is a 3-hour peep-show--a carelessly written and directed hodge-podge of skits

depicting some of the follies of contemporary Western
civilization." Hart attacks especially "the lower middle
class quality of Fellini's unimaginative conceptions of
depravity."

244 HOLLAND, NORMAN N. "The Follies Fellini." Hudson Review,
14, No. 3 (Autumn), 425-31.
The psychoanalytical critic Norman N. Holland argues
that La Dolce Vita is more than a satire of contemporary
social mores. It has a mythic dimension. The central
mythic view is that of "man as helpless and abject before
the gorgon-like, all-powerful image of woman." Holland discusses at length Sylvia as an Aphrodite figure. He also
examines the images of seeing and hearing in the movie.
The essay is reprinted in Renaissance of the Film. Edited
by Julius Bellone. London: Collier-Macmillan, 1970.
Pp. 79-90. And it is incorporated into the longer article
"The Puzzling Movies: Three Analyses and a Guess at Their
Appeal." Journal of Social Issues, 20, No. 1 (January
1964), 71-96.

245 HULL, DAVID STEWART. "Luci del varietà." Film Quarterly, 15,
No. 1 (Fall), 48. Illustrated.
Review of Variety Lights prior to its American release.
Hull sees in it elements of Fellini films that have become
trademarks: "The individual is solitary and must realize
the fundamental ridiculousness of his existence. The
woman is the eternal agent of conscience."

246 KAUFFMANN, STANLEY. "A Catalogue of Deadly Sins." New
Republic, 144, No. 18 (1 May), 22-23.
A balanced review of La Dolce Vita. Kauffmann praises
Fellini's direction of the actors and actresses and praises
his shot selection. Yet, he raises questions about the
narrative: "Fellini has set out to move us with the depravity of contemporary life and has chosen what seems to
me a poor method: cataloguing sins."

247 LANE, JOHN FRANCIS. "La (The) Dolce (Sweet) Vita (Life)."
Films and Filming, 7, No. 9 (June), 30 & 34.
Illustrated.
Lane recounts the process of dubbing La Dolce Vita into
English, a process which he oversaw. He talks also about
the Italian method of dubbing the Italian dialogue after
shooting.

248 LATTUADA, ALBERTO and BRUNELLO RONDI. "Colloquio su Luci del
varietà." Bianco e nero, 22, Nos. 2-3 (February-March),
65-68.

A conversation between Lattuada and Rondi on <u>Variety Lights</u>. Lattuada supplies background material on the film and describes Fellini's contribution to the film.

249 LEFÈVRE, RAYMOND. "<u>Il Bidone</u>." <u>Image et Son</u>, No. 143 (July), pp. 29-30. Brief credits.
This informational "<u>fiche</u>" contains a short biography of Fellini, a brief plot summary of <u>Il Bidone</u>, and a critical discussion of the movie. Lefèvre identifies Augusto's spiritual journey as the main theme and lists other themes as loneliness, money, the depiction of the sordid, and a taste for the sacrilegious.

250 LIZZANI, CARLO. <u>Storia del cinema italiano, 1895-1961</u>. Florence: Parenti editore, pp. 191-215, 373-83 & 563-64. Illustrated. Filmography.
A survey of Italian film history by an Italian writer-director, with a chapter on Fellini. Lizzani discusses the divisive effect Fellini's movies had on the neorealistic movement and traces Fellini's evolution up to <u>Nights of Cabiria</u>. He reprints excerpts of Fellini statements about a visit to Rimini, about his intentions in <u>La Strada</u>, about his attitude toward censorship, and about his intentions in <u>La Dolce Vita</u>.

251 MEKAS, JONAS. "Movie Journal." <u>Village Voice</u>, 6, No. 27 (27 April), 13. Illustrated.
A review of <u>La Dolce Vita</u>. Mekas states that he has always objected to Fellini's sentimentality, but now is attracted to <u>La Dolce Vita</u> as Fellini's "most honest, engaged, moral film." Fellini has a preconceived view of what man is and gives that view in frozen images resembling those of the <u>fumetti</u>. The movie is "human propaganda," not art. "A very great bad film."

252 NEVILLE, ROBERT. "Poet-Director of the Sweet Life." <u>New York Times Magazine</u> (14 May), pp. 17 & 86-87. Illustrated.
A profile of Fellini, treating his past and his methods of working, but concentrating mainly on material about <u>La Dolce Vita</u>. Neville notes the scandal-sheet qualities of the film. Gherardi's sets and costumes were designed to appear as if printed in rotogravure when filmed. Events such as the suicide of Steiner and the transporting of the statue of Christ by helicopter were taken from newspaper stories.

253 PEPPER, CURTIS G. "Rebirth in Italy: Three Great Movie Directors." <u>Newsweek</u>, 58, No. 2 (10 July), 66-68. Illustrated.
Pepper discusses Fellini, Antonioni, and Visconti as the important figures in Italian resurgence in film. All three

are mature men, but they are rebels who are critical of
contemporary society. Fellini is quoted as saying: "We've
ended one part of history and haven't yet begun the next.
We are living in a great gray limbo. We have no great ties
with the past which hold or move us--at least we in Europe.
At the same time, we're unaware of what lies ahead." The
directors are made to appear at each other's throat.
Visconti comments that Fellini's art is nearer caricature
than reality. Fellini remarks on Visconti, "He is too
loaded with the past," and on Antonioni, "I miss the
humanity."

254   PERI, ENZO. "Federico Fellini: An Interview." Film Quarterly,
      15, No. 1 (Fall), 30-33. Illustrated
          Excellent interview. Fellini discusses neorealism in
      terms of its political meaning and calls for a second phase
      to it--that of the poet's vision of the reality discovered
      by the neorealists. He describes La Dolce Vita as the
      "private and confidential confession of a man who speaks of
      himself and his aberration. It is as if a friend were
      telling to other friends his confusion, his contradictions,
      and his own deceptions, trying to clarify for himself his
      own sentimental aridity." The monster at the end of the
      movie, he explains, is taken from a remembrance from child-
      hood. Fellini claims to have undertaken The Temptations
      of Doctor Antonio as a joke against censorship. Peri de-
      scribes Fellini's activities on the set of The Temptations
      of Doctor Antonio.

255   ROEMER, MICHAEL. "Three Hours in Hell." The Reporter, 24,
      No. 7 (30 March), 40-44.
          Mainly favorable review of La Dolce Vita. Roemer calls
      it Fellini's "most inclusive statement" about spiritual
      bankruptcy. "Implicit in the film is the suggestion that
      if most of us had money, and therefore time, we too would
      stand face to face with the unresolved emptiness in which
      we live." Roemer praises Fellini's ability to use the
      faces of actors and extras with striking accuracy to create
      the atmosphere of his scenes. Roemer, however, finds the
      movie too episodic and, therefore, lacking in depth of
      feeling: "a magnificent setting for a story--without a
      story."

256   SOLMI, ANGELO. "Il Film di Fellini ingiustamente bocciato."
      Oggi, 17, No. 33 (17 August), 64.
          Solmi reviews The White Sheik for a second time nearly
      ten years after its original release. He recalls that its
      opening in Milan lasted only three days and that critics
      other than he thought little of it. Now in the light of
      Fellini's later career, he notes The White Sheik has be-
      come accepted as an excellent film.

257 STEEL, RONALD. "Fellini: Moviemaker as Moralist." <u>Christian</u>
      <u>Century</u>, 78, No. 16 (19 April), 488-90.
           A review of <u>La Dolce Vita</u>, in which Steel comments at
      length on the Italian reaction to the film. He recounts
      that the film was given the seal of approval largely through
      the efforts of Cardinal Siri, Archbishop of Genoa and direc-
      tor of Catholic Action. Two Catholic newspapers, <u>Il quoti-</u>
      <u>diano</u> and <u>Il popolo</u>, published generally favorable reviews.
      Then the Vatican newspaper, <u>L'osservatore romano</u>, led an
      attack on the film by publishing two negative articles by
      Count Della Terra, a Roman nobleman. For himself, Steel
      declares the work moralistic. He finds in the movie "the
      beady eye of the moralist and the stricken conscience of
      the puritan."

                            1962

258 ANON. "<u>Boccaccio '70</u>." <u>Newsweek</u>, 60, No. 2 (9 July), 73-74.
      Illustrated.
           Of <u>The Temptations of Doctor Antonio</u>, the reviewer says,
      "Director Fellini has got some wildly hilarious moments
      out of this gargantuan fantasy, but he has taken his
      picture-making too lightly and his theme too seriously.
      When the spoof turns into a sermon on prudery, as it does,
      the fun dries up."

259 ANON. "Mastroianni scherza con la morte in maschera che
      Fellini gli ha preparato." <u>Oggi</u>, 28, No. 44 (1 November),
      14-15.
           A picture spread of four stills of Mastroianni playing
      with a mask of his own face intended for use in $8\frac{1}{2}$. The
      shots were taken during production. The scene was not in-
      cluded in the finished film. It is described here as a
      nightmare in which the hero dreams he has been killed and
      confronts his own face. The title of the movie at this
      stage is reported to be <u>Asa Nisi Masa</u>.

260 BAZIN, ANDRÉ. "<u>Il Bidone</u> ou le salut en question." <u>Qu'est-ce</u>
      <u>que le cinéma?</u> 4. Collection 7e Art. Paris: Éditions du
      cerf, pp. 129-33. Illustrated.
           A reprinting of Bazin's review of <u>Il Bidone</u> which was
      done for the newspaper <u>France-Observateur</u> in March, 1956.
      Bazin discusses the negative reaction the movie received
      at the Venice Film Festival. He, however, praises the
      power of invention and the poetic and moral vision of
      Fellini in the film. He praises the party scene, and he
      comments on the moral ambiguity of Augusto's death.

261 BAZIN, ANDRÉ. "Cabiria ou le voyage au bout du néo-realisme."
    Qu'est-ce que le cinéma? 4. Collection 7e Art. Paris:
    Éditions du cerf, pp. 134-42. Illustrated.
        A reprinting of Bazin's review of Nights of Cabiria,
    which appeared first in Cahiers du Cinéma, No. 76 (November
    1957), pp. 2-7. Later reprinted as "Cabiria: The Voyage
    to the End of Neorealism." What Is Cinema? 2. Translated
    by Hugh Gray. Berkeley: University of California Press,
    1971. Pp. 83-92.

262 _____. "La Profonde Originalité des Vitelloni," in Qu'est-ce
    que le cinéma? 4. Collection 7e Art. Paris: Éditions du
    cerf, pp. 143-45. Illustrated.
        Reprinting of a review of I Vitelloni which Bazin did
    for Radio-Cinema-Television in October, 1957. Bazin finds
    the movie to be original in terms of its conception.
    Fellini has put aside traditional elements of narration.
    He simply records the lifestyle of his characters. Bazin
    calls this "a pure phenomenology of being."

263 _____. "La Strada," in Qu'est-ce que le cinéma? 4. Collection
    7e Art. Paris: Éditions du cerf, pp. 122-28. Illustrated.
        A reprinting of Bazin's review of La Strada which was
    originally published in Esprit, 23, No. 5 (May 1955),
    847-51.

264 BENAYOUN, ROBERT. "De l'ange à l'éclipse: un triomphe du
    fond." Positif, No. 47 (July), pp. 68-74.
        In this report on the Cannes Film Festival, Benayoun
    inserts brief notice of Boccaccio '70. He attacks the
    film as a Goliath of false provocation with scant connec-
    tion to Boccaccio. Fellini's The Temptations of Doctor
    Antonio is labeled a "monumental fiasco," and Fellini's
    special effects are found poor.

265 BRUNO, EDOARDO. "Boccaccio '70." Filmcritica, No. 124
    (August), pp. 425-27.
        A review of Boccaccio '70. Bruno mentions Fellini's
    part only briefly and comments that it fails because of
    its moralizing.

266 CROWTHER, BOSLEY. "Boccaccio '70." New York Times (27 June),
    p. 40. Illustrated. Brief credits.
        Crowther calls The Temptations of Doctor Antonio the
    best of three vignettes. It is a broadly satiric fantasy,
    jabbing at those who lose their sense of proportion in
    figuring out what is decent and what is not.

267 DELCORDE, JACQUES, ed. Entretiens avec Federico Fellini:
    texte extrait des émissions télévisées "La Double Vue."
    Belgium: Radiodiffusion télévision belge, 69 pp.
    Illustrated.

This monograph is an edited version of the texts of four television shows in which Fellini was interviewed. Fellini's remarks are set off against those made by others connected with his work, some of whom are Michelangelo Antonioni, Ennio Flaiano, Piero Gherardi, Otello Martelli, Giulietta Masina, Marcello Mastroianni, Alberto Moravia, Pier Paolo Pasolini, Tullio Pinelli, and Nino Rota. The interview is extremely important in that Fellini offers in it many of the pronouncements and stories which later critics have sought to extend or have quarreled with. It is a basic document. Some of the topics covered are Fellini's childhood in Rimini, his experience at school in Fano, his running away to the circus, his early days in Rome, his meeting with Roberto Rossellini, his film work with Rossellini and with Alberto Lattuada, the genesis of The White Sheik, neorealism, his methods of working with his collaborators and with his actors, his Christianity, the scandal caused by La Dolce Vita, his sense of guilt, and his attitude about criticism, Portions of this interview are translated into English by Rosalie Siegal in Gilbert Salachas' Federico Fellini. New York: Crown Publishers, 1969. Pp. 93-97 & 109-110. A long extract in English of parts of this interview is given in Susanne Budgen's Fellini. London: British Film Institute, 1966. Pp. 85-95.

268   _____. "Federico Fellini: 'Voyons un peu si, pour une fois, j'arrive a dire la vérité." Cinéma 62, No. 67 (June), pp. 4-20. Illustrated.
    A reprinting of extracts from an interview Fellini gave for Radiodiffusion-télévision belge in 1962. See Delcorde, ed. Entretiens avec Federico Fellini. Belgium: Radio-diffusion-télévision belge, 1962. 69 pp.

269   Di CARLO, CARLO and GAIO FRATINI. "Solo uno scherzo." Boccaccio '70 di De Sica, Fellini, Monicelli, Visconti. Rocca San Casciano: Cappelli editore, pp. 105-106.
    A brief interview with Fellini about his reasons for making The Temptations of Doctor Antonio. Fellini insists the film is only a joke made in retaliation for the accusations of immorality launched against La Dolce Vita.

270   FELLINI, FEDERICO. "Federico Fellini: A Self-Portrait." Esquire, 57, No. 2 (February), 92.
    Fellini's responses to a brief questionnaire. His answer to a question about his panaceas: "Imagination, night dreams, recollections of childhood, some very agreeable girls, a trip in a car with a true friend or also with an unknown [person].... In fine, I wish to say that I manage quite easily to console myself." He includes a caricature of himself drawn by him.

271 FELLINI, FEDERICO. "The Screen Answers Back." <u>Films and
Filming</u>, 8, No. 8 (May), 18.
Fellini answers four survey questions about film critics
and film criticism. He states, "Good criticism gives me
strength."

272 _____. "La storia di via Veneto." <u>L'europeo</u>, 18, No. 27
(8 July), 49-61. Illustrated.
In this essay about the Via Veneto, Fellini denies that
he is a "regular" on the street he made famous in <u>La Dolce
Vita</u>. He recounts that when he first came to Rome as a
provincial youth, he was in awe of the glamour of the shops
and cafes and of the conversations he imagined taking place
between intellectuals and writers on Via Veneto. This feeling he tried to capture in <u>Nights of Cabiria</u>. Later after
WWII, Fellini relates, he met with Via Veneto photographers
for several evenings and gleaned from them a large collection of tall tales he used in his film. The street in <u>La
Dolce Vita</u>, however, he argues, was largely a product of
invention, "an allegorical fresco," which, after the success
of the movie, was imitated in real life. Publicity-hungry
stars and promoters began to stage bizarre happenings on
the Via Veneto which would not have occurred earlier. In
the course of the essay, Fellini defends most of his remem-
brances as being essentially true and tries to counter the
impression given of him in Angelo Solmi's biography. The
article is reprinted as "End of the Sweet Parade." <u>Esquire</u>,
59, No. 1 (January 1963), 98-108 & 128. The illustrations
in <u>L'europeo</u> differ from those in <u>Esquire</u>.

273 _____. "The Sweet Beginnings." <u>Atlas</u>, 3, No. 2 (February),
149-52.
Fellini discusses his experiences with Roberto Rossellini
on the filming of <u>Rome, Open City</u> and <u>Paisan</u>. The article
first appeared in Italian in <u>Segnacolo</u> (August 1961). It
is collected in Christian Strich's edition, <u>Fellini on
Fellini</u>. New York: Delacorte Press/Seymour Lawrence,
1976. Pp. 41-46.

274 FITZPATRICK, ELLEN. "<u>Boccaccio '70</u>." <u>Films in Review</u>, 13,
No. 6 (June-July), 363-64.
Fellini's episode in the anthology film is described as
a piece of "puerility."

275 FLAUS, JOHN. "<u>La Dolce Vita</u>." <u>Film Journal</u>, No. 19 (April),
pp. 44-49.
Flaus defines Fellini's "fresco" style in <u>La Dolce Vita</u>
and discusses his abuses of the style. He attacks the use
of Marcello as too individualized to be a "guide figure"
and not individualized enough to be a central character of
depth. Flaus finds the shot compositions "theatrical" and
the editing undynamic.

276 FRATINI, GAIO. "Foglietti di diario." <u>Boccaccio '70 di De</u>
<u>Sica, Fellini, Monicelli, Visconti</u>. Edited by Carlo Di
Carlo and Gaio Fratini. Rocca San Casciano: Cappelli
editore, pp. 29-35.
     A diary of daily events in the filming of <u>The Temptations</u>
<u>of Doctor Antonio</u>. Fratini describes events such as the
decision to use a giant poster of Anita Ekberg, the casting
for some of the parts, and the filming of some of the scenes.

277 GAUTIER, GUY. "<u>La Strada</u>." <u>Image et Son</u>, Nos. 153-54
(Summer), pp. 74-77. Brief credits. Filmography.
     An informational "<u>fiche</u>" on <u>La Strada</u>. Gautier offers a
plot summary, a short biography of Fellini, a summary of
diverse critical reactions, and his own critical discussion.
Gautier describes the movie as a metaphysical fable, with
the characters being abstractions of human qualities.
Gautier detects three major themes: love is the path to
salvation; the redemption of man is possible no matter how
abject his state is; and nothing is useless, that is, all
objects and all beings participate in the great design of
the creator.

278 JOHNSON, IAN. "Anthony Quinn." <u>Films and Filming</u>, 8, No. 5
(February), 13-15 & 42-43.
     The article is a survey of Quinn's career. It contains
a critical appraisal of his role of Zampano in <u>La Strada</u>.

279 KAUFFMANN, STANLEY. "Picaresque and Picturesque." <u>New</u>
<u>Republic</u>, 147, No. 3 (16 July), 28-29.
     A review of <u>Boccaccio '70</u>. Kauffmann calls Fellini's
episode the best and most honest of the three parts of the
film. He says of it: "a <u>tour de force</u> that makes up in
baroque casting, and swift, satirical editing for what the
script lacks in freshness."

280 MEKAS, JONAS. "Movie Journal." <u>Village Voice</u>, 7, No. 36
(28 June), 15.
     Brief notice of <u>Boccaccio '70</u> in which Mekas praises
Fellini's episode as a "satire on Madison Avenue, sex and
I don't know what." It is interesting to note that Mekas
contradicts this position a few weeks later in "Movie
Journal," <u>Village Voice</u>, 7, 41 (2 August), 15. There, he
suggests that only Visconti's episode is worth seeing.

281 MORAVIA, ALBERTO. "Gli amori impossibili del neocapitalism."
<u>L'espresso</u>, 8, No. 10 (11 March), 23.
     A favorable review of <u>Boccaccio '70</u>, by the Italian
novelist. Fellini's episode, <u>The Temptations of Doctor</u>
<u>Antonio</u>, Moravia finds the most amusing. Fellini has
obviously enjoyed making it. Fellini's intent is to satirize the kind of hack-moralists who criticized <u>La Dolce Vita</u>.

Further, Fellini seems to be playing with the same kind of fantasy treated by Charles Baudelaire in his poem "La Géante." [No copy of this review could be located in the U.S.A. A copy was found, however, in the archives of L'espresso in Rome. JCS]

282 PECHTER, WILLIAM S. "Two Movies and Their Critics." Kenyon Review, 24, No. 2 (Spring), 351-62.
       An essay on Fellini's La Dolce Vita and Antonioni's L'Avventura. Pechter attacks Norman Holland's mythic reading of La Dolce Vita and then moves on to attack the movie itself as "redundant." Fellini's method is to pile detail upon detail, "moving quantitatively from the particulars to the generality." Pechter attacks also the idea of the innocent, young girl as the "answer" in the movie. Pechter prefers L'Avventura. The essay is reprinted in Pechter's Twenty-Four Times a Second. New York: Harper and Row, 1971. Pp. 37-50.

283 SOLMI, ANGELO. Storia di Federico Fellini. Milan: Rizzoli editore, 237 pp. Illustrated. Filmography. Bibliography.
       The pioneering work of critical biography of Fellini. The book covers Fellini's career from the beginning through the critical reception of The Temptations of Doctor Antonio in 1962. Solmi is the critic for Oggi and is a friend of Fellini. He prints the legends about Fellini given out by Fellini, but he, then, endeavors to check them through other sources. The first section of the book is speculative. Solmi comments on what he considers to be shaping factors in Fellini's career and major concerns in his work. These include Fellini's tie to neorealism, his interest in the individual, his fear of isolation, his interest in magic and religion, the clash between his symbolism and his moral preoccupations, style, improvisation, and the importance of Giulietta Masina to Fellini's work. This section also includes a summary of the two major critical views in Italy toward Fellini, the Catholic view and the left-wing view. The second section is the most valuable. It is a critical biography of Fellini's career. It deals with Fellini's childhood, his apprentice years in films, and each of Fellini's feature movies through The Temptations of Doctor Antonio. Particularly useful are the discussions of the evolutions of the ideas of the films and the discussions of the production details. The work has been translated into English by Elizabeth Greenwood as Fellini. London: Merlin Press, 1967; New York: Humanities Press, 1968. This English version contains an additional chapter on $8\frac{1}{2}$.

284 TYLER, PARKER. "Love in the City," "La Strada," and "La Dolce Vita." Classics of the Foreign Film: A Pictorial

Treasury. New York: Cadillac Publishing, pp. 214-19 &
244-49. Illustrated
  In this pictorial history of foreign films, Tyler treats
three movies directed in part or totality by Fellini. With
Love in the City, Tyler celebrates the "mere thrill of living bodies that move," caught by the documentary method.
With La Strada, Tyler writes about attacks by neorealists
and Marxist critics on the movie and discusses the essentially religious creed of the work. With La Dolce Vita,
he discusses the play between Fellini's satiric objects and
a kind of autobiographical relish he brings to his description of Rome.

285 VERDONE, MARIO. "Boccaccio '70." Bianco e nero, 23, No. 3
  (March), 58-60. Credits.
  A review of Boccaccio '70, in which Verdone states that
only the portion by De Sica has anything to do with
Boccaccio. The segment by Fellini, argues Verdone, was
created as a rebuttal against the detractors of La Dolce
Vita.

1963

286 ALPERT, HOLLIS. "From ½ Through 8½." New York Times Magazine,
  (21 July), pp. 20-21. Illustrated.
  Essentially a picture spread in which Alpert explains
the counting by which Fellini arrived at the opus number
for 8½.

287 _____. "The Testament of Federico Fellini." Saturday Review,
  46, No. 26 (29 June), 20.
  Strongly favorable review of 8½. Alpert praises
Fellini's imagination and courage in treating the moment
of artistic crisis of a director much like himself.

288 AMENGUAL, BARTHÉLEMY. "Anthologie." Études Cinématographiques, Nos. 28-29 (Winter), pp. 69-77.
  In the special issue of Études Cinématographiques devoted to 8½, Amengual compiles excerpts from reviews by
critics in Italy, the Soviet Union, and Uruguay.

289 _____. "Itinéraire de Fellini: du spectacle au spectaculaire."
  Études Cinématographiques, Nos. 28-29 (Winter), pp. 3-26.
  Illustrated.
  Amengual argues that a basic element of Fellini's art
is his use of staged scenes and scenes with stagelike qualities. We do not view the scenes from out front, but rather
from the wings where we are conscious of their staged qualities. Amengual discusses staged reality especially in 8½.
He digresses briefly on Fellini's obsession with earth-
mothers, his treatment of aged characters, and his movement

away from definitive endings, and he contrasts Fellini's
use of point-of-view with that of Orson Welles.

290   AMENGUAL, BARTHÉLEMY and MICHEL ESTÈVE. "Notes bibliograph-
iques." Études Cinématographiques, Nos. 28-29 (Winter),
pp. 83-85.
    In this special issue of Études Cinématographiques de-
voted to 8½, Amengual and Estève have compiled a bibliography of books on Fellini, screenplays by Fellini, an
interview, reviews, and articles on 8½. There are fifty-
two items listed. Most are in French or Italian.

291   ANON. "Confessione in pubblico: colloquio con Federico
Fellini." Bianco e nero, 24, No. 4 (April), 1-21.
    An important and interesting interview with Fellini and
camera director Gianni di Venanzo by students and instruc-
tors at the Centro sperimentale del cinematografia, after
a showing of 8½. To conjectures about the autobiographical
nature of his films, Fellini responds that the issue is not
important and that autobiography is only a point of departure for him. His motive for making 8½, Fellini insists,
was to present two sides of a character, the realistic and
the fantastic. He comments on how he works with collaborators Ennio Flaiano, Tullio Pinelli, and Brunello Rondi,
denies having been influenced by Last Year at Marienbad,
discusses the two different endings he shot for 8½, argues
that a reversal of direction comes to his protagonist when
he touches the bottom of his abyss, and reaffirms an observation he made previously to journalists that 8½ concerns
the incomprehensible words the Umbrian angel says to
Marcello in La Dolce Vita. di Venanzo describes some of
his solutions to technical problems in 8½. This interview
appears in French, in edited form, as Fellini's article
"Propos sur 8½." Cahiers du Cinéma, No. 164 (March 1965),
pp. 23-24.

292   ANON. "Director on the Couch." Time, 81, No. 26 (28 June),
82. Illustrated.
    A suspicious review of 8½. The reviewer describes the
movie as "self-psychoanalysis" and wonders whether Fellini's
"cinematic catharsis" will be of interest to the viewer who
"may not care to take on the director's doubts and
confusions."

293   ANON. "La Dolce Far Niente." Time, 81 (1 March), 46.
Illustrated.
    Unsigned review of the Italian reactions to the openings
of 8½. At the premiere, there was scattered applause. In
one southern town, however, people nearly beat up the theater manager out of sheer frustration. Intellectual reviewers put the movie in the stream-of-consciousness tradition.

Fellini himself claims the movie is simply about a director who accepts the confusion and doubts of his life and learns "that this chaos is the real force out of which his creativity comes."

294   ANON. "8½: Business Rating $ $ $ Plus." Film Bulletin, 30, No. 357 (8 July), 14.

In this trade journal review, the reviewer predicts 8½ will provide material for analysis to people in the "class market" and sex symbols to whet the appetites of the "mass audience," but he thinks it unlikely the movie will "penetrate very deeply into the hinterlands." The music by Nino Rota, he finds, has "the elements of a commercial click." Then he makes some interesting observations on Fellini's use of blacks and whites in the film.

295   ANON. "Fellini: 8½." Cinema (Beverly Hills), 1, No. 5 (August-September), 19-27. Illustrated.

Brief review of 8½ and interview with Fellini. The reviewer claims Fellini has fallen from favor with intellectuals for his treatment of Steiner in La Dolce Vita. He urges viewers, however, to see 8½ and quotes Fellini's dictum: "Sit back and enjoy the film as an informal discourse between the spectator and the man who is confessing everything." In interview, Fellini denies explicit links between himself and others such as Joyce, Proust, Kierkegaard and Resnais, but leaves open the question of general influences through the culture one lives in.

296   ANON. "Fellini's Masterpiece." Newsweek, 61, No. 25 (24 June), 111-14. Illustrated.

A review of 8½ as an autobiographical film shaped into an artistic masterpiece. Along with autobiographical details, the reviewer stresses the image of the woman in the movie: on the one hand, mother, sister, saint and virtue, and on the other, whore, vice, corruption and sin. The ending of the movie is Guido's "leap of faith."

297   ANON. "Lettere al direttore." Cinema nuovo, 12, No. 164 (July-August), 243-46.

Letters to the editor about 8½. One concerns the morality and symbolism of 8½, and another the issue of Fellini's treatment of religion.

298   ANON. "The Talk of the Town." New Yorker, 39, No. 20 (6 July), 19-20.

Coverage of the American premiere of 8½. The reviewer discusses the mirroring effect of the director in the audience watching a film about a director making a film about a director. Fellini tells the reporter that the movie is more than self-confession; it is a movie about a man

"confronting half a dozen different problems at once."
However, Fellini adds that making a movie about a man like
himself has caused a kind of catharsis: "I have a feeling
that this picture has set me free."

299   ARISTARCO, GUIDO. "Il gattopardo e il telepata." Cinema
nuovo, 12, No. 162 (March-April), 123-29.
   An essay on Visconti's The Leopard and Fellini's 8½.
The Marxist critic identifies Fellini's film as impression-
istic and makes references to the influences of other
artists like Joyce, Bergman, and Antonioni. The second half
of this essay has been translated into French by Barthélemy
Amengual as "L'Intellectual, l'artiste et le télépathe."
Études Cinématographiques, Nos. 28-29 (Winter 1963), 40-46.

300   _____. "L'Intellectual, l'artiste et le télépathe." Trans-
lated by Barthélemy Amengual. Études Cinématographiques,
Nos. 28-29 (Winter), 40-46.
   A French translation of the second part of: "Il gatto-
pardo e il telepata." Cinema nuovo, 12, No. 162 (March-
April 1963), 125-29.

301   BACHMANN, GIDEON. "Fellini Eight and a Half." Film Journal,
No. 21 (April), pp. 116-18.
   Bachmann, friend of Fellini and interviewer, describes
the experience of watching Fellini at work on 8½. (Bachmann
had three different bit parts in the movie.)

302   BAKER, PETER. "Eight and a Half." Films and Filming, 10,
No. 1 (October), 21.
   A brief review in which Baker attacks the ending of 8½.
Apparently Baker feels the movie ends with Guido's
"suicide" and with the decision not to make the scheduled
movie, and he does not see the circling of the characters
as a new beginning. He, therefore, finds the ending too
bitter.

303   BATTEN, MARY. "8½." Film Comment, 1, No. 5 (Summer), 61-62.
Illustrated.
   A review of 8½. Batten describes the movie as a psychoanalysis of a director who "functions against society
rather than with it." Guido withdraws in three ways:
(1) by going to the thermal resort; (2) by retreating into
his past through memory; (3) by going into wish-fulfilling
dreams. Batten attacks the ending for its confusion of
reality and fantasy.

304   BELLOUR, RAYMOND. "La Splendeur de soi-même." Études Cinématographiques, Nos. 28-29 (Winter), pp. 27-30.

Bellour praises $8\frac{1}{2}$ as the first movie to treat seriously as its subject the process of the creation of a movie by its auteur. He compares $8\frac{1}{2}$ to André Gide's The Counterfeiters.

305   BILLARD, PIERRE. "Clôture: confession d'un enfant du siècle." Cinéma 63, No. 77 (June), pp. 62-63. Illustrated.
Laudatory review of $8\frac{1}{2}$ at its showing in the Cannes Film Festival. Billard compares Fellini to other writers and directors such as Alberto Moravia and Michaelangelo Antonioni in the treatment of creative impotency as a modern theme. He comments also on Fellini's treatment of the subconscious of his protagonist and on Fellini's inclusion of self-criticism of his film through the character of the collaborator.

306   BORDE, RAYMOND and ANDRÉ BOUISSY. Nouveau Cinéma italien. Premier Plan No. 30. Lyons: Premier Plan, pp. 5-7, 21-22, 97 & 100-102. Illustrated.
In this monograph on the history of the new Italian cinema after neorealism, Borde and Bouissy consider Fellini's contributions, especially La Dolce Vita and $8\frac{1}{2}$. They feel that La Dolce Vita was a pivotal film. It broke with the puritan morality of neorealism; it took on the problem of the alienation of the individual in the modern world shaped by technology and expansion economics; it was a dazzling piece of cinematography; and it was an enormous success at the box office. Even though the film is idealogically suspect to Borde and Bouissy, they argue it was tremendously influential. $8\frac{1}{2}$, they classify along with Divorce Italian Style and others as part of a movement in Italian cinema toward black comedy.

307   BRUNO, EDOARDO. "Otto e mezzo." Filmcritica, No. 131 (March), pp. 170-73.
A negative review of $8\frac{1}{2}$. Bruno finds the disunity of the film disturbing and its symbolism obvious.

308   CAREY, GARY. "Director in Mid-journey." The Seventh Art, 1, No. 4 (Fall), 12 & 27-28.
A review attacking $8\frac{1}{2}$. For Carey, $8\frac{1}{2}$ is a film about a director at a mid-point in his career, who comes to a self-realization. Carey objects that Guido lacks the depth necessary to be a director we can take seriously and that the comparison between Guido and Fellini gives the film an air of a stunt. Furthermore, he finds this Pirandellian movie lacks Pirandello's compassion. Fellini has concerned himself too much with international mannequins (Claudia Cardinale, Barbara Steele, and Sandra Milo), at the expense of a more interesting, more human woman (Anouk Aimée).

309   CEDERNA, CAMILLA. "La bella confusione." $8\frac{1}{2}$ di Federico
      Fellini. Rocca San Casciano: Cappelli editore, pp. 17-85.
            An introductory essay in an edition of the screenplay of
      $8\frac{1}{2}$. Cederna discusses the making of the film. She begins
      with a conversation she had with Fellini in late 1960 or
      early 1961 about the nature of the hero in $8\frac{1}{2}$. She re-
      prints a letter from Fellini to Brunello Rondi in early
      1961, summing up Fellini's intentions in the film and out-
      lining scenes and main characters. She discusses how
      Fellini divided the work on the project among Rondi, Tullio
      Pinelli, Ennio Flaiano, and Piero Gherardi in the fall of
      1961. Concerning the casting of the film, Cederna recounts
      how Fellini's early wish for Laurence Olivier fell through,
      his subsequent hiring of Mastroianni, and Fellini's search,
      through newspaper announcements, for a fleshy woman to play
      Carla. During the filming itself, she interviews partici-
      pants and describes the shooting of many scenes. At the
      end of the filming, she puts questions to Fellini concern-
      ing his feelings about what he has done. He remarks that
      the film may not be as comic as he had thought and hopes
      that it will not appear to be a presumptuous movie. He
      discusses the two endings--the dining car ending and the
      circus ending, and announces that he feels a joyful sense
      of liberation. The essay is translated into French by H. de
      Mariassy and C. de Lignac as "Une Belle Confusion," in $8\frac{1}{2}$
      de Fellini. Histoire d'un film racontée par Camilla Cederna.
      Paris: René Julliard, 1963. Pp. 9-108. Also translated
      into French and edited by Paul-Louis Thirard in "$8\frac{1}{2}$ de
      Fellini." Cinéma 63, No. 75 (April 1963), pp. 94-109.

310   _____. "Une Belle Confusion." $8\frac{1}{2}$ de Fellini. Histoire d'un
      film racontée par Camilla Cederna. Translated by H. de
      Mariassy and C. de Lignac. Paris: René Julliard,
      pp. 9-108.
            Translation into French of Cederna's essay published
      originally as "La belle confusione," in $8\frac{1}{2}$ di Federico
      Fellini. Rocca San Casciano: Cappelli editore, 1963.
      Pp. 17-85.

311   COHEN, ROBERTA. "A Fresh Interpretation of Fellini's $8\frac{1}{2}$."
      Film, British Federation of Film Societies, No. 38 (Winter),
      pp. 18-19. Illustrated.
            A brief reading of $8\frac{1}{2}$. Cohen argues that Guido is a
      "worrier with a conscience" who questions his life, his
      relationship with women, and himself. In the last scene,
      he understands himself and sees the people in his life in
      perspective.

312   COLLET, JEAN. "Le Plus Long Chemin." Études Cinématograph-
      iques, Nos. 28-29 (Winter), pp. 57-61.

An article on the conflict of <u>animus</u> and <u>anima</u> in $8\frac{1}{2}$. The spirit of <u>animus</u> is represented by the hard lucidity of the French critic Daumier, by heights, and by pure abstractions such as Claudia. The spirit of <u>anima</u> is deeper, confused, and earthy. It is represented by the descents in the movie and the earthy, sensual longings of Guido. In $8\frac{1}{2}$, Fellini affirms the <u>anima</u>.

313   COMUZIO, ERMANNO. "La colonna sonora di <u>Fellini otto e mezzo.</u>" <u>Cineforum</u>, No. 23 (March), pp. 270-72.
      An essay on the sound track of $8\frac{1}{2}$. Comuzio praises the use of sound, noise, and silence in the film, but is critical of some of Nino Rota's musical score, especially his choice of "The Ride of the Valkyries" for the harem revolt.

314   CRIST, JUDITH. "$8\frac{1}{2}$-Brilliant Film, But Strangely Cold." <u>New York Herald Tribune</u>, 123, No. 42,461 (26 June), 15. Illustrated. Brief credits.
      In this review, Crist calls $8\frac{1}{2}$ one of the most brilliant films of the contemporary era, but she finds it strangely cold and uninvolving. It dazzles the mind, but does not touch the heart. For those who are not cultists, seeing the movie is like eavesdropping on the psychoanalysis of a stranger. The review is collected in Crist's <u>The Private Eye, the Cowboy, and the Very Naked Girl</u>. New York: Holt, Rinehart, and Winston, 1968. Pp. 14-16.

315   CROWTHER, BOSLEY. "$8\frac{1}{2}$." <u>New York Times</u> (26 June), p. 36. Illustrated. Brief credits.
      A laudatory review of $8\frac{1}{2}$. Crowther states that the film "sets up a labyrinthine ego for the daring and thoughtful to explore, and it harbors some elegant treasures of wit and satire along the way." He objects, however, to the movie's ending, which he takes to be the hero's realization that he must give, as well as take, love.

316   Di GIAMMATTEO, FERNALDO. "Un caso clinico." <u>Bianco e nero</u>, 24, No. 4 (April), 42-49. Illustrated. Credits.
      Article on $8\frac{1}{2}$. Di Giammatteo praises the film for the masterful way Fellini has eliminated the barrier between fantasy and reality and lists the technical and artistic devices Fellini uses to do this. In addition, Di Giammatteo admires the use of dialogue in $8\frac{1}{2}$ which he feels brings new freedom and naturalness to Italian cinema.

317   DORIGO, FRANCESCO. "Otto e mezzo." <u>Cineforum</u>, No. 23 (March), pp. 247-69. Illustrated. Brief credits.
      A biographical profile of Fellini and a critical essay on $8\frac{1}{2}$. Dorigo traces Fellini's career as a writer-director up to $8\frac{1}{2}$. He gives a sequence-by-sequence synopsis of the film. And he offers an analysis of $8\frac{1}{2}$ in terms of its

development from the original story treatment, in terms of
style and technique, and in terms of theme. Dorigo feels
that Fellini has overreached himself in 8½. He has introduced problems and ideas that he is not prepared to push
to their conclusions. Fellini treats the inability to communicate, the sense of alienation, and the loneliness of a
man caught between the value system of the modern scientific
society of the post-war era and the value system of the
pre-war society more oriented to church and family.

318   FALLACI, ORIANA. "Famous Italian Director." Gli antipatici.
      Milan: Rizzoli editore, pp. 77-98.
         Interview with Fellini conducted during the releasing
      of 8½. Fallaci finds that fame has made Fellini egotist-
      ical, and she slams away at his ego in the interview.
      Topics covered include the autobiographical elements in 8½,
      Fellini's intentions in the movie, his future plans to use
      Giulietta Masina in films, Fellini's Catholic background,
      his interest in Ingmar Bergman and Charlie Chaplin, and his
      assessment of his success. The interview is translated
      into English in Fallaci's Limelighters. London: Michael
      Joseph, 1967. Pp. 49-67. And in Fallaci's The Egotists:
      Sixteen Surprising Interviews. Chicago: Henry Regency,
      1968. Pp. 187-205. It is translated into French and edited
      by Paul-Louis Thirard in "8½ de Fellini." Cinéma 63,
      No. 75 (April 1963), pp. 94-109.

319   FELLINI, FEDERICO. "End of the Sweet Parade." Esquire, 59,
      No. 1 (January), 98-108 & 128. Illustrated.
         Translation into English of Fellini's "La storia di via
      Veneto." L'europeo, 18, No. 27 (8 July), 49-61. The
      illustrations in Esquire differ from those in L'europeo.

320   _____. "Si butto in ginocchio ad abbracciarmi." Cinema
      nuovo, 12, No. 165 (September-October), 360-62.
         An essay by Fellini on the occasion of his being awarded
      a prize for 8½ at the Moscow Film Festival. Fellini com-
      ments on the confused reception of a film which exalts
      man's individuality in a country which celebrates
      collectivity.

321   _____. "What Fellini Thinks Mastroianni Thinks about Women."
      Vogue, 142, No. 3 (15 August), 50, 133 & 135. Illustrated.
         An invented dialogue between Fellini and Mastroianni.
      Fellini projects his own description of ideal women into
      the speech of Mastroianni. Many, if not all of the dif-
      ferent ideals, appear in 8½. Perhaps most interesting is
      the final ideal: "I remember the first impression I had
      of woman, when I was a child. When I was six years old,
      my mother or my nurse was a quiet breathing in the night,
      a port where I could cast my anchor, or the refuge of a
      warm dream."

322 FORD, CHARLES. "Cannes 1963." <u>Films in Review</u>, 14, No. 6
     (June–July), 345.
          Report on the showing of 8½ at the Cannes Film Festival.

323 GILL, BRENDAN. "The Current Cinema." <u>New Yorker</u>, 39 (29
     June), 62.
          Brief laudatory review. Gill states: "8½ is a comedy,
     and the hero's plight and eventual salvation are, to an
     uncanny degree, disguised manifestations of joy."

324 HATCH, ROBERT. "Films." <u>Nation</u>, 197, No. 3 (27 July), 59–60.
          A review in which Hatch labels 8½ "a work of egotism so
     striking as to guarantee its notoriety and almost to assure
     its success." The impulse to make 8½, Hatch says also, is
     "not unlike the schoolboy ruse of writing a paper entitled
     'Why I Have Nothing to Say.'" Yet, the imagery and comment
     of the movie are presented with an "infectious grin." The
     movie is shrewd entertainment finally, not confession and
     therapy.

325 HIRSCHMAN, JACK. "8½." <u>Film Quarterly</u>, 17, No. 1 (Fall),
     43–46. Illustrated.
          A review of 8½ in which Hirschman compares Fellini's
     achievement to that of Joyce and Pirandello. Hirschman
     argues that "the over-riding fact of 8½ is that for the
     hero, as for any man...reality may not exist except as the
     imagination invents it."

326 HOLLAND, NORMAN N. "Fellini's 8½; Holland's <u>11</u>." <u>Hudson
     Review</u>, 16, No. 3 (Autumn), 429–36.
          An interesting essay by the psychoanalytical critic
     Norman N. Holland. Holland finds 8½ too much a piece of
     self-psychoanalysis. He compares it to <u>La Dolce Vita</u> which
     deals with similar psychoanalytical themes, but does so in
     a more generalized, abstracted way. <u>La Dolce Vita</u> has more
     intellectual "meaning" in the traditional moral sense and
     is, therefore, richer." It is also more accessible and less
     private. In a raw, personal way, Fellini continues in 8½
     his interest in the conflict of the male versus the female.
     Men in 8½ are essentially passive, impotent, and dying, but
     concerned with rising and succeeding in terms of money,
     profession, religion, and words. Women "are white, asso-
     ciated with maternal love, healing and forgiveness; they
     are also to be looked at and lusted at." They are
     approached best when they are a little dehumanized. Holland
     feels Fellini is "working out a wish to return to a pre-
     verbal life consisting mostly of looking at mother."

327 _____. "The Puzzling Movies: Their Appeal." <u>Journal of the
     Society of Cinematologists</u>, 3, 17–28.

Holland discusses the recent release of difficult and puzzling movies by Ingmar Bergman, Alain Resnais, Michaelangelo Antonioni, Fellini and others. He theorizes that the "riddling form" of such movies gives "intellectual justification for gratifying the simplest of visual desires, looking at sexy things." More importantly, the films take us back to the child's sense of puzzlement before emotionally complex situations, but convert puzzlement now to an intellectual and aesthetic context so that we may feel confident of "solving" it now as adults. La Dolce Vita is the film by Fellini which is considered in this context. The material in this essay is incorporated into Holland's longer essay "The Puzzling Movies: Three Analyses and a Guess at Their Appeal." Journal of Social Issues, 20, No. 1 (January 1964), 71-96. (Note: Journal of the Society of Cinematologists is now Cinema Journal.)

328 JACOTEY, CHRISTIAN. "Bilan critique." Études Cinématographiques, Nos. 28-29 (Winter), 62-68. Illustrated.
A psychoanalytical essay on 8½. Jacotey discusses the four kinds of childhood factors that mark the adult Guido: (1) the parents; (2) school; (3) Catholic religion; and (4) the discovery of sex. Guido "takes the cure" at the spa in the psychological sense by examining these factors in his dreams and in his movie. Especially interesting are Jacotey's remarks on the curative effect of Guido's symbolic suicide.

329 JOHNSON, IAN. "Boccaccio '70." Films and Filming, 9, No. 7 (April), 29.
Brief review in which Johnson praises especially the opening sequences of The Temptations of Doctor Antonio.

330 KAEL, PAULINE. "The Come-Dressed-As-the-Sick-Soul-of-Europe Parties." Massachusetts Review, 4, No. 2 (Winter), 378-91.
Kael discusses La Dolce Vita, La Notte, and Last Year at Marienbad as European party movies perhaps derived from Renoir's Rules of the Game. She writes: "Fellini and Antonioni ask us to share their moral disgust at the life they show us--as if they are illuminating our lives, but are they? Nothing seems more self-indulgent and shallow than the dissatisfaction of the enervated rich; nothing is easier to attack or expose. The decadence of aristocracy and its attraction to and for Bohemia, are nothing new, not especially characteristic of our age, nor even much of a social problem."

331 KAUFFMANN, STANLEY. "A Jolly Good Fellini." New Republic, 149, No. 2 (13 July), 28-29.
A review of 8½. Kauffmann describes the work as a piece of virtuosity, and as such, he finds it excellent. The

subject matter of a creative crisis encountered and sur-
vived is not explored in depth, rather it provides a frame-
work or an occasion for Fellini's dreamlike sequences.
Kauffmann argues that from La Dolce Vita on, Fellini has
used theme as opportunity rather than as concern. Reprinted in A World on Film. New York: Harper & Row, 1966.
Pp. 322-325.

332 KUHN, HELEN WELDON. "8½." Films in Review, 14, No. 7
     (August-September), 433-35. Illustrated.
        Kuhn states that 8½ presents "incidents of fact, dream,
     fantasy and imagination strung together without reason and
     without art."

333 LANE, JOHN FRANCIS. "A Case of Artistic Inflation." Sight
     and Sound, 32, No. 3 (Summer), 130-35. Illustrated.
        A survey of the state of Italian Cinema in 1962-1963.
     Lane attacks the self-indulgent excesses he finds in De
     Sica's The Condemned of Altona, Visconti's The Leopard,
     and Fellini's 8½. Lane calls 8½ "a Pirandello-like search
     for reality" on the surface. When one looks closer, he
     argues, the film is no more than a "film director's
     notebook."

334 LAURA, ERNESTO G. "L'anti-Marienbad." Bianco e nero, 24,
     No. 4 (April), 54-57.
        An article on 8½, in which Laura defines it as the
     antithesis of Last Year at Marienbad. 8½ offers the stream
     of consciousness of a contemporary man rooted in a society
     at a precise moment. It is not nearly as formally abstract
     as Last Year at Marienbad or as vague.

335 LEPROHON, PIERRE. "Federico Fellini." Histoire du cinéma II,
     l'étape du film parlant. Paris: Éditions du cerf,
     pp. 281-83. Illustrated.
        Brief biographical sketch of Fellini up to the time of
     Boccaccio '70.

336 MADDOCKS, MELVIN. "Fellini Again: 8½." Christian Science
     Monitor, (26 June), p. 6.
        Laudatory review of 8½. Maddocks relishes the light-
     ness and gaiety that Fellini brings to the traditionally
     dour aspects of modern angst: stalled purposes, the ter-
     rors of isolation, miscarriages of communication, spiritual
     suffocation, impotence, and boredom.

337 MANCEAUX, MICHELE. "Fellini en liberté." L'Express, (25
     April), pp. 26-28. Illustrated.
        An interview with Fellini in Rome shortly after 8½ had
     been shown at Cannes. Manceaux follows Fellini on his
     rounds from barber shop to post office to art gallery.

Fellini talks of the meaning of the ending of $8\frac{1}{2}$, his
reasons for making the critic in $8\frac{1}{2}$ French, his attitude
toward psychoanalysis, his sense of guilt, his attitude
about religion, his distrust of the organizing power of
words, and his preference for the spontaneous and the
instinctive.

338   MEKAS, JONAS. "Movie Journal." Village Voice, 8, No. 36
      (27 June), 13.
          Review of $8\frac{1}{2}$. Mekas calls it a film without precedent
      in the commercial cinema. It is a personal film, Fellini's
      equivalent to Cocteau's Blood of a Poet. Mekas especially
      praises Fellini's rendering of childhood.

339   MORAVIA, ALBERTO. "Federico Fellini: Director As Protagonist."
      Atlas, 5, No. 4 (April), 246-48.
          English translation of a review which first appeared as
      "Scopre in se stresso un personaggio," L'espresso, 9, No. 7
      (17 February 1963), 23.

340   _____. "Scopre in se stesso un personaggio." L'espresso, 9,
      No. 7 (17 February), 23.
          Important review of $8\frac{1}{2}$ by one of Italy's leading novel-
      ists. Moravia finds the movie to be an honest treatment of
      "the collapse of creative powers due to lack of vitality."
      This modern neurosis, he maintains, is a theme running
      through our modern culture. Fellini treats it all: "the
      sense of absurdity,...the transformation of life into
      dream and dream into life, the nostalgia for childhood (age
      of energy and vitality which has the further advantage of
      protective maternal love). The horror of the sexual rela-
      tionship that impoverishes and emasculates, creative vel-
      leity, disgust at reality, flight from responsibility and,
      finally, flirtation with suicide." Moravia praises the
      dream sequences as original, "in the metaphorical sense,"
      and compares Fellini to Pirandello and Joyce. This review
      is translated into English as: "Federico Fellini: Director
      As Protagonist,: Atlas, 5, No. 4 (April 1963), pp. 246-48.
      It is translated into French and edited by Paul-Louis
      Thirard in "$8\frac{1}{2}$ de Fellini." Cinéma 63, No. 75 (April 1963),
      pp. 94-109.

341   NAVONE, JOHN J. "Dizzy Doings on a Set." Life, 55, No. 3
      (19 July), 95-97.
          A picture spread of the set of $8\frac{1}{2}$. Seven still
      photographs.

342   _____. "Fellini's La Dolce Italia." Commonweal, 77, No. 25
      (15 March), 639-41.
          An overview of Fellini's Catholic morality, with special
      emphasis on La Dolce Vita. In that film, Navone argues,

Fellini brings his "provincial" and "medieval" morality to bear on the anxiety-ridden modern civilization of Rome. Like many Italian Catholic intellectuals, Fellini is too Catholic for secularists and too modern for clericals.

343 PAOLELLA, ROBERTO. "Un elicottero in Fellini, in Bergman." Bianco e nero, 24, No. 12 (December), 44-45.
     A brief note in which Paolella compares Fellini's use of the image of the helicopter in La Dolce Vita with Bergman's use of it in Through a Glass Darkly.

344 PINEL, VINCENT. "Filmographie de Federico Fellini." Études Cinématographiques, Nos. 28-29 (Winter), pp. 78-82.
     In this special issue of Études Cinématographiques devoted to 8½, Pinel compiles a filmography of Fellini's work. Pinel begins with Rome, Open City in 1944, ignoring earlier work as not essential, and ends with 8½ in 1963.

345 PRICE, JAMES. "Eight and a Half: A Quest for Ecstasy." London Magazine (New Series), 3, No. 8 (November), 58-62.
     Price argues that there are two Fellinis: the satirist and the symbolist poet. It is the symbolist side that bothers Price, because it is beginning to run "a danger of becoming bloodless, repetitive, and naive." With 8½, he especially discusses the pursuit of the girl in white and Fellini's procession ending.

346 RENZI, RENZO. "La 'mezza eta' del socialismo?" Cinema nuovo, 12, No. 162 (March-April), 112-15.
     Renzi draws analogies among the neurotic crisis depicted in 8½, the mal du siècle of modern man, and the aging pains of the socialist movement.

347 RHODE, ERIC. "8½." Sight and Sound, 32, No. 4 (Autumn), 193.
     Laudatory review of 8½. Rhode feels that Fellini made La Dolce Vita to demonstrate to critics he could give a "realistically correct account of Roman society." It was a "creative compromise." In 8½, Fellini shows he is again his own man. Guido demonstrates in the film that "his type of film must be created through his authentic self, and not through the dictates of theory."

348 SADOUL, GEORGES. Histoire du cinéma mondial. Seventh Edition. Paris: Flammarion, pp. 335-36.
     A brief outline of Fellini's career up to and including La Dolce Vita. Sadoul puts Fellini in the category of neorealism, but his remarks about Fellini tend to emphasize Fellini's differences from neorealism. Sadoul notes aspects of comedia dell'arte in La Strada and finds some of the flavor of Chekhov in I Vitelloni.

349 SALACHAS, GILBERT. <u>Federico Fellini</u>. Collection Cinéma
     d'Aujourd'hui. Paris: Seghers, 224 pp. Illustrated.
     Filmography.
          A useful collection of condensed material up to <u>8½</u>. The
     work contains a biographical section which follows and
     quotes from Angelo Solmi's book and a critical section in
     which Salachas attempts to isolate and describe materials
     characteristic of Fellini's movies: processions, public
     squares, unexpected objects in the landscape, fiestas, and
     entertainers. Most useful are excerpts from interviews of
     Fellini collected by Salachas from European journals
     (usually French) that are hard to obtain in the United
     States. Also contained in the work are excerpts of story
     treatments and screenplays, including some material that
     never survived as parts of released movies. The final sec-
     tion is a sampling of French and Italian criticism and of
     comments by those who have worked with Fellini. The book
     in slightly expanded form has been translated into English
     by Rosalie Siegal as <u>Federico Fellini: An Investigation
     into his Films and Philosophy</u>. New York: Crown Publishers,
     1969.

350 _____. "<u>8½</u>" [<u>Huit et demi</u>]. Télécine, No. 112 (October), np.
          Capsule review of <u>8½</u>. Salachas calls the film an over-
     whelming visual and audio presentation. It is also a lucid
     inquiry into the human experience of self-acceptance.

351 SIMON, JOHN. "Fellini's 8½¢ Fancy." <u>New Leader</u>, 46, No. 16
     (5 August), 24-25.
          A negative review of <u>8½</u>. Simon sees the movie as a
     "disheartening fiasco." The present, he argues, is too
     painful to use for autobiography. This form needs tranquil
     recollection. Fellini's tone in <u>8½</u> falters between irony
     and self-pity. Worse, Fellini tries to make his film
     weighty with symbolism and intellectual content, when his
     forte in the past has been character study, local color,
     controlled emotionalism, bittersweet humor, satire, and a
     lyrical view of the world. This review is collected in
     Simon's <u>Private Screenings</u>. New York: Macmillan, 1967.
     Pp. 74-78. And in <u>Film As Film</u>. Edited by Joy Gould
     Boyum and Adrienne Scott. Boston: Allyn and Bacon, 1971.
     Pp. 170-75. Reprinted with study questions in Andrew
     Sarris' The Film. Indianapolis: Bobbs-Merrill, 1968.
     Pp. 53-55.

352 _____. "To Live in Pieces." <u>Acid Test</u>. New York: Stein and
     Day, pp. 17-21.
          Simon compares Fellini's <u>La Dolce Vita</u> and Antonioni's
     <u>L"Avventura</u> as two films which explore the ennui of modern
     life. He finds Fellini's the better of the two films.
     Fellini's careful construction persistently develops the
     point that "there is no cure for human insufficiency and
     unhappiness."

353   SOLMI, ANGELO. "Fellini rivela i retroscena del film più
       atteso dell'anno." <u>Oggi</u>, 19, No. 7 (14 February), 48-51.
       Illustrated.
              A lengthy interview with Fellini before the release of
       <u>8½</u>. Fellini admits that the film takes its departure from
       his own life. The director also insists that the film was
       primarily developed on a day-to-day basis during the shoot-
       ing. He explains what many of the images and fantasies in
       the film mean to him and comments on what he calls the
       "trap of reality."

354   _____. "Mi chiamo Fellini: prendetemi come sono." <u>Oggi</u>, 19,
       No. 9 (28 February), 68-70.
              An interesting review of <u>8½</u>. Solmi identifies the movie
       as Fellini's most courageous and honest one. Solmi sees <u>8½</u>
       as the culmination of a discourse about himself which
       Fellini began with <u>I Vitelloni</u>. <u>8½</u> is a confession of an
       emotional crisis which ends with the hero's self-acceptance.

355   TAYLOR, JOHN RUSSELL. "<u>Boccaccio '70</u>." <u>Sight and Sound</u>, 32,
       No. 2 (Spring), 91-92.
              In the course of this harsh review of the three-part
       movie anthology, Taylor discusses Fellini's original edit-
       ing of <u>The Temptations of Doctor Antonio</u>, which ran the
       feature-length time of an hour and a half.

356   THIRARD, PAUL-LOUIS, ed. "8½ de Fellini." <u>Cinéma 63</u>, No. 75
       (April), pp. 94-109. Illustrated.
              A "dossier" on <u>8½</u>. Thirard edits and translates into
       French material from the following works: Camilla Cederna's
       "La bella confusione," in <u>8½ di Federico Fellini</u>. Rocca
       San Casciano: Cappelli editore, 1963. Pp. 17-85; Oriana
       Fallaci's "Famous Italian Director," in <u>Gli antipatici</u>.
       Milan: Rizzoli editore, 1963. Pp. 77-98; Alberto Moravia's
       "Scopre in se stesso." <u>L'espresso</u>, 9, No. 7 (17 February
       1963), 23; and Mino Argentieri's review in <u>Rinascita</u>, a
       Communist journal. Argentieri finds interesting the film's
       portrait of a Catholic in crisis.

357   TOROK, JEAN-PAUL. "Cannes 63." <u>Positif</u>, Nos. 54-55 (Summer),
       pp. 86-99.
              In the course of this report on the Cannes Film Festival,
       Torok mounts a paragraph-long, blistering attack on <u>8½</u> for
       its exhibitionism: "un des plus sinistres carnages de
       l'histoire du cinéma."

358   VERDONE, MARIO. "L'ora della verità di un artista." <u>Bianco
       e nero</u>, 24, No. 4 (April), 50-53.
              An article on <u>8½</u>. Verdone ponders the reasons why
       Fellini made <u>8½</u> and conjectures that the film was born of

the empty feeling which followed the birth of his masterpiece, La Dolce Vita. As such, 8½ is a moment of truth, a
form of self-therapy for Fellini's artistic life.

359   VIRMAUX, ALAIN. "Les Limites d'une conquête." Études Cinéma-
         tographiques, Nos. 28-29 (Winter), pp. 31-39. Illustrated.
            An important article on 8½. Virmaux discusses the doubl-
         ing principle in the film. It is a film about making a
         film. Referring to heraldry, Virmaux calls the work "en
         abyme," or a shield mounted on a shield. He compares the
         film to previous works by Cocteau, Pirandello, Proust, and
         Gide. He concludes that doubled works can gain aesthetic
         harmony and metaphysical complexity, but he finds 8½ some-
         what simplistic and academic in its use of the possibilities
         of doubling. (This essay forms the basis for a later
         article by Christian Metz on the same subject. See Christian
         Metz's "Mirror Construction in Fellini's 8½," in Film
         Language: A Semiotics of the Cinema. Translated by Michael
         Taylor. New York: Oxford University Press, 1974.
         Pp. 228-34.)

360   ZAND, NICOLE. "Mauvaise conscience d'une conscience chreti-
         enne." Études Cinématographiques, Nos. 28-29 (Winter),
         pp. 47-56. Illustrated.
            An important article on 8½. Zand argues that the funda-
         mental theme is the hero's (and Fellini's) Christian con-
         sciousness. While trying to break from the pronouncements
         of the church, Guido is obsessed with a sense of sin. We
         see this largely in his sexual relationships. He dreams of
         escaping or resolving the conflict between his desires and
         moral dictates. Both endings Fellini devised for the film
         show Guido in such a dream situation. In a sense, Guido
         has not grown emotionally since the moment when he was
         caught with Saranghina when he was made aware of the con-
         flict between the flesh and moral law.

361   ZUCCONI, MARIO. "La musica di 8 e mezzo." Filmcritica,
         No. 138 (October), pp. 641-43.
            An analysis of the use of circus music in 8½. Zucconi
         discusses the psychology of circus music and how this psy-
         chology extends to the film.

                                   1964

362   ANON. "Fellini neuf et demi." Cinéma 64, No. 91 (December),
         pp. 11-13. Illustrated.
            Brief account of Fellini in action filming Juliet of the
         Spirits in his studio on the Palatine Hill in Rome.

363 ANON. "Fellini's Inferno." <u>Newsweek</u> 64, No. 21 (23 November), 117.

Review of <u>Il Bidone</u>. The reviewer finds the movie less successful than <u>La Strada</u> and <u>The Nights of Cabiria</u>, but discusses it as the Inferno in a trilogy, with <u>La Strada</u> as Purgatory and <u>The Nights of Cabiria</u> as Paradise.

364 ANON. "Le Neó-réalisme vu par les auteurs." <u>Études Cinéma-tographiques</u>, Nos. 32-35 (Summer), p. 79.

Fellini's views on neorealism are excerpted in French from George Bluestone's "An Interview with Federico Fellini," <u>Film Culture</u>, 3, No. 3 (October 1957), pp. 3-4 & 21; and from Gideon Bachmann's "Federico Fellini: An Interview," in <u>Film: Book I</u>. Edited by Robert Hughes. New York: Grove Press, 1959. Pp. 99-100.

365 ANON. "Politica cultura impegno." <u>Cinema nuovo</u>, 13, No. 172 (November-December), 429-35.

The article begins with a quotation of Jean-Paul Sartre's credo that politics are not a sentiment that one can abandon or assume at will, but rather a true dimension of the man. There is no individual life but only a collective one. We are born political. After this introduction, Godard, Sadoul, and Fellini are invited to respond. Fellini credits Italian cinema with being the first medium to reflect national consciences in Post-WWII Italy, but acknowledges that he is content with the current tendency to veer away from social commentary to a more subjective study of the internal man.

366 BACHMANN, GIDEON. "Disturber of the Peace: Federico Fellini." <u>Mademoiselle</u>, 60 (November), 152-53, 209-15 & 224.

The first half of this interview with Fellini is a re-editing of material published as: "Interview with Federico Fellini." <u>Sight and Sound</u>, 33, No. 2 (Spring 1964), 82-87. The second half of the interview, however, contains fresh material and reveals the religious, mythical, and perhaps Jungian side of Fellini. Fellini discusses his abhorence of collective solutions. His conception of "salvation" is always individual. It involves the discovery of one's ego without the trappings of dogma, and it involves the possible "re-formation" of the ego. The woman, argues Fellini, can help the male to this "re-formation." Fellini also describes moments when we seem to intuit our place in a harmonious design.

367 ____. "Interview with Federico Fellini." <u>Sight and Sound</u>, 33, No. 2 (Spring), 82-87. Illustrated.

A particularly good interview with Fellini on relationships between the filmmaker and his audience and between the filmmaker and his art. Some specific references to

8½. A re-edited version of this interview appeared as
"Disturber of the Peace: Federico Fellini." <u>Mademoiselle</u>,
60 (November 1964), 152-53, 209-15 & 224.

368 BENNETT, JOSEPH. "Italian Film: Failure and Emergence."
<u>Kenyon Review</u>, 26, No. 4 (Autumn), 738-47.
A survey of the state of Italian filmmaking. Bennett
argues that Fellini has fallen off from the level attained
in <u>I Vitelloni</u>, with its strong sense of physical location.
Fellini, like Hemingway and Faulkner, has been led astray
by intellectual critics and has become pretentious. Bennett
attacks 8½ as "a disgusting piece of self-exhibition."

369 BOYER, DEENA. <u>The Two Hundred Days of 8½</u>. Translated by
Charles Lam Markmann, with an Afterword by Dwight Macdonald.
New York: Macmillan, 218 pp. Illustrated.
A journal of behind the scenes activity in the making of
8½. Boyer reports in some detail on the screen tests,
Fellini's initial conception of the movie, the contents of
the original scenario, the filming of many of the major
sequences, and the two different endings of the movie.
Boyer records, more than analyzes, the material, but her
book is clearly a very important source of information
about 8½ and about Fellini's methods of directing. Macdonald's "Afterword" is a reprinting of his article
"Fellini's Masterpiece." <u>Esquire</u>, 51, No. 1 (January 1964),
149-51.

370 COCKS, JOHN C., JR. "<u>Il Bidone</u>." <u>Film Quarterly</u>, 18, No. 1
(Fall), 55-57.
A harsh review of <u>Il Bidone</u> as the least successful of
Fellini's "trilogy of loneliness." Cocks attacks the sentimentality of Augusto's scenes with his daughter and with
the crippled peasant girl, the abrupt jump-cutting which
destroys "lyric flow," and the attempt to bring spiritual
depth to Augusto only in the last sequence.

371 CROWTHER, BOSLEY. "<u>Il Bidone</u>." <u>New York Times</u> (20 November),
p. 42. Illustrated. Brief credits.
Crowther reviews the film's first showing in the United
States, nine years after its European opening. He states
that the film now can be seen as a "false step" in Fellini's
development. He finds the film a sentimental story of the
small-time swindler who reforms in his last acts. Nevertheless, Crowther praises the first swindle and the
"Gethsemane" scene.

372 FELLINI, FEDERICO. "9½: A Self-Portrait of the Movie Director
as an Artist." <u>Show</u>, 4, No. 5 (May), 86 & 105.
Illustrated.

An important autobiographical essay. Fellini discusses the moment during the shooting of The White Sheik when he asserted himself and became a director. He lists authors who interest him and expresses a feeling of "congeniality" with directors Bergman and Kurosawa. He comments on the historical importance of neorealism. And finally, he defines his own mythos in terms of a desire to break free of his upbringing and to find a new, more personal and individual self-definition.

373 GIANNATTASIO, SANDRA. "I migliori, il linguaggio e le opere a basso costo." Cinema nuovo, 13, No. 168 (March-April) 88-99.

A questionnaire concerning recent films, especially $8\frac{1}{2}$, is put to a wide variety of writers, filmmakers, and critics. Participants are Giulio Carlo Argan, Giorgio Bassani, Carlo Bernari, Carlo Levi, Alberto Moravia, Pier Paolo Pasolini, Giuseppe Patroni-Griffi, and Natalino Sapegno. Argan praises Fellini's gift for parody. Bassani is impressed with the richness of Fellini's language, but wishes he would strive for more clarity in the overall meanings of his films. Pasolini sees nothing new or experimental in Fellini's film. Levi, on the other hand, identifies a new cinematic language in Fellini.

374 GUTTUSO, RENATO. "I migliori, il linguaggio e il film storico." Cinema nuovo, 13, No. 170 (July-August), 273-74.

Guttuso addresses the question of whether or not $8\frac{1}{2}$ is a "positive experience." He affirms that it is. He finds Fellini a sentimental man with an enormous instinct for imagery.

375 HOLLAND, NORMAN N. "The Puzzling Movies: Three Analyses and a Guess at Their Appeal." Journal of Social Issues, 20, No. 1 (January), 71-96.

Holland reprints here in slightly modified form his review of La Dolce Vita, "The Follies Fellini." Hudson Review, 14, No. 3 (Autumn 1961), 425-31; and his essay "The Puzzling Movies: Their Appeal," Journal of the Society of Cinematologists, 3 (1963), 17-28. He combines these with reviews of Bergman's Seventh Seal and Resnais' Last Year at Marienbad. He theorizes that the "riddling form" of these three movies gives us "intellectual justification for gratifying the simplest of visual desires, looking at violent and sexy things." Further, he argues that the films take us back to the child's sense of puzzlement before emotionally complex situations, but convert puzzlement to an intellectual and aesthetic context so that we may feel confident of "solving" it now as adults.

376   LAWSON, JOHN HOWARD. <u>Film: The Creative Process</u>. New York:
Hill and Wang, 236–37, 245–48, et passim.
In this book on film history and theory, Lawson offers
brief discussions of Steiner's suicide as <u>acte gratuit</u>,
an acceptance of the "absurdity" of human existence, and of
Marcello's sense of alienation in <u>La Dolce Vita</u>.

377   MACDONALD, DWIGHT. "Fellini's Masterpiece." <u>Esquire</u>, 51,
No. 1 (January), 149–51.
An essay in which Macdonald summarizes the complaints
brought against 8½ by other American and English critics
of the little magazines and praises it for what they dislike about the movie. The complaints essentially boil down
to the one that the movie lacks intellectual depth. Macdonald defends 8½: "It is a wordly film, all on the surface: humorous, rhetorical, sensuous, hardheaded, lyrical,
full of sharply realistic detail and also of fantastic
scenes...." Macdonald emphasizes the movie's social comedy.
The essay is reprinted in Deena Boyer's <u>The Two Hundred
Days of "8½."</u> Translated by Charles Lam Markmann. New
York: Macmillan, 1964. Pp. 209–18.

378   PENSOTTI, ANITA. "Ho perduto un anno per capire cosa volevo."
<u>Oggi</u>, 20, No. 37 (10 September), 28–31. Illustrated.
An interview with Fellini and his wife about <u>Juliet of
the Spirits</u>. Fellini analyzes the character of Juliet and
discusses his intended meanings in the film. Additional
comments by Giulietta Masina are included, especially anec-
dotes about Fellini's personality and career.

379   RENZI, RENZO. "Gli antenati di Federico Fellini." <u>Cinema
nuovo</u>, 13, No. 169 (May–June), 196–202.
Renzi discusses the influence on Fellini of his native
Romagna, elaborating on its maritime tradition, Oriental
leanings, its mysticism and sensuality, and its poetic
tradition as personified in Pascoli. Renzi concludes the
article with a brief but interesting discussion of the
idiosyncrasies of Italian Roman Catholicism as reflected in
Fellini's movies.

380   RHODE, ERIC. "Fellini's Double City." <u>Encounter</u>, 22, No. 6
(June), 44–49. Illustrated.
Rhode traces and defends Fellini's movement from neorealism to a concern for the inner world of fantasy.
Localities recur in Fellini's films and obsess him as
internal landscapes. Rhode concentrates on Fellini's use
of Rome as both <u>civitas dei</u> and <u>civitas diaboli</u>.

381   RONDI, BRUNELLO. "<u>Lo sceicco bianco</u>: consolidamento dello
stile di Fellini." <u>Bianco e nero</u>, 25, Nos. 4–5 (April–
May), 42–56.

A study of The White Sheik by Fellini's friend and collaborator. Rondi discusses Fellini's interest in the
disparity between man's fantasies and reality and demonstrates how he derives humor from the disparity in The
White Sheik.

382 SARRIS, ANDREW. "Films: Il Bidone." Village Voice, 10,
No. 5 (19 November), 13.
An interesting review of Il Bidone. Sarris regards the
movie as Fellini's most depressing. He lauds Fellini for
not glossing over or over-satirizing the confidence tricks.
The ending, he feels, is ambiguous, for it suspends the
hero between death and deliverance, suggesting an agnostic's
view of Calvary. Sarris finds Fellini most interesting in
his early period, "when his unresolved mysticism grappled
with his dramatic vitality."

383 SCHICKEL, RICHARD. "A Regular Succession of Masterpieces," in
Movies: The History of an Art and an Institution. New
York: Basic Books, pp. 139-63. Illustrated.
In this chapter on post-WWII, European cinema, Schickel
gives an overview of Fellini's career, concentrating on
La Dolce Vita and 8½. The first, he finds an overlong,
simplistic study of ways in which modern man substitutes
absurd action for the old morality, and the second, "an
unsurpassed exercise in cinematic onanism."

384 SIMON, JOHN. "Escapism into Art." New Leader, 47, No. 24
(23 November), 28-29.
In this review, Simon discusses Godard's A Woman Is a
Woman and Fellini's Il Bidone and praises the unassuming
quality of Fellini's movie as opposed to the pretentious-
ness of Godard's. The review is collected in Simon's
Private Screenings. New York: Macmillan, 1967. Pp. 132-36.

385 TAYLOR, JOHN RUSSELL. "Federico Fellini," in Cinema Eye,
Cinema Ear. New York: Hill and Wang, pp. 15-51, 230-33
& 279. Illustrated. Filmography. Credits. Bibliography.
A pioneering work. Taylor is the first critic in
English to attempt an extended critical overview of
Fellini's work. He argues that the structure of sequences
and the use of landscape for psychological "objective cor-
relatives" are fundamental aspects of Fellini's "baroque
art." He describes the structure of a typical sequence in
terms of the characters starting alone, being drawn into a
more and more intricate pattern of action, and then being
unwound from it and left alone to face their own personal
problems. The landscapes Taylor discusses most fully are
the beach by the sea and the city square. His essay contains biographical information and critical readings of

Variety Lights, The White Sheik, I Vitelloni, La Strada,
Il Bidone, Nights of Cabiria, La Dolce Vita, and 8½.

386   WALTER, EUGENE. "Dinner with Fellini." Transatlantic Review,
      No. 17 (Autumn), pp. 47-50.
         Walter, a Fellini translator, describes an evening at
      Fellini's villa in Fregene. The guests play elaborately
      costumed charades, and Fellini describes the movie medium
      in terms of its ability to trigger memories and associations
      in the mind of the viewer. Parts of this essay are incor-
      porated into Walter's "The Wizardry of Fellini." Films and
      Filming, 12, No. 9 (June 1966), 18-26. The essay "Dinner
      with Fellini," with additional remarks on Petronius'
      Satyricon, is reprinted as "Federico Fellini," in Behind
      the Scenes: Theater and Film Interviews from the Trans-
      atlantic Review. Edited by Joseph F. McCrindle. New York:
      Holt, Rinehart, and Winston, 1971. Pp. 167-71.

                              1965

387   ANON. "Federico Fellini." International Film Guide 1965.
      London: Tantivy Press; New York: A. S. Barnes, pp. 11-14.
      Illustrated. Filmography.
         A biographical and critical survey of Fellini's career
      through 8½. The author concludes that Fellini's characters
      often are forced through suffering to try to communicate
      with their fellow human beings.

388   ANON. "Happy Medium." Newsweek, 66, No. 20 (15 November),
      124-25. Illustrated.
         A review of Juliet of the Spirits. The reviewer objects
      to inept plot devices and to the highly abstract presenta-
      tion of Juliet's situation, but praises the movie as inven-
      tive and original, especially in the use of color. The
      review offers a reading of the movie as Juliet's movement
      to free herself from the influences of bourgeois sentiment
      and humiliating religiosity and to redefine her life as her
      own.

389   ANON. "Tra maghi e fantasmi, Fellini ci narra a colori il
      dramma coniugale di Giulietta." Oggi, 21, No. 44 (4
      November), 50-53. Illustrated.
         A picture spread of five color stills and two black and
      white stills from Juliet of the Spirits.

390   ANON. "Variety Lights." Newsweek, 65, No. 20 (17 May), 104.
         Favorable review of Variety Lights on its U.S. opening.
      The reviewer notes how the metaphor of the stage runs
      through La Strada, La Dolce Vita, and 8½, as well as Variety
      Lights. He states that in Variety Lights, co-directors

Fellini and Lattuada show the desperation and the child-like optimism of the vaudeville performers.

391   ARISTARCO, GUIDO. "Gli spiriti e le vaghe stelle." Cinema
      nuovo, 14, No. 178 (November-December), 441-46.
         In this essay on Visconti and Fellini, Aristarco attacks
      Juliet of the Spirits for its baroque tendencies and for
      the influence in it of early twentieth-century poet Gabriele
      D'Annunzio. Aristarco feels that Fellini in his obsession
      to do something new has instead produced a film which con-
      tains a little of each of his previous ones. He suggests
      that Fellini has become too much of a prestidigitator.

392   BACHMANN, GIDEON. "Federico Fellini vous parle." Cinéma 65,
      No. 99 (September-October), pp. 71-89. Illustrated.
         An interview with Fellini as he finishes work on Juliet
      of the Spirits. He talks about his pleasure in developing
      the germ of an idea into a story. He mentions two stories
      that never came to fruition, Moraldo in città and Viaggio
      con Anita. Fellini discusses his methods of using a screen-
      play, of working with collaborators on the screenplay, of
      working with set designer Piero Gherardi, of casting, of
      directing actors, of choosing music, and of selecting shots.
      He comments on the conflict between the element of color
      which is static and the film medium which is one of move-
      ment and change.

393   BRUNO, EDOARDO. "Le visioni di Giulietta." Filmcritica,
      No. 161 (October), pp. 483-85.
         A review of Juliet of the Spirits. Bruno sees the film
      as an extreme consequence of current avant-garde experimen-
      tation with the observation of random events.

394   BRUSTEIN, ROBERT. "La Dolce Spumoni: Juliet of the Spirits."
      The New York Review of Books, 5, No. 10 (23 December),
      22-24.
         Harsh, condemning review of Juliet of the Spirits as
      hollow, specious, and boring. Brustein champions Fellini's
      early movies, and he argues that since La Dolce Vita
      Fellini has had a morally ambivalent attitude toward his
      objects of satire. Juliet of the Spirits is little more
      than a "secularized morality play," and Fellini's "strategic
      error is to superimpose fantasy on romance" without suf-
      ficient difference between the two styles.

395   BUSCO, MARIA TERESA. "Miti contemporanei: Fellini e Bergman."
      Bianco e nero, 26, No. 2 (February), 39-46.
         An excellent article in which Busco compares Fellini
      and Bergman in terms of their social, religious, and
      philosophical viewpoints. She argues that both men have in
      common the theme of alienation, but they present the theme

differently. Fellini depicts twentieth-century neuroses,
while Bergman explores spiritual crises. Both reflect
aspects of Kierkegaard's philosophy of solitude and human
despair. Both directors see love as the only integrating
force and the supreme expression of man's freedom.

396   CAEN, MICHAEL and FRANCIS LACASSIN. "Fellini et les fumetti."
       Cahiers du Cinéma, No. 172 (November), pp. 14-16.
       Illustrated.
           An interview with Fellini on the subject of comic strips.
       Fellini professes his love for strips such as Dick Tracy,
       Mandrake, Flash Gordon, B. C., and Happy Hooligan (the name
       "Gelsomina" came from the Italian version of the last
       strip), and he recounts his situation as an Italian scenar-
       ist of Flash Gordon in Florence under the Fascist regime.
       He ponders ways in which comic strips may have influenced
       him.

397   CASIRAGHI, UGO. "Ritorno alla contemporaneità nel cinema
       jugoslavo." Cinema nuovo, 14, No. 178 (November-December),
       436-40.
           Casirghi comments on the influence of Fellini and
       Antonioni on contemporary Yugoslavian film.

398   CASTELLO, GIULIO CESARE. "Giulietta degli spiriti." Trans-
       lated by Geoffrey Nowell-Smith. Sight and Sound, 35,
       No. 1 (Winter), 18-19. Illustrated.
           A negative review of Juliet of the Spirits. Castello
       feels the movie should conclude Fellini's work with the
       psychoanalytic film. The ending of Juliet of the Spirits
       has the same fault as the ending of 8½: "the opportunistic
       'miracle' solution." He objects also to the discrepancy
       between the narrow-mindedness of the little bourgeoise in
       her daily affairs and the unrestrained extravagances of her
       visions.

399   CRIST, JUDITH. "Make Way for Giulietta of the Rare Spirit."
       New York, The Sunday Herald Tribune Magazine, (7 November),
       p. 33. Illustrated.
           Crist praises Juliet of the Spirits as one of the few
       contemporary films to treat at length the character of
       the adult woman. Although the film resembles 8½ in tech-
       nique, it surpasses the earlier movie in terms of the
       warmth and compassion Giulietta Masina brings to the film.
       This review is collected in Crist's The Private Eye, the
       Cowboy, and the Very Naked Girl. New York: Holt, Rinehart,
       and Winston, 1968. Pp. 138-41.

400   CROWTHER, BOSLEY. "Juliet of the Spirits." New York Times
       (4 November), p. 57. Illustrated. Brief credits.

218

Crowther praises the film as a "bold conglomeration of
visual and aural stimuli." The film does reveal the sources
of Juliet's inhibitions and repressions, but the causes are
not as important as the textures of Juliet's fantasies.

401 DORIGO, FRANCESCO. "Giulietta degli spiriti." Cineforum, 5,
No. 49 (November), 733-54. Illustrated. Brief credits.
A lengthy, negative review of Juliet of the Spirits.
Dorigo finds the movie misconceived. Fellini has over-
filled it with too many elements. The lack of cohesion seen
in 8½ is repeated in Juliet of the Spirits. Fellini attempts to pass off spectacle as poetry. Finally, Dorigo
speculates that the character of Juliet is none other than
Fellini himself.

402 FELLINI, FEDERICO. "Propos sur 8½." Cahiers du Cinéma,
No. 164 (March), pp. 23-24. Illustrated.
An edited version, translated into French, of an interview on 8½ which Fellini gave at the Centro sperimentale di
cinematografia in Rome. It was published first as the following: Anon. "Confessione in pubblico: colloquio con
Federico Fellini." Bianco e nero, 24, No. 4 (April 1963),
1-21. Appended to the French version is a filmography.

403 GOLDBERG, TOBY. Federico Fellini: A Poet of Reality. Boston:
Boston University Broadcasting and Film Division, 115 pp.
Bibliography. Filmography.
Goldberg surveys Fellini's films from Variety Lights to
8½ (excluding A Matrimonial Agency and The Temptations of
Doctor Antonio). She also includes some helpful biograph-
ical material. In her final chapter, entitled "A Personal
Evaluation," Goldberg concludes, as many others have, that
Fellini's greatness lies in his ability to create a person-
alized art which has universal appeal.

404 HART, HENRY. "Juliet of the Spirits." Films in Review, 16,
No. 10 (December), 643. Illustrated.
Hart feels Fellini lacks "artistic integrity." His
films are "incompletions." The "irrelevant incidents"
Fellini piles up in Juliet of the Spirits do not adequately
reproduce the mind of the deserted woman.

405 HARTUNG, PHILIP T. "Fellini, Freud and Frills." Commonweal,
83 (26 November), 244-47.
Laudatory review of Juliet of the Spirits. Hartung
praises especially the use of fantasy in the movie. Juliet
of the Spirits seems to him to have some of the qualities
of Lewis Carroll's Alice works.

406 JACOB, GILLES. "Juliette-des-esprits." Cinéma 65, No. 100
(November), pp. 110-14. Illustrated.

A mixed review of Juliet of the Spirits. Jacob praises
Fellini's energy and inventiveness, but also raises two
objections. He feels the film stays always on the level of
spectacle, and, therefore, we never acquire any sense of
Juliet as a real person with any mental toughness. Also he
feels the movie may be, underneath it all, simply a justification of the husband's infidelity. On the one hand,
Fellini shows Juliet's sexual repression as a possible cause
for the infidelity, and, on the other, Fellini seems to
urge a guilt-free sexual license for his characters which
would exonerate the husband.

407   JACONA, ANTONIO. "Fellini: 'Non posso soffrire la musica.'
      Giulietta: 'La musica è la mia compagna.'" Oggi, 21,
      No. 34 (26 August), 26-30. Illustrated.
          An interview with Fellini and his wife in the form of a
      quiz. They answer a list of twenty-six questions. From
      their answers, personality summaries are extracted.

408   KAEL, PAULINE. "The Come-Dressed-As-the-Sick-Soul-of-Europe
      Parties" and "8½: Confessions of a Movie Director," in I
      Lost It at the Movies. Boston and Toronto: Little, Brown,
      pp. 179-96 & 261-66.
          "8½: Confessions of a Movie Director" is an attacking
      review of 8½. Kael writes: "Someone's fantasy life is
      perfectly good material for a movie if it is imaginative
      and fascinating in itself, or if it illuminates his non-
      fantasy life in some interesting way. But 8½ is neither;
      it's surprisingly like the confectionary dreams of Holly-
      wood heroines, transported by a hack's notions of Freudian
      anxiety and wish fulfillment." "The Come-Dressed-As-the-
      Sick-Soul-of-Europe Parties" is a reprinting from Massa-
      chusetts Review, 4, No. 2 (Winter 1963), 378-91.

409   KARAGANOV, ALEKSANDR. "Taccuino di viaggio di tre cineasti
      sovietici in Italia." Bianco e nero, 26, No. 4, (April),
      iv-x.
          An account of a visit by Russian film critics to the
      Centro sperimentale di cinematografia and to Roman film
      studios. One of the sets they visit is that of Juliet of
      the Spirits. A Russian critic draws Fellini out on the
      issue of how well his audience understands his films.

410   KAST, PIERRE. "Giulietta e Federico: visites à Fellini."
      Cahiers du Cinéma, No. 164 (March), pp. 8-22. Illustrated.
          An interview pieced together by Kast from several con-
      versations with Fellini taped during the filming of Juliet
      of the Spirits. Fellini speaks of the problems of working
      with color, of his manner of altering or expanding his
      screenplay during filming, and of his intentions in Juliet
      of the Spirits. The interview is translated into English

by Rose Kaplin in Cahiers du Cinema in English, No. 5,
(1966), pp. 24-33, and in Interviews with Film Directors.
Edited by Andrew Sarris. Indianapolis: Bobbs-Merrill,
1967. Pp. 141-54.

411 KAUFFMANN, STANLEY. "8½ - Ladies' Size." New Republic, 153,
No. 20 (13 November), 28-32.
     Kauffmann compares Juliet of the Spirits with 8½ and
finds Juliet of the Spirits to be decidedly inferior. He
attacks Fellini's definition of Juliet's character as pallid
and his use of color as often blatant or old-fashioned.
The years have decreased the depth of Fellini's work but
they have increased the dazzle of his style, at least up to
8½. Kauffmann calls for more play, more humor, from Fellini
than is evident in Juliet of the Spirits. Reprinted as
"Juliet of the Spirits" in A World on Film. New York:
Harper and Row, 1966. Pp. 325-29.

412 _____. "To Tell the Truth." New Republic, 152, No. 20 (15
May), 32-33.
     Kauffmann calls attention to the New Yorker Theater's
importation of Variety Lights. He advises that many of
Fellini's qualities made famous in later films are to be
found in embryo in Variety Lights. Reprinted in A World on
Film. New York: Harper & Row, 1966. P. 325.

413 KEZICH, TULLIO. "The Long Interview," translated by Howard
Greenfeld, in Juliet of the Spirits. New York: Orion
Press, pp. 11-65.
     English translation of Kezich's interview with Fellini
at the time of the filming of Juliet of the Spirits. First
published in Giulietta degli spiriti. Rocca San Casciano:
Cappelli editore, 1965. Pp. 20-72.

414 _____. "La muraglia cinese," in Giulietta degli spiriti.
Rocca San Casciano: Cappelli editore, pp. 20-72.
     A long and important interview with Fellini at the time
of the filming of Juliet of the Spirits. Topics covered include Fellini's account of the beginning of his career as a
filmmaker, his lack of competitiveness, the importance of
dreams, personality formation during childhood, his experiment with LSD, the relationship between narrative invention
and graphic representation in his imagination, his attitudes
about the use of color in films, and his methods with the
screenplay, with actors, set designers, and cameramen. On
Juliet of the Spirits, Fellini discusses the male's difficulty in portraying the female point of view, Giulietta
Masina's embodiment for him of nostalgia for innocence, the
germination of the idea of the film from the discovery of a
nun's diary during the shooting of La Strada, and attitudes
about marriage in Italy. Translated into English by Howard

Greenfeld in <u>Juliet of the Spirits</u>. New York: Orion Press, 1965. Pp. 11-65.

415   LIBER, NADINE. "A New Fantasy by the 8½ Man." <u>Life</u>, 59, No. 9 (27 August), 50-54. Illustrated.
        Pre-release report on <u>Juliet of the Spirits</u>. The article includes six excellent color stills, three of which come from the beach scene. Fellini comments that the vision on the beach represents "frightening things adults tell children they will see when they become adults--war, sickness, bad women and death." He also talks about the original impulses or ideas which start him off composing his film stories.

416   McANANY, EMILE G., S. J. and ROBERT WILLIAMS, S. J. "<u>La Strada</u>," in <u>The Filmviewer's Handbook</u>. Glen Rock, N.J.: Paulist Press, pp. 103-109. Brief credits.
        <u>La Strada</u> is presented as a film that might be shown and discussed by a film society. McAnany and Williams present background material on Fellini's career up to <u>The Temptations of Doctor Antonio</u>. They suggest that the problems of communication and interpersonal relationships in <u>La Strada</u> could provide a starting point for discussion of the film. They put forward the possibility of interpreting the movie in a Christian framework, with the Fool as a Christ figure. And they state that the visual presentations of scenes perform three functions: to give realistic settings for lower class life, to set moods, and to symbolize some things beyond the immediate confines of the story.

417   MAZZOCCHI, G. "How I Create." Translated by Heather Gordon-Horwood. <u>Atlas</u>, 9, No. 3 (March), pp. 182-85. Illustrated.
        An interview with Fellini in which he discusses his manner of making a film. He outlines several stages: the original idea or image, work with collaborators on a screenplay, the process of selecting actors and faces, work with the set designer, and final decisions during the shooting. Fellini comments that his episode in <u>Love in the City</u> was a joke on Marxist, neorealistic critics and that his episode in <u>Boccaccio '70</u> was another one on the Jesuit critics of <u>La civiltà cattolica</u>. He speaks briefly about parallels between film authors and literary ones.

418   MORAVIA, ALBERTO. "Federico del barocco." <u>L'espresso</u>, 11, No. 44 (31 October), 12-13. Illustrated.
        An interview with Fellini by the Italian novelist generally on the subject of <u>Juliet of the Spirits</u>. Moravia describes <u>Juliet of the Spirits</u> as combining the objective point of view presented in <u>La Dolce Vita</u> with the subjective one in <u>8½</u>. Fellini disagrees slightly with Moravia's claim of "objective reality" for <u>La Dolce Vita</u>, and he

expresses unhappiness over the word "fresco" which he himself has used. He insists La Dolce Vita shows a world "completely invented." Moravia compares Juliet to Alice in Wonderland. Fellini states that his most difficult problem with the character of Juliet as played by Giulietta Masina was to block out all references to the previous parts of Gelsomina and Cabiria which she played in his movies. Moravia suggests that in some of the episodes Fellini's point of view intrudes on the character's, especially Fellini's attitude toward the bourgeoisie and his linkage of the monstrous with the erotic. The two men discuss Fellini's use of art nouveau materials in the film and his use of color. Finally, Moravia defines Fellini's style as "baroque" in the sense that he exceeds traditional forms in order to astonish the viewer and to create new meanings. [No copy of this review could be located in the U.S.A. A copy was found, however, in the archives of L'espresso in Rome. JCS]

419 MORTIER, MICHAEL. "Juliette des esprits." Téléciné, No. 125 (November), pp. 25-37. Illustrated. Credits.
     An informational "fiche" on Juliet of the Spirits. It contains notes on the structure of the film, on the cinematography, on color, and on sound, a discussion of the characters, and a critical overview. Mortier defends Fellini's attempt to study the inner world of an upper middle class woman, even if Fellini transposes many of his own obsessions to her. Mortier sees Juliet as moving toward acceptance of herself in defiance of the inhibiting factors of her mother, her religious upbringing, and her marriage. Briefly, he discusses the sexual images as cathartic.

420 MOURLET, MICHEL. "Fellini et Masina," in Sur un art ignoré. Paris: La Table ronde, pp. 200-202.
     An attack on Fellini's art when he chooses to use his wife, Giulietta Masina, as a central character. Mourlet states that Masina can present only grotesque caricatures of actions. Fellini's mistake is to use her when he wants to create a lyrical tone.

421 PHILIPPE, PIERRE. "Pour reparler de Juliette-des-esprits." Cinéma 65, No. 101 (December), pp. 128-30.
     An essay on Juliet of the Spirits in which Philippe argues that Fellini is turning away from traditional narrative and is turning toward the form of the poetic essay. This is the form usually practiced by experimental filmmakers such as Kenneth Anger. Philippe argues that Juliet of the Spirits is "a meditation on the air-conditioned horror" of the modern world. He sees Fellini as a more desperate filmmaker than Antonioni.

422 RONDI, BRUNELLO. <u>Il cinema di Fellini</u>. Rome: Edizione di
<u>Bianco e nero</u>, 418 pp. Illustrated. Filmography.
    A critical study of Fellini's work through <u>Juliet of the
Spirits</u> by Fellini's friend and collaborator. The book is
divided into three sections. The first is an overview in
which Rondi discusses Fellini's personality, work style, and
the influence on him of Ingmar Bergman. The second concerns
Fellini's artistic growth through his first seven films
from <u>Variety Lights</u> to <u>Nights of Cabiria</u>. The third treats
his mature period of <u>La Dolce Vita</u>, 8½, <u>The Temptations of
Doctor Antonio</u>, and <u>Juliet of the Spirits</u>. Rondi identifies
twelve major themes in Fellini's work: (1) alienation;
(2) misogyny; (3) bourgeois experience, with the family as
ultimate totem; (4) conflict of fantasy and reality;
(5) solitude, especially in terms of Kierkegaard's solution
in <u>La Strada</u>; (6) choral society; (7) urban corruption;
(8) religious reversals and paradoxes; (9) allegorical
journeys; (10) sex, especially frigid sexual games and sex
as spectacle; (11) grotesques and Rabelaisian imagery; and
(12) baroque sentiment of death.

423 ROSS, LILLIAN. "Profiles: 10½." <u>New Yorker</u>, 41, No. 37
(30 October), 63-107.
    A profile on Fellini at the time of the editing of
<u>Juliet of the Spirits</u>. The essay is done in the form of a
screenplay. In a flashback, Ross describes Fellini's childhood in Rimini and his experiences as a young man in Rome,
working for <u>Marc' Aurelio</u>, the satiric journal, during WWII.
In the present, she describes him choosing a sound to be
dubbed into <u>Juliet of the Spirits</u>, talking with a friend in
Fellini's house in Fregene during the weekend, going to
dinner with businessmen, and returning to work after the
weekend. Fellini talks on a variety of subjects including
his wife, his attitude toward women expressed in <u>Juliet of
the Spirits</u>, his fear of competing, his distrust of intellectuals, his problems with producers, his childhood delight in American comic strips, his admiration for Pope
John, and his anxieties about being a director in his
forties.

424 SADOUL, GEORGES. "Fellini, Federico." <u>Dictionnaire des
cinéastes</u>. Paris: Éditions du seuil, pp. 85-86. Illustrated. Filmography.
    An outline of Fellini's career up to and including 8½.
Sadoul emphasizes Fellini's break with neorealism in
<u>La Strada</u>.

425 SALACHAS, GILBERT. "Fellini: <u>Giulietta des esprits--8½</u>."
<u>Télécine</u>, No. 124 (October), pp. 41-44. Illustrated.
    A reprinting of the last chapter of the second edition
of Salachas' <u>Federico Fellini</u>. Cinema d'aujourd'hui.

Paris: Seghers, 1965. It is a comparison of <u>Juliet of the Spirits</u> and $8\frac{1}{2}$. Both, Salachas says, are surrealistic rhapsodies, with musical lines, variations and counter-points from previous works. These elements include the suffocating contemporary world, a conservative view of the church, decadent spectacles, the sea, the ennui of the rich, extravagant fashions, generously proportioned women, spiritualists, childhood memories, and the circus.

426 SARRIS, ANDREW. "Films: <u>Juliet of the Spirits</u>." <u>Village Voice</u>, 11, No. 4 (11 November), 23 and No. 5 (18 November), 23.

A two-part review of <u>Juliet of the Spirits</u> in which Sarris attacks the inflated quality of Fellini's movie. When Fellini deals with the stiffling influence of the church, he is both dramatically successful and socially relevant. But Sarris questions what liberation will bring to Fellini's passive heroine, other than loneliness. He questions further the mixture of objective situations with subjective interpretations. The movie is a "dazzling dead end." This review is collected in Sarris' <u>Confessions of a Cultist: On the Cinema 1959-1969</u>. New York: Simon and Schuster, 1970. Pp. 215-19.

427 SIMON, JOHN. "Wherefore Art Thou, Juliet?" <u>New Leader</u>, 48, No. 24 (6 December), 32-33.

A negative review of <u>Juliet of the Spirits</u>. Simon calls the movie "dreadful." Fellini, he states, has "sold out," but not for money, rather for intellect. Somewhere in the middle of <u>La Dolce Vita</u> the decline began. In <u>Juliet of the Spirits</u>, the central problem of the marriage itself is never investigated. Worst of all is Juliet's too easy liberation, "with just one dream." As in $8\frac{1}{2}$, Fellini sheds no light on the problems and ambiguities of his main character. There is no set of values implicit in his treatment of Juliet. The review is collected in Simon's <u>Private Screenings</u>. New York: Macmillan, 1967. Pp. 193-98.

428 SOLMI, ANGELO. "Fellini: il favolista che ama la realtà." <u>Oggi</u>, 21, No. 44 (4 November), 100-101. Illustrated.

A review of <u>Juliet of the Spirits</u>. Solmi stresses Fellini's ability to synthesize fantasy with reality. However, Fellini announces to Solmi his intention to abandon fantasy in his future films.

429 _____. "Fellini non è un divo ma un artista." <u>Oggi</u>, 21, No. 37 (16 September), 82.

A passionate defense of Fellini's artistic integrity after his controversial withdrawal of <u>Juliet of the Spirits</u> from the Venice Film Festival.

430 SOLMI, ANGELO. "Il vero e solo padre dei film è il regista."
   Oggi, 21, No. 26 (1 July), 84–85.
      Solmi contrasts the role of the Italian film director
   (Fellini in particular) with the American director. He
   argues that in Italy the director has become more and more
   the real "author" of the film, and he uses the case of
   Fellini to illustrate his point. He offers reasons why the
   American director's role is less encompassing.

431 WALTER, EUGENE. "Federico Fellini: Wizard of Film." *Atlantic*,
   216, No. 6 (December), 62–67.
      A biographical profile of the director by Walter, a jour-
   nalist and the translator of *Fellini Satyricon*. The essay
   includes a description of Rimini, Fellini's native town, and
   an interview with Fellini's mother and sister. Most interesting is the inclusion of three caricatures by Fellini.
   They show Giulietta Masina as Cabiria, as Gelsomina, and with
   Sandra Milo as Juliet and Suzy. Some of the material in
   this essay was published previously in Walter's "The Private
   Jokes of Federico Fellini." *Vogue*, 146 (1 September 1965),
   274–75 & 282. The essay "Federico Fellini: Wizard of
   Film" is the basis for Walter's expanded biographical essay
   "The Wizardry of Fellini." *Films and Filming*, 12, No. 9
   (June 1966), 18–26.

432 _____. "The Private Jokes of Federico Fellini." *Vogue*, 146
   (1 September), 274–75 & 282.
      Article describing a visit to the set of *Juliet of the
   Spirits*. Walter describes the costumes in some detail and
   comments on two themes he sees in the movie: the differences between what people think, what they say, and what
   they do; and the search for an island of peace amidst the
   hurly-burly of modern life. He notes some secret jokes in
   Fellini's casting of aristocrats as servants in $8\frac{1}{2}$ and his
   casting of beach boys as nuns in *Juliet of the Spirits*.
   Material from this essay has been reused by Walter in
   "Federico Fellini: Wizard of Film." *Atlantic*, 216, No. 6
   (December 1965), 62–67. And in "The Wizardry of Fellini."
   Films and Filming, 12, No. 9 (June 1966), 18–26.

433 WEILER, A. H. "*Variety Lights*." *New York Times*, (7 May),
   p. 34. Illustrated. Brief credits.
      Laudatory review of *Variety Lights*. Weiler notes aspects
   of Fellini's art that have become well established in his
   films made later than *Variety Lights*: emphasis on faces,
   indications of loneliness, "the rootlessness and brassiness
   of little people in a tough world."

434 WOLF, WILLIAM. "The Fellinis Visit New York." *Cue*, 34,
   No. 45, (6 November), 14. Illustrated.

A biographical sketch of the marriage and careers of
Fellini and Giulietta Masina, written in connection with a
publicity trip the two took to New York for the opening of
Juliet of the Spirits.

1966

435   ANON. "Juliette des esprits." L' Avant-Scène, No. 63
(October), pp. 95-98. Illustrated. Credits.
Photo-spread on Juliet of the Spirits. Some interview
material and excerpts from reviews in the French press are
included.

436   ANON. "Playboy Interview: Federico Fellini." Playboy, 13,
No. 2 (February), 55-66.
A lengthy interview with Fellini who touches often on
$8\frac{1}{2}$ and Juliet of the Spirits. Fellini discusses Guido's
need in $8\frac{1}{2}$, Juliet's need in Juliet of the Spirits, and
Fellini's own need to gain "freedom" from the inhibitions,
guilt feelings, and misinformation taken on in childhood.
He also talks about his attitudes toward the Catholic church,
idealizations of women, and death. He describes working
with his wife, Giulietta Masina, his ritual of looking at
portrait photos, and his manner of using a scenario. He
comments briefly on Kurosawa, Bergman, Antonioni, De Sica,
and neorealism and tells why he has avoided opportunities
to work in Hollywood.

437   ANON. "Sept personnages en quête d'Antonioni." Positif,
No. 76 (June), pp. 16-22.
Seven people comment on the work of Michelangelo
Antonioni. One is Fellini. He comments that what pleases
him about Antonioni is his unswerving fidelity to his own
type of filmmaking, even though the public in recent years
has turned away from him.

438   BOFFA, FRANCO. "La splendida automaniera di Fellini." Cineforum, 6, No. 54 (April), 304-19. Illustrated.
A lengthy review of Juliet of the Spirits. Boffa begins
with a study of Fellini's artistic development from his
earliest films and states that La Strada and $8\frac{1}{2}$ are the
two major achievements of his career. In this context, he
finds Juliet of the Spirits a kind of cerebral game, decorative, but without poetic and narrative impetus.

439   BORDE, RAYMOND. "Juliette des esprits: le péché original."
Positif, No. 74 (March), pp. 101-104. Illustrated. Brief
credits.
An ambivalent review. Borde objects to Fellini the
moralizer, but praises him as one who can transcend his

intellectual limitations to give an audience a striking
sense of a visual world. Borde finds Juliet's virtue, like
Gelsomina's, cloying and castrating, but he enjoys Fellini's
ability to merge paranoid vision with reality in certain
scenes.

440 BUDGEN, SUZANNE. _Fellini_. London: British Film Institute,
128 pp. Illustrated. Filmography. Credits.
An excellent critical study of Fellini's movies from
The White Sheik through _Juliet of the Spirits_. Budgen
stresses Fellini's use of comedy as a means of expressing his
compassion for his characters, and she stresses the physical
immediacy of his images. She finds _La Strada_ a film of
central importance in Fellini's work. It shows his compassion for the dispossessed, his comic fantasy, his preoccupation with circus life, his love for the sea, and his
ability to suggest an air of mystery beneath surface reality.
The journey of Gelsomina is a movement from childhood and
innocence through womanhood and knowledge, to death and a
kind of apotheosis. In _Nights of Cabiria_, Fellini treats a
creature with a capacity for giving love but no one to give
it to. _I Vitelloni_, _The White Sheik_, and _Il Bidone_ all
deal with organized living and some form of refusal of its
norms. _La Dolce Vita_ and _8½_ deal with the individual's, or
the artist's, search for self-definition. Budgen sees
Steiner as a false ideal in _La Dolce Vita_, because he has
removed himself too far from the assertiveness of life. She
defends Sylvia as a personification of vitality and energy.
In _8½_, Claudia is a Platonic Ideal from which Guido must
turn in order to confront the disorderly elements of his
life as it is. Budgen asserts that _Juliet of the Spirits_
marks a new departure for Fellini. Instead of following
his usual method of seeing normal things in an abnormal way,
he seems interested in this film in creating elaborately
artificial sets. The movie presents Juliet's attempt to
break through the myths surrounding women and marriage to a
fuller sense of self-definition. Budgen also treats some
elements running through many of Fellini movies--his use of
disguises as release from one's identity, his use of parties
as moments of "corporate high spirits," and his treatment
of the church. Appended to the book is an English version
of part of the farm wedding sequence of _La Strada_; and ex-
tracts in English of part of Delcorde's _Entretiens avec
Federico Fellini_. Brussels: Les Cahiers R. T. B. Serie
Telecinema, 1962; and of part of Fellini's "Su _La dolce
vita_ la parola a Fellini." _Bianco e nero_, 21, Nos. 1-2
(January-February 1960), 1-18.

441 DAVIS, MELTON S. "First the Pasta, Then the Play." _New York
Times Magazine_ (2 January), pp. 10-11, 13-14 & 16.
Illustrated.

A carefully done biographical sketch of Giulietta Masina. Davis outlines the phases of her career and discusses her marriage with Fellini. Masina offers her thoughts about acting and about the character of Juliet.

442 ELLISON, HARLAN. "Juliet of the Spirits." Cinema (Beverly Hills), 3, No. 3 (July), 46.
      A review of Juliet of the Spirits as "an hysterical act of confusion." Ellison argues that Fellini is too self-indulgent and that he has gotten too far away from traditional storytelling devices.

443 FIESCHI, JEAN-ANDRE. "Cabiria Lobotomized." Cahiers du Cinema in English, No. 2, pp. 76-77.
      An English translation of Fieschi's review of Juliet of the Spirits published in: Cahiers du Cinéma, No. 174 (January 1966), pp. 77-78.

444 _____. "Cabiria trépanée." Cahiers du Cinéma, No. 174 (January), pp. 77-78. Illustrated.
      A review of Juliet of the Spirits. Fieschi maintains that although the number and size of the defects in the movie make it a failure, he finds it a generous, indulgent and candid film. It is not an ambitious movie. Fellini is content to film the terrors, the domestic demons of a middle class Roman woman who is not very young or very intelligent. The review is translated into English in Cahiers du Cinema in English, No. 2 (1966), pp. 76-77.

445 GAUTEUR, CLAUDE. "Masina contre Fellini." Image et Son, No. 193 (April), pp. 33-41. Illustrated.
      An essay on the careers of Giulietta Masina and Federico Fellini since their success in La Strada in 1954. Gauteur finds Masina an intelligent woman, but a limited actress. Her facial gestures are few. She plays only three roles: prostitute, simple soul, and unhappy wife. These roles overlap, and she has repeated them too often. Her career has been one of deterioration. Fellini, on the other hand, has progressed, although his career is not without its ups and downs. Gauteur calls 8½ his masterpiece. It is his Don Juan.

446 HARCOURT, PETER. "The Secret Life of Federico Fellini." Film Quarterly, 19, No. 3 (Spring), 4-19. Illustrated.
      In this study of Fellini, Harcourt covers a variety of subjects. First, he argues that Fellini films often involve a journey or movement without an established goal. During the journey, however, there occur two kinds of encounters: with the freshness and unexpectedness of innocence and with something threatening and dreadful. He discusses this pattern mainly in La Strada and La Dolce Vita. In addition,

Harcourt argues for the need to approach Fellini's images
with the same methods of visual analysis that the art
critic uses with painting. He compares shot compositions
in Fellini's movies with paintings by Jean Carzou and
Giorgio de Chirico. Finally, he discusses Fellini's successful use of tough, rational self-questioning in 8½ and
his unsuccessful attempt to transfer his own obsessions to
the psyche of a gentle <u>bourgeoise</u> in <u>Juliet of the Spirits</u>.
The article reappears in a slightly altered and expanded
form in Harcourt's <u>Six European Directors</u>. Harmondsworth,
England and Baltimore: Penguin Books, 1974. Pp. 183-211.

447 JOMY, ALAIN. "Fellini entre deux portes." <u>Cahiers du Cinéma</u>,
No. 180 (July), p. 13. Illustrated.
Brief recounting of a conversation Jomy had with Fellini
about LSD and <u>Juliet of the Spirits</u>.

448 KAST, PIERRE. "Visits with Fellini." Translated by Rose
Kaplin. <u>Cahiers du Cinema in English</u>, No. 5, pp. 24-33.
A translation of an interview which appeared first in
French in <u>Cahiers du Cinéma</u>, No. 164 (March 1965), pp. 6-22.

449 KAUFFMANN, STANLEY. "<u>La Dolce Vita</u>," "8½," "<u>Variety Lights</u>,"
and "<u>Juliet of the Spirits</u>," in <u>A World on Film</u>. New York:
Harper & Row, pp. 320-22, 322-25 & 325-29.
A reprinting of four reviews. "<u>La Dolce Vita</u>" appeared
first as "A Catalogue of Deadly Sins." <u>New Republic</u>, 144,
No. 18 (1 May 1961), 22-23. "<u>8½</u>" as "A Jolly Good Fellini."
<u>New Republic</u>, 149, No. 2 (13 July 1963), 28-29. "<u>Variety
Lights</u>" as "To Tell the Truth." <u>New Republic</u>, 152, No. 20
(15 May 1965), 32-33. "<u>Juliet of the Spirits</u>" as "8½--
Ladies' Size." <u>New Republic</u>, 153, No. 20 (13 November
1965), 28-32.

450 LEFÈVRE, RAYMOND. "<u>Juliette des esprits</u>." <u>Image et Son</u>,
No. 192 (March), pp. 105-108. Brief credits.
A mixed review of <u>Juliet of the Spirits</u>. Lefèvre argues
that the movie does not give entry to the feminine psyche
as intended. It repeats the masculine concerns of characters of earlier films by Fellini. It is a masculine view
of the feminine ego. He states that the movie works on
three levels: the real, the archetypal, and the level of
memory of childhood. He deplores Fellini's misogyny in
converting the women around Juliet into a gallery of monsters and describes the archetypal images that assail
Juliet at the end as comprising a carnival of moralistic
terrors. He praises, however, the handling of Juliet's
sense of enchantment in Suzy's house and the handling of
Juliet's memories of her grandfather.

451   LEPROHON, PIERRE. <u>Le Cinema italien</u>. Paris: Seghers,
        pp. 155-60, 177-81, 217-19 & 274. Illustrated. Filmography.
          Leprohon tries to define Fellini's place in the histor-
        ical evolution of Italian films by discussing the new
        dimensions Fellini brought to neorealism and to the "new
        cinema" of the 1960s. The book has been translated into
        English by Roger Greaves and Oliver Stallybrass as <u>The</u>
        <u>Italian Cinema</u>. New York: Praeger, 1972. <u>See</u> pp. 141-47,
        167-70, 204-206 & 228.

452   LEVINE, IRVING R. "'I Was Born for the Cinema': A Conversa-
        tion with Federico Fellini." <u>Film Comment</u>, 4, No. 1 (Fall),
        77-84.
          The text of a filmed interview with Fellini at the Saffa
        Palatine Studios. The interview is wide-ranging and inter-
        esting. Although it goes over some ground covered else-
        where, it does have some unique material too. Fellini
        discusses at length his yearning for liberation, a theme
        that permeates <u>La Dolce Vita</u>, $8\frac{1}{2}$, and <u>Juliet of the Spirits</u>.
        He wants to urge modern man "to accept and love life the
        way it is without idealizing it, without creating concepts
        about it, without projecting oneself into idealized images
        on a moral or ethical plane. I want to give back to man a
        virginal availability, his innocence as he had in child-
        hood." He talks also of being shaped by emotional experi-
        ences in his own life more than by other filmmakers, of his
        interest in New York City, and of the problems and advantages
        of working with color.

453   LYON, NINETTE. "Giulietta Masina, Federico Fellini: A Second
        Fame: Good Food." <u>Vogue</u>, 147, No. 1 (1 January), 152-54.
        Illustrated.
          An interview with Fellini and Masina about their favorite
        foods. It is of some slight biographical interest, since
        Fellini describes his mother as a severe and religious woman
        who fussed about the healthfulness of her childrens' diet.

454   MANVELL, ROGER. <u>New Cinema in Europe</u>. London: Studio Vista,
        pp. 30-37. Illustrated.
        Brief sketch of Fellini's career up to $8\frac{1}{2}$.

455   MEEHAN, THOMAS. "Fantasy, Flesh, and Fellini." <u>Saturday</u>
        <u>Evening Post</u>, 239, No. 1 (1 January), 24-33. Illustrated.
          A lengthy, two-part article. In the first part, Meehan
        discusses Fellini's work on <u>Juliet of the Spirits</u>, his
        general methods of nurturing a story idea into a screenplay,
        of casting his films, and of working with actors. The
        second part is an interesting biographical essay, dealing
        with the financial side, as well as the personal and artis-
        tic sides, of Fellini's career.

456   METZ, CHRISTIAN. "La Construction 'en abyme' dans <u>Huit et</u>
      <u>demi</u> de Fellini." <u>Revue d'esthétique</u>, 19, No. 1 (January-
      March), 96-101.
          Metz sees <u>8½</u> as a movie that <u>triples</u> the device of the
      play-within-a-play. Fellini is making a movie about Guido
      who is making a movie about a director. (Translator Michael
      Taylor supplies the metaphor of a double mirror, reflecting
      itself.) Metz argues that an important aspect of the ending
      is Guido's entry into the circle of characters he has been
      directing. The place of the director, thus relinquished by
      Guido, he suggests, "can only be occupied by a character
      external to the action of the film: by Fellini himself."
      Metz is intrigued by the possibilities of a film with three
      levels of parallels rather than the more conventional two,
      and his essay is richly suggestive. The essay is reprinted
      in French in <u>Essais sur la signification au cinéma</u>. Paris:
      Editions Klineksieck, 1968. Pp. 223-28. It is translated
      into English by Michael Taylor as "Mirror Construction in
      Fellini's <u>8½</u>." <u>Film Language: A Semiotics of the Cinema</u>.
      New York: Oxford University Press, 1974. Pp. 228-34.

457   PAINE, WINGATE, FRANÇOISE SAGAN, and FEDERICO FELLINI. <u>Mirror</u>
      <u>of Venus</u>. New York: Ridge Press, 157 pp. Illustrated.
          A volume of photographs of three models. The photo-
      graphs were taken by Wingate Paine. Captions were added by
      Fellini and Françoise Sagan. Generally, these captions are
      banal. Occasionally Fellini displays some wit, as when he
      remarks about a picture of a model splashing in the surf
      with a parasol: "I once tried to recapture a moment like
      this in the bathtub. <u>Dio mio! Che disastro!</u>"

458   PAOLUCCI, ANNE. "The Italian Film: Antonioni, Fellini,
      Bolognini." <u>Massachusetts Review</u>, 7, No. 3 (Summer),
      556-67.
          An overview of the state of Italian cinema. Fellini is
      lauded for finding a film idiom comparable to poetic
      metaphor.

459   PESCE, ALBERTO. "Il matrimonio nel cinema italiano." <u>Cine-</u>
      <u>forum</u>, 6, No. 55 (May), 366-83.
          Pesce considers the cinematic treatment of marriage as
      a continuing social dialogue and traces the evolution of
      the treatment from silent films to the 1960s. He devotes
      two pages to Fellini's handling of marriage from <u>The White</u>
      <u>Sheik</u> to <u>Juliet of the Spirits</u>.

460   QUAGLIETTI, LORENZO. "Les 3 Grands du cinéma italien sont 4."
      Translated by Paul-Louis Thirard. <u>Image et Son</u>, No. 196
      (July), pp. 31-44. Illustrated.
          A review of four recent films by the three directors
      Visconti, Antonioni, and Fellini. <u>Juliet of the Spirits</u>

is the film by Fellini which is considered. Quaglietti
states that Juliet of the Spirits resembles 8½ in that both
treat the theme of a protagonist's escape from a repressive
childhood education. Quaglietti finds the theme intellectually thin.

461 RHODE, ERIC. "Federico Fellini," in Tower of Babel: Specula-
     tions on the Cinema. Philadelphia and New York: Chilton
     Books, pp. 121-34.
        This essay treats Fellini's departure from neorealism
     and his search for the authentic self through fantasy. In
     particular, Rhode discusses the image of Rome as civitas
     diaboli in Fellini's movies.

462 RONDI, GIAN LUIGI. Italian Cinema Today, 1952-1965. New York:
     Hill and Wang, pp. 92-111. Illustrated.
        Brief critical survey of Fellini's films from I Vitelloni
     to 8½ and photographic essay of them from I Vitelloni to
     Juliet of the Spirits.

463 VERDONE, MARIO. "Giulietta degli spiriti." Bianco e nero, 27,
     Nos. 1-2 (January-February), 150-54. Illustrated. Credits.
        A review of Juliet of the Spirits. Verdone discusses
     Fellini's treatment of the culture of the era of mass com-
     munications and his treatment of the interior journey of
     one of the "little people" in the culture. The movie cele-
     brates the small victory of the small individual.

464 WALTER, EUGENE. "The Wizardry of Fellini." Films and Filming,
     12, No. 9 (June), 18-26. Illustrated.
        A biographical profile of Fellini, in which Walter draws
     together material published elsewhere. He describes
     Fellini's home town of Rimini and interviews Fellini's
     mother and sister who continue to live there. He explains
     several inside jokes and biographical references in
     Fellini's movies. Walter talks about Fellini's manner on
     the set of Juliet of the Spirits and about the contributions
     of costume and set designer Piero Gherardi. Finally he re-
     counts the events at a dinner party at Fellini's home.
     Walter draws on parts of the following articles that he had
     published previously. "Dinner with Fellini." Transatlantic
     Review, No. 17 (Autumn 1964), pp. 47-50. "The Private
     Jokes of Federico Fellini." Vogue, No. 146 (1 September
     1965), pp. 274-75 & 282. "Federico Fellini: Wizard of
     Film." Atlantic Monthly, 216, No. 6 (December 1965), 62-67.

465 ZIMMER, C. "Federico Fellini," in Dictionnaire du cinéma.
     Edited by Raymond Bellour et al. Paris, Éditions univer-
     sitaires, pp. 264-67.
        Brief essay on Fellini's films up to and including
     Juliet of the Spirits. Zimmer feels that Fellini's main

concerns are the past and youth. Fellini seeks the "truth of childhood" as a state of grace.

1967

466   BACHMANN, GIDEON. "Giulietta degli spiriti." International Film Guide 1967. London: Tantivy Press; New York: A. S. Barnes, pp. 107-108. Brief credits.
      Brief notice of Juliet of the Spirits. Bachmann argues that "the film represents a search for stability and reason." As spectacle and as play with color harmonies, he finds the movie successful. The character of Juliet, however, lacks the strength to become the dramatic heroine the plot requires her to be.

467   CURTIS, JEAN-LOUIS. "Enfin Fellini fut." Cinéma. Paris: Julliard, pp. 165-72.
      An essay on Juliet of the Spirits in which Curtis deplores the change in Fellini's movies since La Dolce Vita. Curtis praises Fellini's early films for their handling of the pathos of quotidian life. He attacks Fellini's interest in artificial life styles in La Dolce Vita and 8½, and sees Juliet of the Spirits as an unsuccessful attempt to get back to the wellspring of his early successes.

468   FALLACI, ORIANA. "Federico Fellini: Famous Italian Director." Limelighters. Translated by Pamela Swinglehurst. London: Michael Joseph, pp. 49-67.
      English translation of an interview of Fellini originally published in Fallaci's Gli antipatici. Milan: Rizzoli editore, 1963. Pp. 77-98. The translation is also reprinted in Fallaci's The Egotists: Sixteen Surprising Interviews. Chicago: Henry Regency, 1968. Pp. 187-205.

469   FELLINI, FEDERICO. "Anouk Aimée: A Face of the Hour." Vogue, 150 (1 October), pp. 160-61.
      Fellini writes that if a filmmaker wishes to express certain feelings, he has to use faces. Faces are to the filmmaker as adjectives to the writer. Anouk Aimée has the face of a new woman, a mature companion for the adult male, one who saves him from infantilism. Also, Fellini discusses Jung's idea of woman as the dark side of the man.

470   _____. "The Bitter Life--of Money." Film Makers on Film Making. Edited by Harry M. Geduld. Bloomington and London: Indiana University Press, pp. 191-94.
      Reprinting of an essay published previously in Films and Filming, 17, No. 4 (January 1961), 13 & 38.

471 _____. La mia Rimini. Edited by Renzo Renzi. Bologna:
Cappelli editore, 244 pp. Illustrated.
The book is an illustrated volume about Fellini's home
town of Rimini. It contains essays and poems by several
hands about Rimini's past and present. Most important is
Fellini's own autobiographical essay entitled "Il mio
paese" [My Home Town]. The essay is Fellini's best statement about his youth. He recalls the people, the aspects,
and the events of Rimini which seized his imagination. Many
of the characters and events discussed here appear later in
movies like The Clowns and Amarcord: the episodes of
Fellini touching Gradisca's knee in the movie theatre, of
watching the dancers on the terraces of The Grand Hotel, of
fearing Fascist harrassment of his father, and of listening
to Giudizio, the backward fellow who offers to make love to
the beautiful foreign lady for fifty lire. Fellini also
discusses his summers in Gambettola, his first love, and
his early caricaturing work. Finally he recounts his return
to Rimini greatly changed after the war. The illustrations
combine photographs of actual events, people, and landscapes of Rimini with Fellini's sketches and stills from
his movies. Fellini's essay is translated in Christian
Strich's Fellini on Fellini. Translated by Isabel Quigley.
New York: Delacorte Press/Seymour Lawrence, 1976. Pp. 1-40.

472 KAST, PIERRE. "Interview with Fellini," translated by Rose
Kaplin, in Interviews with Film Directors. Indianapolis:
Bobbs-Merrill, pp. 141-54.
A translation of an interview which appeared first in
French in Cahiers du Cinéma, No. 164 (March 1965), pp. 6-22.

473 LEWIS, LEON. "Fellini: The Psychology of the Self," in The
Landscape of Contemporary Cinema. Edited by William David
Sherman and Leon Lewis. Buffalo: Spectrum Press, pp. 9-12.
Lewis discusses the psychological portraits of Guido in
$8\frac{1}{2}$ and Giulietta in Juliet of the Spirits. $8\frac{1}{2}$ is a masterpiece, recalling Joyce's use of stream-of-consciousness
technique and his idea of "epiphanies," sudden moments of
illumination. But Juliet fails to provide a sympathetic
central character or a controlling vision. (Lewis is so
little impressed with Giulietta Masina that he repeatedly
misspells her name.)

474 PELLEGRINI, GLAUCO, ed. "Viaggio attraverso la musica del
cinema italiano." Bianco e nero, 28, Nos. 3-4 (March-
April), 18-33.
Transcript of a RAI-TV program on the history of music
in Italian films. Fellini and Nino Rota, composer and
music director of most of Fellini's films, are among those
commenting on musical scores. They discuss briefly their
collaborations.

235

475   SIMON, JOHN. "Favorites," "Fellini's 8½¢ Fancy," "Escapism
      into Art," and "Wherefore Art Thou, Juliet?" in Private-
      Screenings. New York: Macmillan, pp. 17-37, 74-78, 132-
      36 & 193-98.
          In "Favorites," Simon cites films that have defied "the
      rules" to become excellent films. He discusses The White
      Sheik and I Vitelloni as movies that are masterpieces
      despite their quotidian subject matter. He stresses the
      perfect mixture of laughter and tears in the films and
      Fellini's control of elements. "Fellini's 8½¢ Fancy" is a
      reprinting of a review first published in New Leader, 46,
      No. 16 (5 August 1963), 24-25. "Escapism into Art" in New
      Leader, 47, No. 24 (23 November 1964), 28-29. "Wherefore
      Art Thou, Juliet?" in New Leader, 48, No. 24 (6 December
      1965), 32-33.

476   SOLMI, ANGELO. Fellini. Translated by Elizabeth Greenwood.
      London: Merlin Press; New York: Humanities Press, 183 pp.
      Illustrated. Filmography. Bibliography.
          A translation into English of Solmi's Storia di Federico
      Fellini. Milan: Rizzoli editore, 1962. This English
      version contains an additional chapter on 8½ not in the
      first Italian version.

477   WOOD, ROBIN. "The Question of Fellini Continues." December,
      9, Nos. 2-3, 140.
          Wood raises questions about the merits of La Dolce Vita
      and 8½. He finds both dazzling in terms of Fellini's tech-
      nique and inventiveness, but both lacking in terms of con-
      tent and "grandeur of spirit."

                            1968

478   ANON. "Bergman e Fellini insieme." Cineforum, 8, No. 80
      (December), np & 711.
          A news item. The reporter raises the question of Fellini
      and Bergman doing a film together. Fellini admits to being
      interested by the idea.

479   ANON. "Federico Fellini ed un collega." Cineforum, 8, No. 74
      (April), np & 217.
          A news item in which a friend asks Fellini the greatest
      opportunity he ever missed. Fellini answers that he regrets
      missing in the past moments of freedom which he enjoys now.

480   ANON. "Federico Fellini richiesto dei motivi." Cineforum, 8,
      No. 79 (November), np.
          A news item. The reporter asks Fellini why he chose
      Petronius' Satyricon as the source for a movie. Fellini
      admits that he has little knowledge of, or empathy for, the

ancient Romans. He likens the choosing of a film subject
to taking a vacation, only the immediate pretext is known,
not the hidden motivations.

481 ANON. "Il tanto sospirato film di Federico Fellini, Il viaggio
di G. Mastorna." Cineforum, 8, No. 72 (February), np.
A news item that Fellini's much anticipated film, The
Voyage of G. Mastorna, is about to be shot and that Danny
Kaye has been chosen to act in it. [The film, in fact, was
never made. JCS]

482 ANON. "Toby Dammit." Cinema nuovo, 17, No. 194 (July-August),
np.
Picture spread of six stills from Toby Dammit.

483 BETTI, LILIANA. "Alla ricerca di Toby Dammit," in Tre Passi
nel delirio di Federico Fellini, Louis Malle, Roger Vadim.
Bologna: Cappelli editore, pp. 31-59.
A long and careful essay on the evolution of Fellini's
Toby Dammit. Betti discusses Fellini's troubled dealings
with producer Dino De Laurentiis and Fellini's transfer of
attention away from The Voyage of G. Mastorna to Toby
Dammit. She offers details on the casting and preparation
of Toby Dammit.

484 BLUMER, RONALD. "Tales of Mystery and Imagination." Take One,
1, No. 12 (July-August), 23.
Brief review of Toby Dammit. Blumer praises Fellini's
ability to capture truths en passant through the use of
extras, some of whom in the airport sequence were painted
on backdrops.

485 COMUZIO, ERMANNO. "Tre passi nel delirio." Cineforum, 8,
No. 80 (December), 781-82. Brief credits.
A lukewarm review of Spirits of the Dead. Comuzio points
out that none of the three parts of the film has much to do
with the Poe stories they are derived from. He finds, however, that Toby Dammit, Fellini's section, does reveal a
certain surrealistic fantasy.

486 CRIST, JUDITH. "Cold Brilliance of 8½," and "Giulietta of the
Rare Spirit," in The Private Eye, the Cowboy, and the Very
Naked Girl. New York: Holt, Rinehart, and Winston, pp. 14-
16 & 138-41.
In this book, Crist collects two reviews published
earlier. The first appeared as "8½ - Brilliant Film, But
Strangely Cold." New York Herald Tribune, 123, No. 42,
461 (26 June 1963), 15. The second as "Make Way for
Giulietta of the Rare Spirit." New York, The Sunday Herald
Tribune Magazine (7 November 1965), p. 33.

487 FALLACI, ORIANA. "Federico Fellini: Famous Italian Director,"
in The Egotists: Sixteen Surprising Interviews. Translated
by Pamela Swinglehurst. Chicago: Henry Regency, pp. 187-205.
English translation of an interview of Fellini originally
published in Fallaci's Gli antipatici. Milan: Rizzoli
editore, 1963. Pp. 77-98. The translation first appeared
in Fallaci's Limelighters. London: Michael Joseph, 1967.
Pp. 49-67.

488 FINK, GUIDO. "Tre passi nel delirio." Cinema nuovo, 17,
No. 195 (September-October), 378-80.
A generally unfavorable review of Spirits of the Dead.
Only Fellini's section, Toby Dammit, is found to achieve
any of the original sinister quality of Poe's fiction.

489 GILI, JEAN A. "Histoires extraordinaires." Cinéma 68,
No. 129 (October), pp. 127 & 130-31. Brief credits.
A review of Spirits of the Dead. Gili finds the three
different sketches and three different directorial styles
make the movie a disparate amalgam. He praises Fellini,
however, for finding cinematic equivalents for the literary
skills of Poe. Fellini's Toby Dammit deals with dissolute-
ness, with neurosis, and with the loneliness of a creative
person in a world that does not recognize his creativity.
Gili states that Fellini uses color more deftly in Toby
Dammit than in Juliet of the Spirits.

490 HUSS, ROY and NORMAN SILVERSTEIN. The Film Experience. New
York: Harper and Row, pp. 94-98. Illustrated.
As part of a general discussion of imagery, the authors
describe the image of water in La Dolce Vita. They find
its usual associations - romanticism, purification, baptism,
and the origin of life - are treated ironically.

491 IVALDI, NEDO, ed. "Histoires extraordinaires di Vadim, Malle,
Fellini." Bianco e nero, 29, Nos. 5-6 (May-June), 43-46.
A collection of reviews of Spirits of the Dead by five
newspaper reviewers. In general, Fellini's episode is
found to be the best, because the subject matter suits both
Fellini's imagination and Poe's.

492 KAEL, PAULINE. "Notes on 280 Movies," in Kiss Kiss Bang Bang.
Boston: Little, Brown, pp. 318, 351, 365-66 & 368.
Kael's book contains brief notes on Nights of Cabiria,
La Strada, Variety Lights, I Vitelloni, and The White Sheik.
She praises Nights of Cabiria, in particular, for Masina's
portrayal of a gullibility which is the character's saving
grace, and comments in regard to Variety Lights that the
magic of show business, for Fellini, lies in self-delusion.

493 LEFÈVRE, RAYMOND. "Histoires extraordinaires." Image et Son,
     No. 221 (November), pp. 103-104. Illustrated.
     A brief review of Spirits of the Dead. Lefèvre praises
     Toby Dammit as a torrent of fearful images, exposing our
     suicide-prone society. He comments specifically on Fellini's
     use of the Ferrari as an image of decadence.

494 METZ, CHRISTIAN. "La Construction 'en abyme' dans Huit et
     demi de Fellini," in Essais sur la signification au cinema.
     Paris: Editions Klincksieck, pp. 223-28.
     A reprinting in French of Metz' article which appeared
     first in Revue d'esthetique, 19, No. 1 (January-March
     1966), 96-101. The article is translated into English by
     Michael Taylor as "Mirror Construction in Fellini's 8½," in
     Film Language: A Semiotics of the Cinema. New York:
     Oxford University Press, 1974. Pp. 228-34.

495 MORAVIA, ALBERTO. "Un assassino pieno di scrupoli."
     L'espresso, 14, No. 39 (29 October), 23.
     A review of Spirits of the Dead, by the Italian novelist.
     Moravia maintains that the excellence of Edgar Allan Poe's
     work lies not in literary style, but in his probing of
     psychological and psychoanalytical materials. He dismisses
     the adaptations of Vadim and Malle as works merely echoing
     Poe's style, and he praises Fellini's Toby Dammit as an
     attempt to match and even surpass, in terms of psychological
     analysis, Poe's treatment of the Faustian bargain. [No
     copy of this review could be located in the U.S.A. A copy
     was found, however, in the archives of L'espresso in Rome.
     JCS]

496 SARRIS, ANDREW, ed. The Film. Indianapolis: Bobbs-Merrill
     pp. 53-64.
     Reprinting with study questions of John Simon's "Fellini's
     8½¢ Fancy." New Leader, 46, No. 16 (5 August 1963), 24-25;
     and Dwight Macdonald's "Afterword," in Deena Boyer's The
     Two Hundred Days of 8½. New York: Macmillan, 1964.
     Pp. 209-18.

497 SCHIRALDI, VITTORIO. "Io al cinema mi annoio." Oggi, 24,
     No. 37 (12 September), 38-39. Illustrated.
     An interview with Fellini which begins with some of his
     comments on his intentions in Fellini Satyricon and closes
     with a discussion of his favorite actors. Also included
     are his ideas on the implications of sex and violence in
     modern films.

498 SHIVAS, MARK. "Fellini's Back, and Mae West's Got Him." New
     York Times, 118, No. 40,440 (13 October), Section II, 21.
     Illustrated.

An interview with Fellini as he prepares for the shooting of Fellini Satyricon. Fellini announces that he wishes to sign Terence Stamp, Piette Clementi, Michael J. Pollard, Danny Kaye, Groucho Marx, the Beatles, Jimmy Durante, and Mae West. Danny Kaye, Fellini assures Shivas, will play a merchant of monsters, and Mae West an erotic witch, the mother of an empress. In this interview, Fellini states that he does not wish to compare the contemporary era with ancient Rome. The idea of evoking a lost world interests him mainly on the expressive plane.

499   SINEUX, MICHEL. "Histoires extraordinaires: une oasis de fatalité dans un Sahara d'erreurs." Positif, No. 98 (October), pp. 58-60. Illustrated. Brief credits.
      Sineux argues that man and his double comprise a theme running through the three episodes of the anthology film. Only Fellini, however, succeeds in building a frightening fantasy which is in the tradition of Poe and which is at the same time in Fellini's own style.

500   SOLMI, ANGELO. "Fellini: 'Tutti i matti del mundo vengono da me.'" Oggi, 24, No. 43 (24 October), 91-92. Illustrated.
      An interview with Fellini while he was in the process of making A Director's Notebook, a TV documentary about his methods of making films. He will concentrate, he announces, on how he selects people for his films.

501   _____. "Tre registi nel delirio di Poe." Oggi, 24, No. 45 (7 November), 121 & 123.
      A review of Spirits of the Dead. After negative comments on the episodes directed by Vadim and Malle, Solmi praises Fellini's episode, Toby Dammit. He argues that Fellini's character of the English actor is closest to Poe's kind of stricken characters.

502   VERDONE, MARIO. "Tre passi nel delirio." Bianco e nero, 29, Nos. 11-12 (November-December), 283-85. Credits.
      In this review, Verdone calls Spirits of the Dead a commercial film, not an artistic one. He states that Toby Dammit has little to do with Poe and much to do with Fellini's previous film experiences.

503   VOLTA, ORNELLA. "Come è nato Tre passi nel delirio." Tre passi nel delirio di Federico Fellini, Louis Malle, Roger Vadim. Bologna: Cappelli editore, pp. 25-28.
      An article on how European film producer Raymond Eger conceived of the idea for Spirits of the Dead.

504   WILLIAMS, FORREST. "Fellini's Voices." Film Quarterly, 21, No. 3 (Spring), 21-25.

Williams discusses the way dialogue is used satirically
by Fellini in Juliet of the Spirits. Fellini "has produced
an auditory Inferno which exactly parallels the visual
phantasmagoria." The historical cause for the emptiness of
the dialogue of the characters may be the development of a
flavorless, standardized Italian through broadcasting.

505 ZAPPONI, BERNARDINO. "Edgar Poe e il cinema." Tre passi nel
     delirio di Federico Fellini, Louis Malle, Roger Vadim.
     Bologna: Cappelli editore, pp. 15-19.
        In this essay, Zapponi, Fellini's collaborator on Toby
     Dammit, outlines the major characteristics of Edgar Allan
     Poe as a writer and discusses reasons why filmmakers are
     attracted to his works. Zapponi gives a short history of
     films of Poe's works.

                              1969

506 ALPERT, HOLLIS. "Fellini at Work." Saturday Review, 52
     (12 July), 14-17.
        A behind-the-scenes report on Fellini at work on Fellini
     Satyricon. Fellini comments briefly on the economics of
     the filming, his intentions in the movie, and his ideas
     about casting.

507 ANON. "Fellini on Fellini on Satyricon." Cinema (Beverly
     Hills), 5, No. 3 (Fall), 2-11. Illustrated.
        A culling of remarks by Fellini and of illustrations
     from Fellini Satyricon. Fellini comments on his general
     method of expanding from a screenplay during the filming
     and notes that he was much more restricted to advance prep-
     aration in Fellini Satyricon. He states that his aim was
     to recreate the pre-Christian era in a new way in Fellini
     Satyricon. He sees the early Roman era as differing from
     the Christian era in respects ranging from gestures to con-
     ceptions of charity and conscience. He also discusses his
     obsession with faces.

508 ANON. "Fellini Satyricon." Films and Filming, 16, No. 2
     (November), 26-31. Illustrated.
        A compilation of background material on the production
     of Fellini Satyricon and of quotations of remarks by
     Fellini on his intentions in the movie. Fellini comments
     on his sources, the characters of his young protagonists,
     and his difficulty in avoiding a Christian and Catholic
     point of view toward the Romans.

509 ANON. "An Interview with Fellini." Cinema (Beverly Hills),
     5, No. 3 (Fall), 12-13. Illustrated.

An interview during the filming of <u>Fellini Satyricon</u>. Fellini comments on differences between the Christian era and the pagan era, on superstition, on his antipathy for being typed, and on his distrust of conceptions of "ideals."

510 ANTONIONI, MICHELANGELO. "Licenziosità come ribellione." <u>Cinema nuovo</u>, 18, No. 202 (November-December), 414-15.
    An open letter from Antonioni to producer Gianluigi Polidoro reassuring him that <u>Fellini Satyricon</u> is not pornographic.

511 ARECCO, SERGIO. "<u>Fellini satyricon</u> di Federico Fellini." <u>Filmcritica</u>, No. 200 (September), p. 262. Illustrated.
    Brief negative review of <u>Fellini Satyricon</u>. Arecco describes the film as asymmetrical and insular. He dismisses it as "kitsch."

512 ARISTARCO, GUIDO. "La nostra epoca e il lutto del cielo." <u>Cinema nuovo</u>, 18, No. 202 (November-December), 412-17.
    In this discussion of <u>Fellini Satyricon</u>, Aristarco raises the issue of grace as it is developed in many of Fellini's films. The moral tone of <u>Fellini Satyricon</u> convinces Artistarco to view <u>La Dolce Vita</u> as a prologue to it.

513 BENAYOUN, ROBERT. "Les Conquérants de la planète mère." <u>Positif</u>, No. 111 (December), pp. 22-26. Illustrated.
    A review of <u>Fellini Satyricon</u>. Benayoun discusses the movie as a science-fiction voyage into a futuristic world beyond the world of traditional Christian morality. He celebrates Fellini's own liberation from the sort of "double game" he had played with the church in previous movies.

514 BEZZOLA, GUIDO. "Il racconto storico." <u>Bianco e nero</u>, 30, Nos. 11-12 (November-December), 46-51.
    An article on historical films, especially <u>Fellini Satyricon</u> and <u>The Leopard</u>. According to Bezzola, <u>Fellini Satyricon</u> is neither the conventional historical film which uses history as a backdrop for the action of the characters, nor an historical film like <u>The Leopard</u> which critically examines a historical period. Instead, <u>Fellini Satyricon</u> is a personalized version of history. It is a slow-moving, noisy film dominated by Fellini's obsessive concern with sin.

515 BRUNO, EDOARDO. "Manifesto dell' essenzialità." <u>Filmcritica</u>, No. 200 (September), pp. 252-56.
    A general discussion of the films at the Venice Film Festival in terms of their "essential" drives. In <u>Fellini Satyricon</u>, Bruno identifies the "essential" need to push images to the point of hallucination.

516   CANALI, LUCA. "Friderico profante." <u>Fellini Satyricon di Federico Fellini</u>. Edited by Dario Zanelli. Bologna: Cappelli editore, pp. 277-78.
    The Latin scholar who served as consultant for <u>Fellini Satyricon</u> comments on the use of Latin in the film.

517   CANBY, VINCENT. "<u>Spirits of the Dead</u> at Rivoli and Pacific East." <u>New York Times</u>, (4 September), p. 51. Illustrated. Brief credits.
    Review in which Canby praises <u>Toby Dammit</u> as a short, but major movie. He compares Fellini's work with the Poe short story on which it was based.

518   CORBUCCI, GIANFRANCO. "<u>Satyricon</u>." <u>Cinema nuovo</u>, 18, No. 201 (September-October), 383-85.
    A review of <u>Fellini Satyricon</u> in which Corbucci accuses Fellini of betraying the poetic essence of Petronius' original work with his moralizing.

519   EASON, PATRICK. "Notes on Double Structure and the Films of Fellini." <u>Cinema</u> (London), 2 (March), 22-24. Illustrated.
    Eason argues for a structuralist approach to cinema and uses his version of the approach on <u>La Strada</u>, <u>Il Bidone</u>, and <u>8½</u>. He states that Fellini uses a double structure in his films, that is, he organizes each film on two different levels or in two different parts and gains resonance from the interaction of the two levels or two parts.

520   FAVAZZA, ARMANDO. "Fellini: Analyst Without Portfolio," in <u>Man and the Movies</u>. Edited by W. R. Robinson. Baltimore: Penguin Books, pp. 180-90.
    Favazza is a psychiatrist, and he discusses <u>8½</u> and <u>Juliet of the Spirits</u> as Fellini's means of working out his problems with creativity and religion.

521   FELLINI, FEDERICO. "L'Introduction au <u>Satyricon</u>." Translated by Paul-Louis Thirard. <u>Positif</u>, No. 111 (December), pp. 18-20.
    French translation of Fellini's introduction to <u>Fellini Satyricon</u>. Edited by Dario Zanelli. Bologna: Cappelli editore, 1969. Pp. 107-110. And it appears in English in <u>Fellini's Satyricon</u>. Translated by Eugene Walter and John Matthews. New York: Ballantine Books, 1970. Pp. 43-46.

522   _____. "I miei amici Poe e Petronio." <u>Cinema nuovo</u>, 18, No. 201 (September-October), 373.
    A brief note in which Fellini refutes Roberto Rossellini's statement that cinema is dead, comments on the effect current social and political upheavals have had on him, and describes his attitudes about borrowing from Poe and Petronius.

523 FELLINI, FEDERICO. "Premessa," in *Fellini satyricon di Federico Fellini*. Edited by Dario Zanelli. Bologna: Cappelli editore, pp. 107-110.
In this preface to *Fellini Satyricon*, Fellini describes the parallels he finds between Petronius' ancient Rome before the arrival of Christianity and our modern society. There is a disconcerting modernity about Petronius' work. Fellini states his intention to draw on other classical texts too for his film. He wishes to create a Roman world that will seem strange to and removed from our comprehension, even while parallel to our world. The essay is translated into English in *Fellini's Satyricon*. Edited by Dario Zanelli and translated by Eugene Walter and John Matthews. New York: Ballantine Books, 1970. Pp. 43-46. It appears in French as "L'Introduction au *Satyricon*." *Positif*, No. 111 (December 1969), pp. 18-20.

524 GOW, GORDON. "*La Strada*." *Films and Filming*, 16, No. 1 (October), 58. Brief credits.
A review of *La Strada* on the occasion of its re-release. Gow describes it as a transitional film in Fellini's career. It is a film still to some extent in the neorealistic idiom, but its heroes are primatives whose problems are more universal or elemental than the particularized social problems usually found in neorealistic films. Gow describes elements in *La Strada* that reappear in later Fellini movies.

525 GROSS, ROBERT. "The Telltale Heart." *Newsweek*, 74, No. 11 (15 September), 102.
A review of *Spirits of the Dead*. Gross states that in *Toby Dammit* Fellini gives "a harrowing experience of obsession and terror by projecting the inner fantasies of his protagonist on the screen." He discusses the effect gained by Fellini in using the conventionally innocent figure of a young girl as a threatening image.

526 HERMAN, DAVID. "Federico Fellini." *American Imago*, 26, (Fall), 251-68. Illustrated.
A psychoanalytical study of Fellini's movies from *Variety Lights* to *Juliet of the Spirits* (with the exception of *Il Bidone*). Herman's thesis is that the artist uses the creative process to reassure himself about and to atone for "crimes" committed in his early fantasies. He takes up such elements as scoptophilia, exhibitionism, and narcissism in Fellini's work, and he comments briefly on Fellini's fear of heights, his stereotypes of women, and his interest in mysticism.

527 HUGHES, EILEEN. "Old Roma alla Fellini." *Life*, 67 (15 August), 56-61. Illustrated.

A behind-the-scenes visit to Fellini Satyricon. Hughes discusses mainly the casting and making up of the actors and the set designing. The material here is included in her book, On the Set of Fellini Satyricon: A Behind-the-Scenes Diary. New York: Marrow Press, 1971.

528 KAUFFMANN, STANLEY. "Spirits of the Dead." New Republic, 161, No. 13 (27 September), 22.

Kauffmann urges his readers to see Fellini's episode, Toby Dammit, in the three-part anthology. He states: "His horror is joyous." Kauffmann argues that Fellini is in his second period: "the first in which his cinematic mind serves his humanist concerns; the second, in which his humanist concerns are the base for stylistic exultation." La Dolce Vita is the transitional film. Reprinted in Figures of Light. New York: Harper & Row, 1971. Pp. 196-98.

529 LANGMAN, BETSY. "Il mio amore con Fellini." Fellini satyricon di Federico Fellini. Edited by Dario Zanelli. Bologna: Cappelli editore, pp. 91-104.

An account by a young, American actress of her experience playing a small role under Fellini's direction in Fellini Satyricon. The essay appears in English as "Working with Fellini." Mademoiselle, 70 (January 1970), 74-75 & 130-33.

530 LEFÈVRE, RAYMOND. "Venise." Image et Son, No. 232 (November), pp. 53-59. Illustrated.

Brief mention of the showing of Fellini Satyricon at the Venice Film Festival. The reviewer calls it one of the high points of the festival: "the apocalypse of sex, the death of voluptuousness, the defeat of woman as erotic object."

531 MARTIN, MARCEL. "Fellini Satyricon." Cinéma 69, No. 140 (November), pp. 55-57. Illustrated.

Brief notice of the showing of Fellini Satyricon at the Venice Film Festival. Martin states that the movie is visually inventive, but also frozen. Fellini has put into the Roman world his obsessions, including the flesh as sin and the problem of creative impotence. Martin finds the treatment of nudity singularly chaste.

532 MORAVIA, ALBERTO. "Roma prende la cicuta." L'espresso, 15, No. 34 (24 August), 12-13. Illustrated.

A review of Fellini Satyricon by the Italian novelist. Moravia discusses first the "open" structure of Petronius' Satyricon. Fellini's adaptation is a kind of farewell to the classical antiquity of Petronius' time. Fellini depicts antiquity as incomprehensible, partially erased, absurd, mysterious, and dreamlike. Moravia attaches great importance to Fellini's statement that the film is a "documentary

of a dream." According to Moravia, Fellini ignores much of
what has been written about antiquity and concentrates on
what has been depicted in the visual arts. Moravia finds a
strong aesthetic sense in the film, with influences such as
primitive, Pompeian, surreal, expressionistic, and pop art.
He argues also that the movie has in it the kind of dis-
sociation found in Renaissance art where the violence of
depicted events contrasts with the serenity of the characters involved in the events. Fellini's actors do not become
characters, but remain apparitions in a dream. Finally,
Moravia asserts that Fellini puts into his version of antiquity his own religious attitude. Like medieval Christians,
Fellini tends to think of antiquity as a corrupted world.
He peoples it with the monstrous and the impure. Moravia
finds a decadence in Fellini's interest in such a world.
[No copy of this review could be located in the U.S.A. A
copy was found, however, in the library of the Centro sperimentale di cinematografia in Rome. JCS]

533 RENZI, RENZO. "Fellini che va, fanciullino che viene."
     Cinema nuovo, 18, No. 199 (May-June), 186-93.
        A reprinting of the lively debate between Renzi and
     Fellini which appeared as "Fellini che va, Fellini che
     viene," in Il primo Fellini. Bologna: Cappelli editore,
     1969. Pp. 13-19.

534 _____. "Fellini che va, Fellini che viene." Il primo Fellini.
     Bologna: Cappelli editore, pp. 13-19.
        In interview, Renzi plans to confront Fellini with a
     critical problem he recognizes in Fellini's work, namely
     its retrogressive and contradictory nature. Renzi identi-
     fies this inclination as a "return to the womb." He asks
     Fellini if he does not feel that his work is reminiscent of
     a serpent biting its own tail. Fellini discusses the image
     as the Oriental symbol for wisdom and points out that past
     experiences put the future in perspective. Renzi argues
     that the image is alien and contradictory to the Christian
     symbol of the cross. Fellini disagrees and reasserts his
     idea that past and future, nostalgia and hope, are linked
     in important ways. Renzi concludes that Fellini's final
     words only confirm the circular and contradictory philosophy
     of his work. This lively debate is reprinted as "Fellini
     che va, fanciullino che viene." Cinema nuovo, 18, No. 199
     (May-June 1969), 186-93.

535 RICHARDSON, ROBERT. Literature and Film. Bloomington:
     Indiana University Press, pp. 106-16.
        Richardson compares Fellini's La Dolce Vita with T. S.
     Eliot's The Waste Land in terms of each author's intention
     to break down traditional narrative structures and to re-
     arrange narrative elements the better to treat the theme of
     the breakdown of traditional order.

536 SALACHAS, GILBERT. <u>Federico Fellini: An Investigation into his Films and Philosophy</u>. Translated by Rosalie Siegal. New York: Crown Publishers, 224 pp. Illustrated. Filmography.

    A translation into English of Salachas' <u>Federico Fellini</u>. Collection Cinema d'Aujourd'hui. Paris: Seghers, 1963. This version is slightly expanded to cover <u>Juliet of the Spirits</u>. (<u>Toby Dammit</u> and <u>Fellini Satyricon</u> are mentioned only in an editor's note.)

537 _____. "Federico Fellini: 'Comme ce verre d'eau est bon.'" <u>Télécine</u>, No. 156 (October-November), pp. 10-12. Illustrated.

    An interview with Fellini at the Venice Film Festival, largely on subjects related to <u>Fellini Satyricon</u>. Fellini discusses the ending of the movie and his attempt for a detached point of view in the film. He explains that his major concern in most of his films is the individual's sense of harmony with himself. He praises the youth movements and revolutions of the contemporary era as steps toward such interior harmony on a broad, social scale.

538 _____. "<u>Fellini Satyricon</u>." <u>Télécine</u>, No. 156 (October-November), pp. 5-9. Illustrated. Credits.

    A publication of a chapter on <u>Fellini Satyricon</u> to be added to the third edition of Salachas' <u>Federico Fellini</u>. Collection Cinéma d'Aujourd'hui. Paris: Seghers, 1970. Salachas places great weight on Encolpius' final decision to break from the decadent life of the Roman Empire. With Encolpius' breaking away, comes the dawn of a new era and a new hope. The breaking away sets up a moral point of view on the preceding episodes. Salachas sees the film as a parable of contemporary Western Society. Fellini's view is apocalyptic. The essay is followed by eleven excerpts from reviews of <u>Fellini Satyricon</u> from the French press.

539 SARRIS, ANDREW. "<u>Spirits of the Dead</u>." <u>Village Voice</u>, 14, No. 48 (11 September), 51 & 55.

    Sarris finds the movie as a whole useless and pointless. Poe's prose style runs parallel to the film's <u>mise-en-scene</u> and "never intersects it at a point of mutual expressiveness." In his episode, Fellini is "content merely to flourish his own very formidable style to the point of self-parody." All the doubt and self-hatred of $8\frac{1}{2}$ reappear. This review is collected in Sarris' <u>Confessions of a Cultist: On the Cinema 1959-1969</u>. New York: Simon and Schuster, 1970. Pp. 459-61.

540 SOLMI, ANGELO. "Anche negli errori riesce geniale." <u>Oggi</u>, 25, No. 41 (8 October), 135 & 137. Illustrated.

A review of Fellini Satyricon. Solmi describes the
financial success of the movie and the wide split of popular
opinion about it. Solmi himself evokes the names of Goya,
Bosch, and Brueghel to describe the mixture of the macabre
and of the lyrical in the movie. He feels the suggestive
power of the film compensates for its lack of balance and
of logical connections.

541   SOLMI, ANGELO. ["Il festival cinematografico di Venezia 1969:
      la notte del Satyricon."] Oggi, 25, No. 38 (17 September),
      62-65. Illustrated.
      Solmi reports on the showing of Fellini Satyricon at the
      Venice Film Festival. He interviews Fellini about the film
      and then partly agrees with some of the film's detractors
      that the film relies too heavily on visual effects and
      violence.

542   VERDONE, MARIO. "Venezia 1969: un rogo per ricominciare."
      Bianco e nero, 30, Nos. 9-10 (September-October), 67-84.
      Illustrated. Credits.
      In this attack on the safe, conventional attitudes of
      the organizers of the Venice Film Festival, Verdone praises
      Fellini Satyricon as a ground-breaking film which demon-
      strates how rapidly cinema is evolving. He praises the
      almost totally visual way Fellini treats the decomposition
      of an epoch.

543   VOLTA, ORNELLA. "Le Voyage de Fellini." Translated by Paul-
      Louis Thirard. Positif, No. 111 (December), pp. 20-22.
      Illustrated.
      Brief article on the Roman world created by Fellini in
      Fellini Satyricon. Volta discusses the cultural and
      psychological differences between that world before
      Christianity and the modern world. Fellini's descent into
      this world is like Dante's descent into Hell.

544   ZANELLI, DARIO. "Dal pianeta Roma," in Fellini satyricon di
      Federico Fellini. Bologna: Cappelli editore, pp. 13-79.
      A lengthy article on Fellini Satyricon emphasizing back-
      ground information on the film and the evolution of
      Fellini's thoughts about the film. Much of the material
      comes from observations Zanelli made on the set and from
      interviews with Fellini. Fellini explains how he selected
      Petronius' work for his film, his impression of Petronius'
      characters, the liberties he has taken with the source,
      and his wish to achieve a sense of estrangement in the
      world he creates in his film through the use of unknown
      actors, of static camera work, and of dubbing out of syn-
      chronization. Fellini talks also about analogies he sees
      between ancient Rome and modern times and between his heroes

and modern youths. Zanelli interviews the film's producer, Fellini's co-writer, his consultant in Latin, and other associates on the film about such diverse matters as production costs, property rights, historical background, and even press reaction to the filming. Zanelli reproduces sections of an interview between Fellini and Alberto Moravia in which Moravia tells Fellini he has projected his Christian prejudices and modern sensibilities onto his version of Roman antiquity. A portion of this material has been translated into English by Eugene Walter and John Matthews in "From the Planet Rome," in Fellini's Satyricon. New York: Ballantine Books, pp. 3-20.

545 ZAPPONI, BERNARDINO. "Lo strano viaggio." Fellini satyricon di Federico Fellini. Edited by Dario Zanelli. Bologna: Cappelli editore, pp. 83-88.
An account by Fellini's co-writer of the evolution of Fellini Satyricon and of Fellini's method of collaborating. Zapponi describes a visit he and Fellini paid to Italy's leading scholar of Petronius, Ettore Paratore, and he describes a visit to the set of Fellini Satyricon paid by Ingmar Bergman.

1970

546 ANON. "Fellini--Satyricon." L'Avant-Scène, No. 102 (April), pp. 55-66. Illustrated. Credits. Filmography.
A photographic supplement on Fellini Satyricon. The supplement contains a brief synopsis of the film, complete credits, some information about Fellini's activities before and after Fellini Satyricon, quotations of remarks by Fellini about the film, information about the Satyricon of Petronius Arbiter, and a collection of excerpts from French reviews of the movie.

547 ANON. "Fellini segreto: per cinque ore ha fatto il clown prima di girare il suo film." Oggi, 26, No. 38 (22 September), 68-69.
A picture spread of five color stills of Fellini making himself up as a "white clown" and as an "Augusto." The event was in connection with the theater release of The Clowns.

548 ANON. "Rome, B.C., A.F." Time, 95, No. 11 (16 March), 76-81. Illustrated.
A brief review of Fellini Satyricon. The reviewer calls the movie Jungian, but does not discuss the idea in detail. Instead, he discusses the film as social satire.

549 BARNESCHI, RENATO. "Dovevo lavarmi nella sua acqua." <u>Oggi</u>,
26, No. 49 (7 December), 89. Illustrated.
A brief biographical essay about Fellini's brother,
Riccardo, who discusses his situation of living in his
famous brother's shadow.

550 BAUDRY, PIERRE. "Un Avatar du sens." <u>Cahiers du Cinéma</u>,
No. 219 (April), pp. 56-57. Illustrated. Brief credits.
A review of <u>Fellini Satyricon</u>. Baudry scoffs at other
reviewers who have put the movie in a Christian moral tradition. He offers a Freudian reading. He finds that
Fellini suspends the world of sense and then has his young
hero seek to overcome his castration complex. Baudry calls
the movie a sexual <u>bildungsroman</u>.

551 BONGIOANNI, MARCO. "Antipaganesimo nel nuovo <u>Satyricon</u>."
<u>Cineforum</u>, 9, No. 90 (March), 651-60.
Bongioanni argues that one cannot understand <u>Fellini
Satyricon</u> unless one recognizes the anxiety of spiritual
liberation which pervades so much of Fellini's work. He
discusses Fellini's background in the Romagna area and the
nature of his Catholic upbringing. In addition, Bongioanni
offers information on Petronius' <u>Satyricon</u> and on the
history of various editions of the work.

552 BURKE, TOM. "Fellini Finds 'An Unknown Planet for Me to
Populate!'" <u>New York Times</u> (8 February), pp. 15 & 20.
Fellini covers familiar ground in this interview on
<u>Fellini Satyricon</u> and his approach to filmmaking. He makes
some very interesting observations, however, on two collaborative efforts. He reveals that <u>Love Duet</u>, which was to
have been directed by Fellini and Ingmar Bergman, was can-
celled because of Bergman's unavailability. Concerning
<u>Spirits of the Dead</u>, he says that originally the episodes
were to be directed by Bergman, Buñuel, and himself. (The
final directors were Fellini, Roger Vadim, and Louis Malle.)

553 CANBY, VINCENT. "<u>Fellini Satyricon</u>." <u>New York Times</u> (12
March), p. 48. Illustrated. Brief credits.
A review in which Canby praises <u>Fellini Satyricon</u> as a
"surreal epic" which is descriptive rather than narrative.
He remarks that Fellini's casual way of synchronizing
dialogue with lip movements gives the movie an incantory
affect, and he comments that the movie is not about homosexuality, although it shows homosexuality.

554 _____. "Fellini's Magical Mystery Tour." <u>New York Times</u>
(15 March), Section II, p. 1.
A second review of <u>Fellini Satyricon</u> in which Canby
reiterates his views expressed in "<u>Fellini Satyricon</u>."
<u>New York Times</u> (12 March 1970), p. 48.

555 CIMENT, MICHEL. "Venise, 1970." <u>Positif</u>, No. 121 (November), pp. 8-21. Illustrated.
   In this report on the Venice Film Festival, Ciment reviews <u>The Clowns</u>. He finds much vitality in the unassuming TV film. It concerns the death of an art form and sheds a good deal of light on Fellini and the nature of his imagination.

556 COX, HARVEY G., JR. "The Purpose of the Grotesque in Fellini's Films," in <u>Celluloid and Symbols</u>. Edited by John C. Cooper and Carl Skrade. Philadelphia: Fortress Press, pp. 89-106.
   The professor from Harvard's Divinity School recounts amusingly a visit to the set of <u>Fellini Satyricon</u>, where he is given the coat of G. Mastorna to put on and as a result feels the call of the actor momentarily. In a serious vein, Cox discusses Fellini's love for grotesque characters as his love for the mysterious, the non-regular, and the non-rational in life. It may even be, Cox suggests, a part of his love for the transcendental and the holy.

557 CULKIN, JOHN M., S.J. "<u>Fellini Satyricon</u>--Pro." <u>Show</u>, 1, No. 4 (April), 20. Illustrated.
   Half of a two-part, pro and con debate with Molly Haskell about <u>Fellini Satyricon</u>. Culkin defends the movie as one "for painters rather than for literary men" and compares it briefly to <u>La Dolce Vita</u>. He notes "almost every major scene is climaxed with a death scene."

558 de LAUROT, EDOUARD. "<u>La Strada</u>--A Poem on Saintly Folly," in <u>Renaissance of the Film</u>. Edited by Julius Bellone. London: Collier-Macmillan, pp. 264-76. Illustrated.
   A reprinting of de Laurot's review of <u>La Strada</u> originally published in <u>Film Culture</u>, 2, No. 1 (1956), 11-14.

559 del BUONO, ORESTE. "Da Fortunello a Giudizio passando per Little Nemo," in <u>I clowns</u>. Edited by Renzo Renzi. Bologna: Cappelli editore, pp. 73-76. Illustrated.
   An essay in which del Buono discusses the influences of comic strips on Fellini's films. del Buono outlines the historical development of comic strips. Fellini acknowledges his indebtedness to his early reading of comic strips and to his early drawing of cartoons. Fellini sees similarities between comic strip heroes and clowns.

560 _____. "I due Federici," in <u>Federico a.c., disegni per il Satyricon di Federico Fellini</u>. Edited by Liliana Betti. Milan: Milano libri edizioni, pp. 5-21.
   del Buono's essay serves as a preface to Liliana Betti's collection of Fellini's sketches for <u>Fellini Satyricon</u>. The essay is a survey of Fellini's work from <u>Variety Lights</u> to <u>Fellini Satyricon</u>. (<u>A Matrimonial Agency</u> and <u>The</u>

Temptations of Doctor Antonio are excluded; <u>Toby Dammit</u> and
the unrealized project <u>The Voyage of G. Mastorna</u> are included.) del Buono feels that all of Fellini's movies are
basically a dialogue with himself. The modern Italian man
as depicted by Fellini, argues del Buono, is contemporary
only by chronology, not by mores. Fellini's "modern
Italian" is as antiquated in his values, as provincial, and
as sentimental as he ever was.

561 ETAIX, PIERRE and ANNIE FRATELLINI. "Che cosa mangia un clown?"
     in <u>I clowns</u>. Edited by Renzo Renzi. Bologna: Cappelli
     editore, p. 260.
        A letter to Fellini in which Pierre Etaix and Annie
     Fratellini give their conception of what a clown is and of
     the world he lives in. They feel that clowns belong to
     mythology. When Annie Fratellini was asked by a child what
     clowns eat, she did not know how to answer, because she did
     not want to violate the world of illusion in which clowns
     live.

562 FELLINI, FEDERICO. "L'Autre Nuit au Colisée." Translated by
     Max Tessier. <u>Cinéma 70</u>, No. 142 (January), pp. 110-13.
        A translation into French of remarks Fellini made to an
     interviewer for <u>Il dramma</u> which are printed in Italian in
     Dario Zanelli's "Dal pianeta Roma," in <u>Fellini satyricon di
     Federico Fellini</u>. Bologna: Cappelli editore, 1969.
     Pp. 29-31. This material was cut from Zanelli's essay
     when the essay was translated into English in <u>Fellini's
     Satyricon</u>. New York: Ballantine Books, 1970. In the
     interview, Fellini discusses his feelings about ancient Rome
     and possible reasons for undertaking the film. He tells of
     seeing the Colosseum lit at night by the moon, like an im-
     mense skull, and thinking for a moment he was in the
     presence of a civilization from another planet.

563 _____. "Fellini's <u>Formula</u>." <u>Esquire</u>, 74, No. 2 (August), 62
     & 18. Illustrated.
        A wide-ranging personal essay by Fellini on such subjects
     as <u>The Clowns</u>, television, his antipathy to making films
     outside of Italy, his reasons for giving fabrications to
     journalists, his beginning film experiences, his methods
     with actors, and his interest in the American youth
     movements.

564 _____. "Preface," in <u>Fellini's Satyricon</u>. Edited by Dario
     Zanelli. Translated by Eugene Walter and John Matthews.
     New York: Ballantine Books, pp. 43-46.
        The preface is a statement of Fellini's intentions in
     <u>Fellini Satyricon</u>, written before filming. He writes of
     the similarities between the Roman world of Petronius and
     our own society and between Encolpius and Ascyltus and

modern hippies. He intends to stress these parallels, but he also wishes to evoke an air of fantasy. To do the latter, he will allow himself the freedom to draw on materials from Apuleius, Horace, and Suetonius.

565 _____. "Satyricon: Pictorial Essay." Playboy, 17, No. 5 (May), 105-11 & 210. Illustrated.
Fellini discusses his first realization of the visual style he would follow in Fellini Satyricon when at night he saw the Colosseum as a "horrendous lunar catastrophe of stone" suggesting "a civilization with a different destiny." He compares his youthful heroes to modern hippies and discusses at some length his understanding of the hippies' kind of social revolution.

566 _____. "Un viaggio nell'ombra," in I clowns. Edited by Renzo Renzi. Bologna: Cappelli editore, pp. 27-56.
An interesting and extended introductory essay to The Clowns. First Fellini outlines the circumstances under which he came to make the television film. Then he discusses the importance of the circus for him. It is not just a spectacle but a life experience, for it captures the essence of many of life's events: the threat of death, excitement, speed, risk, travel, and stepping into the limelight. He distinguishes between the white clown and the Augusto. The former is authority, the adult, beauty, grace, and intelligence--in short, "what should be done." The Augusto is the rebellious child, the mocker, and the mocked--"a fantastic creature who expresses the irrational aspect of man." Fellini reproduces comments made by the clown Bario in which Bario describes his routine for recalling his dead partner by his trumpet. (Fellini uses this routine for the ending of The Clowns.) And Fellini reproduces some episodes that do not appear in the final version of the movie. This essay has been reprinted in Fellini TV. Block-notes di un regista. I clowns. Edited by Renzo Renzi. Bologna: Cappelli editore, 1972. Pp. 105-30. It has been translated into English by Isabel Quigley as "Why Clowns?" in Fellini on Fellini. New York: Delacorte Press/Seymour Lawrence, 1976. Pp. 115-39.

567 FRIENDLY, ALFRED, JR. "Now ! In the Center Ring!! Fellini!!!" New York Times (19 July), p. 13.
Fellini interviewed on The Clowns and his attitude toward television. He states: "When you think of all those people watching while they argue or eat or put the children to bed it's very upsetting.... I am not adapted to it. Just not adapted."

568 GARDIES, RENÉ. "Le Tournant baroque de Fellini." Image et Son, No. 238 (April), pp. 51-54. Illustrated.

Gardies argues that <u>Fellini Satyricon</u> is a baroque masterpiece in which literary narrative has little importance and visual style has a great deal of importance. Fellini's visual style is founded on oppositions. Other characteristics are infinite repetitions of a complex motif, a taste for <u>trompe-l'oeil</u>, and a pervasive sense of theatricality.

569 GOW, GORDON. "<u>Fellini Satyricon</u>." <u>Films and Filming</u>, 17, No. 2 (November), 47-48. Illustrated. Credits.
Laudatory review of <u>Fellini Satyricon</u>. Gows comments on the use of grotesques and on the sense of spectacle in the film. He finds fault with the use of a cockney accent in the dubbing of Trimalchio.

570 HARCOURT, PETER. "Fellini's <u>Satyricon</u>." <u>Queen's Quarterly</u>, 77, No. 3 (Autumn), 447-53.
Harcourt discusses Fellini's movement toward overtly surreal art. He notes the decrease of "pure" children and the increase of the "Gioconda smile" in Fellini's films. He finds Fellini more and more concerned with the disastrous things which follow surrender to physical love. The material in this essay is expanded in Harcourt's <u>Six European Directors</u>. Harmondsworth, England and Baltimore: Penguin Books, 1974.

571 HART, HENRY. "<u>Fellini Satyricon</u>." <u>Films in Review</u>, 21, No. 4 (April), 239-41. Illustrated.
An all-out attack on Fellini's intentions in this movie. Hart sees Fellini as propagandizing for homosexuality, abetting social disintegration, enhancing his reputation among anarcho-nihilists, and regurgitating a life-long anti-humanism!

572 HASKELL, MOLLY. "<u>Fellini Satyricon</u>-Con." <u>Show</u>, 1, No. 4 (April), 21. Illustrated.
Half of a two-part, pro and con debate with John M. Culkin about <u>Fellini Satyricon</u>. Haskell attacks the movie as "gratuitously grotesque." The more remote Fellini's material is from his own dreams and demands, the more artificial and purely decorative are its metaphors. <u>Fellini Satyricon</u> lacks the tension found in Fellini's best movies-- the tension between the yearning to be emotionally free and the restraints imposed by a given society.

573 HIGHET, GILBERT. "Whose <u>Satyricon</u>, Petronius' or Fellini's?" <u>Horizon</u>, 12, No. 4 (Autumn), 42-47. Illustrated.
The classicist compares incidents and intentions in Petronius' <u>Satyricon</u> with those in <u>Fellini Satyricon</u>. In particular, he discusses incidents invented by Fellini: the earthquake; the story of Oenothea; the scene with the

nymphomaniac; the sexual failure of Encolpius with Ariadne; the worship of the hermaphrodite; Lichas' "marriage" to Encolpius; and several action sequences. He finds Fellini's views of Roman life in the first century and of contemporary life profoundly pessimistic.

574 HOLLAND, NORMAN N. "The Follies Fellini," in Renaissance of the Film. Edited by Julius Bellone. London: Collier-Macmillan, pp. 79-90. Illustrated.
A reprinting of Holland's essay on La Dolce Vita from Hudson Review, 14, No. 3 (Autumn 1961), 425-31.

575 KAEL, PAULINE. "Fellini's Mondo Trasho." New Yorker, 46 (14 March), 134-40.
Kael argues that Fellini Satyricon is based on Fellini's (and a youthful audience's) superstitious belief that depravity and deformity are related and that ugliness is God's punishment for disobedience.

576 KAUFFMANN, STANLEY. "Fellini Satyricon." New Republic, 162, Nos. 14-15 (4 & 11 April), 24 & 38.
A review in which Kauffmann speculates on Fellini's reasons for making Fellini Satyricon. He disagrees with Alberto Moravia's statement that Fellini has "completely surmounted the personal crisis" treated in previous films. Because of a sense of incompetence to deal with the modern world's "amplified experience," Fellini has emigrated to the past, as Antonioni emigrated to a different place and a different generation in Zabriskie Point. In the past, with Petronius' material, Fellini's "sense of futility and oppression was relieved of the necessity of point and could express itself as a function of film-making itself." Reprinted in Figures of Light. New York: Harper & Row, 1971. Pp. 250-54.

577 LANGMAN, BETSY. "Working with Fellini." Mademoiselle, 70 (January), pp. 74-75 & 130-33. Illustrated.
English version of Langman's article, "Il mio amore con Fellini," in Fellini satyricon di Federico Fellini. Edited by Dario Zanelli. Bologna: Cappelli editore, pp. 91-104.

578 LEFÈVRE, RAYMOND. "Le Satyricon." Image et Son, No. 237 (March), pp. 134-37. Illustrated. Brief credits.
Laudatory review of Fellini Satyricon. Lefèvre praises Fellini's effort to recreate a pre-Christian world without any biases of the Christian world. Fellini shows the "decadent" period of Rome as an era dominated by a taste for spectacle. It is an era of death for art and philosophy.

579 LINDEN, GEORGE W. "Film Form: Situation, Articulation, Revelation," in Reflections on the Screen. Belmont, California: Wadsworth Publishing, pp. 258-65.

An excellent discussion of $8\frac{1}{2}$. Linden argues against
Pauline Kael's contention that the film is narcissistic
and incomprehensible. Linden feels that Fellini has
"objectified" the autobiographical elements to make them
applicable, by extension, not only to all creative persons,
but to all men. He finds $8\frac{1}{2}$ to be "mystical," not "mysterious." Linden states that the film works on five levels:
(1) the realistic level; (2) the level of masculine viewpoint; (3) the level of fantasy and imagination; (4) the
level of memory; and (5) the level of mystic vision. The
theme of the film is "the difficulty, if not impossibility,
of emotional commitment in the modern world."

580   MARTIN, MARCEL. "Les Clowns." Cinéma 70, No. 147 (September-
       October), pp. 58-59.
           Brief notice of the showing of The Clowns at the Venice
       Film Festival. Martin praises the mixture of the documentary form with Fellini's subjective point of view. The
       film, he finds, is a sympathetic look at a world which is
       in the process of disappearing.

581   MICHALEK, BOLESLAW. "Oscurità, caos, demoni." Translated by
       Elena Barbaro. Filmcritica, No. 206 (April), pp. 171-74.
           A comparison of Fellini Satyricon with Visconti's The
       Damned. Michalek sees in each common elements of amorality
       and self-destructiveness which suggest works profoundly out
       of touch with their own times.

582   MORAVIA, ALBERTO. "Documentary of a Dream: A Dialogue between
       Alberto Moravia and Federico Fellini," in Fellini's Satyricon. Edited by Dario Zanelli. Translated by Eugene Walter
       and John Matthews. New York: Ballantine, pp. 23-30.
           A different translation with slightly different editing
       of Moravia's dialogue with Fellini about Fellini Satyricon,
       which was published as "Fellini on Satyricon: Agony, Indulgence, Enigma, Dream—a Talk with Moravia." Vogue, 155
       (1 March 1970), 168-71, 207 & 220.

583   _____. "Dreaming up Petronius." Translated by Raymond
       Rosenthal. New York Review of Books, 14, No. 6 (26 March),
       40-42.
           Review of Fellini Satyricon. The Italian novelist compares Fellini's work with Petronius' and finds Fellini an
       expressionist and Petronius a realist. Fellini regards
       classical antiquity as an "era of a fallen and corrupt
       nature, teeming with physical and moral monsters." Moravia
       comments also on Fellini's use of ancient art as a source
       and on his use of dreamlike "dissociation."

584 _____. "Fellini on Satyricon: Agony, Indulgence, Enigma,
Dream--a Talk with Moravia." Translated by Simona Morini.
Vogue, 155 (1 March), 168-71, 207 & 220. Illustrated.
    A dialogue between Fellini and Moravia about Fellini
Satyricon. Fellini explains that he wishes to make a film
about pagan Rome showing it as mysterious and alien. He
wishes to avoid the myths that have shaped our thinking
about it for two thousand years. The film will have qualities of a dream, but a dream viewed in a dispassionate,
analytical way. Hence it will be a "documentary of a
dream." Moravia argues that this is not the case. He feels
that Fellini sees pagan Rome as the early Christians did,
as "pure nature, but fallen into the lowest degree of corruption." He adds that Fellini has used Freud's conception
of the libido and Jung's conception of cultural archetypes.
He concludes that Fellini has transferred to his ancient
world his own anxieties and sensibilities as a modern man.
The review was originally prepared for the Italian edition
of Vogue. A slightly different version in English appears
as "Documentary of a Dream: A Dialogue between Alberto
Moravia and Federico Fellini," in Fellini's Satyricon.
Edited by Dario Zanelli. New York: Ballantine Books, 1970.
Pp. 23-30.

585 MORGENSTERN, JOSEPH. "Roman Carnival." Newsweek, 75, No. 12
(23 March), 102. Illustrated.
    An attacking review of Fellini Satyricon. With the ex-
ception of a few scenes, Morgenstern finds the movie a
repetitive and surprisingly solemn discourse on society
heading for an apocalypse.

586 MYHERS, JOHN. "Fellini's Continuing Autobiography." Cinema
(Beverly Hills), 6, No. 2 (February), 40-41.
    The screenwriter and actor argues that Fellini's Satyricon
is an allegory of Fellini's early career. Encolpius' relationship with Eumolpus parallels Fellini's relationship
with Rossellini; the beheading of Lichas parallels the
demonstration of Mussolini's body in Milan; and the death of
the hermaphrodite parallels the death of Fellini's infant
son. While the argument in a general sense may have merit,
the particular examples seem somewhat forced.

587 NOVI, MARIO, ed. Fellini TV: I clowns. Rome: RAI radio-
television italiana, 37 pp.
    A pamphlet in which are collected various documents con-
cerning Fellini's work on television up to 1970. The
documents include credits and an outline for The Clowns
and the script of an interview with and on Fellini, conducted by Sergio Zavoli in May 1964. Among those interviewed, along with Fellini, are Fellini's mother; his
friend from Rimini, Luigi Benzi; Alberto Sordi; Georges

Simenon; Giulietta Masina; the screenwriter Sergio Amidei,
who worked with Fellini on Rome Open City; and the Russian
film critic Gherassimov. The interview is directed mainly
toward biographical material.

588 OLDRINI, GUIDO. "Considerazioni estetiche sulle tendenze del
film italiano." Cinema nuovo, 19, No. 207 (September-
October), 356-71.
A discussion of the relative merits of two mainstreams
in cinema: realism and avant-garde. Oldrini identifies
himself as a champion of realism and proceeds to develop a
comparison between the careers of realistic director
Visconti and of Fellini whom Oldrini considers avant-garde.
The article concludes with an analysis of the aesthetic
defects of the "formal irrationalism" of filmmakers like
Fellini.

589 OXENHANDLER, NEAL. "The Distancing Perspective in Satyricon."
Film Quarterly, 23, No. 4 (Summer), 38-42.
Oxenhandler contends that Fellini Satyricon resembles
the wish-fulfillment dream of the adolescent. The young
heroes of the movie confront a series of monstrous creatures
or events and triumph over them, thanks to youth and beauty.
Fellini's use of theatrical spectacles, history, and dis-
tortions of Mediterranean types and his style set the work
at a distance proper for his meditation on the fable of the
monstrous. Reprinted in The Classic Cinema: Essays in
Criticism. New York, Chicago, San Francisco, Atlanta:
Harcourt Brace Jovanovich, 1973. Pp. 328-32.

590 PENSOTTI, ANITA. "Giulietta Masina: 'Chiudo un occhio sui
suoi flirt.'" Oggi, 26, No. 24 (1 June), 78-80.
Illustrated.
An interview with Fellini's wife about her reactions to
the other women in his life. To some extent, the interview
corroborates Fellini's portrait of himself in 8½.

591 PIERI, FRANÇOISE and GILBERT SALACHAS. "Fellini Satyricon."
Télécine, No. 162 (May-June), pp. 5-20. Illustrated.
Credits.
An informational "fiche" on Fellini Satyricon. It contains the following sections: a sequence outline; a history
of the development of the idea for the film; a discussion
of the disjunctive, dreamlike quality of the structure; a
consideration of the sets, with emphasis on their stage-
bound qualities; notes on lighting, color, movement, and
music; discussions of the major characters; and a critical
overview. Pieri and Salachas feel that Fellini's work has
evolved from realistic representation to more abstract,
expressive representations of his inner world. Fellini
Satyricon presents us with his obsessions and nightmares.
It is a vision of his private Hell.

592   ROLLIN, BETTY. "Fellini: He Shoots Dreams on Film." Look,
       34 (10 March), 48-53. Illustrated.
            The article describes a visit to the set of Fellini
       Satyricon. Primarily it is a pictorial spread on Fellini's
       grotesques.

593   SARRIS, ANDREW. "Cabiria," "Italy's Big Four," "Juliet of the
       Spirits," and "Spirits of the Dead," in Confessions of a
       Cultist: On the Cinema 1959-1969. New York: Simon and
       Schuster, pp. 23-29, 29-33, 215-19 & 459-61.
            In this book, Sarris collects four previously written
       reviews. "Cabiria" appeared first as "Nights of Cabiria."
       Film Culture, 4, No. 1 (January 1958), 18-21. "Juliet of
       the Spirits" first appeared in The Village Voice, 11,
       No. 4 (11 November 1965), 23, and No. 5 (18 November 1965),
       23. "Spirits of the Dead" in The Village Voice, 14, No. 48
       (11 September 1969), 51 & 55. Although "Italy's Big Four"
       was published originally in Showbill (January 1961), it
       can be located now only in Sarris' book. In this essay,
       Sarris weighs the achievements of Rossellini, Visconti,
       Antonioni, and Fellini. Fellini is the only one with a
       flair for comedy. His tone, however, is often one of a
       tragicomic lyricism. With La Dolce Vita, Fellini has en-
       larged his subject matter but has not expanded his ideas.

594   ____. "Films in Focus: Fellini Satyricon." Village Voice,
       15, No. 12 (19 March), 51.
            Sarris argues that Fellini Satyricon can be seen only in
       terms of Fellini's personal dream world. The movie appar-
       ently about the pre-Christian era, in fact, reminds Sarris
       of Fellini's well established treatments of the provincial
       on the road to Rome and of the mindless vanity, lust,
       gluttony, superstition, and cruelty of the modern Romans
       who now infest Via Veneto.

595   SCHMIDT, GIULIO. "Individuo e società." Cineforum, Nos. 88-
       89 (January-February), pp. 552-56.
            A review of Fellini Satyricon along with four other films
       shown at the Venice Film Festival. Schmidt praises Fellini
       Satyricon as an expression of Fellini's interior world. He
       notes a series of scenes alternating between the celebra-
       tion of vitality and the presentation of death and failure.
       Throughout Fellini's work in general, Schmidt argues, there
       are to be found the fear of death and the exaltation of
       life. In Fellini Satyricon, Encolpius is the emblem of the
       human thirst for new things and for self-renewal. He travels
       through corrupt situations, but remains innocent of the cor-
       ruptions he has participated in.

596 SETLOWE, RICK. "Ask Fellini about 'Symbolism': He Says There
     Is None; Lets Press Amuse Selves." Variety, 257, No. 10
     (21 January), 6.
          A report on a question and answer session held at the
     American Film Institute as part of Fellini's U.S. promo-
     tional tour for Fellini Satyricon.

597 SILKE, JAMES R. Federico Fellini. Discussion. No. 1, Beverly
     Hills: American Film Institute, 15 pp.
          This monograph is a transcript of an interview with
     Fellini at the American Film Institute's Center. Fellini
     responds to questions from those present. Fellini Satyricon
     had been shown earlier in the day, and many of the questions
     are directed at that film. Fellini discusses the following
     general subjects: his methods for choosing actors and work-
     ing with them; his manner of making adjustments from the
     screenplay during shooting; the structure of Fellini
     Satyricon; his use of film music; and the editing of his
     films. Anthony Quinn, also present, describes his experi-
     ence of working with Fellini on La Strada.

598 SIMON, JOHN. "Fellini Satyricon." New York Times, (10 May)
     Section II, p. 11.
          A blistering attack on Fellini Satyricon. Simon feels
     that Fellini has degraded Petronius' work into a series of
     random images "dredged up from Fellini's subconscious."
     "Undigested dreams," Simon states, "do not make telling works
     of art." Reprinted in Movies Into Film. New York: Dell,
     1971. Pp. 216-19.

599 SKELTON, RICHARD "RED." "Ecco perchè ho cercato di diventare
     un clown senza trucco," in I clowns. Edited by Renzo
     Renzi. Bologna: Cappelli editore, p. 303.
          A letter to Fellini from Red Skelton in which Skelton
     offers his conception of a clown as the saddest and loneli-
     est of individuals.

600 SOLMI, ANGELO. "Per tre mesi sono stato più povero e meno
     fesso." Oggi, 26, No. 46 (16 November), 68 & 71.
     Illustrated.
          An interview in which Fellini describes the circum-
     stances surrounding the making of The Clowns for NBC-TV.

601 SUFRIN, MARK. "I Vitelloni." Film Society Review, 5, No. 9
     (May), 42-45. Illustrated. Brief credits.
          A brief introductory essay on I Vitelloni. Sufrin de-
     scribes the movie as a case of the "middleclass blues." He
     discusses the youthful longings and "weak" rebellions of
     the vitelloni and finds that all except Moraldo sink back
     into the confines of middle class existence and the melan-
     choly of completed lives at the end of the movie.

602   TERNO, SAM. "Federico, Federico!" Bianco e nero, 31, Nos. 11-
       12 (November-December), 101.
         A defense of the television showing of The Clowns against
       charges published in Il circo, a circus monthly. The
       attacker objects to Fellini's assumption that the circus is
       dead and ponders his reasons for mingling horrifying images
       from the world of his childhood with the atmosphere of
       physical beauty of the circus. Sam Terno defends Fellini's
       right to pursue his personal vision of the circus.

603   TESSIER, MAX. "Fellini Satyricon." Cinéma 70, No. 142
       (January), pp. 110-14. Brief credits.
         A review of Fellini Satyricon. Tessier expresses delight
       that Fellini has survived a period of doubt and is making
       films again, but Tessier sees Fellini as a successful artist
       condemned to repeat himself. Fellini Satyricon is a magnif-
       cent visual fresco. Yet, it is still a reworking of the
       traditional Fellini themes of the search for virility and
       of the equation of the flesh with sin (purity existing only
       in suicide).

604   ZANELLI, DARIO. "From the Planet Rome," in Fellini's Satyricon.
       Edited by Dario Zanelli. Translated by Eugene Walter and
       John Matthews. New York: Ballantine Books, pp. 3-20.
         A highly edited, cut, English version of Zanelli's "Dal
       pianeta Roma," in Fellini satyricon di Federico Fellini.
       Bologna: Cappelli editore. Pp. 13-79. In this version of
       his essay, Zanelli relates Fellini's wish to achieve a sense
       of estrangement in the Roman world by casting unknown
       actors, using static shots, and dubbing voices out of syn-
       chronization. Zanelli describes the shooting of the heroes'
       work through the suburra, the feast sequence, and the final
       beach sequence.

605   ZAPPONI, BERNARDINO. "A Parigi, una recherche del circo
       perduto," in I clowns. Edited by Renzo Renzi. Bologna:
       Cappelli editore, pp. 81-84.
         Fellini's collaborator, Zapponi, gives an account of a
       trip he and Fellini took to Paris to do research for The
       Clowns. The article provides some information about the
       history of clowns, as well as information about Fellini's
       activities on the trip.

606   _____. "The Strange Journey," translated by John Matthews,
       in Fellini's Satyricon. Edited by Dario Zanelli. New York:
       Ballantine Books, pp. 33-39.
         English version of Zapponi's "Lo strano viaggio," in
       Fellini satyricon di Federico Fellini. Edited by Dario
       Zanelli. Bologna: Cappelli editore, pp. 83-88.

1971

607   ALPERT, HOLLIS. "The Testament of Federico Fellini," in Film
      as Film. Edited by Joy Gould Boyum and Adrienne Scott.
      Boston: Allyn and Bacon, pp. 178-80.
          A reprinting, with discussion questions, of Alpert's
      review of 8½ which appeared first in Saturday Review, 46,
      No. 26 (29 June 1963), 20.

608   ANON. "Black-and-White T.V. Showing of 'Clowns' Kills Theatre
      B. O. of Fellini Color Pic." Variety, 261, No. 10 (20
      January), 2 & 62.
          This article presents Fellini's negative reactions to
      the theatrical release of The Clowns two days after the
      initial black and white television showing on December 25,
      1970. The article also contains Fellini's comments on the
      limitations of television and production information on
      Roma.

609   ANON. "Rome's Biggest Summer Spectacle: Fellini's Filming of
      Symbolic Roma." Variety, 264, No. 2 (25 August), 27.
          This interesting article on the filming of Roma dis-
      cusses: the excitement in the city during the shooting of
      the motorcycle cavalcade; the financial problems surround-
      ing Giuseppe Pasquale and Ultra Film; and the immense pop-
      ularity of Fellini, who calls Roma "an informal chat about
      one of the most fascinating cities in the world."

610   ARMES, ROY. Patterns of Realism. New York: A. S. Barnes,
      passim.
          The book is an historical study of Italian neorealism.
      Although no single, extended section is devoted to Fellini,
      his ties with the movement, especially through his work
      with Rossellini, are discussed at several points. See the
      index.

611   BACKÈS-CLEMENT, CATHERINE. "Le Sanglier, ou une érudition
      déplacée." L'Arc (Aix-en-Province), No. 45, pp. 61-62.
          A comparison of Fellini's treatment of the scene of the
      roasted pig at Trimalchio's feast in Fellini Satyricon with
      Petronius' treatment of the roasted boar. Backès-Clement
      argues that Fellini transferred the bi-sexuality implicit
      in Petronius' story of the boar over to the sequence about
      the oracle in Fellini Satyricon.

612   BALDELLI, PIO. "Dilatazione visionaria del documento e
      nostalgia della madre chiesa in Fellini," in Cinema dell'
      ambiguità: Rossellini, De Sica e Zavattini, Fellini. Rome:
      Edizioni Samonà e Savelli, pp. 285-379. Filmography.
          In this chapter of his film book, Baldelli discusses
      Fellini's mature work (after Nights of Cabiria). He

summarizes five central themes or aspects in Fellini's
movies: (1) exploration of the idea of true spirituality;
(2) exploitation of autobiographical material; (3) sentimentality verging on the point of histrionics; (4) a taste
for day-to-day events and details; and (5) the mistaken and
decadent lifestyle of citizens of the contemporary era.
From this last aspect, Baldelli develops his ideas about
Fellini's religious stance. He notes that the Marxists
claim Fellini's films reveal the decadence of all capital-
istic institutions including the church, and that the
Ecclesiastics claim Fellini's films show how low man has
sunk since he abandoned God. Baldelli finds both viewpoints defective and goes on to describe the religious
stances which he finds in La Dolce Vita, 8½, and Juliet of
the Spirits.

613   BARNESCHI, RENATO. "Il mio amore per Roma cominciò con tre
sputi in testa." Oggi, 27, No. 35 (30 August), 58-62.
Illustrated.
An interview with Fellini during shooting on location of
Roma. Fellini outlines his plan to reveal Rome at three
levels: Rome as viewed by the provincial; Rome as one first
comes to it; and Rome today.

614   BAZIN, ANDRÉ. "Cabiria: The Voyage to the End of Neorealism,"
in What Is Cinema? II. Translated by Hugh Gray. Berkeley,
Los Angeles, London: University of California Press,
pp. 83-92.
English translation of the article published originally
as "Cabiria ou le voyage au bout du néorealisme." Cahiers
du Cinéma, No. 76 (November 1957), pp. 2-7.

615   BESSET, MARTINE. "Biofilmographie de Federico Fellini."
Image et Son, No. 246 (January), pp. 43-48. Illustrated.
Credits. Filmography.
A filmography with extensive credits covering Fellini's
career from Variety Lights through Fellini Satyricon. Men-
tion of The Clowns.

616   BORDERIE, ROGER, ed. Fellini. L'Arc (Aix-en-Province),
No. 45, 79 pp. Illustrated. Filmography.
An issue of the review L'Arc devoted to Fellini. It
contains articles, interview material, and "testimony."
Contributors are Fellini, Jean Roudaut, J.M.G. Le Clézio,
Claude Ollier, René Micha, Robert Lapoujade, Catherine
Backès-Clement, Marcel Martin, Ornella Volta, Bernardino
Zapponi, Henry Miller, Georges Simenon, and Max Born.
Annotations may be found under the headings of the individ-
ual authors, with the exceptions of Roudaut's impression-
istic rendering of a walk through Cinecittà, and Ollier's
material on two actresses preparing for a scene. The
illustrations include caricatures drawn by Fellini.

617 BORDERIE, ROGER, HENRI RONSE, and JEAN ROUDAUT. "Entretien
     avec Federico Fellini." Cahiers du Cinéma, No. 229 (May-
     June), pp. 52-53.
        An interview with Fellini, loosely related to The Clowns.
     Fellini talks about the general subjects of inspiration and
     improvization. He states that The Clowns has three elements:
     his memories, a documentary, and a series of "numbers" in
     the form of an allegory on the death of the clown. He men-
     tions his dislike for television as a medium, and he comments
     on his preference for dubbing films after they have been
     shot. The material of this interview is included by Ornella
     Volta in "Federico Fellini: Propos." L'Arc (Aix-en-
     Province), No. 45 (1971), pp. 65-69.

618 BORN, MAX. "Témoignage." L'Arc (Aix-en-Province), No. 45,
     p. 40.
        Letter to Fellini from Max Born who played the part of
     Giton in Fellini Satyricon. He asks Fellini if Fellini can
     find work for Born in Rome so that Born can go to India to
     study Hatha Yoga.

619 BORY, JEAN-LOUIS. "Pour et contre Fellini," in Des Yeux pour
     voir. Paris: Union générale d'éditions, pp. 48-58.
        This collection of Bory's essays written between 1961
     and 1966 contains essays on 8½ and Juliet of the Spirits.
     Bory describes 8½ as a depiction of the interior life of
     the consciousness of a director (who is very much like
     Fellini) at a point of artistic crisis. Bory finds this
     interior life utterly banal, and he finds the form of the
     movie weakly imitative of Resnais and Robbe-Grillet. In
     Juliet of the Spirits, Fellini attempts to show the interior
     life of the consciousness of a bourgeois housewife at a
     crisis point, but in fact repeats his own fantasies slightly
     transformed. Nevertheless, Bory enjoys the dignity accorded
     Juliet at the end when she gains a measure of self-control.

620 BUDGEN, SUZANNE. "Fellini," in A Concise History of the
     Cinema, 2. Edited by Peter Cowie. London: A. Zwemmer;
     New York: A. S. Barnes, pp. 138-43.
        A brief biographical sketch of Fellini's career up to
     Fellini Satyricon (1969).

621 CANBY, VINCENT. "The Clowns Recollects Circus Experiences."
     New York Times (15 June), p. 50. Brief credits.
        Canby finds The Clowns only partially successful. He
     praises the child's vision of clowns and the funeral of
     Augusto, but finds the movie, overall, not adventurous
     enough.

622 COVI, ANTONIO. "Federico Fellini," in Dibattiti di film.
     Padua: Gregoriana editrice, pp. 15-60. Illustrated.
     Filmography. Brief bibliography.

In this chapter of his book on Ialian cinema, Covi sets
out to trace the development of Fellini's work. He divides
the work into three periods. The first period (1951-53)
consists of recollections of a provincial world and attempts
to escape from it. The second period (1954-57) deals with
attempts to escape from individual isolation through contact with others. The third period (1960-69), Covi describes as an ascending and then descending parabolic curve.
It begins with an attack on decadence and then reveals an
increasing submission on Fellini's part to death and
fatality. Covi offers detailed analyses of films in the
downward curve. $8\frac{1}{2}$ is formally splendid but thematically
ambivalent. Juliet of the Spirits is an awkward fusion of
dream and reality. Spirits of the Dead is a pretext for
revolt against the fatuous world of cinema. Fellini
Satyricon is formidable in imagery but fails in terms of its
moral emptiness. And The Clowns is a poetic and human farewell to the circus world.

623   COWIE, PETER. "Fellini-Satyricon," in International Film Guide
      1971. London: Tantivy Press; New York: A. S. Barnes,
      p. 185. Illustrated. Brief credits.
            Brief notice of Fellini Satyricon. Cowie remarks on
      the heroes' search for a nameless goal and the movie's
      comparison of Roman society with modern times. He finds
      that Fellini has not brought to bear enough "moral interro-
      gation" on his materials.

624   DILLARD, R. H. W. "If We Were All Devils." Contempora, 1,
      No. 5 (January-April), 26-32.
            Dillard considers Fellini Satyricon as a Christian horror
      film. He compares the film to James Whale's Frankenstein
      classics in both manner and intention, and he discusses
      prefigurings of Christianity in Fellini's film. Appended
      to the article is a bibliography prepared by George P.
      Garrett.

625   FELLINI, FEDERICO. "Rimini." L'Arc (Aix-en-Province), No. 45,
      pp. 7-18. Illustrated.
            Edited French version of Fellini's essay "Il mio paese,"
      in Il mio Rimini. Bologna: Cappelli editore, 1967.
      Pp. 23-43. The article also appears in English as "My
      Home Town," in Fellini on Fellini. Edited by Christian
      Strich. New York: Delacorte Press/Seymour Lawrence, 1976.
      Pp. 1-46.

626   FOFI, GOFFREDO. Il cinema italiano: servi e padroni. Milan:
      Feltrinelli editore, pp. 95-105, et passim.
            Fofi's pamphlet is a radical left-wing attack on the
      Italian film industry. His aim is to demonstrate, through
      a criticism of modern film production, a new way for artists

to work in a cinema "which contributes to a culture for the
revolution." His analysis of the history of Italian cinema
starts from post-war neorealism and ends around the beginning of the seventies. He feels that with the center-left
governments of the sixties, the Italian "left-wing" diluted
its social criticism, and the Italian cinema was able to
become totally disengaged. The three most important directors of that era were Visconti, Antonioni, and Fellini.
They are all criticized by Fofi, but Fellini somewhat less
than the others, for he recognized his provincialism and
he refused to take the film industry seriously. Fofi labels
La Dolce Vita a "mad Catholic caldron." He finds 8½ an
arbitrary film on privacy and self-exaltation. Toby Dammit
is all oneiric. In Juliet of the Spirits, Fellini tried to
tell the story of his wife's psychoanalysis and "entered
quite thoroughly into the mental universe of a foolish
provincial woman suddenly become rich." The Clowns is an
effort by Fellini to mock his own death in the death of the
clown. Fellini Satyricon is a badly controlled and organized film which mirrors the chaos of today. Like Visconti
and Antonioni, Fellini wears a mask, but Fofi finds that his
mask, unlike theirs, is sincere and modern.

627   FOVEZ, JEAN, PIERRE LOUBIÈRE, GUILLAUME LOURIS, and YVES
      GUEGAN. "Post-scriptum: Les Clowns." Téléciné, No. 169
      (May), pp. 36-37.
         Brief reactions to The Clowns by four regular contribu-
      tors to Téléciné and by six critics from French newspapers.
      Perhaps most interesting is Louris' observation that Fellini
      seems to give himself most free reign to dream when he
      undertakes a documentary style.

628   GARDIES, RENÉ. "Les Clowns." Image et Son, No. 247 (February),
      pp. 109-11. Illustrated.
         A review of The Clowns. Gardies offers a series of
      subtle propositions about the movie. He argues that the
      informing principle of composition is distortion. The
      subject of clowns is seen through the prism of Fellini's
      point of view. But this point of view is in fact three
      points of view: Fellini as child, Fellini as adult, and
      Fellini as creator. Put in terms of the action, these view-
      points may be considered as fantasy, reality, and creation.
      Fellini as cinematic creator synthesizes the dialectic of
      the real and fantastic. He affirms the supreme role of the
      creator and affirms the power of the kind of imagination
      discussed by Gaston Bachelard as the source of great poetic
      works.

629   GARRETT, GEORGE P. "Fellini: A Selected Checklist of Available
      Secondary Materials Published in English." Contempora, 1,
      No. 5 (January-April), 33.

A checklist of screenplays, books, interviews, and critical pieces. The list contains thirty-seven items in total.

630 HAMBLIN, DORA JANE. "Which Face Is Fellini?" <u>Life</u>, 71, no. 5 (30 July), 58-61. Illustrated.
Hamblin discusses <u>The Clowns</u> and includes comments by Fellini on the differences between the white clown and the Augusto. On the tension between the objective, documentary elements and the subjective, fictionalized elements in the film, Fellini comments: "In the middle of <u>The Clowns</u>, I realized, I am not really doing a documentary, I am doing the world inside my mind."

631 HART, HENRY. "<u>The Clowns</u>." <u>Films in Review</u>, 22, No. 6 (June-July), 367-69. Illustrated.
A review of <u>The Clowns</u>. Hart describes it as "Fellini's only completely honest film to date." He discusses the clowns' appeal to the individual's unconscious, and he reproduces some of Fellini's words on the differences between the Augusto and the white clown.

632 HATCH, ROBERT. "<u>8½</u>." <u>Film as Film</u>. Edited by Joy Gould Boyum and Adrienne Scott. Boston: Allyn and Bacon, pp. 175-77.
A reprinting, with discussion questions, of Hatch's review of <u>8½</u> which appeared first in <u>Nation</u>, 197, No. 3 (27 July 1963), 59-60.

633 HUGHES, EILEEN LANOUETTE. <u>On the Set of Fellini Satyricon: A Behind-the-Scenes Diary</u>. New York: William Morrow, 248 pp. Illustrated.
The book is a running account of events on the set from November 12, 1968 to July 11, 1969. It contains interviews with Fellini, the actors, the cinematographer, the set designer, the music director, the script collaborator, and others connected with the filming. Hughes gives a picture of Fellini's methods of directing. She speculates only briefly on Fellini's overall intentions in the film.

634 JAFFE, IRA S. "<u>The Clowns</u>." <u>Film Quarterly</u>, 25, No. 1 (Fall), 53-55.
In this review, Jaffe discusses the circus as "an emotionally painful ritual, initiating the young into life through the fierce mockery of bodily injury and death."

635 JULIA, JACQUES. "Psychanalyse de Fellini." <u>Cinéma 71</u>, No. 156 (May), pp. 45-50. Illustrated.
An interesting psychoanalytical study of Fellini's films up to and including <u>Fellini Satyricon</u>. Julia stresses the films after <u>La Dolce Vita</u>. He argues that the monster from the sea in <u>La Dolce Vita</u> provides Marcello with such a

strong image of his unconscious fears that he is unable to
accept the optimism offered by Paola. From this point on,
Fellini's treatment of the unconscious is more explicit.
Julia discusses the entanglements of Guido's childhood attitudes about sexuality, sin, religion, and mother which
lead to his repressed state in 8½. Juliet of the Spirits
is a parallel film in which Fellini takes up the feminine
version of the same repression. Fellini Satyricon provides
a broader canvas. The whole of the picture is presented as
a dream state.

636 KAUFFMANN, STANLEY. "The Clowns." New Republic, 165, No. 1
     (3 July), 22 & 33-34.
         Favorable review of The Clowns. Kauffmann notes: "The
     idea of the human being as clown, seen affectionately as
     fellow-grotesque, has always been central to Fellini's
     vision." Kauffmann discusses such elements as European
     clowns versus American clowns, the free-flowing form of the
     movie, deep-focus composition, the interplay of image and
     sound, tributes to Chaplin, and Fellini's sentimentality.
     The review is reprinted in Kauffmann's Living Images. New
     York: Harper & Row, 1975. Pp. 59-61.

637 _____. "Fellini Satyricon," and "Spirits of the Dead," in
     Figures of Light. New York: Harper & Row, pp. 250-54 &
     196-98.
         A reprinting of two reviews. "Fellini Satyricon" appeared
     first in New Republic, 162, Nos. 14-15 (4 & 11 April 1970),
     24 & 38. "Spirits of the Dead" in New Republic, 161, No. 13
     (27 September 1969), 22.

638 LAPOUJADE, ROBERT. "Du montage au 'montrage.'" L'Arc (Aix-en-
     Province), No. 45, pp. 57-60.
         A brief article on the experimentation with structure in
     Fellini's films, from a phenomenological point of view.
     Lapoujade seeks to put Fellini in the tradition of le
     nouveau roman and in the tradition of avant-garde poetry.
     He concentrates mainly on Fellini Satyricon and Toby Dammit,
     and he emphasizes Fellini's break with conventional, linear
     narrative in favor of experimentation with ways of
     perceiving.

639 LAUDER, ROBERT E. "A Priest Looks at Fellini." New York
     Times (4 July), Section II, 11. Illustrated.
         An appreciation of The Clowns. Lauder praises Fellini
     for his "hopeful humanism." With the exception of
     Fellini Satyricon, all his movies reveal Fellini's "love of
     human beings, who themselves are struggling to love."

640 Le CLÉZIO, J.M.G. "L'Extra-terrestre." L'Arc (Aix-en-
     Province), No. 45, pp. 27-29.

Brief, appreciatory essay on Fellini Satyricon.
Le Clézio declares that Fellini's films all treat the discovery of the ugliness and corruption of the world by an
adolescent who, in his innocence, is like an extraterres-
trial being. Society in Fellini's films in general and in
Fellini Satyricon in particular is in the process of breaking up in order to redefine itself differently. Le Clézio
praises especially Fellini's experimentation with narrative
form in Fellini Satyricon to project us into a fictive world
beyond conventional logic and psychological assumptions,
where all is flux and uncertainty.

641 LEFÈVRE, RAYMOND. "Fellini." Image et Son, No. 246 (January),
pp. 1-42. Illustrated.
A lengthy study of Fellini's work through Fellini
Satyricon. The article is a pastiche of plot summaries,
observations made by Lefèvre in previous reviews, and some
new comparisons he draws for this essay. Some of the
themes treated are Fellini's use of the circus or the show
in La Strada, realism in I Vitelloni, the mixture of realism
and moral statement in Il Bidone, the treatments of illusion
in Nights of Cabiria and The White Sheik, decadence in Toby
Dammit, Fellini Satyricon, and La Dolce Vita, censorship
in The Temptations of Doctor Antonio, the depiction of women
in Juliet of the Spirits and 8½, and Guido's desire to
reconcile pure and impure love in 8½.

642 MARTIN, MARCEL. "Un Artiste sous le chapiteau: perplexe."
L'Arc (Aix-en-Province), No. 45, pp. 73-76.
This number devoted to Fellini reprints Martin's article
of the same title from Cinéma 71, No. 156 (May 1971),
pp. 38-44.

643 _____. "Un Artiste sous le chapiteau: perplexe." Cinéma 71,
No. 156 (May), pp. 38-44. Illustrated.
An interesting, speculative article in which Martin
traces Fellini's development as a director. Martin's approach is, to a certain extent, psychoanalytical. He sees
Fellini's first four films as realistic and his next three
films as mystical. La Dolce Vita, however, marks a change.
Here Fellini makes himself more clearly the subject of the
film. The monster from the sea and Steiner's suicide reveal
unconscious fears. With 8½ and Juliet of the Spirits,
Fellini deals more openly with creative impotence and the
incapacity to live. At this point in his career, working
on The Voyage of G. Mastorna, Fellini seems to undergo the
kind of creative failure he depicted earlier in 8½. Martin
sees Toby Dammit as Fellini's means of working through his
crisis. The Clowns reveals him again at the top of his
form. In the circus, Martin sees three aspects important to

Fellini: the spectacle, the journey, and "vitellonism."
The article is reprinted in L'Arc (Aix-en-Province), No. 45,
1971, pp. 73-76.

644 MICHA, RENÉ. "Le Clair et l'obscur." L'Arc (Aix-en-Province),
No. 45, pp. 42-56. Illustrated.
An essay on 8½ in a monograph devoted to Fellini. Micha's
point of view is that of auteur criticism. He sees 8½ as
self-analysis designed in part to "seduce" viewers. Micha
comments on elements from Fellini's childhood in the movie
and on his images of women. Micha stresses Fellini's concern with sin and death and Fellini's nostalgic longing for
a Garden of Eden (the harem sequence). Interestingly, Micha
argues that the circus ring ending of 8½ embodies a false
longing of Guido, like the harem sequence--the last tempta-
tion, to which Guido succumbs, but not Fellini.

645 _____. "Toby Dammit." L'Arc (Aix-en-Province), No. 45,
pp. 36-37. Illustrated.
Brief, appreciatory essay on Toby Dammit. Micha finds
that Fellini keeps the bitterness and the sense of intoxica-
tion of Poe. Interestingly, he remarks that Terence Stamp,
the actor, resembles Poe, and a sketch of Stamp as Poe,
drawn by Fellini, included with the essay, bears out the
observation quite literally.

646 MILLER, HENRY. "Témoignages." L'Arc (Aix-en-Province),
No. 45, p. 39.
Brief testimony from the writer of his pleasure in seeing
Fellini Satyricon. Miller compares the experience of see-
ing Fellini's film with that of seeing Buñuel's L'Age d'or.
He praises Fellini's insistence on doing exactly as he
pleases.

647 O'MEALY, JOSEPH. "Fellini Satyricon: A Structural Analysis."
Film Heritage, 6, No. 4 (Summer), 25-29.
O'Mealy finds Fellini Satyricon to be organized as six
episodes each involving the themes of doom, death, and
decay and involving similar expressionistic manipulations
of light and setting. In both regards, Fellini Satyricon
resembles German expressionistic films of the early
twenties. O'Mealy's six groupings are as follows: city
life; country life; national disorder; sexual disorder;
mythic parody; and escape to a new world.

648 PAINI, DOMINIQUE. "Lettre sur Les Clowns." Cahiers du
Cinéma, No. 229 (May-June), pp. 64-65.
A letter on The Clowns. Paini offers suggestions for a
Marxist interpretation of the film. He theorizes that the
decline of the world of the clown may reflect the decline
of the values of the liberal bourgeoisie, of which Fellini
is a spokesman.

649   PECHTER, WILLIAM S.   "Two Movies and Their Critics" and "$8\frac{1}{2}$
      Times Two," in Twenty-four Times a Second.   New York,
      Evanston, and London: Harper & Row, 37-50 & 77-84.
         In "$8\frac{1}{2}$ Times Two," Pechter discusses his experience on
      seeing $8\frac{1}{2}$ for the second time.   At the first viewing, he had
      thought the movie a series of brilliant, but disparate
      sequences.   At the second viewing, however, he was struck
      with Fellini's skill in interweaving memories, hallucina-
      tions, dreams, and fantasies to comment on the way in which
      art and life interpenetrate.   "Two Movies and Their Critics,"
      is reprinted from Kenyon Review, 24, No. 2 (Spring 1962),
      351-62.

650   PIERRE, SYLVIE.   "L'Homme aux clowns."   Cahiers du Cinéma,
      No. 229 (May-June), pp. 48-51.   Illustrated.
         An interesting Freudian study of The Clowns.   Pierre sees
      the opening sequence as a metaphoric representation of a
      primal castration scene.   The clowns are presented as
      attacking, castrating figures like the wolves in the dream
      of Freud's famous patient known as the "Wolf Man."

651   RESNAIS, ALAIN.   "Deux questions."   L'Arc (Aix-en-Province),
      No. 45, p. 26.
         Two questions put to Fellini by Resnais.   The first con-
      cerns Resnais' feeling that Fellini Satyricon has in the
      film medium the kind of freeness and invention which the
      comic strip has in the literary medium.   The second concerns
      a statement Fellini had made fifteen years earlier about
      fearing the consequences of opening a door to his inner life
      in his films.   Fellini answers the first question and par-
      ries the second.

652   SALACHAS, GILBERT.   "Les Clowns."   Téléciné, No. 168 (March-
      April), p. 21.
         Capsule review of The Clowns.   Salachas announces that
      Fellini has tricked his producers as usual.   The film is
      not about clowns as much as it is about Fellini.   Salachas
      praises the mixture of memories, dreams, and imaginative
      creations as richly evocative.

653   SARRIS, ANDREW.   "Films in Focus: The Clowns."   Village Voice,
      16, No. 26 (1 July), 47.
         In this review, Sarris quotes from and comments on
      Fellini's program notes to The Clowns.   Fellini discusses
      in his notes the importance of the circus to him and the
      distinction between the white clown and the Augusto clown.
      Sarris finds the movie more modest than the notes and
      praises Fellini's light touch.

654   SIMENON, GEORGES.   "Témoignage."   L'Arc (Aix-en-Province),
      No. 45, pp. 39-40.

Letter to Fellini from the French writer, expressing
Simenon's feeling of rapport with Fellini while reading
Fellini's remarks during an interview for the Paris
L'Express.

655 SIMON, JOHN. "Fellini's 8½¢ Fancy," in Film As Film. Edited
by Joy Gould Boyum and Adrienne Scott. Boston: Allyn and
Bacon, pp. 170-75.
A reprinting, with discussion questions, of Simon's
review of 8½ which appeared first in New Leader, 46, No. 16
(5 August 1963), 24-25.

656 TERMINE, LIBORIO. "I clowns." Cinema nuovo, 20, No. 209
(January-February), 58-59.
Termine argues that Fellini conceives of clowns as
demons and the circus itself as hell. The Clowns, therefore, is tinged with ferocious moral judgments against the
objects of Fellini's early, infantile fears.

657 TESSIER, MAX. "Les Clowns." Cinéma 71, No. 155 (April),
pp. 110-111 & 114. Brief credits.
An ecstatically favorable review of The Clowns. Tessier
states that Fellini has taken the criticism against him that
he is a Barnum of the cinema and converted the criticism to
his favor. The Clowns is a study of the birth, life, and
death of an art form. It is a meditation on the fragility
of art. Tessier finds in the work Fellini's "lucid pessimism" which has deepened over the years.

658 VOLTA, ORNELLA, ed. "Federico Fellini: propos." L'Arc (Aix-
en-Province), No. 45, pp. 4-6, 30-33 & 63-70. Illustrated.
Remarks on a wide range of topics by Fellini, gathered
by Ornella Volta from a variety of previous sources.
Fellini speaks of his personal likes and dislikes and of
his work habits. He emphasizes his need for external stimulation, and, therefore, he declares that the medium of
film, with the various types of collaboration and inter-
action it requires, is the medium best suited to him. He
speaks also of his abhorence of false "ideals" and classifi-
cations. A major source of material for this collection is
the interview conducted by Roger Borderie, Henri Ronse, and
Jean Roudaut and published as "Entretien avec Federico
Fellini." Cahiers du Cinéma, No. 229 (May-June 1971),
pp. 52-53.

659 WALTER, EUGENE. "Federico Fellini." Behind the Scenes:
Theater and Film Interviews from the "Transatlantic Review."
Edited by Joseph F. McCrindle. New York: Holt, Rinehart and
Winston, pp. 167-71.
A reprinting of Walter's interview published previously
as "Dinner with Fellini." Transatlantic Review, No. 17

(Autumn 1964), 47-50. Added are some remarks by Fellini on Petronius' Satyricon.

660 ZAPPONI, BERNARDINO. "Temoignages." L'Arc (Aix-en-Province), No. 45, pp. 38-39.
Zapponi describes briefly his experiences collaborating with Fellini on Toby Dammit and on Fellini Satyricon. Interesting is the stress Zapponi puts on Fellini's sense of mathematical order and geometrical necessity.

661 ZIMMERMAN, PAUL. "The Nose-Thumbers." Newsweek, 77, No. 25 (21 June), 86. Illustrated.
Laudatory review of The Clowns. Zimmerman argues that Fellini is searching beneath the world of clowns for the essence of his own primal art.

1972

662 AMIEL, MIREILLE. "Fellini Roma." Cinéma 72, No. 168 (July), pp. 57-65. Illustrated.
A laudatory review of Roma. Amiel feels that Fellini has reached a high point in his career in terms of the form and internal coherence he gives to Roma. It is a work that is directly cinematic as opposed to a translation from another medium. Roma shows the death of a culture and hints at a possible rebirth. Amiel discusses the three illusions of Rome: church, state, and cinema.

663 ANON. "Federico Fellini: biofilmographie." L'Avant-Scène, No. 129 (October), pp. 71-72. Filmography.
A brief biographical sketch, followed by a filmography up to 1972. Roma is the last film listed.

664 ANON. "Fellini Roma." Films and Filming, 19, No. 1 (October), 41-44. Illustrated.
A spread of photographs of Roma.

665 BACHMANN, GIDEON. "Fellini Roma." Film Quarterly, 26, No. 2 (Winter), 37-39.
A negative review of Roma in which Bachmann suggests that Fellini's involvement with the self and with subjective fantasy has become destructive.

666 BARNESCHI, RENATO. "Wallace mi insegnò a fare il ladro di polli." Oggi, 28, No. 7 (12 February), 47-50. Illustrated.
An interesting and wide-ranging interview. Fellini speaks about the persons he admires the most. His list includes Jung, Picasso, and Moravia. Fellini also talks about his grandmother, about Gradisca, a Rimini vamp he knew during his childhood, and about his sentimental attachment to clowns.

273

667   CANALI, LUCA. "Una trilogia su Roma," in Roma di Federico
       Fellini. Edited by Bernardino Zapponi. Rocca San Casciano:
       Cappelli editore, pp. 77-84.
            An essay on Fellini's Roma. Canali stresses the three
       eras of Roman history treated in the movie: (1) the silver
       age of Latin letters; (2) the late Renaissance; and (3) the
       capitalistic, atomic age. Canali feels these are periods
       when man has felt isolated and when he has been preoccupied
       with death.

668   CONTI, ISABELLA. "Fellini 8½ (A Jungian Analysis)." Ikon,
       23, No. 80 (January-March), 43-76; and Nos. 82-83 (July-
       December), 123-70.
            Part I is Conti's reproduction of the movie 8½ with a
       few comments of her own on character motivation. She trans-
       lates into English large portions of description from the
       Italian screenplay and large portions of dialogue taken
       directly from the finished movie. Her amalgamation of
       screenplay and continuity script is quite useful in the
       absence of published versions of either the screenplay or
       the continuity script in English. Part II is her Jungian
       analysis of the movie. She argues that Guido's crisis in
       the movie follows the pattern of Jung's "individuation pro-
       cess," that is, the process by which the person confronts
       consciously personifications of his unconscious. Conti dis-
       cusses Daumier and Mezzabotta as challenging "shadow"
       figures, Claudia as archetypal inspiration, and the magician
       as a figure of creative genius. The two psychological tasks
       for Guido, she states, are to assimilate diverse "anima"
       figures such as Saraghina, Carla, Louisa, and Rossella and
       to confront the fear of death (or to descend into Hades).

669   DAMIANI, BRUNO. "Il re è nudo." Cineforum, 12, Nos. 115-16
       (July-August), 140-43. Brief credits.
            A review of Roma. Damiani accuses Fellini of having
       finally chosen the hallucinatory and distorted world of
       his films as a way of life. He suggests that we put aside
       our reverential deference to Fellini and avoid the easy
       excuse for him of labeling Roma an atmosphere film.

670   de VILALLONGA, JOSÉ LUIS. "Les Esprits de Fellini," in Gold
       Gotha. Paris: Éditions du seuil, pp. 307-63.
            Author-actor de Vilallonga played the role of the Spanish
       lover José in Juliet of the Spirits. Here in his book of
       portraits of famous and controversial people, he offers an
       interesting, biographical interview with Fellini. On the
       subject of his youth in Rimini, Fellini discusses the
       vitelloni, the changes of season in the resort town, his
       early reading of Ariosto and Dante, his relationship with
       his parents, his encounter on the beach with la Saraghina,
       his Catholicism, his brief flight at age fifteen with the

girl Bianchina, and his first visit to the circus. On his days in Rome as a young man, Fellini describes his experiences under the Fascist regime and his meeting with Giulietta Masina.

671 DURGNAT, RAYMOND. <u>Sexual Alienation in the Cinema</u>. London: Studio Vista, pp. 24-61. Illustrated.

Durgnat discusses <u>Fellini Satyricon</u> as part of a study of emotional and sexual debilitation in modern movies. He argues that <u>Fellini Satyricon</u> has for its main theme the "devirilization" and regeneration of Encolpius. Durgnat discusses Fellini's handling of bi-sexuality and the sexual nature of the various figures who challenge and confuse Encolpius.

672 FELLINI, FEDERICO. "Come non detto," in <u>Fellini TV. Block-notes di un regista. I clowns</u>. Bologna: Cappelli editore, pp. 209-13.

Fellini outlines his feelings about television. He states that originally he labored under the misconception that through television a writer-director would achieve a more intimate rapport with his audience by entering their homes than could a movie author who must reach his audience in a theater. After working on television, he realizes that such a view is simplistic. He offers three reasons for the superiority of the film medium for an author. (1) Unlike the case with movies, the TV audience is in charge of the medium, not the director. The audience can turn off the set immediately if not pleased. (2) The sacred rituals of the theater (darkened theater, curtains, tickets, etc.) are absent on television, and, therefore, the sense of spectacle is diminished. (3) Certain technical problems exist with television that do not exist with films. Long shots are impossible on television, as is lighting for mood. Fellini concludes that television is a good medium for journalists, but not for writer-directors.

673 _____. "<u>Fellini Roma</u>: texte écrit par Federico Fellini durant la préparation du film." <u>Cinéma 72</u>, No. 168 (July), pp. 66-71. Illustrated.

An interesting essay by Fellini on his intentions in <u>Roma</u>, written during the preparation of the film. Fellini wishes to evoke the story of the city as it appears to its citizens as well as to foreigners. He describes the image of the city which he held as a provincial youth in Rimini and describes its impressions on him when he first went to Rome in 1938. He discusses an evening in a Roman street, the scepticism of the Romans, and the spectacle of the Jovinelli vaudeville hall. He wonders about the attitudes of the hippy youths who congregate by the Spanish Steps in the present time. And he speculates that in his film he

will play off against each other a group of young documentary filmmakers who seek objectivity and an "amateur" who
cannot disengage himself from his subject.

674　FELLINI, FEDERICO. "Madame Roma." L'espresso E, 18, No. 1
　　　(2 January), 4-15. Illustrated.
　　　　　A fond and poetic article on Rome and the filming of
　　　Roma. Fellini describes Rome as "a mother who has too many
　　　children to devote herself to one.... Thus she receives you
　　　when you come and lets you go at will." As such, Fellini
　　　acknowledges that Rome is the "ideal mother." He feels that
　　　it is not necessary to leave Rome to find the strange or un-
　　　expected. After filming Roma, he discovered that he had
　　　not exhausted his material, but instead had hardly pene-
　　　trated it. He discusses at length the stages of filmmaking
　　　from original conception to shooting.

675　　　　　. "La prima idea è stata di scappare." L'espresso, 18,
　　　No. 37 (10 September), 13.
　　　　　A review by Fellini of Stanley Kubrick's A Clockwork
　　　Orange. Fellini expresses alarm at the film's violent, de-
　　　structive energy. He acknowledges, however, that the
　　　energy is a part of modern society.

676　　　　　. "Le rovine di Mastorna." Fellini TV. Block-notes di
　　　un regista. I clowns. Bologna: Cappelli editore,
　　　pp. 35-37.
　　　　　An interesting letter from Fellini to American TV pro-
　　　ducer Peter Goldfarb about Fellini: A Director's Notebook.
　　　Fellini explains that making a film is like doing battle
　　　and that films are made both by building ideas and by
　　　destroying them. In Fellini: A Director's Notebook,
　　　Fellini wants to show not only what he puts in a film but
　　　what he leaves out.

677　　　　　. "Un viaggio nell'ombra." Fellini TV. Block-notes di
　　　un regista. I clowns. Edited by Renzo Renzi. Bologna:
　　　Cappelli editore, pp. 105-30.
　　　　　A reprinting of an essay published originally in I
　　　clowns. Edited by Renzo Renzi. Bologna: Cappelli editore,
　　　1970. Pp. 27-56. The essay has been translated into
　　　English by Isabel Quigley as "Why Clowns?", in Fellini on
　　　Fellini. New York: Delacorte Press/Seymour Lawrence, 1976.
　　　Pp. 115-39.

678　GREENSPUN, ROGER. "Fellini's Roma." New York Times, (16
　　　October), p. 46. Brief credits.
　　　　　Greenspun praises Roma as Fellini's most enjoyable film
　　　in a dozen years. The movie, he states, is three-quarters
　　　Fellini and one-quarter Rome. The movie puts us in the
　　　presence of what excites the director's imagination.

679 HARCOURT, PETER. "The Loss of Community: Six European Directors." Cinema Journal, 12, No. 1 (Fall), 2-10.
In this interesting article, Harcourt describes Fellini as a traditionalist who looks back longingly not to a historical period, but to an interior past of childhood and adolescence. He discusses also Fellini's interest in the surrender of individual feeling in his group scenes and his delight in the incomprehensible, the irrational, and the magical. Fellini, he feels, affirms life through his affirmation of the state of childhood. Only by looking backward can he escape the anxiety and the sense of loss of a nurturing community which the modern adult feels. This article reappears in Harcourt's Six European Directors. Harmondsworth, England; Baltimore: Penguin Books, 1974. Pp. 255-67.

680 HOFMANN, PAUL. "Roma." New York Times (1 May), p. 40.
A report from Italy on Roma prior to its U.S. release. Hofmann states that the Marxists objected to Fellini's lack of sociological interest, that reviews, in general, were "lukewarm," but that box-office ratings were high.

681 KAEL, PAULINE. "The Current Cinema." New Yorker, 48, No. 35 (21 October), 137-40.
Kael finds Roma an "ambivalent celebration of decay." It is one more example of Fellini's continuing insistence upon the grotesque excesses of his own imagination. This review is collected in Kael's Reeling. Boston: Little, Brown, 1976. Pp. 25-27.

682 KAUFFMANN, STANLEY. "Fellini's Roma." New Republic, 167, No. 17 (4 November), 22.
Review of Roma in which Kauffmann attacks Fellini for repeating familiar material and techniques. "He is a victim of this age's gravest disease for artists: the inability to synthesize new subject matter out of experience, the shattering of creative confidence by the immensity of modern consciousness." Reprinted in Kauffmann's Living Images. New York: Harper & Row, 1975. Pp. 148-50.

683 KINDER, MARSHA and BEVERLE HOUSTON. Close-Up: A Critical Perspective on Film. New York, Chicago, San Francisco, Atlanta: Harcourt Brace Jovanovich, pp. 246-54 & 313-31. Illustrated.
Kinder and Houston discuss Fellini's mixture of past, present, and imagination in 8½, concentrating on the chaotic and challenging aspects of the opening sequence, the harem sequence, the press conference sequence, and the ending sequence. They compare La Dolce Vita and Fellini Satyricon as myths concerning the survival of heroes in unpredictable and challenging worlds. And finally they

argue that The Clowns is a culminating work in Fellini's
career, a work that insists on a "comic acceptance of the
chaos and contradictions of experience."

684 KOVÁCS, STEVEN. "Fellini's Toby Dammit: A Study of Characteristic Themes and Techniques." Journal of Aesthetics and
Art Criticism, 31, No. 2 (Winter), 255-61. Illustrated.
A richly suggestive article, albeit a loosely organized
one, in which Kovács uses Toby Dammit as a starting point
to discuss three general aspects of Fellini's movies: his
preoccupation with "stars" of public media; his use of music
(Ruby, in this case) as a unifying factor integrated with
the form and meaning of his films; and his concern about
the corruption of the pure qualities of children.

685 LAJEUNESSE, JACQUELINE. "Fellini Roma." Image et Son,
No. 262 (June-July), p. 156.
Brief notice of Roma. Lajeunesse describes the film as
one in which the presence of Fellini's point of view sup-
plants the importance of Rome as an entity. She remarks
on his obsessions, his provoking and provocative taste for
the vulgar, and his propensity toward easiness.

686 LEPROHON, PIERRE. The Italian Cinema. Translated by Roger
Greaves and Oliver Stallybrass. New York: Praeger,
pp. 117-18, 141-47, 167-70, 204-206 & 228.
A translation of Leprohon's Le Cinéma italien. Paris:
Seghers, 1966. See pp. 155-60, 177-81, 217-19 & 274.

687 LÉVY-KLEIN, STEPHANE and DENIS TARANTO. "Entretien avec
Fellini sur Roma." Positif, No. 140 (July-August),
pp. 8-11. Illustrated.
In this interview on Roma, Fellini defines Rome as a
splendid woman, both mother and lover. He outlines three
points of view toward Rome which appear in his movie: the
viewpoint of those in a provincial village; the viewpoint
of a young man who arrives in Rome from the provinces; and
the more objective viewpoint of a film director. Also, he
discusses the construction of a section of freeway in
Cinecittà for the film and his love for special effects
using fog, steam, or smoke which create a phantasmagorical
atmosphere.

688 LUCATO, CLAUDIO. "L'autobiografia di narciso." Cineforum,
12, Nos. 115-16 (July-August), 132-39. Illustrated.
A review of Roma. Lucato finds it uneven stylistically,
but noteworthy from the standpoint of what it reveals about
Fellini, the man.

689 McBRIDE, JOSEPH. "Director as Superstar." Sight and Sound,
41, No. 2 (Spring), 78-81.

McBride discusses <u>Fellini: A Director's Notebook</u> as an entry into Fellini's creative process.

690   MALAPELLE. "Metti un Fellini sotto vetro." <u>Oggi</u>, 28, No. 43 (24 October), 12–13. Illustrated.
      Brief interview with Giulietta Masina about her life with Fellini. Superficial and anecdotal.

691   MORAVIA, ALBERTO. "Un défilé col cardinale." <u>L'espresso</u>, 18, No. 13 (26 March), 23.
      A review of Fellini's <u>Roma</u>. Moravia outlines what he considers to be some of the essential characteristics of Fellini's work. Among these characteristics are Fellini's obsession with Rome, not as a film locale or background, but as the film's protagonist itself. However, the city of Rome as identified by Fellini, Moravia contends, is partially myth because of Fellini's emphasis on the baroque and his fascination with corruption.

692   MORIN, GERALD. "L'autopsia di un eterno spettacolo," in <u>Roma di Federico Fellini</u>. Edited by Bernardino Zapponi. Rocca San Casciano: Editrice Licinio Cappelli, pp. 87–91.
      A short, interpretive article on Fellini's conception of Rome. Morin finds in <u>Roma</u> an emphasis on the element of spectacle associated with Rome, be it religious, gustatory, or social spectacle.

693   PENSOTTI, ANITA. "Vorrei Fellini contadino." <u>Oggi</u>, 28, No. 34 (8 August), 28–29. Illustrated.
      An interview with Giulietta Masina about her personal feelings and her life with Fellini. Anecdotal and superficial.

694   PERRY, TED. "Signifiers in Fellini's $8\frac{1}{2}$." <u>Forum Italicum</u>, 6, No. 1 (March), 79–86.
      Using the terms of French semiologists, Perry discusses the <u>signifieds</u> and the <u>signifiers</u> in $8\frac{1}{2}$. Those things which are signified are Guido's feelings of estrangement, entrapment, and confusion. Those things which do the signifying are the use of the subjective camera, the inter-mingling of various realities and times, the juxtaposition of Guido with other people with whom he cannot interact, the use of magic, and the use of dancing. Much of the material in this essay appears in expanded form in Perry's mono-graph, <u>Filmguide to $8\frac{1}{2}$</u>. Bloomington: Indiana University Press, 1975.

695   PERUZZI, GIUSEPPE. "<u>Roma</u>." <u>Cinema nuovo</u>, 21, No. 217 (May–June), 213–17.

Peruzzi identifies in Roma two of Fellini's principle
themes: death and the need for a new social order. Peruzzi
compares Fellini with the Roman poet Gioachino Belli.

696 PIRO, SINIBALDO. "Fellini, irrazionalismo, e ipotesi di
     salvezza." Cinema nuovo, 21, No. 218 (July–August), 247–49.
         A review of Roma. Piro states that the film contains
     many elements typical of all Fellini films: loose struc-
     ture, tender nostalgia, autobiography which is dangerously
     close to auto-enchantment, and irrationalism.

697 REILLY, CHARLES PHILLIPS. "Fellini's Roma." Films in Review,
     23, No. 9 (November), 566.
         Favorable review of Roma. Reilly stresses Fellini's
     satiric jabs at the Romans.

698 RENZI, RENZO. "Dal nostro inviato in memoryland," in Fellini
     TV. Block-notes di un regista. I clowns. Bologna:
     Cappelli editore, pp. 13–31.
         Ostensively an article about the nature of Fellini's art
     when it has been reduced for the TV screen. The bulk of
     the article, however, concerns the history of Rome and
     Fellini's often unfavorable impressions of Romans expressed
     on TV and in film. At the conclusion of the essay, Renzi
     does outline the limitations television places on Fellini
     in stifling his humor and reducing his use of panorama.

699 SADOUL, GEORGES. "Fellini," in Dictionary of Film Makers.
     Translated, edited, and updated by Peter Morris. Berkeley
     & Los Angeles: University of California Press, pp. 80–81.
     Filmography.
         Brief biographical sketch. Sadoul praises Fellini's
     ability to bring "types" to life.

700 SAMUELS, CHARLES THOMAS. Encountering Directors. New York:
     Putnams, pp. 117–41. Illustrated.
         A three-part interview with Fellini, which touches on
     his films from Variety Lights to Roma. It also deals with
     such subjects as Fellini's belief that realization dimin-
     ishes dream, his attitudes about the label "neorealistic,"
     and his attitudes about the usefulness of critics. Most
     interesting is the battle of wills between Samuels who
     defends the role of the critic and who asks bold questions
     of motivation and Fellini who defends the importance of
     intuitive creation and seeks to evade questions of why he
     does what he does.

701 SARNE, MIKE. "Fellini's Toby Dammit." Films and Filming, 19,
     No. 2 (November), 20–24. Illustrated.
         Actor Mike Sarne describes the rejuvenation he experi-
     ences when he watches Toby Dammit. He identifies strongly

with the British "star" in the film and is purged by watching a depression similar to his own created by Fellini.

702   SARRIS, ANDREW. "Films in Focus: <u>Fellini's Roma</u>." <u>Village
       Voice</u>, 17, No. 50 (14 December), 81.
           In this review, Sarris states that <u>Roma</u> carries <u>auteurism</u>
       to absurdity. It is an "100 per cent projection of the
       director's personality." Sarris points out that the young
       man who plays Fellini is more beautiful than any of the
       women in the film and suggests Fellini is in his narcissis-
       tic period. Sarris praises, however, the sequence of the
       ecclesiastical fashion show.

703   SOLMI, ANGELO. "Fellini va a nozze con Roma." <u>Oggi</u>, 28,
       No. 13 (25 March), 103. Illustrated.
           A review of <u>Roma</u>. Solmi describes the movie as an
       attempt to synthesize a world view into one city. He
       adds that <u>Roma</u> is a disjointed film without plot or logic.

704   _____. "8 e mezzo in TV non prende più di 4." <u>Oggi</u>, 28,
       No. 50 (5 December), 181-82. Illustrated.
           A commentary on the failure of 8½ to capture a large
       audience for its first showing on Italian TV. Solmi attacks
       the method of poll-taking and also blames substandard TV
       programming which does not prepare a sophisticated enough
       audience to understand a film such as 8½.

705   SOLOMON, STANLEY J. "Structuring an Expanding Visual Idea:
       <u>Fellini Satyricon</u>," in <u>The Film Idea</u>. New York, Chicago,
       San Francisco, Atlanta: Harcourt Brace Jovanovich, 370-76.
           Solomon discusses <u>Fellini Satyricon</u> as a work with a
       non-Aristotelian structure. It is a work constructed
       around an expanding visual representation of a society in
       the process of spiritual collapse.

706   TASSONE, ALDO. "In udienza dal papa con Ferreri, Fellini e
       Zeffirelli." <u>Cineforum</u>, 12, No. 113 (April), 41-54.
           Tassone considers three directors' views of the papacy:
       Zeffirelli's in <u>Brother Sun, Sister Moon</u>, Ferreri's in
       <u>L'Udienza</u>, and Fellini's in <u>Roma</u>. Fellini's view, Tassone
       contends, is ambiguous. Fellini is repulsed by the concep-
       tion of an absolute and theocratic monarch, but attracted
       to the Pope as the vicar of Christ.

707   VOLTA, ORNELLA. "Sur <u>Roma</u> de Federico Fellini." <u>Positif</u>,
       No. 135 (February), pp. 68-71. Illustrated.
           This descriptive review of <u>Roma</u> emphasizes Fellini's
       growing concern for the past and his inability to accept
       the present.

708 ZAPPONI, BERNARDINO. "Il fiume." L'espresso E, 18, No. 1
     (2 January), 10. Illustrated.
          An anecdote recorded by Zapponi. He recalls a visit he
     and Fellini made to the home of a Roman scholar in order to
     learn more about the river Tiber for their film Roma.

709 _____. "Il metro." L'espresso E, 18, No. 1 (2 January), 14.
     Illustrated.
          An anecdote. Zapponi recalls a visit he and Fellini made
     to the Roman metro as part of their research for Roma.

710 _____. "Le nuvole." L'espresso E, 18, No. 1 (2 January), 7.
     Illustrated.
          An anecdote. Zapponi recalls a proposed trip with
     Fellini by helicopter to study cloud formations over Rome
     as part of their research for Roma.

711 _____. "Roma e Fellini," in Roma di Federico Fellini. Edited
     by Bernardino Zapponi. Rocca San Casciano: Editrice
     Liciano Cappelli, pp. 11-73.
          A very detailed account of the researching, financing,
     scriptwriting, costuming, set designing, casting, and shoot-
     ing of Roma, written by Fellini's collaborator.

712 ZIMMERMAN, PAUL D. "Digging the Eternal City." Newsweek, 80,
     No. 18 (30 October), 112-13. Illustrated.
          A laudatory review of Roma. Zimmerman finds the movie a
     series of set-pieces that build toward a "strangely exhilar-
     ating vision of impending doom." He traces the breaking
     apart of social cohesion in contemporary Rome in the last
     episodes of the movie.

                              1973

713 ANON. "Amarcord." Cinema nuovo, 22, No. 224 (July-August),
     np.
          A spread of photographs from Amarcord.

714 ARMES, ROY. "Rome, from Rimini." London Magazine, 12, No. 6
     (February-March), 116-22. Illustrated.
          A review of Roma. Armes discusses Fellini's balance of
     spectacle and documentary statement. He finds Roma a
     chronicle of a "society going noisily to its own destruc-
     tion." The church and state are represented as "farcical or
     brutal." The "extravert side of Italian life" is revealed
     as escapist. It is "existence conceived as show."

715 ARMSTRONG, MICHAEL. "Tales of Mystery." Films and Filming,
     20, No. 2 (November), 54.
          Laudatory review of the Toby Dammit section of Spirits
     of the Dead.

*716   BACHMANN, GIDEON. "Federico Fellini." Cinemages (1973).
        [This issue of Cinemages is very rare. No copy of it
        could be located by me after an extensive search. However,
        it is cited by Ted Perry in Filmguide to 8½. Bloomington,
        London: Indiana University Press, 1975. P. 73. Perry
        describes the issue as being devoted to Fellini and to
        Ciao, Federico!, Bachmann's documentary on Fellini. The
        issue includes credits and the script of the documentary.
        Perry consulted Bachmann's issue of Cinemages (1973) for
        his information. JCS]

717   BARNESCHI, RENATO. "No a Fellini, sì al marito." Oggi, 29,
        Nos. 4-5, 63-65. Illustrated.
        An article about Sandra Milo's withdrawal from the role
        of Gradisca in Amarcord.

718   BAYER, WILLIAM. "La Dolce Vita," "8½," and "La Strada," in
        The Great Movies. New York: Grosset & Dunlap, pp. 154-57,
        176-78 & 183-84. Illustrated. Brief credits.
        In a pictorial history of sixty great movies, Bayer con-
        siders three Fellini films. He describes La Dolce Vita as
        a film of social comment which was "the first in a phalanx
        of pictures that disected the milieu of the rich and the
        successful, and helped to smash public confidence in the
        social order." 8½, Bayer discusses as a film about the
        psychic process by which the film was conceived. And he
        describes La Strada as lyric and personal.

719   CASTY, ALAN. "Fellini, Pasolini, and Surreal Expressionism,"
        in Development of the Film, An Interpretive History. New
        York, Chicago, San Francisco, Atlanta: Harcourt Brace
        Jovanovich, pp. 291-305. Illustrated.
        In this introductory text, Casty defines "surreal expres-
        sionism" and then traces the developments of Fellini and
        Pasolini toward "surreal expressionism" from neorealism.
        Beginning with Fellini's involvement with Rossellini, Casty
        follows Fellini's work up to Fellini Satyricon.

720   DOSS, JANET C. "Fellini's Demythologized World," in The
        Classic Cinema: Essays in Criticism. Edited by Stanley J.
        Solomon. New York, Chicago, San Francisco, Atlanta:
        Harcourt Brace Jovanovich, pp. 332-38.
        Doss discusses Fellini Satyricon. She argues that the
        death of the Hermaphrodite, the representation of inspira-
        tion, is important to an understanding of the movie. The
        ancient myths become grotesque parodies. She treats espec-
        ially the battle of Encolpius with the Minotaur, the mar-
        riage of Encolpius to Lichas, and the death of Eumolpus.
        Also she deals with various of Fellini's devices for set-
        ting the work at a distance from the viewers.

721 ETHIER, JEAN-RENÉ. "Roma." Sequences (Montreal), No. 72
(April), pp. 39-40.
A laudatory review of Roma. Ethier finds in the film
the "calculated incoherence" of the circus. He praises
Fellini's playfulness with the different pieces of his
vision of Rome.

722 FELLINI, FEDERICO. "As Fellini Sees Rome: A City of Desola-
tion, Fossilized Ruins, and Children." New York Times
(3 June), Section 10, p. 3. Illustrated.
Fellini describes Rome from three different points of
view, the first two positive and the third negative. He
calls Rome "a horizontal city, stretched out," which is an
"ideal platform for fantastic vertical flights" of the be-
holder's imagination. It is for him, also, like a mother
with many children who offers a mixture of warmth and
indifference. Finally, he finds in Rome a quality of com-
fortableness which inhibits growth and development in its
citizens. He states, "It is a city of willful children,
skeptical and rude; even a little deformed, since to pre-
vent growth is unnatural."

723 _____. "Preface to the Screen Treatment of Satyricon," in The
Classic Cinema: Essays in Criticism. New York, Chicago,
San Francisco, Atlanta: Harcourt Brace Jovanovich,
pp. 321-23.
A reprinting of the preface originally published in
English in Fellini's Satyricon. Edited by Dario Zanelli.
Translated by Eugene Walter and John Matthews. New York:
Ballantine Books, 1970. Pp. 43-46.

724 FELLINI, FEDERICO, with José Luis de Vilallonga. "My Dolce
Vita." Oui, 2, No. 3 (March), 35-36 & 108-110.
An interesting autobiographical essay covering a range
of topics. Fellini describes the summer courtships of
female tourists by the vitelloni of Rimini. He discusses
his feelings for the church and recounts a fantasy play
about confession, which he claims to have made up at age
ten. He tells the escapade of running away for a day at
age fifteen with the girl Bianchina Sorianis. (The incident is denied by Bianchina in Angelo Solmi's Fellini.
London: Merlin Press, 1967. P. 65.) He talks about his
experiences as a journalist and as a cartoonist. Finally,
he recounts events surrounding the medical examinations to
determine his eligibility for the draft in WWII.

725 FREE, WILLIAM. "Fellini's I Clowns and the Grotesque."
Journal of Modern Literature, 3, No. 2 (April), 214-27.
Free defines two traditions of the grotesque: the
tradition of Peter Brueghel, which involves comic distribution and irreverent attitude, and the tradition of

Hieronymous Bosch, which involves terrifying distortion and a demonic sense. Free places the art of clowns and the films of Fellini in the first tradition, as opposed to much of modern literature which he places in the second. This done, he studies three basic themes in The Clowns: (1) the ambiguity of the clown and the average man; (2) Fellini's abortive attempt to find the "reality" of clowns through the documentary method; and (3) Fellini's acknowledgement that the clown is dead and his wish to resurrect him imaginatively.

726   GOW, GORDON. "Fellini's Roma." Films and Filming, 19, No. 3 (January), 46-47.
        Laudatory review of Roma, with an extensive summary of the movie's contents.

727   KAEL, PAULINE. "Fellini's Mondo Trasho," in Deeper Into Movies. Boston: Little, Brown, pp. 127-32.
        Reprint of the review of Fellini Satyricon which first appeared in The New Yorker, 46, No. 4 (14 March 1970), 134-40.

728   KINDER, MARSHA and BEVERLE HOUSTON. "A Film from Fellini's Mythology," in The Classic Cinema: Essays in Criticism. Edited by Stanley J. Solomon. New York, Chicago, San Francisco, Atlanta: Harcourt Brace Jovanovich, pp. 324-28.
        A reprinting of an essay originally published in Marsha Kinder and Beverle Houston's Close-Up: A Critical Perspective on Film. New York, Chicago, San Francisco, Atlanta: Harcourt Brace Jovanovich, 1972. Pp. 313-19.

729   LANE, JOHN FRANCIS. "Fellini Looks Back Again." Films and Filming, 19, No. 12 (September), 30-31. Illustrated.
        A brief behind-the-scenes visit to the set for Amarcord on the Cinecittà lot. Lane notes that an early title for the film was L'uomo invaso [Man Profaned], that Sandra Milo was originally intended for the part of la Gradisca, and that Fellini had represented Amarcord in a sketch as a Noah's Ark.

730   LEDUC, JEAN. "Roma." Cinema (Quebec), 2 (January-February), 44-45. Illustrated.
        A brief review of Roma. Two aspects are stressed. First is the juxtaposition which Fellini makes between past and present time, as in the sequence where the motorcyclists drive through the deserted square and in the sequence where the ancient Roman house is discovered during subway excavations. Second is Fellini's "multiplication of human space" from a few people to a large gallery in the boarding house sequence and the music hall sequence.

731   MONT-SERVAN, JEAN-PAUL. "Federico Fellini: Chacun de mes
      films se rapporte a une saison de ma vie." Ecran 73,
      No. 18 (September-October), pp. 4-8. Illustrated.
         An interview with Fellini during the filming of Amarcord.
      Fellini discusses the steps by which the film began to take
      shape. He mentions that he first considered the title The
      Man Profaned and that he thought the film would be about a
      person totally conditioned by false learning. Fellini com-
      ments also on his proclivity for working in a studio as
      opposed to working on location, and he talks of his reli-
      gious feelings and of the hopeful notes in his films.

732   MORAVIA, ALBERTO. "Un bouquet di fiori appassiti." L'espresso,
      19, No. 51 (23 December), 23.
         A review of Amarcord. Moravia identifies this film as
      one of Fellini's finest for its Taoist vision of the world,
      a vision of the world in which history and nature become
      intermingled. Amarcord, says Moravia, expresses a nostalgia
      for the inexperience of youth. Moravia insists that the
      film is not autobiographical, because the audience learns
      nothing of the man Fellini.

733   ORTMAYER, ROGER. "Fellini's Film Journey," in Three European
      Directors. Edited by James M. Wall. Grand Rapids:
      William B. Eardmans, pp. 67-107.
         Ortmayer is the Executive Director of the Department of
      Church and Culture for the National Council of Churches,
      and he attempts a general introduction to the movies of
      Fellini in the broad context of Western Culture. He sees
      Fellini as a proponent of the twentieth-century arts which
      have broken with earlier conceptions of stasis and com-
      munication. La Strada and Juliet of the Spirits are the
      works treated at the greatest length. The essay seems
      intended for those with little background in film studies.

734   RIVA, VALERIO. "La balia in camicia nera." L'espresso, 19,
      No. 40 (7 October), 12-13. Illustrated.
         A most important interview in which Fellini drops his
      mask of perpetual geniality and shows himself at his most
      concerned with social, moral, and psychological issues.
      The interview is on the subject of Fascism in Amarcord.
      Fellini defines Fascism as a psychological state of delayed
      adolescence in which the individual wishes to give the dis-
      charging of his responsibilities to someone else, be it a
      parent figure, the state, or the church. This delayed
      adolescence, he wishes to attack in Amarcord. It is a major
      part of the provincial town that many people carry within
      themselves. Riva talks of the yearnings for power in the
      people of Amarcord as a part of the picture of Fascism, and
      Fellini extends his remark to sections of Roma. This inter-
      view appears as: "Il fascismo tentro di noi," in Il film

<u>Amarcord di Federico Fellini</u>. Bologna: Cappelli editore, 1974. Pp. 101-107. And as: "Entretien avec Federico Fellini." Translated by Paul-Louis Thirard. <u>Positif</u>, No. 158 (14 April 1974), pp. 10-14.

735 ROSENTHAL, STUART. "<u>Roma</u>." <u>International Film Guide 1973</u>. London: Tantivy Press; New York: A. S. Barnes, pp. 229-30. Illustrated. Brief credits.

Brief notice of <u>Roma</u>. Rosenthal defines the movie as a portrait of what the city has meant to Fellini. He finds a tension between nostalgic, affectionate humanism and a fatalistic pessimism.

736 SHARPLES, WIN, JR. "Fellini's <u>Roma</u>: The Audacious Image." <u>Filmmaker's Newsletter</u>, 6, No. 4 (February), 51-52. Illustrated.

Sharples attempts to trace briefly three elements of Fellini's films up to their presentation in <u>Roma</u>: the image of the church, the girl in white, and the procession. The girl in white, he finds, is replaced by the girls in the bordello and by the suspicious star, Anna Magnani. He fails to note that such figures have existed side by side with the girl in white previously. More successful are his treatments of the image of the church and of the procession.

737 TASSONE, ALDO. "Entretien avec Tonino Guerra." <u>Image et son</u>, No. 279 (December), pp. 67-82. Illustrated.

Interview with the poet and screenwriter who has collaborated with Fellini, Michaelangelo Antonioni, and Elio Petri. About three pages are devoted to <u>Amarcord</u>, his one collaboration with Fellini. Guerra describes the film as the story of a village, a family, and a boy in the year 1936. The film is not nostalgic or consolatory. It is a mocking, irreverent reminiscence. Guerra says that the village is Italy in the contemporary era as well as in the past. He compares the film briefly to <u>Roma</u> and discusses his relationship with Fellini.

738 WARHOL, ANDY and PAT HACKETT. "Fellini." <u>Interview</u>, No. 35 (August), pp. 6-7.

Interview on the set of <u>Amarcord</u> in which Fellini talks of his manner of adding sound in the editing stage.

739 WERBA, HANK. "Fellini, Now Lensing <u>Amarcord</u>, Raps Stiff Terms of Italo Unions' New Pact." <u>Variety</u>, 270, No. 4 (7 March), 32 & 34.

The title of the article is a good annotation. The article contains some production information and Fellini's complaint that union standardization (a five-day week and a ten-hour day) destroys artisan habits and attitudes.

740   WINSTON, DOUGLAS GARRETT. "Federico Fellini and the Psycho-
      analytic Technique in Film," in The Screenplay As Literature.
      Rutherford, Madison, Teaneck, N.J.: Fairleigh Dickinson
      University Press, pp. 140-61.
         Winston treats Fellini's psychoanalytic method in $8\frac{1}{2}$ and
      Juliet of the Spirits. Each movie involves the process of
      resolving or bringing to the surface of consciousness con-
      flicts begun in childhood. Free-association is the method
      used by Fellini to uncover the conflicts. Winston treats
      especially Guido's dream of the visit to the family tomb,
      his memories of the bath in the wine vat and of Saraghina,
      Juliet's hallucination on the beach, her vision of the
      beautiful circus artist, her memory of the religious pageant,
      and her final fantasy of release. In both movies, a con-
      flict between religious upbringing and sexuality is at the
      source of the problem.

741   YOUNG, JEAN. "Fellini's Roma." Film, British Federation of
      Film Societies, No. 2 (May), pp. 10-11.
         A review of Roma. Young states that the film is about
      Fellini himself and how he sees Rome imaginatively. The
      movie is a continuation of his personal, non-narrative
      method of filmmaking.

                              1974

742   AMIEL, MIREILLE. "Amarcord." Cinéma 74, No. 188 (June),
      pp. 93-94. Illustrated.
         Brief laudatory review of Amarcord on its showing at the
      Cannes Film Festival. Amiel describes it as a film about
      adolescence, the people of a town, and dispossession. The
      world of the town is beset by Fascism, the change of the
      seasons, and death. Amiel discusses in particular the
      sequence about the oceanliner Rex.

743   _____. "La (Tres) Pudique Agonie de Federico Fellini."
      Cinéma 74, Nos. 190-91 (September-October), pp. 223-30.
      Illustrated.
         A retrospective view of Fellini's career since La Dolce
      Vita. Amiel describes Fellini's agony at the demise of his
      town, his country, and his culture, all of which Fellini
      treats in his films. He seems to stand on the edge of a
      new culture, unable to enter it, but capable of loving it.
      Similarly, he has broken from traditional narrative and
      from realism. His movies have moved toward the form of the
      poetic essay, and he has chosen to exploit the illusionistic
      aspects of cinema. In short, he is an artist on the outer
      limits of his culture and his art.

744 ANGELUCCI, GIANFRANCO. "Fellini 15 e ½ e la poetica
dell'onirico," in Il film Amarcord di Federico Fellini.
Bologna: Cappelli editore, pp. 9-46.
  An interesting article on the oneiric character ("oneir-
ical poetics" and "prophesying oneiris") in Fellini films
from The White Sheik to Amarcord. Angelucci declares that
Fellini shows the difficulty of modern man in perceiving
the "indecipherable and mysterious reality" of the modern
world. Angelucci attempts to rebutt some of the charges
against Fellini by left-wing critics in Italy and insists
on the artist's right to be ambiguous. For 8½, Angelucci
draws a close comparison with Joycean stream of consciousness. He discusses the use of color in Juliet of the
Spirits and Fellini Satyricon. Amarcord concludes an
effort, begun by Fellini in La Dolce Vita, to abolish human
figures as such and to replace them with situations and
places.

745 ANON. "Amarcord: un film de Federico Fellini." L'Avant-
Scène, No. 153 (December), pp. 58-60. Illustrated. Credits.
  A brief photo-spread on Amarcord. The article contains
a synopsis of the film and a short sampling of French
reviews.

746 ANON. "Federico Fellini's Amarcord." Films and Filming, 20
(June), 37-41. Illustrated. Credits.
  A spread of photographs from Amarcord.

747 ANON. "Talk of the Town." New Yorker, 50, No. 33 (7 October),
33-35.
  The New Yorker reporter describes the experience of meeting Fellini at the airport on Fellini's visit to America to
promote Amarcord. Fellini compares the American musical
anthology That's Entertainment to his Amarcord and mentions
his liking for the "great American writers--the ones who
write 'Dick Tracy' and 'Popeye.'"

748 ARBASINO, ALBERTO. "Fellini." Translated by Richard Alleman.
Vogue, 164, No. 4 (October), 220, 222 & 246-47.
Illustrated.
  A brief interview with Fellini about Amarcord and
Casanova. In the former, Fellini claims to have looked
back on his childhood in Rimini in the thirties with "a
little melancholy, a little irritation, and a good deal of
critical hindsight." He speaks of life wasted in the small
town. He discusses also his interest in light and structure. Concerning the latter film project, he describes
Casanova's existence as, "A life not lived, a sea of indifference, human eyes which never see anything, erotic gestures repeated mechanically."

749   BACHMANN, GIDEON. "Amarcord." Take One, 4, No. 2 (19 March),
      35. Illustrated. (Although the issue is marked "Nov.-
      Dec. 1972," it was actually published 19 March 1974.)
          A review of Amarcord. Bachmann laments the deterior-
      ation of Fellini's films since 8½ and Juliet of the Spirits.
      In part, he attributes this deterioration to the loss of
      collaborators Gianni di Venanzo (cinematographer), Piero
      Gherardi (set designer), and Leo Cattozzo (editor).
      Fellini's recent films, including Amarcord, argues Bachmann,
      lack the sense of measure, the constantly mounting rhythm
      and dramatic structure of the earlier films. The article
      appears in French as "Lettre de Rome: Amarcord est sorti."
      Cinéma 74, No. 187 (May 1974), pp. 28-30.

750   _____. "Lettre de Rome: Amarcord est sorti." Cinéma 74,
      No. 187 (May), pp. 28-30. Illustrated.
          A translation into French of a review published first in
      English as "Amarcord." Take One, 4, No. 2 (19 March), 35.

751   BENDERSON, ALBERT EDWARD. Critical Approaches to Federico
      Fellini's "8½." New York: Arno Press, 239 pp.
      Bibliography.
          A published dissertation originally submitted at the
      State University of New York at Buffalo. Benderson con-
      siders 8½ according to contextual analysis (or "new criti-
      cism") and archetypal analysis. He also discusses the
      fallacy of an autobiographical approach, and he offers an
      analysis of 8½ seen against the background of other films
      by Fellini. Most interesting is the long section on con-
      textual analysis. Benderson demonstrates the movie's
      resemblance to subjective, first-person narration, consid-
      ering such elements as camera movement, music, the lack of
      establishing shots, the exaggeration of perspective empha-
      sizing the vanishing point, night and day lighting, and
      gestures, as well as more traditional literary concerns.
      He discusses the character of Guido in terms of the obses-
      sion Guido has with death and old age, the adolescent and
      escapist qualities of his fantasies, the influence the
      church has on him, and the kind of alienated, subject-
      object relationships Guido has with those around him. In
      the section on archetypal analysis, Benderson extends his
      arguments by drawing on Jung's conceptions of the "anima,"
      the mandala, and individuation. He concludes that Guido's
      development toward psychic wholeness is incomplete since he
      stops short of facing the reality of his situation and
      fantasizes a Luisa more compliant than his wife really is.
      Appended to Benderson's book is a short section on the
      Pinocchio motif in 8½. This appendix has been reprinted in
      altered and expanded form as "The Pinocchio Motif in
      Federico Fellini's 8½." Film Studies Annual (1976),
      pp. 215-24.

752   BETTI, LILIANA. "Un dramma anche qui," in Il film Amarcord di
       Federico Fellini. Bologna: Cappelli editore, pp. 111-17.
              Notes put together by Betti while working at an editing
       viewer to establish a final version of the screenplay of
       Amarcord. She discusses differences between a film and a
       written account of it and notes Fellini's hostility to writ-
       ten accounts of films. Very briefly, she mentions the way
       in which a film differs from its original screenplay. She
       remarks that Fellini cut out a great deal of material during
       the editing stages of Amarcord. To discover the coherence
       of the film, the viewer must recognize thematic links among
       seemingly diverse sequences (e.g., the tendency of the
       characters to lose themselves in wish-fulfilling dreams).
       She finds that the film has "a splendid formal carelessness."

753   _____. "Introduction," in Federcord: disegni per Amarcord
       di Federico Fellini. Milan: Milano libri edizioni,
       pp. 26-79.
              An introductory essay to a volume of Fellini's sketches
       for Amarcord. Betti describes behind-the-scenes work on
       Amarcord. She deals mainly with the casting and with the
       shooting of certain scenes. Some of the scenes she discusses
       are those involving the character Biscein, those taking
       place in the school, those concerning the prince and
       Gradisca, and those dealing with the oceanliner Rex. She
       reproduces some statements by participants, and she re-
       counts some of her own experiences as assistant director of
       the film.

754   BONITZER, PASCAL. "Memoire de l'oeil." Cahiers du Cinéma,
       Nos. 251-52 (July-August), pp. 75-76.
              An interesting review of Amarcord from a Marxist point
       of view. Bonitzer argues that the carnivalesque aspects of
       Fellini movies tend to overturn joyfully the repressive
       order of the power structure.

755   CALVINO, ITALO. "Autobiografia di uno spettatore," in
       Quattro film [by Federico Fellini]. Turin: Giulio
       Einaudi editore, pp. ix-xxiv.
              An interesting, speculative essay by the Italian novelist
       Italo Calvino, which serves as an introduction to four
       screenplays by Fellini. In his youth, Calvino states, he
       was drawn to American films as a world held at a distance
       from that of his provincial town of San Remo. Modern films
       in general and Fellini's autobiographical films in particu-
       lar now reverse that appeal. The viewer now must confront
       himself and his quotidian existence. In Fellini's auto-
       biographical films, Calvino finds as subjects his provincial
       town and himself as a youth, with both the town and himself
       continually measuring themselves against the world of the
       cinema. Calvino discusses also Fellini's use of comic

strip styles to gain an assertive image, and he insists on
the true bases of Fellini's caricatures of Italian Fascists.
He briefly comments on Fellini's religious upbringing.
Calvino concludes that Fellini has used the provincial town
of Rimini, especially in Amarcord, to establish a symptoma-
tology of Italian neuroses. The essay is translated into
French by Sylvette Legrand as "Autobiographie d'un spectateur." Positif, No. 181 (May 1976), pp. 13-23.

756 CANBY, VINCENT. "Amarcord." New York Times (20 September),
     P. 32. Illustrated. Brief credits.
         Laudatory review of Amarcord. Canby praises the mixture
     of comedy and dreamlike evocations of the past. Fellini is
     fascinated with and puts to good use the artificialities of
     the studio to get the right tone. Canby expands on these
     ideas in a follow-up review on September 29, 1974.

757 _____. "Amarcord." New York Times (29 September), pp. 1 & 34.
     Illustrated.
         Canby's second review of Amarcord. He reiterates on a
     slightly larger scale the points he made earlier in his
     review on September 20, 1974.

758 CERVONI, ALBERT. "Les Feux du music-hall." Cinéma 74,
     Nos. 190-91 (September-October), pp. 310-11. Brief credits.
         An essay describing Cervoni's experience on reseeing
     Variety Lights after the passage of many years. He finds
     new viewpoints with which to approach the film. It docu-
     ments an historical period, and it shows stages in the
     developments of Fellini and Lattuada as directors. But most
     of all the film remains for Cervoni complete, beautiful and
     precise.

759 COCKS, JAY. "Fellini Remembers." Time, 104, No. 15 (7
     October), 7-11. Illustrated.
         Laudatory review of Amarcord as a successful synthesis
     of reminiscence and fantasy. Cocks feels that there is a
     strong political subcurrent in the movie, but argues that
     it is only a part of the whole. Fellini is exploring his
     childhood world of Rimini as he has done before. This time,
     however, he does it with heightened powers.

760 CODELLI, LORENZO. "Nuit et gel." Positif, No. 158 (April),
     pp. 15-17.
         A review of Amarcord. Codelli attacks the movie as too
     much in the conventional mode of recent Italian fiction
     which stresses regionalism and dialect. Fellini merely
     plays with the charm of the horrible of the peculiar in
     provincial life much as he has played before with the affect
     of physically monstrous people.

761   del BUONO, ORESTE. "Vita (presunta, provvisoria, precaria) con Federico Fellini," in <u>Federcord: disegni per Amarcord di Federico Fellini</u>. Milan: Milano libri edizioni, pp. 5-24.
       An introductory essay to a volume of Fellini's drawings for <u>Amarcord</u>. Del Buono gives a behind-the-scenes account of some aspects of Fellini's work on <u>Roma</u>, <u>Amarcord</u>, and <u>Casanova</u>. He finds that Fellini often plays the role of the beleaguered director who won't be able to finish his film successfully. Del Buono describes some of the casting interviews for <u>Amarcord</u> and the final shooting of the scene with the mad uncle in the tree. <u>Amarcord</u> is for del Buono a depiction of the Italy of yesterday that lives in the Italy of the present. The film shows Italy as a medieval village shut off from the rest of the world, isolated within its own walls. He finds the movie Fellini's strongest social statement. Only through imagination can Titta, the protagonist, find a release from his limited world of the small town. Fellini's plans for <u>Casanova</u> are described by del Buono as a continuation of his treatment of "Italianity." In this movie, Fellini will attack a false ideal of Italians.

762   ELLEY, DEREK. "<u>Amarcord</u>." <u>Films and Filming</u>, 20, No. 12 (September), 41-42.
       Laudatory review of <u>Amarcord</u>. Elley finds best the time-less events of a childhood world and regrets the intrusion of specific historical events concerning Fascism.

763   ESCOBAR, ROBERTO. "<u>Amarcord</u>." <u>Cineforum</u>, 14, No. 131 (April), 269-82. Illustrated. Brief credits.
       A lengthy review of <u>Amarcord</u>. Escobar uses the film as the basis for a discussion of the following four themes which he finds throughout Fellini's films: (1) recovery of the past, especially Fellini's past; (2) bad conscience, usually related to sexual repression; (3) death, viewed in early films as tragedy, but in <u>Amarcord</u> with resignation; and (4) hope, tied with fantasies about the future.

764   FARBER, STEPHEN. "<u>Amarcord</u> and <u>Lacombe Lucien</u>: Illuminations of Things Past." <u>New York Times</u> (3 November), Section II, p. 15.
       Farber compares Fellini's film with Malle's as two works which probe the situations in provincial towns under Fascism. With <u>Amarcord</u>, Farber concentrates on the sequence about the arrest of Titta's father, and he notes how the docility and insularity of the townspeople permit Fascism to flourish.

765   FELLINI, FEDERICO. <u>Federcord: disegni per Amarcord di Federico Fellini</u>. Edited by Liliana Betti and Oreste del Buono. Milan: Milano libri edizioni, 79 pp. Illustrated.

Sketches by Fellini for <u>Amarcord</u>. The volume is introduced by essays by Liliana Betti and Oreste del Buono.

766 FELLINI, FEDERICO. "Fellini dit <u>Amarcord</u>." <u>Cinema</u> (Quebec),
4, No. 1, 43-44.
A printing in French of Fellini's letter to Italian
critic Gian Luigi Rondi about how Fellini conceives and
develops his film ideas in general and about his intentions
in <u>Amarcord</u> in particular. The film is a picture of the
closed world of a small Italian town under the church and
under Fascism. The condition of this world is similar to
the state of adolescence in the individual.

767 _____. "Ma in fondo un attore cos'è?" <u>L'espresso</u>, 20, No. 11
(17 March), 83.
Fellini comments that a good actor's greatest gift is
his unconscious and childlike acquaintanceship with everyday things. He feels that the moment an actor becomes too
intellectually aware of himself, he is finished. Culture,
self-awareness, and intelligence are of no value to the
actor. It is the director's job to pull out the actor's
unconscious qualities.

768 FINETTI, UGO. "<u>Amarcord</u>." <u>Cinema nuovo</u>, 23, No. 227
(January-February), 57-59. Brief credits.
A review of <u>Amarcord</u>. Finetti questions the validity
of the political and nostalgic elements of <u>Amarcord</u>. He
prefers to view the film as a more general commentary on
small-town life and the cyclical nature of life.

769 GILI, JEAN A. "<u>Amarcord</u>." <u>Ecran 74</u>, No. 25 (May), pp. 61-63.
Illustrated. Brief credits.
A laudatory review of <u>Amarcord</u>. Gili feels that Fellini
has reconstructed his version of an Italian provincial town
in the 1930s as a comparison for the present. Fellini
presents a bitter-sweet depiction of the past and asks if
we have changed for the better or the worse. Especially
interesting is Gili's discussion of Italian Fascism as an
occasion for collective irresponsibility.

770 _____. "<u>Les Feux du music-hall</u>." <u>Ecran 74</u>, No. 29 (October),
pp. 77-78. Brief credits.
A review of <u>Variety Lights</u>. Gili finds the movie more
in the style of Alberto Lattuada than in the style of
Fellini. The film reveals the economic depression of the
world through which the vaudeville performers move. There
is more realism in the film than one usually finds in a
film by Fellini.

771 GORBMAN, CLAUDIA. "Music As Salvation: Notes on Fellini and
Rota." <u>Film Quarterly</u>, 28, No. 2 (Winter), 17-25.

A study of the use of music for narrative purposes in
Nights of Cabiria. Gorbman traces the uses of four musical
themes in the film. She argues for the importance of the
musicians on the road and the theme they play in demonstrat-
ing Cabiria's salvation at the end of the movie.

772 HARCOURT, PETER. "The Secret Life of Federico Fellini" and
"Conclusion," in Six European Directors. Harmondsworth,
England and Baltimore: Penguin Books, pp. 183-211 & 255-67.
These two sections of Harcourt's book are reprintings
in slightly altered form of two articles. "The Secret Life
of Federico Fellini" appeared first in Film Quarterly, 19,
No. 3 (Spring 1966), 4-19; and "Conclusion" was originally
"The Loss of Community: Six European Directors" in Cinema
Journal, 12, No. 1 (Fall 1972), 2-10.

773 HASKELL, MOLLY. From Reverence to Rape. New York: Holt,
Rinehart and Winston, pp. 309-12.
One of Haskell's main theses is that women in films
"generally emerge as the projections of male values."
Fellini's women, she argues, tend to be "emanations of his
sexual fears." They tend to be demonesses or virgins. The
figure played by Giulietta Masina, however, is an exception.
Before Juliet of the Spirits, she is sexually neutral, a
resilient tramp. In Juliet of the Spirits, she is a persona
for the author-director.

774 HYMAN, TIMOTHY. "$8\frac{1}{2}$ As an Anatomy of Melancholy." Sight and
Sound, 43, No. 3 (Summer), 172-75. Illustrated.
Hyman states that each of us has a "fundamental recur-
rent 'pattern,' to which his experience largely conforms."
$8\frac{1}{2}$ is the mapping out of one such pattern. The pattern of
Guido's experience is cyclical. It involves crisis,
liberation, and fall. Fellini's language for portraying
the cycle is his oscillation of light and dark scenes.

775 KAUFFMANN, STANLEY. "Amarcord." New Republic, 171, No. 13
(28 September), 22 & 33-34.
Laudatory review of Amarcord. Kauffmann praises Fellini
for confronting and giving shape to memories of his youth
that have been haunting him in his adult life. Kauffmann
compares Amarcord to Winesburg, Ohio, Spoon River Anthology,
and Our Town. Fellini is using his film as "psychic
explorer" of his "obsessing dream."

776 LÉVY, DENIS. "Amarcord." Télécine, No. 190 (July-August),
pp. 24-25. Illustrated. Brief credits.
Review of Amarcord. Lévy argues that the movie should
not be taken as a documentary of the recent past or as a
piece of autobiography. Rather the movie should be seen
as "cultural experience" which is common to ours, but which

enriches ours with new elaborations. Lévy deals specifically with the sequence of the oceanliner Rex and with the sequence of the grandfather lost in the fog.

777   METZ, CHRISTIAN. "Mirror Construction in Fellini's 8½," in
      Film Language: A Semiotics of the Cinema. Translated by
      Michael Taylor. New York: Oxford University Press,
      pp. 228-34.
          A translation into English of Metz' article which appeared
      first as "La Construction 'en abyme' dans Huit et demi de
      Fellini." Revue d'esthetique, 19, No. 1 (January-March
      1966), 96-101. The article appears also in French in Essais
      sur la signification au cinéma. Paris: Éditions Klinck-
      sieck, 1968. Pp. 223-28.

778   MONTEMAGGI, AMEDEO. "Mi sveglia in piena notte e dice: 'Corri,
      mi sento solo.'" Oggi, 30, No. 7 (13 February), 37-40.
      Illustrated.
          An interview with Luigi Benzi, one of Fellini's oldest
      and best childhood friends. The interviewer identifies him
      as the inspiration for Amarcord and the model for its
      protagonist.

779   MOSCATO, ALFONSO, S.J. "Amarcord, di Fellini." La civiltà
      cattolica, 125, No. 2 (4 May), 259-62.
          An attacking review of Amarcord as the third in a series
      of movies about Fellini's past. (The Clowns and Roma are
      the other two films in the series.) Moscato finds Fellini's
      reminiscences superficial, narcissistic, and repetitive.

780   PECORI, FRANCO. Federico Fellini. Florence: "La nuova Italia"
      editrice, 133 pp. Filmography.
          A short collection of statements by Fellini about him-
      self, a short biographical essay on Fellini's life up to
      the time of Variety Lights, and a biographical-critical
      survey of Fellini's career from Variety Lights to Amarcord.
      Pecori concerns himself mainly with the personal and auto-
      biographical vision of Fellini.

781   REILLY, CHARLES PHILLIPS. "Amarcord." Films in Review, 25,
      No. 9 (November), 566.
          Laudatory review. Reilly praises Fellini for returning
      to the subject of people and their responses to life. The
      town of Amarcord is a "Rabelaisian world where the grotesque
      is not unusual and man's animal nature is part of his life."

782   RIVA, VALERIO. "Entretien avec Federico Fellini." Translated
      by Paul-Louis Thirard. Positif, No. 158 (1 April),
      pp. 10-14. Illustrated.

A translation of an Italian interview with Fellini which appeared originally as "La balia in camicia nera." L'espresso, 19, No. 40 (7 October 1973), 12-13.

783 _____. "Il fascismo dentro di noi," in Il film Amarcord di Federico Fellini. Bologna: Cappelli editore, pp. 101-107.
A reprinting in Italian of an interview with Fellini which appeared originally as "La balia in camicia nera." L'espresso, 19, No. 40 (7 October 1973), 12-13.

784 SARRIS, ANDREW. "Federico to a Fare-Thee-Well." Village Voice, 19, No. 38 (19 September), 83-84.
A review of Amarcord. Sarris quotes Bazin's pronouncement that the long descriptive sequences of no apparent effect in the development of the "action" constitute the most important sections of Fellini's film. Now, Sarris feels, Fellini's films consist almost entirely of such "priviledged moments." He offers the idea that Fellini is in his third and least stimulating period, one of ostentatious introspection. The movie, furthermore, vacillates between personal autobiography and official history.

785 SICILIANO, ENZO. "In teatro persino il mare," in Il film Amarcord di Federico Fellini. Bologna: Cappelli editore, pp. 89-97.
An important interview with Fellini during the final stages of editing Amarcord in 1973. Fellini outlines the steps by which he brings a film to life: (1) the initial vision, where the film is perceived as a cloudy, vague, and indistinct, but seemingly whole entity; (2) the financial arrangements; (3) the screenplay where the initial vision is transformed into literary rhythms; (4) casting when Fellini seeks out the faces to match or change his mental images; (5) production work when sets are made to match or change his mental images; (6) direction of actors and crew while the scene is shot; and (7) final editing. Each step, Fellini argues, alters the film and makes it different from his initial conception. Fellini also states that his films are autobiographical only in the sense that they are his invention. The interview appeared first as "Fellini: io e il film." Il mondo (13 September 1973). It is translated into English by Isabel Quigley in slightly altered form as "The Birth of a Film," in Fellini on Fellini. Edited by Christian Strich. New York: Delacorte Press/Seymour Lawrence, 1976. Pp. 159-66.

786 SIMON, JOHN. "The Tragic Deterioration of Fellini's Genius." New York Times (24 November), Section II, pp. 17 & 19.
A review of Amarcord. Simon laments a change in Fellini and in his work as he has grown older and more successful. Fellini is now "too crudely despotic a creature to have

much of the artist left about him." His films have always
been autobiographical, but beginning with La Dolce Vita
they have become self-centered. And Fellini's humor which
was warm in his early films has become more cruel: "the
chief joke is human ugliness." To back up his argument,
Simon traces various treatments of the character Giudizio,
of wedding feasts, of large, fleshy women, of statues of
large heads, and of grotesques.

787   SOLMI, ANGELO. "Un Fellini maiscolo." Oggi, 30, No. 1 (2
      January), 73-74. Illustrated.
          A review of Amarcord. Solmi praises it as Fellini's
      most compact and unified film. He commends it, in particu-
      lar, for its nostalgic depiction of provincial Italian life
      of the 1930s. The reviewer offers his own reminiscences
      too.

788   _____. "Impossibile non premiare Fellini." Oggi, 30, No. 28
      (10 July), 91-92. Illustrated.
          An article which outlines the events and the in-fighting
      surrounding Fellini's winning of the Rizzoli Prize of 1974
      for Amarcord.

789   TAYLOR, JOHN RUSSELL. "Amarcord." Sight and Sound, 43, No. 4
      (Autumn), 244-45. Illustrated.
          Condemning review of Amarcord. Taylor remarks that we
      know "Fellini's imaginative world inside out." It remains
      only to see what he can do with it on a given occasion. He
      finds Amarcord too tasteful. All the sequences are played
      down. Only the scene where the townspeople go to sea to
      stare at the passing of the liner Rex gains his approval:
      "Its apparition has the effect of a sort of religious
      experience." Otherwise, it seems to Taylor that Fellini is
      tired of his traditional material.

790   TURRONI, GIUSEPPE. "Amarcord." Filmcritica, No. 245 (May),
      pp. 201-202.
          A review of Amarcord, written in an elliptical, lyrical
      style. Turroni states that the movie deals with the pass-
      ing of the seasons, the significance of memories, the beat
      of the human heart, and the sense of mathematical exactness
      and destiny. The movie both uses and reflects movie
      images of the 1930s, from Morocco, Laurel and Hardy movies,
      Anthony Adverse, The Wedding Night, and others.

791   VOLTA, ORNELLA. "Le Journal des rêves de Federico Fellini."
      Positif, No. 158 (April), pp. 2-9. Illustrated.
          Fourteen drawings from a dream notebook kept by Fellini.
      The commentary is mainly descriptive, rather than evalu-
      ative. The drawings often show Fellini's persona threatened
      or overwhelmed. Most of his dreams would be considered
      anxiety dreams.

792 WALSH, MOIRA. "Holiday Nostalgia and Fantasy." <u>America</u>, 131,
No. 20 (21 December), 411.
  Brief, negative review of <u>Amarcord</u>. Walsh finds the
movie brilliant in form, but marred by self-indulgence and
deficient substance.

793 ZIMMERMAN, PAUL. "Growing up Fellini." <u>Newsweek</u>, 84, No. 14
(30 September), 106-107. Illustrated.
  A review of <u>Amarcord</u>. Zimmerman calls the movie Fellini's
most beautiful, and he claims it is a landmark in the history
of film. He argues that since <u>8½</u>, Fellini has been moving
toward a new kind of film in which the director's imagination replaces the single protagonist as hero. <u>Amarcord</u> is
the culmination of that movement. Zimmerman also discusses
Fellini's treatment of the family in the movie.

1975

794 ANON. "Fellini Abandons <u>Casanova</u> Project." <u>Variety</u>, 277,
No. 11 (22 January), 42.
  A brief note on the apparent termination of <u>Casanova</u>
because of irreconcilable differences between Fellini and
producers Andrea Rizzoli and Dino De Laurentiis. Interestingly, the disagreements centered around Fellini's refusal
to cast an American male star and direct an original English
version.

795 ANON. "Pix Pessimism Out of Style in Italy." <u>Variety</u>, 279,
No. 1 (14 May), 5 & 43.
  This survey of the Italian film industry finds it in a
very healthy condition with all of the major directors
working. Fellini's <u>Casanova</u>, in production under producer
Alberto Grimaldi, is seen as leading the way of this
present revival.

796 BETTI, LILIANA and GIANFRANCO ANGELUCCI. <u>Casanova, rendez-</u>
<u>vous con Federico Fellini</u>. Milan: Bompiani, 209 pp.
  A collection of material about Casanova gathered while
Fellini was making his film <u>Casanova</u>. In the first section,
the authors interview four contemporary Italian seducers in
order to discover the attitudes of the Casanova type. In
the second section, they ask various Italian intellectuals
to comment on the Casanova myth. This section concludes
with an account of Fellini's dealings with the various producers of <u>Casanova</u> and an interview with Fellini conducted
by Aldo Tassone in which Fellini makes clear his dislike
for his protagonist. The third and final section is the
script of a television "special" organized by Betti and
Angelucci on Fellini's conception of Casanova. It is a
documentary. Again various people, including writers,

actors, intellectuals, and seducers are interviewed.
Fellini participates briefly in the program. (Liliana Betti
was assistant director on the film <u>Casanova</u>.)

797 GREENBERG, HARVEY R. "8½--The Declensions of Silence," in <u>The</u>
<u>Movies on Your Mind</u>. New York: <u>Saturday Review</u> Press and
E. P. Dutton, pp. 138-68.
    A thoughtful and interesting psychoanalytical study of
8½. Greenberg discusses Guido's fear of age and creative
impotence, his lack of a supportive paternal image, and his
split view of the maternal image as seducer-accuser or pure,
docile nurse. Greenberg finds the apparent harmony of the
ending fantasy to be deceiving. Guido has, in fact, severed
relations with Luisa, relinquished Claudia, his muse, and
given up a film project. The ending, says Greenberg, "bears
the mark of an abortive attempt at restitution." Greenberg
discusses briefly Fellini's life in parallel with Guido's
and traces the desperateness he sees in 8½ through Fellini's
later movies.

798 KAUFFMANN, STANLEY. "<u>The Clowns</u>" and "Fellini's <u>Roma</u>," in
<u>Living Images</u>. New York: Harper & Row, pp. 59-61 & 148-50.
    The first review is reprinted from <u>New Republic</u>, 165,
No. 1 (3 July 1971), 22 & 33-34. The second from <u>New</u>
<u>Republic</u>, 167, No. 17 (4 November 1972), 22.

799 KEYSTER, LESTER J. "Three Faces of Evil: Fascism in Recent
Movies." <u>Journal of Popular Film</u>, 4, No. 1, 21-31.
    Keyster examines three current films (Louis Malle's
<u>Lacombe, Lucien</u>, Fellini's <u>Amarcord</u>, and Liliana Cavani's
<u>Night Porter</u>) which attempt to present some insight into
the nature of Fascism. He finds <u>Amarcord</u> "an impression-
istic mood piece" which locates the roots of Fascism in the
day-to-day routines of the family, the church, and the
state. Fellini's Fascists are not to be feared because
they "do little more than use castor oil for their third
degree."

800 MICCICHÈ, LINO. "Italy," in <u>International Film Guide 1975</u>.
London: Tantivy Press; New York: A. S. Barnes, 232-39.
Illustrated.
    In the midst of his discussion of Italian cinema,
Miccichè discusses favorable critical reactions to <u>Amarcord</u>
in Italy by left-wing critics and by moderates.

801 MORAVIA, ALBERTO. "Casanova era un insetto." <u>L'espresso</u>, 21,
No. 49 (7 December), 105.
    An article written by Moravia after visiting Fellini on
the set of <u>Casanova</u>. Fellini has insisted that he is filming <u>Casanova</u> only because he is under contract to do so.
If he had read Casanova's <u>Memoirs</u> first, he would have

refused to do the film. Moravia accepts Fellini's words but with some qualifications. He suggests four other reasons why Fellini might have been tempted to do this film: (1) Casanova was an eminently social creature, and Fellini is an avid observer of society; (2) Casanova is a monster, an anomaly, and Fellini is fascinated by exceptions to the general social order; (3) Casanova represents what Italians are typically reputed to be--a population of actors, always on stage; and (4) Casanova is a kind of reversal of psycho-analytical principles, that is, he has no apparent sexual hangups despite the fact that he is emotionally empty. The article is reprinted in Gianfranco Angelucci's "Un film di carta stampata," in Il Casanova di Federico Fellini. Edited by Liliana Betti and Gianfranco Angelucci. Bologna: Cappelli editore, 1977. Pp. 55-56.

802 _____. "Roma, mille film orsono." L'espresso, 21, No. 41 (12 October), 85.
A philosophical look at Fellini's La Dolce Vita in which Moravia asserts that the film is not so much a commentary on the decadence of Italian society, as it is a documentary that myths are the reality of Italian society, at least for Fellini. Reality for Fellini and society today consists of spectacle, and spectacle is the tangible by-product of Fellini's mythological concept of reality. Spectacle is a consumer good.

803 PERRY, TED. Filmguide to 8½. Filmguide Series. Bloomington and London: Indiana University Press, 89 pp. Filmography. Credits. Bibliography.
This monograph contains an outline of scenes of 8½, production notes, a biographical essay on Fellini, and a fifty-page essay of analysis of the movie. Perry argues that the movie is about the mental processes of the hero and about the processes of filmmaking. He states, "8½ seems to be a rendering of the mind trying to see, know, and reflect upon itself." In his analysis of the movie, Perry concentrates on camera strategies and on visual meaning. His analysis is a detailed "reading" of the movie, scene by scene.

804 RENZI, RENZO. "Il fascismo involontario (a proposito di Amarcord)," in Il fascismo involontario e altri scritti. Bologna: Cappelli editore, pp. 131-81. Illustrated.
An essay in the form of an open letter to Fellini, with regard to Amarcord. Fellini's film has stirred up many memories of Renzi's own youthful experiences with Fascism, and Renzi discusses them at length. Renzi feels Amarcord is important for its accurate representation of a "cultural substratum" of Italy that has continued into the present time.

805   RIZZO, EUGENE. "Fellini's Musical Alter Ego, Nino Rota: How
      They Work." Variety, 279, No. 2 (21 May), 28.
            An interesting biographical sketch of the composer Nino
      Rota, notes on his collaboration with Fellini and other
      directors, and comments by Rota himself.

806   STUBBS, JOHN C. "Study Guide to 8½." Journal of Aesthetic
      Education, 9, No. 2 (April), 96-108. Bibliography.
            Brief critical and biographical essay on Fellini's career
      up to Roma. Sequence outline and study questions for 8½.

                              1976

807   BENDERSON, ALBERT. "The Pinocchio Motif in Federico Fellini's
      8½." Film Studies Annual, pp. 215-24.
            A revised and expanded version of Benderson's "Appendix
      B," in Critical Approaches to Federico Fellini's 8½. New
      York: Arno Press, 1974. Pp. 224-32. Benderson points out
      instances where he feels that Fellini has drawn on elements
      from Carlo Lorenzini's satiric tale, Pinocchio, for Fellini's
      depiction of Guido's growth toward self-realization. The
      general argument is an interesting one, although some of
      Benderson's points of comparison seem forced. Also in this
      article, Benderson discusses Jung's theory of individuation
      as applied to 8½.

808   BETTI, LILIANA. Fellini. Zurich: Diogenes Verlag, 302 pp.
      Illustrated.
            A book-length portrait of Fellini in German by the woman
      who has served as assistant director to Fellini on several
      films.

809   CALVINO, ITALO. "Autobiographie d'un spectateur." Translated
      by Sylvette Legrand. Positif, No. 181 (May), pp. 13-23.
      Illustrated.
            Translation into French of Calvino's essay which appeared
      first in Italian as "Autobiografia di uno spettatore," in
      Federico Fellini's Quattro film: I vitelloni, La dolce
      vita, 8½, Giulietta degli spiriti. Turin: Giulio
      Einaudi editore, 1974. Pp. ix-xxiv.

810   CHEMASI, ANTONIO. "Fellini's Casanova: The Final Nights."
      American Film, 1, No. 10 (September), 8-16. Illustrated.
            Chemasi describes work on the set of Casanova during
      the final days of filming. He records Fellini's scornful
      description of Casanova's life as one "that has in fact
      been lived under ice," and he interviews Donald Sutherland
      on the experience of working with Fellini.

811 CHESSA, PASQUALE. "Casanova cassa vuota." L'espresso, 22,
     No. 2 (11 January), 48-51. Illustrated.
          A lengthy article about the financing of Casanova, com-
     paring its budget to other contemporary spectacles like
     Barry Lyndon. The article also goes behind the scenes to
     treat the strife of filmmaking in terms of technical prob-
     lems and personality conflicts between Fellini and his
     producer, Alberto Grimaldi.

812 DRAGADZE, PETER. "Movies...Italian Style!" Town and Country,
     130, No. 4647 (September), 120 & 52-55.
          In the course of this general survey of contemporary
     Italian cinema, Dragadze interviews Fellini. Fellini dis-
     cusses the character of Casanova, his set for Casanova, the
     fact that Casanova is his first film in English, the break-
     ing up of modern society, the circus as a microcosm, and
     his interest in subjectivity.

813 FELLINI, FEDERICO. Letter to Andrea Zanzotto, in Filò: per
     il Casanova di Fellini by Andrea Zanzotto. Venice:
     Edizioni del Ruzante, pp. 7-10.
          Fellini's letter to the well-known, Italian poet Zanzotto
     inviting him to compose poems in early Venetian dialect for
     use in Casanova. Fellini discusses the two scenes where he
     wishes to use dialect: the carnival in Venice at the begin-
     ning of the movie and the scene with the giantess in her
     bath in London later in the film.

814 JANOS, LEO. "The New Fellini: Venice on Ice." Time, 107,
     No. 20 (17 May), 75-77. Illustrated.
          An article on Casanova, written during the last days of
     filming. Janos describes Fellini at work on the set. He
     discusses Fellini's conception of Casanova as "all shop
     front, a public figure striking attitudes...in short, a
     braggart Fascist," and Fellini's somewhat despotic manner
     of handling actor Donald Sutherland. The article gives
     many of the production figures.

815 KAEL, PAULINE. "Fellini's Roma," in Reeling. Boston: Little,
     Brown, pp. 25-27.
          Reprint of a review which appeared in New Yorker, 48,
     No. 35 (21 October 1972), 137-40.

816 KETCHAM, CHARLES B. Federico Fellini: The Search for a New
     Mythology. New York: Paulist Press, 94 pp.
          In the first part of this provocative examination of
     Fellini's "religious observations and ideas," Ketcham sur-
     veys various interviews with Fellini, including his own
     previously unpublished discussion with the director.
     Ketcham finds Fellini's existentialist beliefs similar to
     those of Sören Kierkegaard. He calls Fellini an

"ontological realist" who sees life as a continual process of living and questioning. This may explain Fellini's "improvisational" approach to filmmaking (Ketcham labels it "attentive passivity"). He also sees "ontological realism" as fundamental to Fellini's insistence on his own experiences in his films to illuminate universal experience. In the second half of the book Ketcham applies these observations to La Strada, La Dolce Vita, and 8½. He discusses the many Christian symbols which are central to La Strada. He provides an ingenious reading of La Dolce Vita based on the sacraments of the Roman Catholic Church. He isolates seven central sequences which correspond to the sacraments; but instead of leading Marcello to salvation, each episode chronicles his "spiritual death." Concerning 8½, Ketcham declares that "the religious statement has shifted from an objective biography to a subjective autobiography."

817   MORAVIA, ALBERTO. "Il seduttor scortese." L'espresso, 22, No. 52 (26 December), 90-91.
      A generally favorable review of Casanova. Moravia discusses the relationship between Casanova's physical energy and the moribund state of the dying, eighteenth-century world he lives in. Fellini depicts Casanova's dying world by using obviously artificial elements and by setting many scenes at night.

818   MURRAY, EDWARD. Fellini the Artist. New York: Frederick Ungar Publishing, 256 pp. Illustrated. Bibliography. Brief filmography.
      A critical book on Fellini's full-length films from The White Sheik through Amarcord. The first section is a biographical sketch of Fellini, and the second is a summary of Fellini's attitudes toward his art of filmmaking. In both sections, Murray draws extensively on the vast body of interview material previously published. The third and longest section is a film-by-film analysis of the form and content of Fellini's work. In this section, Murray offers close observation of how Fellini handles point of view, creates mood, and develops character and theme. Especially interesting are Murray's various observations about the effects Fellini achieves through camera angle, camera movement, and framing. The overview of Fellini which Murray offers in his concluding fourth section is that of a romantic artist concerned with the interplay of the real, what is, with the ideal, what ought to be. He finds Fellini influenced by his early Catholic background to the extent that redemption and hope are major themes for him. Further, Murray discusses the "personal" and "inclusive" qualities of Fellini's art. He finds a deterioration in Fellini's work since Fellini Satyricon, attributable at least in part to Fellini's turning away from the use of strong central characters.

819   PASCO, ALLAN H. "The Thematic Structure of Fellini's
      Amarcord." Film Studies Annual, pp. 259-71.
          In this reading of Amarcord, Pasco discusses the symbols
      inherent in the names of the characters, the many allusions
      to Italian literature, and the historical significance of
      much of the narrative action. However, his main interest
      concerns the way Fellini has structured his examination of
      the opposing forces of illusion and reality. Pasco finds a
      very tight structure, based on analogy, in which "each of
      the scenes turns around a conflict between true human values
      and those ever renewed dreams--whether sexual, intellectual,
      religious, or political--which dehumanize man."

820   RIVA, VALERIO. "Casanova, in arte Pinocchio." L'espresso,
      22, No. 22 (30 May), 90-105. Illustrated.
          An article on Casanova which Riva saw on an editing viewer
      during final cutting. He gives production costs and figures
      and discusses Donald Sutherland's make-up for the role of
      Casanova. Supported by some remarks made by Fellini, Riva
      argues that sex in the various sequences seems to satisfy
      the female protagonists, but exhaust or deplete Casanova.
      He describes sex as a "petite mort" for Casanova. Riva
      further stresses the symbolic importance of the giant,
      wooden head, seemingly held prisoner beneath the canal in
      Venice, as an image of Casanova. In interview, Fellini
      discusses a slight change in his attitude toward Casanova
      during the filming, a change from abhorrence of the charac-
      ter to a more tolerant view of him. The article is re-
      printed in condensed form in Gianfranco Angelucci's "Un
      film di carta stampata," in Il Casanova di Federico Fellini.
      Edited by Liliana Betti and Gianfranco Angelucci. Bologna:
      Cappelli editore, 1977. Pp. 71-73.

821   ROSENTHAL, STUART. The Cinema of Federico Fellini. London:
      Tantivy Press; New York: A. S. Barnes, 190 pp.
      Illustrated. Filmography. Credits.
          An excellent critical study of Fellini's works from
      Variety Lights through Amarcord. In the first chapter,
      Rosenthal deals with Fellini's use of objectivity (neutral
      point of view), subjectivity (a character's point of view),
      and personalism (the director's point of view). Especially
      interesting are Rosenthal's discussion of the function of
      the reporter as a subjective viewpoint in A Matrimonial
      Agency and his comparison of Fellini's films with those of
      Ingmar Bergman. In the second chapter, Rosenthal treats
      Fellini's symbolic use of locations, characters, objects,
      and animals to extend meaning or create tone. Some of the
      specific elements Rosenthal comments on are the forest,
      the sea, the city, the sea creature in La Dolce Vita, the
      horse in La Strada, Toby Dammit's Ferrari, and the peacock
      in Amarcord. Chapter Three covers Fellini's use of

spectacle to magnify the emotion and significance of a life
or an event, or to satirize something through exaggeration.
Rosenthal compares Fellini's spectacles with those of Busby
Berkeley. Chapter Four concerns Fellini's main characters,
especially Gelsomina, Cabiria, Juliet, Augusto, Marcello,
and Guido. Rosenthal argues that Fellini's characters are
people shut off from others. Fellini is concerned with
their need for relationships with other human beings and
concerned with the personal and social factors which frus-
trate the fulfillment of this need. Rosenthal discusses
also the tendency of the characters to cling to the security
and clarity of childhood as opposed to facing the uncertainty
of adult experience. In the fifth chapter, Rosenthal examines Fellini's treatments of the past in The Clowns, Roma,
and Amarcord. He finds in Amarcord a harder attitude toward
the past, provincial life, and childish fantasies than
Fellini has shown in other, previous films. All of
Rosenthal's arguments are carefully worked out. Perhaps
as important as his main arguments, though, are the separate
insights he provides into the individual films. Rosenthal
is extremely good at the close observation of films.

822   SNYDER, STEPHEN. "Color, Growth, and Evolution in Fellini
       Satyricon." Film Studies Annual, pp. 272-87.
         Snyder identifies and discusses two color patterns that
serve metaphoric purposes in Fellini Satyricon. The first
pattern, he calls "assimilative." The pattern calls attention to Enclopius' need to assimilate or immerse himself in
the physical world of nature. Snyder finds that four
colors (blue, red, white, and brown) dominate different
sections of the film and that these colors are analogous to
elements which Encolpius assimilates (water, fire, air, and
earth). The second pattern is "generative." Three times
in the film, Fellini follows a pattern of beginning with
black and white, establishing the three subtractive primary
colors (red, blue, and yellow), and then generating a pro-
fusion of secondary and tertiary colors from the primaries.
This "chromatic expansion," Snyder finds analogous to
Encolpius' need to expand or release his "procreative
capacities."

823   STRICH, CHRISTIAN, ed. Fellini on Fellini. Translated from
       the Italian by Isabel Quigley. New York: Delacorte Press/
       Seymour Lawrence, 180 pp. Illustrated. Filmography.
       Credits.
         An excellent compilation of essays by Fellini and inter-
views with him. Many of the pieces are translated into
English here for the first time. Also many of the pieces
are from Italian newspapers and journals which are difficult or impossible to obtain in the U.S.A. Some of the
major essays and interviews are the following. "Rimini,

My Home Town," which appeared first as "Il mio paese," in
La mia Rimini. Edited by Renzo Renzi. Bologna: Cappelli
editore, 1967. Pp. 23-43. "Sweet Beginnings," which was
first available in English in Atlas, 3, No. 2 (February,
1962), 149-52. "Via Veneto: Dolce Vita," which first
appeared as "La storia di via Veneto." L'europeo, 18,
No. 27 (8 July 1962), 49-61. "The Bitter Life--of Money,"
which appeared first in Films and Filming, 17, No. 4
(January 1961), 13 & 38. "Why Clowns?" which appeared first
as "Un viaggio nell'ombra," in I Clowns. Edited by Renzo
Renzi. Bologna: Cappelli editore, 1970. Pp. 27-56. "Whom
Do You Most Admire?" which appeared first as Renato
Barneschi's "Wallace mi insegno a fare il ladro di polli."
Oggi, 28, No. 7 (12 February 1972), 47-50. "The Birth of a
Film," which appeared earlier as "In teatro persino il
mare," in Il film Amarcord di Federico Fellini. Bologna:
Cappelli editore, 1974. Pp. 89-97. [All of the above are
annotated under the earlier entry.] Additional material
deals with Fellini's attitudes toward Marxist criticism of
La Strada, with his religious point of view in La Strada,
with the reception of 8½ in Moscow, with Fellini's attitude
toward censorship, and with his fondness for comic strips.

824   _____, ed. Fellini's Filme. Zurich: Diogenes Verlag, 344 pp.
Illustrated. Credits.
    Illustrations, descriptions, and credits from Fellini's
films from Variety Lights to Casanova. A brief introduction
by Georges Simenon. The texts are in German.

825   _____, ed. Fellini's Zeichnungen. Zurich: Diogenes Verlag,
136 pp. Illustrated.
    Drawings by Fellini ranging from sketches for early films
such as The White Sheik, I Vitelloni, and La Strada to
sketches for Casanova. Incidental caricatures and drawings
are also included. There is a brief foreword in German by
Roland Topor.

826   TASSONE, ALDO. "Entretien avec Federico Fellini." Translated by Françoise Pieri. Positif, No. 181 (May),
pp. 4-12, and No. 182 (June), pp. 34-43. Illustrated.
    French translation of an interview Tassone held with
Fellini in Rome during August, 1975, during work on
Casanova. In his introduction, Tassone states that Fellini's
major qualities are irony, imagination, and ambiguity. In
the interview, Fellini describes the void of Casanova's life.
For Fellini, Casanova passed through his life of apparent
adventure and intellectual stimulation with virtually no
human response. Fellini expresses revulsion for such a
man. The film will be an exposure of the void of Casanova's
life, and it will be anti-cinematic. Fellini, however,
hopes to avoid falling back on utopian discourses. His aim

must be no less than to unmask the lie, to identify the inauthentic, and to dismantle pseudo-absolutes. He comments briefly on the false distinction in films between form and content, on his apoliticalness in the narrow sense of the word "political," on the impact of the myths of the Catholic church on him, on his liking for the films of Kubrick and Buñuel, on his feelings about music, on his aversion to seeing rushes because they only approximate his hopes, on the play of memory and invention in his works, on lighting, and on the constant complaints in Italy that the cinema is on its last legs. Included among the illustrations are some sketches by Fellini.

827 VOLTA, ORNELLA. "Fellini 1976." *Positif*, No. 181 (May), pp. 2-3. Illustrated.
    Volta speculates that Fellini's work is growing darker. *Fellini Satyricon*, *Roma*, and *Amarcord* demonstrate his interest in the "biography" of a society (as opposed to an individual). The society evolves and changes almost in contempt of the individuals who make it up. *Casanova*, she argues, will extend this tendency. It will be a cold, opaque film with little reassurance offered to the audience about the human condition.

1977

828 ANGELUCCI, GIANFRANCO. "Un film di carta stampata," in *Il Casanova di Federico Fellini*. Edited by Liliana Betti and Gianfranco Angelucci. Bologna: Cappelli editore, pp. 15-76.
    Angelucci traces the evolution of Fellini's *Casanova* chronologically by means of newspaper and magazine articles about it. What unfolds is a typical Fellini film venture replete with thorny casting problems and disagreements with producers over money. Most interesting of the articles are: Alberto Moravia's "Casanova era un insetto." *L'espresso*, 21, No. 49 (7 December 1975), 105; and Valerio Riva's "Casanova, in arte Pinocchio." *L'espresso*, 22, No. 22 (30 May 1976), 90-105.

829 CANBY, VINCENT. "Sometimes the Decor Is The Thing." *New York Times* (27 February), p. 17.
    A brief discussion of production design techniques in Fellini's *Casanova*, Alain Resnais' *Providence*, and Wim Wenders' *The Goalie's Anxiety at the Penalty Kick*. Canby finds *Casanova* "dazzling to look at but... surprisingly pious."

830 CRIST, JUDITH. "Fellini without Feeling." *Saturday Review*, 4, No. 10 (19 February), 40-41. Illustrated.

A review of <u>Casanova</u>. Crist describes the film as "a stunning studio creation, a fascination for the eye, a bemusement for the intellect, and a void for the heart." She notes Fellini's self-detachment from his protagonist, but praises his depiction of the world Casanova passes through. Fellini's fantasy is "so deeply textured that it counteracts the director's alienation."

831   DAVIS, MELTON S. "Conversation with Federico Fellini." <u>Oui</u>, 6, No. 1 (January), 91-92 & 154-56.
       An interview with Fellini, largely about <u>Casanova</u>. Fellini describes his relations with producers in the past and on the Casanova project. Fellini sees Casanova as a man who never existed in any meaningful sense of the word. Fellini feels that Casanova's memoirs were an attempt by Casanova to convince himself that he really did live. Casanova avoided responsibility and lived in the comfortable conviction that everything would come from on high. In his attitude toward women, Casanova was infantile and rhetorical; he asserted his virility and had a sexist attitude toward women. He exalted women, treated them as objects, and finally discarded them. Fellini talks briefly of the theft of some of the film shot for the movie, his reasons for choosing Donald Sutherland, and his distaste for a version of the script done by Gore Vidal. He tells a fine tall tale about communicating with Casanova through a medium.

832   HATCH, ROBERT. "Films." <u>Nation</u>, 224, No. 8 (26 February), 252-53.
       An unfavorable review of <u>Casanova</u> which questions Fellini's distaste for his main character. "Casanova was a scoundrel but he was not a buffoon, and to play him as though he were drains the film of what zest it might have."

833   JOHNSON, ALBERT. "Fellini's <u>Casanova</u>: Con." <u>Film Quarterly</u>, 30, No. 4 (Summer), 30-31. Illustrated.
       Second part of a two-part series on <u>Casanova</u>. Johnson attacks the film as "an obvious pandering to the lowest popular taste." The subject is the emotional impotence of Casanova. Johnson states: "The sophomoric tone keeps every sexual nuance lingering between a snicker and a sneer; Fellini's cynicism...represents the triumph of misogyny over art." Johnson does praise the sequence where DuBois stages a mock opera-ballet as discreetly witty. Also, he praises the set designs of Danilo Donati, especially in the opening sequence in Venice which reminds Johnson of the paintings of Tiepolo.

834   KAUFFMANN, STANLEY. "Fellini's <u>Casanova</u>." <u>New Republic</u>, 176, No. 10 (5 March), 28-29.

Kauffmann divides Fellini's career in two: the neo-realist films of 1950-1959 and the more "ornate" films which followed. When Fellini fails in either period, it is because of the distance of the story from his own life (e.g., La Dolce Vita and Fellini Satyricon). Kauffmann says this is why Casanova is "the closest thing to a completely boring work that Fellini has done."

835 KROLL, JACK. "A Sterile Casanova." Newsweek, 89, No. 4 (24 January), 60-61. Illustrated.
An attacking review of Casanova. Kroll describes the film as Fellini's attempt "to exorcise the antiself he recognizes in Casanova." Casanova's History of My Life, Kroll finds "perhaps our most encyclopedic account of the sheer attempt to live life amid the storm of circumstance." He laments that Fellini has reduced these memoirs to a lecture on the emptiness of lechery. Casanova is the "first Fellini movie in which there is no joy." The movie seems to Kroll a "horror movie" because of Fellini's life-less and mechanical depictions of his characters.

836 PORTERFIELD, CHRISTOPHER. "Waxwork Narcissus." Time, 109, No. 8 (21 February), 70. Illustrated.
An attacking review of Casanova. Porterfield discusses possible aspects of Casanova's career that could have been treated by Fellini and expresses disappointment at Fellini's reductive treatment of the man. Porterfield finds the film a sombre meditation on Casanova's life. Sin is made re-pellent, and the episodes are made inert and static.

837 ROBBINS, FRED. "Sutherland on Fellini." Oui, 6, No. 1 (January), 156-57. Illustrated.
An interview with Donald Sutherland, largely about his work with Fellini on Casanova. Sutherland states that he is more sympathetic to Casanova than Fellini is. For Fellini, Casanova "represents the epitome of an Italian masculine trait: infantile shallowness." For Sutherland, however, Casanova was "a great wit." He would fall in love, have great expectations, and then cool off shortly after-wards. Pathetically, Casanova's life would repeat this pattern over and over. Sutherland talks also of the experi-ence of working under Fellini's direction.

838 SCHWARTZMAN, PAUL. "Fellini's Unlovable Casanova." New York Times Magazine (6 February), pp. 21-22, 24, 28 & 32-33. Illustrated.
Schwartzman describes Fellini's methods of handling actors on the set of Casanova. He discusses particularly the relationship between Fellini and Donald Sutherland. In addition, Schwartzman defines Casanova as "modern man: self-preoccupied, yet alienated from himself; plunging into

experience, yet alienated from others." Casanova lacks
tragically the trait so prominent in Fellini himself, critical self-awareness.

839   WELSH, JAMES M. "Fellini's Casanova." Films In Review, 28,
      No. 4 (April), 245-46.
         A favorable review of Casanova which stresses the co-
      herence of Fellini's "disturbingly bleak vision of the human
      animal trapped in a systemic universe."

840   WESTERBECK, COLIN L., JR. "The Screen." Commonweal, 104,
      No. 8 (15 April), 240-41; 104, No. 9 (29 April), 277-78.
         A review of Casanova. Westerbeck finds Casanova a per-
      fect character for Fellini precisely because the director
      is so scornful of him. "Fellini works best when he works
      by a kind of aversion." Casanova is yet another in the long
      line of Fellini's grotesques and clowns.

841   WILLIS, DON. "Fellini's Casanova: Pro." Film Quarterly, 30,
      No. 4 (Summer), 24-30. Illustrated.
         One part of a two-part series on Casanova. Willis de-
      fends the film. Willis states, "Fellini's Casanova is a
      comic hero, an idealist lost in a world of sensualists.
      His gallantry undercuts that world's crassness; its blunt-
      ness undercuts him." Willis finds the "core metaphor" of
      the film to be man-as-machine. He stresses Fellini's use
      of circular motion and of bird imagery. Willis attacks
      the dubbing in the film. He feels that the flatness of the
      dialogue detracts from the film's visual density.

Writings, Performances
and Other Film Related Activity

<u>Published Screenplays and Dialogues of</u>
<u>Films Directed by Fellini</u>

1952

842 FELLINI, FEDERICO, ENNIO FLAIANO, and TULLIO PINELLI. "<u>I</u>
     <u>Vitelloni</u>." <u>Cinema</u> (nuova serie), 8, Nos. 99-100 (15-31
     December), 289-93. Illustrated.
          The story treatment of <u>I Vitelloni</u>. [No copy of <u>Cinema</u>
     (nuova serie) could be found in the U.S.A. A copy was
     located, however, at the <u>Centro sperimentale di cinema-</u>
     <u>tografia</u> in Rome. JCS]

1954

843 FELLINI, FEDERICO, ENNIO FLAIANO, and TULLIO PINELLI. <u>Moraldo</u>
     <u>in città</u>. <u>Cinema</u> (nuova serie), 12, No. 139 (10 August),
     459-62; No. 142 (10 October), 593-94; No. 144 (10 November),
     657-58; No. 145 (25 November), 686; Nos. 146-47 (10-25
     December), 718 & 743-44.
          Screenplay of Fellini's unrealized film project <u>Moraldo</u>
     <u>in the City</u>. The film was intended as a continuation of
     the story of Moraldo, the character in <u>I Vitelloni</u>, after
     his flight from his provincial town to Rome. [No copies of
     <u>Cinema</u> (nuova serie) containing the screenplay could be
     located in the U.S.A. A copy was found, however, in the
     library of the <u>Centro sperimentale di cinematografia</u> in
     Rome. JCS]

844 FELLINI, FEDERICO and TULLIO PINELLI. "10,000 lire per una
     moglie." <u>Cinema nuovo</u>, 3, No. 39 (15 July), 14.
     Illustrated.
          Dialogue of the opening sequence of <u>La Strada</u>.

845 _____. <u>La strada</u>. <u>Bianco e nero</u>, 15, Nos. 9-10 (September-
     October), 9-178. Illustrated.

The original screenplay in Italian. The screenplay contains material not contained in the final version, such as
a scene where Gelsomina must push Zampano's vehicle, a scene
in which Gelsomina watches a lady in her home through a window and listens to the music of the lady's radio, and a
scene in which Gelsomina speaks with an ox which she is
told sees ghosts. Two drawings of Gelsomina by Fellini are
included.

1955

846   BASTIDE, FRANÇOIS-RÉGIS, JULIETTE CAPUTO, and CHRIS MARKER,
eds. La Strada. Paris: Éditions du seuil, 119 pp.
Illustrated. Filmography.
    This work contains the cutting continuity and dialogue
of La Strada in slightly condensed form, numerous photographs, reproductions of parts of the musical score, of
sketches of Gelsomina by Fellini, and of early cartoons by
Fellini, and a long interview with Giulietta Masina and
Fellini.

847   PINELLI, TULLIO. "Ce que disait 'le fou.'" Translated by
Laura Mauri. Cahiers du Cinéma, No. 45 (March), pp. 16-19.
    French translation of the original dialogue spoken be-
tween Gelsomina and the Fool in La Strada, in which the
Fool explains that everything in the universe may have a
purpose. This original dialogue has been shortened in the
film. A version translated into English by Rosalie Siegel
appears in: Gilbert Salachas. Federico Fellini. New York:
Crown, 1969. Pp. 125-31.

1956

848   FELLINI, FEDERICO, ENNIO FLAIANO, and TULLIO PINELLI. Il
Bidone. Translated by Dominique Delouche. Paris:
Flammarion, 228 pp. Illustrated.
    The screenplay in French.

1957

849   FELLINI, FEDERICO. "Les Femmes libres de Magliano." Cahiers
du Cinéma, No. 68 (February), pp. 8-14. Illustrated.
    French version of Fellini's treatment of Mario Tupino's
book of the same title. The project was never realized.
An English translation of the treatment by Rosalie Siegel
appears in: Gilbert Salachas. Federico Fellini. New York:
Crown, 1969. Pp. 163-70.

850   _____. <u>Le notti di Cabiria di Federico Fellini</u>. Edited by
       Lino del Fra. Rocca San Casciano: Cappelli editore,
       239 pp. Illustrated. Credits.
          Screenplay in Italian. Also included are an introduction
       by Lino del Fra and essays by Giulietta Masina, Tullio
       Pinelli, and Pier Paolo Pasolini.

851   _____. "<u>Les Nuits de Cabiria</u>: extraits du dernier film de
       <u>Fellini</u>." <u>Cahiers du Cinéma</u>, No. 68 (February), pp. 15-24.
       Illustrated.
          French version of the script for the sequence in <u>Nights</u>
       <u>of Cabiria</u> where Cabiria spends the night in the movie
       star's villa.

1960

852   FELLINI, FEDERICO. <u>La Dolce Vita</u>. Edited by Giuseppe Lo Duca.
       [Paris]: J. J. Pauvert, 170 pp. Illustrated.
          A photographic reconstruction of the movie. Most of the
       photographs are stills, but there are also some frame en-
       largements. Captions and pieces of dialogue provide
       continuity.

853   _____. <u>La dolce vita di Federico Fellini</u>. Edited by Tullio
       Kezich. Bologna: Cappelli editore, 279 pp. Illustrated.
       Credits.
          Screenplay in Italian of <u>La Dolce Vita</u>, preceded by a
       lengthy diary by Tullio Kezich about the filming from pre-
       liminary preparations to completion.

854   _____. <u>La Douceur de vivre</u>. Edited by Giuseppe Lo Duca.
       Translated by Marie-Charlotte Guillaume. Paris: Julliard,
       1960. 227 pp.
          French translation of the screenplay of <u>La Dolce Vita</u>.
       The preface is Lo Duca's heartfelt, if bombastic, hymn to
       Fellini's courage in making his film a denunciation of the
       modern world's vacuity.

1961

855   FELLINI, FEDERICO. <u>La Dolce Vita</u>. Translated by Oscar DeLiso
       and Bernard Shir-Cliff. New York: Ballantine Books,
       276 pp. Illustrated. Credits.
          English translation of the screenplay. The preface is
       a reprinting of Hollis Alpert's review: "Adventures of a
       Journalist." <u>Saturday Review</u>, 44, No. 15 (15 April 1961),
       33.

1962

856   FELLINI, FEDERICO. Boccaccio '70 di De Sica, Fellini,
      Monicelli, Visconti. Edited by Carlo Di Carlo and Gaio
      Fratini. Rocca San Casciano: Cappelli editore, 226 pp.
      Illustrated. Credits.
            Screenplay in Italian of Boccaccio '70. Screenplays for
      the original four parts are included. [One directed by
      Mario Monicelli was cut from the film just prior to expor-
      tation. JCS] Part of the prefatory matter is a diary by
      Gaio Fratini covering day-to-day events in the filming of
      the parts, especially The Temptations of Doctor Antonio.
      The story treatment and a statement by the director pre-
      cede each screenplay.

1963

857   FELLINI, FEDERICO. 8½ de Fellini. Histoire d'un film raconté
      par Camilla Cederna. Translated by H. de Mariassy and
      C. de Lignac. Paris: Rene Julliard, 218 pp. Illustrated.
      Credits.
            French translation of 8½ di Federico Fellini. Edited by
      Camilla Cederna. Rocca San Casciano: Cappelli editore,
      1963.

858   _____. 8½ di Federico Fellini. Edited by Camilla Cederna.
      Rocca San Casciano: Cappelli editore, 155 pp. Illustrated.
      Credits.
            Screenplay in Italian. The screenplay differs from the
      finished film. It contains, for example, Fellini's orig-
      inal ending in the dining car of a train. Many of the
      scenes with Claudia differ from those in the released film.
      The sequence of the screen tests in the movie theater comes
      earlier in the screenplay. And the harem sequence con-
      cludes with two scenes not contained in the film.

1965

859   FELLINI, FEDERICO. Giulietta degli spiriti. Edited by Tullio
      Kezich. Rocca San Casciano: Cappelli editore, 177 pp.
      Illustrated. Credits.
            The screenplay in Italian of Juliet of the Spirits.
      The finished film differs in several details from the
      screenplay. For example, the grandfather in the screenplay
      flies in a balloon as opposed to the bi-plane of the movie,
      and Suzy makes her first entrance by helicopter as opposed
      to the barge in the film. The edition contains an inter-
      view of Fellini conducted by Kezich.

860   _____. <u>Juliet of the Spirits</u>. Edited by Tullio Kezich.
Translated by Howard Greenfeld. New York: Orion Press,
181 pp. Illustrated. Credits.
    Screenplay in English. Included is an introduction by
Tullio Kezich and an interview of Fellini by Kezich.

861   _____. <u>8½ di Federico Fellini</u>. Edited by Camilla Cederna.
Rocca San Casciano: Cappelli editore, 190 pp. Illustrated.
Credits.
    A reprinting of <u>8½ di Federico Fellini</u>. Edited by
Camilla Cederna. Rocca San Casciano: Cappelli editore,
1963. This edition has added to it the screenplay of <u>The
Temptations of Doctor Antonio</u>.

1966

862 FELLINI, FEDERICO. "<u>Huit et demi</u>." <u>L'Avant-Scène</u>, No. 63
(October), pp. 1-92. Illustrated. Credits. Filmography.
    The screenplay in French. The screenplay contains some
material (carefully marked) which is not included in the
released movie. It contains, for example, Fellini's alternate ending, set in a train's dining car. Short introductory essays by Gilbert Salachas and René Gibson and excerpts
from reviews in the French and Italian papers and journals
are included.

863   _____. <u>Juliet of the Spirits</u>. Edited by Tullio Kezich.
Translated by Howard Greenfeld. Transcription of the
final screenplay by John Cohen. New York: Ballantine
Books, 318 pp. Illustrated. Credits.
    Screenplay in English and a transcription in English of
the final continuity script.

1968

864 FELLINI, FEDERICO, LOUIS MALLE, and ROGER VADIM. <u>Tre passi
nel delirio</u>. Edited by Liliana Betti, Ornella Volta, and
Bernardino Zapponi. Bologna: Cappelli editore, 227 pp.
Illustrated. Credits.
    Screenplay in Italian of <u>Spirits of the Dead</u>. Also in-
cluded are introductory essays by Liliana Betti, Bernardino
Zapponi, and Ornella Volta and an Italian translation of
Edgar Allan Poe's "Don't Bet the Devil Your Head."

1969

865 FELLINI, FEDERICO. <u>Fellini Satyricon di Federico Fellini</u>.
Edited by Dario Zanelli. Bologna: Cappelli editore, 303 pp.
Illustrated. Credits.

Screenplay in Italian. Material cut from the film is noted. Also included are the story treatment, pages of the Latin dialogue and introductory essays by Dario Zanelli, Bernardino Zapponi, Luca Canali, and actress Betsy Langman.

866   FELLINI, FEDERICO. <u>Il primo Fellini. Lo sceicco bianco, I vitelloni, La strada, Il bidone</u>. Edited by Renzo Renzi. Bologna: Cappelli editore, 326 pp. Illustrated. Credits.
    Screenplays in Italian of <u>The White Sheik</u>, <u>I Vitelloni</u>, <u>La Strada</u>, and <u>Il Bidone</u>. Also included is an introductory essay by Renzo Renzi.

1970

867   FELLINI, FEDERICO. <u>I clowns</u>. Edited by Renzo Renzi. Bologna: Cappelli editore, 414 pp. Illustrated. Credits.
    A large, deluxe edition of the screenplay of <u>The Clowns</u>. Included in the volume is Fellini's essay "Un viaggio nell'ombra," Oreste del Buono's essay "Da Fortunello a Giudizio, passando per Little Nemo," Bernardino Zapponi's essay "A Parigi, una recherche del circo perduto," and Liliana Betti's essay "Un'entrata di Federico e le rivelazioni di un maghino in trance." The edition includes also letters to Fellini in 1970 by Red Skelton, by Pierre Etaix and Annie Fratellini, and by Groucho Marx. (Groucho Marx, however, disclaims any real knowledge of clowns.) Numerous documents on the history and the art of clowns, in addition, are contained in the volume, including Ornella Volta's "Breve dizionario enciclopedio dei clowns." Illustrations in color of shots from <u>The Clowns</u> and illustrations in black and white of materials from clown history.

868   _____. <u>Fellini's Satyricon</u>. Edited by Dario Zanelli. Translated by Eugene Walter and John Matthews. New York: Ballantine Books, 280 pp. Illustrated. Credits.
    Screenplay in English. Material cut from the film is noted. Also included are the story treatment and introductory essays by Dario Zanelli, Alberto Moravia, Bernardino Zapponi, and Fellini.

869   _____. <u>La Strada</u>. <u>L'Avant-Scène</u>, No. 102 (April), pp. 1-52. Illustrated. Credits.
    The cutting continuity and dialogue of <u>La Strada</u>. This version contains some scenes, clearly marked, which were deleted from the final version of the film. The deletions include scenes where Gelsomina must push the caravan of Zampano; where she hears for the first time, while standing in shelter from the rain, the song which she will make hers; and where she discovers in the barn where she is to sleep,

318

an ox who trembles because he sees ghosts. The script is followed by brief excerpts from French and Italian reviews.

870 _____. Three Screenplays. Translated by Judith Green. New York: Orion Press, 287 pp. Illustrated. Credits.
Screenplays in English of I Vitelloni, Il Bidone, and The Temptations of Doctor Antonio.

1971

871 FELLINI, FEDERICO. Early Screenplays: Variety Lights, The White Sheik. Translated by Judith Green. New York: Grossman Publishers, 198 pp. Illustrated.
Screenplays in English of Variety Lights and The White Sheik.

1972

872 FELLINI, FEDERICO. Fellini TV. Block-notes di un regista. I clowns. Edited by Renzo Renzi. Bologna: Cappelli editore, 213 pp. Illustrated.
Screenplays in Italian of A Director's Notebook and The Clowns. Also included are introductory essays by Renzo Renzi and Fellini.

873 _____. Roma. L'Avant-Scène, No. 129 (October), 5-72. Illustrated.
The cutting continuity and dialogue of Roma. This version contains some scenes which were deleted from the final version of the film. (They are clearly marked as deletions.) Two such scenes are interviews in Trastevere with Marcello Mastroianni and with Alberto Sordi. The script is followed by brief excerpts of French reviews and a filmography.

874 _____. Roma. Paris: Raoul Solar, 220 pp.
French edition of Roma. The edition is the dialogue and continuity of the edited film.

875 _____. Roma di Federico Fellini. Edited by Bernardino Zapponi. Rocca San Casciano: Editrice Licinio Cappelli, 374 pp. Illustrated. Credits.
Two drafts of the screenplay in Italian. Also included are introductory articles by Bernardino Zapponi, Luca Canali, and Gerald Morin.

1973

876   FELLINI, FEDERICO and TONINO GUERRA. Amarcord. Milan:
       Rizzoli editore, 156 pp.
            Story treatment in Italian of Amarcord, written as a
       novel. Significantly different from the final film ver-
       sion. The story treatment, for example, contains a sequence
       about a summer squall that strikes the village, which is
       not contained in the final film.

1974

877   FELLINI, FEDERICO. Il film Amarcord di Federico Fellini.
       Edited by Gianfranco Angelucci and Liliana Betti. Bologna:
       Cappelli editore, 330 pp. Illustrated. Credits.
            The screenplay in Italian of Amarcord. Also included
       are introductory essays by Gianfranco Angelucci, Enzo
       Siciliano, and Liliana Betti and Fellini's essay on Rimini,
       "Il mio paese" published originally in La mia Rimini.
       Bologna: Cappelli editore, 1967. Pp. 23-43.

878   _____. Quattro film: I vitelloni, La dolce vita, 8½,
       Giulietta degli spiriti. Turin: Giulio Einaudi, 493 pp.
       Illustrated.
            Screenplays of I Vitelloni, La Dolce Vita, 8½ and Juliet
       of the Spirits, with an introductory essay by Italian
       novelist Italo Calvino. There are some differences between
       the screenplays and the finished movies. 8½, for instance,
       contains a scene of the marriage between Guido and Luisa
       and a final sequence in a dining car of a train, both of
       which are cut from the film, and La Dolce Vita contains
       scenes between Marcello and a middle-aged female writer
       named Dolores, which are not in the film.

879   FELLINI, FEDERICO and BERNARDINO ZAPPONI. Il Casanova di
       Fellini: sceneggiatura originale. Turin: Einaudi editore,
       155 pp. Illustrated.
            Original screenplay in Italian for Casanova. In the
       actual filming, some of the material in this version was
       cut or altered, and some additional material was added.
       For example, a sequence set in Turkey described in the
       original screenplay does not survive in the finished film.
       The ending of the sequence with the giantess is altered and
       softened from the original screenplay in the film. And the
       dance with the mechanical doll on the frozen canal, which
       ends the movie, is an addition. It was not contained in
       the original screenplay.

880   FELLINI, FEDERICO and TONINO GUERRA. Amarcord: Portrait of a
       Town. Translated by Nina Rootes. London: Abelard-Schuman,
       124 pp.

320

Story treatment in English of <u>Amarcord</u>, written as a
novel. Significantly different from the final film version.
The story treatment, for example, contains a sequence about
a summer squall that strikes the village, which is not contained in the final film.

881 ZANZOTTO, ANDREA. <u>Filò: per il Casanova di Fellini</u>. Venice:
Edizioni del Ruzante, 97 pp. Illustrated.
An edition containing the poems in early Venetian dialect
by Zanzotto for Fellini's <u>Casanova</u>. The edition contains
five sketches by Fellini. Fellini's letter to Zanzotto in-
viting him to compose the songs and poems serves as a preface to the edition.

1977

882 FELLINI, FEDERICO and BERNARDINO ZAPPONI. <u>Il Casanova di</u>
<u>Federico Fellini</u>. Edited by Gianfranco Angelucci and
Liliana Betti. Bologna: Cappelli editore, 206 pp.
Illustrated. Credits.
Screenplay of the film in Italian, as transcribed by
Liliana Betti from the film. The screenplay is prefaced by
an essay by Gianfranco Angelucci.

883 ZAPPONI, BERNARDINO. <u>Casanova: In un romanzo la storia del</u>
<u>film di Fellini</u>. Milan: Mondadori editore, 146 pp.
A version of <u>Casanova</u> in Italian written in the form of
a novel.

Work as Screenwriter

1939

884 <u>Lo vedi come sei?</u> [Do You Know What You Look Like?], directed
by Mario Mattoli, for the comedian Erminio Macario.
Fellini was a gag writer.

1940

885 <u>Non me lo dire</u> [Don't Tell Me], directed by Mario Mattoli, for
Erminio Macario. Fellini was a gag writer.

886 <u>Il pirato sono io</u> [I Am the Pirate], directed by Mario Mattoli,
for Erminio Macario. Fellini was a gag writer.

1941

887   <u>Documento Z3</u> [Document Z3], directed by Alfredo Guarini.
       Fellini collaborated on the screenplay.

1942

888   <u>Avanti, c'è posto</u> [Come On, There's Room], directed by Mario
       Bonnard, with Aldo Fabrizi. Fellini collaborated on the
       screenplay.

889   <u>Chi l'ha visto?</u> [Who Has Seen Him?], directed by Goffredo
       Alessandrini. Fellini collaborated on the story treatment
       and the screenplay.

890   <u>Quarta pagina</u> [The Fourth Page], directed by Nicola Manzari
       and Domenico Gambino. Fellini collaborated on the story
       treatment and screenplay.

1943

891   <u>Apparizione</u> [Apparition], directed by Jean de Limur. Fellini
       collaborated on the screenplay.

892   <u>Campo dei fiori</u> [Field of Flowers], directed by Mario Bonnard,
       with Aldo Fabrizi. Fellini collaborated on the screenplay.

893   <u>Tutta la città canta</u> [The Whole City Sings], directed by
       Riccardo Freda. Fellini collaborated on the screenplay.

894   <u>L'ultima carrozzella</u> [The Last Merry-Go-Round], directed by
       Mario Mattoli, with Aldo Fabrizi. Fellini collaborated on
       the screenplay.

1945

895   <u>Roma, città operta</u> [Rome, Open City], directed by Roberto
       Rossellini. Fellini collaborated on the screenplay.

1946

896   <u>Paisà</u> [Paisan], directed by Roberto Rossellini. Fellini col-
       laborated on the story treatment and the screenplay.

1947

897 Il delitto di Giovanni Episcopo [Flesh Will Surrender],
     directed by Alberto Lattuada. Fellini collaborated on the
     screenplay. The film was adapted from a novel by Gabriele
     d'Annunzio.

898 Il passatore [Bullet for Stefano], directed by Dulio Coletti.
     Fellini collaborated on the screenplay with Tullio Pinelli.

1948

899 Il miracolo [The Miracle], an episode in L'amore [Love],
     directed by Roberto Rossellini. Fellini wrote the story
     treatment by himself and collaborated on the screenplay.

900 Il mulino del Po [The Mill on the Po], directed by Alberto
     Lattuada. The film was adapted from a novel of the same
     name by Riccardo Bacchelli. Fellini collaborated on the
     screenplay. Tullio Pinelli also worked on the screenplay.

901 In nome della legge [In the Name of the Law/Mafia], directed
     by Pietro Germi. The movie is adapted from the novel
     Piccola pretura by G. E. Losciavo. Fellini and Tullio
     Pinelli collaborated on the screenplay.

902 Senza pietà [Without Pity], directed by Alberto Lattuada.
     Fellini collaborated on the screenplay along with Tullio
     Pinelli.

1949

903 Francesco, giullare di Dio [Flowers of St. Francis], directed
     by Roberto Rossellini, with Aldo Fabrizi. Otello Martelli
     was the camera director. The movie was based on I fioretti
     di Francesco d'Assisi. Fellini collaborated on the
     screenplay.

1950

904 Il cammino della speranza [The Path of Hope], directed by
     Pietro Germi. The film is adapted from Nino di Maria's
     novel Cuori su gli abissi. Fellini collaborated on the
     story treatment and the screenplay. Tullio Pinelli also
     worked on the screenplay.

1951

905   La città si difende [Passport to Hell/Four Ways Out], directed
       by Pietro Germi. Fellini collaborated on the story treat-
       ment and the screenplay.

1952

906   Il brigante di Tacca del Lupo [The Brigand of Tacca del Lupo],
       directed by Pietro Germi. The movie was adapted from a
       story by Riccardo Bacchelli. Fellini collaborated on the
       screenplay.

907   Europa '51, directed by Roberto Rossellini. Fellini collabo-
       rated on the screenplay. Giulietta Masina plays a part in
       the film.

1958

908   Fortunella, directed by Eduardo De Filippo. Fellini collabo-
       rated on the screenplay. Tullio Pinelli and Ennio Flaiano
       also worked on the screenplay. Giulietta Masina stars in
       the film.

Work as Assistant Director

1945

909   Roma, città aperta [Rome, Open City], directed by Roberto
       Rossellini.

1946

910   Paisà [Paisan], directed by Roberto Rossellini.

1948

911   Il miracolo [The Miracle], an episode in L'amore [Love],
       directed by Roberto Rossellini.

1949

912   Francesco, giullare di Dio [Flowers of St. Francis], directed
       by Roberto Rossellini.

Work as Actor

1948

913   Il miracolo [The Miracle], directed by Roberto Rossellini.
      with his hair dyed blond, Fellini plays the part of a
      stranger who is mistaken by a simple shepherdess (Anna
      Magnani) for St. Joseph. Fellini does not speak.

1970

914   Alex in Wonderland, directed by Paul Mazursky. Fellini appears
      briefly as himself.

Note: Fellini appears on camera as himself in three of his movies:
Fellini: A Director's Notebook, The Clowns, and Roma. [It has been
claimed that he played a very small part as a client in the agency of
A Matrimonial Agency, but after repeated viewings, I could not con-
firm this. ML]

Unfinished Film Projects

1954

915   Moraldo in città [Moraldo in the City].
      This was written by Fellini, Ennio Flaiano, and Tullio
      Pinelli as a sequel to I Vitelloni. Material from it was
      used in La Dolce Vita. The screenplay has been published
      in Italian in Cinema (nuova serie), No. 139 (10 August 1954),
      pp. 459-62; No. 142 (10 October 1954), pp. 593-94; No. 144
      (10 November 1954), pp. 657-58; No. 145 (25 November 1954),
      p. 686; Nos. 146-47 (10-25 December 1954), pp. 718 & 743-
      44. [No copies of these issues of Cinema (nuova serie)
      could be found in the U.S.A. However, copies were located
      in the Centro sperimentale di cinematografia in Rome. JCS]

1957

916   Le donne libere di Magliano [The Free Women of Magliano].
      This project was to be based on Mario Tupino's book of the
      same title. The film deals with a doctor who begins work
      in an insane asylum. The story treatment was published in
      French in Cahiers du Cinéma, No. 68 (February 1957), pp. 8-
      14. An English version appears in Gilbert Salachas'
      Federico Fellini: An Investigation into His Films and
      Philosophy. Translated by Rosalie Siegel. New York:
      Crown Publishers, 1969. Pp. 163-70.

1966-1967

917   Il viaggio di G. Mastorna [The Voyage of G. Mastorna].
      A film about a 'cello player's flight into a world of
      fantasy. Avant-garde writer Dino Buzzatti was a collabo-
      rator. Marcello Mastroianni was cast as Mastorna. Parts
      of the set were filmed in Fellini's documentary, Fellini:
      A Director's Notebook.

Documentaries About Fellini

1970

918   Ciao Federico!, directed by Gideon Bachmann. Color. 60
      minutes. American Distributor: Macmillan/Audio Brandon
      Films, Mount Vernon, N.Y.
      The movie consists of interviews with Fellini shot on
      the set of Fellini Satyricon. It is especially good in
      showing Fellini at work.

919   Fellini: The Director As Creator. Edited by Michael Misch.
      Black and white. 27 minutes. American distributor:
      Harold Mantell, Inc., New York, N.Y. "Films for the
      Humanities."
      On Fellini's manner of directing. Much of the footage
      shows behind-the-scenes work on Juliet of the Spirits. The
      narrator comments on Fellini's fascination with faces, the
      balance of improvisation and use of screenplay in Fellini's
      directing, the balance of tyranny and playfulness on a
      Fellini set, the teamwork of Fellini and Giulietta Masina,
      Fellini's vanity, and Fellini's tendency to get his ideas
      at night. Fellini himself speaks only briefly in interview.

Records of Music from Fellini's Films

920   Recordings have been made of La Strada, Nights of Cabiria,
      La Dolce Vita, Boccaccio '70, 8½, and Juliet of the Spirits.
      La Strada was issued by seventeen different companies;
      Nights of Cabiria, by two; La Dolce Vita, by fourteen com-
      panies; Boccaccio '70, by one; 8½, by seven; and Juliet of
      the Spirits, by two. Information on these records and on
      the producing companies is readily obtainable in James L.
      Limbacher's "Recorded Musical Scores," in Film Music: From
      Violins to Video. Metuchen, N.J.: Scarecrow Press, 1974.
      Pp. 688-828. Unfortunately, these recordings are out of
      print. The titles listed below are those which were in
      print during the time this book was compiled.

1969

921   Fellini Satyricon. United Artists 5208.

1970

922   The Clowns. Columbia 30772.

1972

923   Roma. United Artists LA052G.

1973

924   Amarcord. RCA ARL 1-0907.

1976

925   Il Casanova di Federico Fellini. CAM SAG 9075.

926   Concerto di musiche da film di Nino Rota. CAM ZNLA 33040.
       (The record includes music from Casanova, La Strada, La
       Dolce Vita, Boccaccio '70, 8½, and The Clowns.)

927   Tutti i film di Fellini. CAM SAG 9053.

Archival Sources

928   Information and Documentation Department, British Film Institute, 127/133 Charing Cross Road, London WI. Head of Department: Brenda Davies; Deputy: Gillian Hartnoll; Phone: (01) - 437-4355.

929   The National Film Archive, British Film Institute, 81 Dean Street, London WI. Curator: David Francis; Film Viewings Supervisor: Jeremy Boulton; Phone: (01) - 437-4355.
    The library of BFI's Information and Documentation Department has a strong collection of journals and books with information on Fellini and of published scripts of his films. An excellent file of material on Fellini lists forty-eight items. The National Film Archive has a stills collection and a film collection. The archive lists The White Sheik (16mm) and La Strada (35mm) as "viewable copies." It lists I Vitelloni (35mm), Variety Lights (16mm), Nights of Cabiria (35mm), La Dolce Vita (35mm), Boccaccio '70 (35mm), and Juliet of the Spirits (35mm) as "preservation copies," not generally available. (At time of inquiry [July 1977] the National Film Archive was unwilling to allow any of these films to be used by non-residents of Great Britain.)

Italy

930   Cineteca nazionale, Centro sperimentale di cinematografia, Via Tuscolana 1524, 00173 Rome. Director: Dr. Lodoletta Lupo; Phone: 74-00-46.
    The library contains an outstanding collection of Italian, French, and English film journals. It has a good collection of critical books on Fellini (mainly in Italian) and a collection of twelve published film scripts of Fellini's films (again mainly in Italian). The Cineteca has a good gathering of stills. Prints of the following films directed by

Fellini are available for study: <u>Variety Lights</u>, <u>The White Sheik</u>, <u>I Vitelloni</u>, <u>Love in the City</u>, <u>Il Bidone</u>, <u>La Dolce Vita</u>, <u>8½</u>, <u>Juliet of the Spirits</u>, and <u>Fellini Satyricon</u>. In addition, the Cineteca holds prints of the following films on which Fellini worked as writer or assistant: <u>Field of Flowers</u>, <u>Rome, Open City</u>, <u>Paisan</u>, <u>The Miracle</u>, <u>Without Pity</u>, <u>The Mill on the Po</u>, <u>In the Name of the Law</u>, <u>The Path of Hope</u>, <u>Flowers of St. Francis</u>, and <u>The Brigand of Tacca del Lupo</u>. The films are in 35mm.

United States--California

931 American Film Institute, 501 Doheny Road, Beverly Hills, California 90210. Librarian: Anne G. Schlosser; Phone: (213) 278-8777.

The library has extensive holdings of books and published scripts in English. Two manuscripts are a transcript of a discussion Fellini held with Fellows of the AFI on January 12, 1970, mainly on the subject of <u>Fellini Satyricon</u>, and a translation of <u>La Strada</u> into English by Cecily Gittes. [The first has been published, but the second, Gittes' translation, has not been published. It is, at this time, the only translation of <u>La Strada</u> into English. JCS]

932 Special Collections Library, Room 206, Doheny Library, University of Southern California, University Park, Los Angeles, California 90007. Director: Robert Knutson; Phone: (213) 746-6058.

This library is an outstanding resource center for work with secondary materials. Its holdings in English, Italian, and French film journals and critical books is very extensive. The card catalogue lists fifty-four entries for Fellini. That figure includes twenty-two published scripts in English, Italian, French, and German.

933 Theater Arts Library, UCLA, 405 Hilgard Avenue, Los Angeles, California 90024. Librarian: Audree Malkin; Phone: (213) 825-4880.

The library holds an extensive collection of film journals. The staff maintains a file of clippings on Fellini with articles taken at random from periodicals. They have six books on Fellini and seventeen published scripts of Fellini's films in English, Italian, French, and German. In addition, the library has stills and slides on Fellini's movies.

Archival Sources

United States--Illinois

934   Library, University of Illinois, Urbana, Illinois 61801. Film
librarian: Nancy Allen; Phone: (217) 333-3479.

       The University of Illinois Library has a good collection
of English language books on Fellini and of published
scripts of his movies in English. The collection of books
and scripts in French and Italian is better than average
and is growing. The card catalogue for books lists twenty-
five entries on Fellini. Of that number, fifteen are published scripts in English, French, Italian, and German.
The library also holds six press books for Fellini films
and a mimeographed copy of the English shooting script for
Casanova.

United States--New York

935   Film Study Center, Museum of Modern Art, 11 West 53rd Street,
New York, New York 10019. Supervisor: Charles Silver;
Phone: (212) 956-4212.

       The Museum of Modern Art has 35mm. prints of the follow-
ing films which are available for study purposes: The
White Sheik, I Vitelloni, La Dolce Vita, and 8½. It has an
extensive collection of stills from Fellini's movies, and
it maintains a file of such things as clippings, press
releases, and program notes for each film. Most interesting
holdings are a press book in Italian on I Vitelloni and
press releases on production information for 8½ and Love
in the City.

Note: Much of the material which might be called "primary" material,
that is, drawings by Fellini and early versions of screenplays, has
been published. Additional material, of course, remains in the hands
of the director, his collaborators, and his producers. Literary
rights to Fellini's manuscript material are handled by Daniel Keel,
Diogenes Verlag, Sprecherstrasse 8, CH-8032 Zurich, Switzerland.

Film Distributors

936 ART CINEMA BOOKING SERVICE, 1501 Broadway, New York, NY 10036, (212) 947-2445.
  I Vitelloni, Variety Lights, The White Sheik

937 AVCO EMBASSY PICTURES, 1301 Avenue of the Americas, New York, NY 10019, (212) 956-5500.
  Boccaccio '70 (The Temptations of Doctor Antonio)

938 CONTEMPORARY/McGRAW-HILL FILMS, Princeton Road, Highstown, NJ 08520, (609) 448-1700; 828 Custer Avenue, Evanston, IL 60202, (312) 869-5010; 1714 Stockton Street, San Francisco, CA 94133, (415) 362-3115.
  I Vitelloni, Variety Lights, The White Sheik

939 FILMS INCORPORATED, 5589 New Peachtree Road, Atlanta, GA 30341, (404) 451-7431; 441 Park Avenue South, New York, NY 10016, (212) 889-7910; 5625 Hollywood Boulevard, Hollywood, CA 90028, (213) 466-5481; 733 Green Bay Road, Wilmette, IL 60091, (312) 256-6600.
  Amarcord, The Clowns, Fellini: A Director's Notebook

940 IVY FILMS/16, 165 West 46th Street, New York, NY 10036, (212) 765-3940.
  Il Bidone

941 JANUS FILMS, 745 Fifth Avenue, New York, NY 10022, (212) 753-7100.
  La Strada

942 MACMILLAN/AUDIO BRANDON FILMS, 34 MacQuesten Parkway South, Mount Vernon, NY 10550, (914) 664-5051; 3868 Piedmont Avenue, Oakland, CA 94611, (415) 658-9890; 1619 North Cherokee, Los Angeles, CA 90028, (213) 463-0357; 8400 Brookfield Avenue, Brookfield, IL 60513, (312) 485-3925; 2512 Program Drive, Dallas, TX 75229, (214) 357-6496.
  $8\frac{1}{2}$, I Vitelloni, Il Bidone, Juliet of the Spirits, La Dolce Vita, La Strada, Love In the City (A Matrimonial Agency), Variety Lights, The White Sheik

943   MASS MEDIA ASSOCIATES, 2116 North Charles Street, Baltimore, MD 21218, (301) 727-3270.
La Strada

944   MODERN SOUND PICTURES, 1402 Howard Street, Omaha, NB 68102, (402) 341-8476.
Spirits of the Dead (Toby Dammit)

945   MOTTAS FILMS, 1318 Ohio Avenue NE, Canton, OH 44705, (216) 454-8821.
Spirits of the Dead (Toby Dammit)

946   NBC EDUCATIONAL ENTERPRISES, 30 Rockfeller Plaza, New York, NY 10020, (212) 247-8300.
Fellini: A Director's Notebook

947   PYRAMID FILMS, P.O. Box 1048, Santa Monica, CA 90406, (213) 828-7577.
Fellini: A Director's Notebook

948   TWYMAN FILMS, 329 Salem Avenue, Dayton, OH 45401, (513) 222-4014.
Fellini: A Director's Notebook

949   UNITED ARTISTS/16, 729 7th Avenue, New York, NY 10019, (212) 575-4715.
Fellini Satyricon, Fellini's Roma

950   UNITED FILMS, 1425 South Main Street, Tulsa, OK 74119, (918) 583-2681.
Spirits of the Dead (Toby Dammit)

951   UNIVERSITY OF CALIFORNIA, Extension Media Center, 2223 Fulton Street, Berkeley, CA 94720, (415) 845-6000.
Fellini: A Director's Notebook

952   VISUAL AIDS SERVICE, University of Illinois, 1325 South Oak Street, Champaign, IL 61820, (217) 333-1360.
Fellini: A Director's Notebook

953   WESTCOAST FILMS, 25 Lusk Street, San Francisco, CA 94107, (415) 362-4700.
Spirits of the Dead (Toby Dammit)

Film Title Index

This index covers Sections III-VII.
Numbers given are item numbers.

A

Un agenzia matrimoniale. See
  A Matrimonial Agency.
Alex in Wonderland, 914
Amarcord, 17, 214, 471, 625, 713,
  717, 729, 731, 732, 734, 737-
  739, 742-750, 752-757, 759-
  761, 763-766, 768, 769, 775,
  776, 778-790, 792, 793, 799,
  800, 804, 809, 818, 819, 821,
  823, 824, 827, 876, 877, 880,
  924, 939
L'amore. See The Miracle.
Amore in città. See A Matrimo-
  nial Agency.
Apparition, 283, 476, 891
Apparizione. See Apparition.
Avanti, c'è posto. See Come On,
  There's Room.

B

Il Bidone, 6, 61, 67, 72, 73, 77,
  80-84, 86, 87, 93-95, 99, 100,
  102, 103, 105, 106, 122, 125,
  131, 134, 138, 144, 149, 151,
  159, 173, 176, 178, 180, 190,
  194, 206, 216, 223, 231, 235,
  249, 250, 260, 283, 349, 363,
  370, 371, 380, 382, 384, 385,
  387, 403, 422, 440, 446, 451,
  462, 465, 475, 476, 519, 536,
  560, 615, 641, 686, 700, 719,
  744, 772, 780, 806, 818, 821,
  823, 824, 848, 866, 870, 930,
  940, 942

Block-notes di un regista. See
  Fellini: A Director's
  Notebook.
Boccaccio '70. See The Tempta-
  tions of Doctor Antonio.
The Brigand of Tacca del Lupo,
  283, 476, 906, 930
Il brigante di Tacca del Lupo.
  See The Brigand of Tacca del
  Lupo.
Bullet for Stefano, 898

C

Cabiria. See Nights of Cabiria.
Il cammino della speranza. See
  The Path of Hope.
Campo dei fiori. See Field of
  Flowers.
Casanova, 18, 214, 748, 761, 794-
  796, 801, 810-814, 817, 820,
  824-841, 879, 881-883, 925,
  926, 934
Chi l'ha visto? See Who Has Seen
  Him?
Ciao, Federico!, 716, 918
La città si difende. See Pass-
  port to Hell.
I clowns. See The Clowns.
The Clowns, 15, 471, 547, 555,
  559, 561, 563, 566, 567, 580,
  587, 599, 600, 602, 605, 608,
  615, 617, 621, 622, 625-628,
  630, 631, 634, 636, 639, 642,
  643, 648, 650, 652, 653, 656,
  657, 661, 677, 683, 700, 725,

335

728, 743, 744, 772, 779, 780,
798, 806, 818, 821, 823, 824,
867, 872, 922, 926, 939
Come On, There's Room, 283, 476,
888

D

Il delitto di Giovanni Episcopo.
  See Flesh Will Surrender.
Document Z$_3$, 283, 476, 887
Documento Z$_3$. See Document Z$_3$.
La Dolce Vita, 8, 175, 185, 187,
189, 191-193, 197-208, 211-
225, 227-234, 236-244, 246,
247, 250-252, 254, 255, 257,
267, 269, 272, 275, 281-285,
291, 295, 306, 319, 326, 327,
330, 331, 342, 343, 347, 349,
352, 358, 375, 376, 380, 383,
385, 387, 390, 402, 403, 408,
418, 422, 440, 446, 449, 451,
452, 454, 459, 461, 462, 465,
467, 470, 476, 477, 490, 512,
526, 528, 535, 536, 557, 560,
574, 593, 612, 615, 626, 635,
637, 641-643, 649, 679, 683,
686, 700, 718, 719, 728, 743,
744, 772, 780, 786, 802, 806,
816, 818, 821, 823, 824, 834,
852-855, 878, 915, 920, 926,
929, 930, 935, 942
Le donne libere di Magliano. See
  The Free Women of Magliano.
Don't Tell Me, 283, 476, 885
Do You Know What You Look Like?,
283, 476, 884

E

8½, 10, 259, 286-318, 320-326,
328, 331-334, 336-341, 345-
347, 349-351, 353, 354, 356-
361, 366-369, 373, 374, 377,
380, 383, 385, 387, 390, 398,
402, 403, 408, 411, 422, 425,
432, 436, 440, 445, 446, 449,
451, 452, 454, 456, 459-462,
465, 467, 468, 473, 475-477,
486, 487, 494, 496, 519, 520,
526, 536, 539, 560, 579, 590,

607, 612, 615, 619, 622, 626,
632, 635, 641-644, 649, 655,
668, 679, 683, 686, 694, 700,
704, 718, 719, 728, 740, 743,
744, 749-751, 772, 774, 777,
778, 780, 793, 797, 803, 806,
807, 816, 818, 821, 823, 824,
857, 858, 861, 862, 878, 920,
926, 930, 935, 942
Europa '51, 283, 476, 907

F

Fellini: A Director's Notebook,
13, 500, 676, 744, 821, 823,
872, 917, 939, 946-948, 951,
952
Fellini: The Director as Creator,
919
Fellini Roma. See Roma.
Fellini Satyricon, 14, 220, 480,
497, 498, 506-516, 518, 521-
523, 527, 529-532, 537, 538,
540-546, 548, 550-554, 556,
557, 560, 562, 564, 565, 568-
573, 575-578, 581-586, 589,
591, 592, 594-598, 603, 604,
606, 611, 615, 618, 622-624,
626, 633, 635, 637-641, 646,
647, 651, 660, 671, 683, 700,
705, 719, 720, 723, 727, 728,
743, 744, 772, 780, 806, 818,
821-824, 827, 834, 865, 868,
921, 930, 931, 949
Fellini's Roma. See Roma.
Field of Flowers, 283, 476, 892,
930
Flesh Will Surrender, 283, 476,
897
Flowers of St. Francis, 283, 476,
610, 719, 903, 912, 930
Fortunella, 283, 476, 908
The Fourth Page, 283, 476, 890
Four Ways Out. See Passport to
  Hell.
Francesco, giullare di Dio. See
  Flowers of St. Francis.
The Free Women of Magliano, 349,
536, 849, 916

G

Giulietta degli spiriti. See
Juliet of the Spirits.

H

Histoires extraordinaires. See
Toby Dammit.

I

I Am the Pirate, 283, 476, 886
In nome della legge. See In the
Name of the Law.
In the Name of the Law, 283, 476,
901, 930
I Remember. See Amarcord.

J

Juliet of the Spirits, 11, 362,
378, 388, 389, 391-394, 398-
401, 404-406, 409-411, 413-
415, 418, 419, 421-423, 425-
429, 431, 432, 434-436, 438-
444, 446-452, 454, 455, 459,
460, 462-467, 472, 473, 475,
486, 489, 504, 520, 526, 536,
560, 593, 612, 615, 619, 622,
626, 635, 641-643, 686, 700,
719, 733, 740, 743, 744, 749,
750, 772, 773, 780, 806, 818,
821, 823, 824, 859, 860, 863,
878, 920, 929, 930, 942

L

The Last Merry-Go-Round, 283,
476, 894
Lo vedi come sei? See Do You
Know What You Look Like?
Love Duet, 552
Love in the City. See A Matri-
monial Agency.
Luci del varietà. See Variety
Lights.

M

Mafia. See In the Name of the
Law.

A Matrimonial Agency, 4, 32, 41,
44, 54, 62, 105, 118, 134,
156, 163, 173, 190, 195, 223,
283, 284, 349, 387, 417, 422,
459, 476, 536, 615, 700, 744,
780, 821, 824, 930, 935, 942
The Mill on the Po, 283, 476,
610, 900, 930
The Miracle, 267, 283, 349, 476,
536, 610, 719, 823, 899, 911,
913, 930
Il miracolo. See The Miracle.
Moraldo in città. See Moraldo
in the City.
Moraldo in the City, 40, 45, 105,
144, 187, 223, 250, 283, 392,
476, 700, 843, 915
Il mulino del Po. See The Mill
on the Po.

N

Nights of Cabiria, 7, 92, 113,
114, 117, 119, 120, 122-124,
127, 128, 130-137, 142, 144,
147, 148, 151, 153-155, 161,
164, 165, 168-170, 172-174,
176, 177, 179-182, 190, 194,
206, 208, 210, 216, 223, 231,
235, 250, 261, 272, 283, 349,
363, 380, 385, 387, 403, 422,
431, 440, 446, 451, 454, 459,
462, 465, 476, 492, 526, 536,
560, 593, 612, 614, 615, 641,
679, 686, 700, 719, 771-773,
780, 806, 818, 821, 823, 824,
850, 851, 920, 929
Non me lo dire. See Don't Tell
Me.
Le notti di Cabiria. See Nights
of Cabiria.

O

Otto e mezzo. See 8½ (Eight and
a Half).

P

Paisà. See Paisan.

Paisan, 164, 165, 182, 210, 267,
273, 283, 476, 610, 823, 896,
910, 930
Il passatore. See Bullet for
Stefano.
Passport to Hell, 283, 476, 905
The Path of Hope, 283, 476, 904,
930
Il pirato sono io. See I Am the
Pirate.

Q

Quarta pagina. See The Fourth
Page.

R

The Road. See La Strada.
Roma, 16, 608, 609, 613, 662,
664, 665, 667, 669, 673, 674,
678, 680-682, 685, 687, 688,
691, 692, 695-697, 700, 702,
703, 706-712, 714, 721, 722,
726, 730, 734-737, 741, 743,
744, 761, 772, 779, 780, 798,
806, 815, 818, 821, 823, 824,
827, 873-875, 923, 949
Roma, città aperta. See Rome,
Open City.
Rome, Open City, 273, 283, 349,
476, 536, 587, 610, 823, 895,
909, 930

S

Satyricon. See Fellini
Satyricon.
Lo sceicco bianco. See The White
Sheik.
Senza pietà. See Without Pity.
Spirits of the Dead. See Toby
Dammit.
The Spivs. See I Vitelloni.
La Strada, 5, 31, 35, 39, 42, 47-
50, 52, 53, 55-58, 60-66, 68,
69, 74-76, 78, 79, 84, 86, 89,
90, 94, 98, 101, 104, 105,
107-109, 111, 114, 115, 118,
125, 126, 130, 131, 134, 135,
138, 144, 147-150, 159, 162,

164, 165, 168, 173, 174, 180,
182, 184, 190, 194, 206, 210,
216, 223, 226, 231, 235, 250,
263, 277, 278, 283, 284, 348,
349, 363, 364, 380, 385, 387,
390, 396, 403, 416, 522, 424,
431, 440, 445, 446, 451, 454,
461, 462, 465, 476, 492, 519,
524, 526, 536, 558, 560, 597,
610, 615, 641, 686, 700, 718,
719, 733, 744, 772, 773, 780,
806, 816, 818, 821, 823, 824,
825, 844-847, 866, 869, 920,
926, 929, 931, 941-943
The Sweet Life. See La Dolce
Vita.
The Swindle. See Il Bidone.

T

Tales of Mystery. See Toby
Dammit.
The Temptations of Doctor Antonio,
9, 254, 258, 264-266, 269, 274,
276, 279-281, 283, 285, 329,
349, 355, 380, 417, 422, 446,
459, 461, 462, 476, 526, 536,
615, 641, 744, 772, 780, 821,
824, 856, 861, 870, 920, 926,
929, 937
Le tentazioni del Dottor Antonio.
See The Temptations of Doctor
Antonio.
Toby Dammit, 12, 482-485, 488,
489, 491, 493, 495, 499, 501-
503, 505, 517, 522, 525, 528,
539, 552, 560, 593, 615, 622,
626, 637, 638, 641-643, 645,
660, 684, 700, 701, 715, 744,
772, 780, 821, 823, 824, 864,
944, 945, 950, 953
Tre passi nel delirio. See Toby
Dammit.
Tutta la città canta. See The
Whole City Sings.

U

L'ultima carrozzella. See The
Last Merry-Go-Round.

V

Variety Lights, 1, 19-22, 86, 105,
143, 144, 149, 160, 173, 176,
190, 209, 216, 223, 226, 245,
248, 250, 267, 283, 349, 385,
387, 390, 403, 412, 422, 433,
448, 451, 476, 492, 526, 536,
560, 615, 686, 700, 719, 758,
770, 780, 806, 821, 823, 824,
871, 929, 930, 936, 938, 942
Viaggio con Anita. See Voyage
with Anita.
Il viaggio di G. Mastorna. See
The Voyage of G. Mastorna.
I Vitelloni, 3, 29-31, 33, 34,
36, 37, 40, 45, 51, 59, 61,
69, 74, 76, 78, 84-86, 88, 90,
91, 94, 96, 105, 110, 111,
125, 134, 138, 144, 159, 173,
176, 186, 190, 194, 196, 206,
219, 223, 250, 262, 283, 348,
349, 354, 368, 380, 385, 387,
403, 422, 440, 446, 451, 454,
462, 465, 475, 476, 492, 526,
536, 560, 601, 610, 615, 641,
679, 686, 700, 719, 744, 772,
780, 806, 818, 821, 823-825,
842, 866, 870, 878, 915, 929,
930, 935, 936, 938, 942

The Voyage of G. Mastorna, 481,
483, 556, 560, 642, 643, 700,
823, 917
Voyage with Anita, 283, 392, 476

W

The White Sheik, 2, 23-28, 33, 55,
70, 76, 78, 84, 86, 97, 101,
105, 111, 122, 125, 134, 144,
146, 173, 190, 194, 206, 216,
223, 226, 250, 256, 267, 283,
349, 372, 380, 381, 385, 387,
403, 422, 440, 446, 451, 459,
461, 475, 476, 492, 526, 536,
560, 615, 641, 686, 700, 719,
744, 772, 780, 806, 818, 821,
823-825, 866, 871, 929, 930,
935, 936, 938, 942
Who Has Seen Him?, 283, 476, 889
The Whole City Sings, 283, 476,
893
Without Pity, 283, 476, 610, 902
930

Y

The Young and the Passionate.
See I Vitelloni.

Author Index

This index covers items listed in Sections IV
and V-A.   Numbers given are item numbers.

A

Agel, Geneviève, 38, 86, 112
Agel, Henri, 87, 197, 231
Allombert, Guy, 113
Alpert, Hollis, 232, 286, 287,
    506, 607
Amengual, Barthélemy, 288-290
Amiel, Mireille, 662, 742, 743
Angelucci, Gianfranco, 744, 796,
    828
Anon., 19, 61, 88-90, 114-117,
    164-167, 182, 198, 199, 233,
    258, 259, 291-298, 362-365,
    387-390, 435-437, 478-482,
    507-509, 546-548, 608, 609,
    663, 664, 713, 745-747, 794,
    795
Antonioni, Michelangelo, 510
Arbasino, Alberto, 748
Arbois, Janick, 118
Archer, Eugene, 91
Arecco, Sergio, 511
Aristarco, Guido, 21, 23, 39,
    62, 119, 120, 200, 299, 300,
    391, 512
Armes, Roy, 610, 714
Armstrong, Michael, 715
Astre, Georges-Albert, 201
Aubier, Dominique, 63
Autera, Leonardo, 121, 122

B

Bachmann, Gideon, 183, 301, 366,
    367, 392, 466, 665, 716, 749,
    750

Backès-Clément, Catherine, 611
Baker, Peter, 168, 302
Baldelli, Pio, 612
Baragli, Enrico, S. J., 202, 203
Barneschi, Renato, 549, 613, 666,
    717
Bastide, François-Régis, 64, 846
Batten, Mary, 303
Baudry, Pierre, 550
Bayer, William, 718
Bazin, André, 65, 123, 260-263,
    614
Bellour, Raymond, 304
Benayoun, Robert, 66, 124, 204,
    264, 513
Benderson, Albert Edward, 751,
    807
Benedetti, Benedetto, 40, 92
Bennett, Joseph, 368
Berger, Rudi, 29
Bergtal, Eric, 234
Besset, Martine, 615
Betti, Liliana, 483, 752, 753,
    796, 808
Bezzola, Guido, 514
Bianchi, Pietro, 125
Billard, Pierre, 305
Bluestone, George, 126
Blumer, Ronald, 484
Boffa, Franco, 438
Bongioanni, Marco, 551
Bonitzer, Pascal, 754
Borde, Raymond, 93, 306, 439
Borderie, Roger, 616, 617
Born, Max, 618
Bory, Jean-Louis, 619
Bouissy, André, 306

Boyer, Deena, 369
Bruno, Edoardo, 24, 41, 42, 67,
    127, 205, 265, 307, 393, 515
Brustein, Robert, 394
Buache, Freddy, 184
Budgen, Suzanne, 440, 620
Burke, Tom, 552
Busco, Maria Teresa, 395

C

Caen, Michael, 396
Calvino, Italo, 755, 809
Canali, Luca, 516, 667
Canby, Vincent, 517, 553, 554,
    621, 756, 757, 829
Caputo, Juliette, 64, 846
Carey, Gary, 308
Carpi, Fabio, 169
Casiraghi, Ugo, 397
Castello, Giulio Cesare, 25, 30,
    94, 398
Casty, Alan, 719
Cattivelli, Giulio, 128
Cavicchioli, Luigi, 43, 129, 185
Cederna, Camilla, 206, 309, 310
Celli, Teodoro, 186
Cervoni, Albert, 758
Chardère, Bernard, 59, 68, 95
Chemasi, Antonio, 810
Chessa, Pasquale, 811
Chevallier, Jean, 69, 70, 130
Chiarini, Luigi, 131
Ciment, Michel, 555
Cocks, Jay, 759
Cocks, John C., Jr., 370
Codelli, Lorenzo, 760
Cohen, Roberta, 311
Collet, Jean, 312
Comuzio, Ermano, 313, 485
Conti, Isabella, 668
Corbin, Louise, 132
Corbucci, Gianfranco, 518
Corich, Nevio, 235
Covi, Antonio, 622
Cowie, Peter, 623
Cox, Harvey G., Jr., 556
Crist, Judith, 314, 399, 486, 830
Crowther, Bosley, 96, 97, 133,
    236, 266, 315, 371, 400
Culkin, John M., S. J., 557

Curtis, Jean-Louis, 467

D

"D., G.," 44
Damiani, Bruno, 669
Davis, Melton S., 441, 831
Delcorde, Jacques, 267, 268
de Laurot, Edouard, 98, 558
del Buono, Oreste, 559, 560, 761
Del Fra, Lino, 134, 135
Delouche, Dominique, 99, 100, 136,
    137, 170, 207, 208
De Vilallonga, José-Luis, 670,
    724
Di Carlo, Carlo, 269
Di Giammatteo, Fernaldo, 22, 316
Dillard, R. H. W., 624
Dorigo, Francesco, 317, 401
Doss, Janet C., 720
Dragadze, Peter, 812
Duprey, Richard A., 237
Durgnat, Raymond, 209, 238, 671

E

Eason, Patrick, 519
Elley, Derek, 762
Ellison, Harlan, 442
Escobar, Roberto, 763
Estève, Michel, 290
Etaix, Pierre, 561
Ethier, Jean-René, 721

F

Fabrini, Ivano, 45
Fallaci, Oriana, 318, 468, 487
Farber, Stephen, 764
Favazza, Armando, 520
Fellini, Federico, 31, 46, 47,
    71, 138, 139, 171, 187, 188,
    210, 239, 270-273, 319-321,
    372, 402, 457, 469-471, 521-
    523, 562-566, 625, 672-677,
    722-724, 765-767, 813, 842-
    845, 848-880, 882
Ferrara, Giuseppe, 140
Ferruzza, Alfredo, 189, 211
Fieschi, Jean-Andre, 443, 444
Finetti, Ugo, 768
Fink, Guido, 488

Fitzpatrick, Ellen, 274
Flaiano, Ennio, 48, 842–844
Flaus, John, 275
Fofi, Goffredo, 626
Ford, Charles, 322
Fovez, Jean, 627
Franchi, R. L., 240
Fratellini, Annie, 561
Fratini, Gaio, 269, 276
Free, William, 725
Friendly, Alfred, Jr., 567

G

Gardies, René, 568, 628
Garrett, George P., 629
Gauteur, Claude, 445
Gautier, Guy, 277
Ghelli, Nino, 26, 32, 33, 72
Giacosi, Luigi, 49
Giannattasio, Sandra, 373
Gili, Jean A., 489, 769, 770
Gill, Brendan, 323
Goldberg, Toby, 403
Gorbman, Claudia, 771
Gow, Gordon, 141, 524, 569, 726
Grandi, Libero, 212
Greenberg, Harvey R., 797
Greenspun, Roger, 678
Grenier, Cynthia, 213
Gross, Robert, 525
Guegan, Yves, 627
Guerra, Tonino, 880
Guttoso, Renato, 374

H

Hackett, Pat, 738
Hamblin, Dora Jane, 630
Harcourt, Peter, 241, 242, 446,
    570, 679, 772
Hart, Henry, 243, 404, 571, 631
Hartung, Philip T., 405
Haskell, Molly, 572, 773
Hatch, Robert, 324, 632, 832
Herman, David, 526
Highet, Gilbert, 573
Hirschman, Jack, 325
Hofmann, Paul, 680
Holland, Norman N., 244, 326,
    327, 375, 574
Houston, Beverle, 683, 728

Hovald, Patrice G., 190
Hughes, Eileen, 527, 633
Hull, David Stewart, 245
Huss, Roy, 490
Hyman, Timothy, 774

I

Ivaldi, Nedo, 491

J

Jacob, Gilles, 406
Jacona, Antonio, 407
Jacotey, Christian, 328
Jaffe, Ira S., 634
Janos, Leo, 814
Johnson, Albert, 833
Johnson, Ian, 278, 329
Jomy, Alain, 447
Julia, Jacques, 635

K

Kael, Pauline, 330, 408, 492, 575,
    681, 727, 815
Karaganov, Aleksandr, 409
Kast, Pierre, 410, 448, 472
Kauffmann, Stanley, 246, 279, 331,
    411, 412, 449, 528, 576, 636,
    637, 682, 775, 798, 834
Kerans, James, 172
Ketcham, Charles B., 816
Keyster, Lester J., 799
Kezich, Tullio, 214, 413, 414
Kinder, Marsha, 683, 728
Knight, Arthur, 142
Kovács, Steven, 684
Koval, Francis, 34, 50, 73
Kroll, Jack, 835
Kuhn, Helen Weldon, 332

L

Labarthe, André, 143
Lacassin, Francis, 396
Lajeunesse, Jacqueline, 685
Lambert, Gavin, 74
Lane, John Francis, 144, 215,
    247, 333, 729
Langman, Betsy, 529, 577
Lapoujade, Robert, 638

Lattuada, Alberto, 248
Lauder, Robert E., 639
Laugier, Jean-Louis, 216
Laura, Ernesto, 145, 217, 334
Lawson, John Howard, 376
Le Clézio, J. M. G., 640
Leduc, Jean, 730
Lefèvre, Raymond, 101, 146, 173, 218, 249, 450, 493, 530, 578, 641
Leprohon, Pierre, 335, 451, 686
Levine, Irving R., 452
Lévy, Denis, 776
Lévy-Klein, Stephane, 687
Lewis, Leon, 473
L'Her, Yves, 75
Liber, Nadine, 415
Linden, George W., 579
Lizzani, Carlo, 250
Loubière, Pierre, 627
Louris, Guillaume, 627
Lucato, Claudio, 688
Lyon, Ninette, 453

M

McAnany, Emile G., S. J., 416
McBride, Joseph, 689
Macdonald, Dwight, 377, 496
Maddocks, Melvin, 336
Malapelle, 690
Malle, Louis, 863
Manceaux, Michele, 337
Mangini, Cecilia, 76, 77
Manvell, Roger, 454
Mardore, 219
Marker, Chris, 64, 846
Marroncle, Jeannine, 78
Martin, André, 51, 79, 80
Martin, Marcel, 102, 147, 531, 580, 642, 643
Martini, Stelio, 35
Masina, Giulietta, 52, 148, 174
Mauriac, Claude, 149
Mayer, Andrew C., 150
Mazzocchi, G., 417
Meehan, Thomas, 455
Mekas, Jonas, 251, 280, 338
Metz, Christian, 456, 494, 777
Miccichè, Lino, 800
Micha, René, 644, 645

Michalek, Boleslaw, 581
Mida, Massimo, 20, 27
Miller, Henry, 646
Montemaggi, Amedeo, 778
Montesanti, Fausto, 53
Mont-Sevran, Jean-Paul, 731
Moravia, Alberto, 81, 151, 220, 281, 339, 340, 418, 495, 532, 582-584, 691, 732, 801, 802, 817
Morgenstern, Joseph, 585
Morin, Gerald, 692
Mortier, Michael, 419
Moscato, Alfonso, S. J., 779
Moullet, Luc, 152
Mourlet, Michel, 420
Mucchi, Gabriele, 54
Murray, Edward, 818
Murray, William, 153
Myhers, John, 586

N

Navone, John J., 341, 342
Neville, Robert, 252
Novi, Mario, 587

O

Oldrini, Guido, 588
O'Mealy, Joseph, 647
Ortmayer, Roger, 733
Oxenhandler, Neal, 589

P

Paine, Wingate, 457
Paini, Dominique, 648
Paolella, Roberto, 343
Paolucci, Anne, 458
Pasco, Allan H., 819
Pasolini, Pier Paolo, 154, 221
Pechter, William S., 282, 649
Pecori, Franco, 780
Pellegrini, Glauco, 474
Pensotti, Anita, 175, 191, 192, 222, 378, 590, 693
Pepper, Curtis G., 253
Peri, Enzo, 254
Perry, Ted, 694, 803
Peruzzi, Giuseppe, 695

Pesce, Alberto, 459
Philippe, Pierre, 176, 421
Pieri, Françoise, 591
Pierre, Sylvie, 650
Pinel, Vincent, 344
Pinelli, Tullio, 55, 155, 842–845, 847, 848
Piro, Sinibaldo, 696
Poix, Georges, 177
Porterfield, Christopher, 836
Price, James, 345
Prouse, Derek, 103

Q

Quaglietti, Lorenzo, 460

R

Ranchal, Marcel, 156
Reichley, James, 104
Reilly, Charles Phillips, 697, 781
Renzi, Renzo, 82, 83, 105, 157, 223, 346, 379, 533, 534, 698, 804
Resnais, Alain, 651
Rhode, Eric, 224, 347, 380, 461
Richardson, Robert, 535
Riva, Valerio, 734, 782, 783, 820
Rizzo, Eugene, 805
Robbins, Fred, 837
Roemer, Michael, 255
Rollin, Betty, 592
Rondi, Brunello, 56, 158, 225, 226, 248, 381, 422
Rondi, Gian Luigi, 462
Ronse, Henri, 617
Rosenthal, Stuart, 735, 821
Ross, Lillian, 423
Rossi, Moraldo, 57
Rotha, Paul, 159, 178
Roudaut, Jean, 617

S

Sadoul, Georges, 84, 348, 424, 699
Sagan, Françoise, 457

Salachas, Gilbert, 85, 106, 160, 181, 227, 349, 350, 425, 536–538, 591, 652
Samuels, Charles Thomas, 700
Sarne, Mike, 701
Sarris, Andrew, 179, 382, 426, 496, 539, 593, 594, 653, 702, 784
Schickel, Richard, 383
Schiraldi, Vittorio, 497
Schmidt, Guido, 595
Schwartzman, Paul, 838
Setlowe, Rick, 596
Sharples, Win, Jr., 736
Shivas, Mark, 498
Siciliano, Enzo, 785
Silke, James R., 597
Silverman, Dore, 228
Silverstein, Norman, 490
Simenon, Georges, 654
Simon, John, 351, 352, 384, 427, 475, 496, 598, 655, 786
Sineux, Michel, 499
Skelton, Richard "Red," 599
Snyder, Stephen, 822
Solmi, Angelo, 28, 36, 58, 161, 193, 229, 256, 283, 353, 354, 428–430, 476, 500, 501, 540, 541, 600, 703, 704, 787, 788
Solomon, Stanley J., 705
Stanbrook, Alan, 194
Steel, Ronald, 257
Strich, Christian, 823–825
Stubbs, John C., 806
Sufrin, Mark, 601
Swados, Harvey, 107

T

Tailleur, Roger, 59
Taranto, Denis, 687
Tassone, Aldo, 706, 737, 826
Taylor, John Russell, 355, 385, 789
Termine, Liborio, 656
Terno, Sam, 602
Tessier, Max, 603, 657
Thirard, Paul-Louis, 180, 356
Thuillier, Pierre, 181
Torok, Jean-Paul, 357
Tozzi, Romano, 195

Tranchant, François, 196
Turroni, Giuseppe, 790
Tyler, Parker, 284

U

Ubezio, Stefano, 60

V

Vadim, Roger, 863
Verdone, Mario, 285, 358, 463,
   502, 542
Vice, 37
Virmaux, Alain, 359
Visconti, Luchino, 162
Vogel, Amos, 163
Volta, Ornella, 503, 543, 658,
   707, 791, 827

W

Walsch, Moira, 792
Walter, Eugene, 386, 431, 432,
   464, 659
Warhol, Andy, 738
Weaver, William, 230
Weiler, A. H., 108, 433

Welsh, James M., 839
Werba, Hank, 739
Westerbeck, Colin L., Jr., 840
Williams, Forest, 504
Williams, Robert S. J., 416
Willing, Diana, 109, 110
Willis, Don, 841
Winston, Douglas Garrett, 740
Wolf, William, 434
Wood, Robin, 477

Y

Young, Jean, 741
Young, Vernon, 111

Z

Zand, Nicole, 360
Zanelli, Dario, 544, 604
Zanzotto, Andrea, 881
Zapponi, Bernadino, 505, 545,
   605, 606, 660, 708-711, 879,
   882, 883
Zimmer, C., 465
Zimmerman, Paul, 661, 712, 793
Zucconi, Mario, 361